T0335684

This book gives an account of computability that embraces not only the general theory created by Turing and others in the 1930s, but also the theory of finite functions and relations initiated by Post, the theory of regular languages from a number of points of view (finite automata, regular expressions, logical expressions, etc.), and the theory of other families of languages (especially context-free languages). These are addressed from the classical perspective of their generation by grammars and from the more modern perspective as rational cones.

The treatment of the classical theory of computable functions and relations takes the form of a tour through basic recursive function theory, starting with an axiomatic foundation and developing the essential methods to survey the most memorable results of the field.

This authoritative, up-to-date account will be required reading for graduate students and researchers in theoretical computer science and mathematics.

# THEORIES OF COMPUTABILITY

# THEORIES OF COMPUTABILITY

### NICHOLAS PIPPENGER
*University of British Columbia*

# CAMBRIDGE
## UNIVERSITY PRESS

32 Avenue of the Americas, New York NY 10013-2473, USA

Cambridge University Press is part of the University of Cambridge.

It furthers the University's mission by disseminating knowledge in the pursuit of education, learning and research at the highest international levels of excellence.

www.cambridge.org
Information on this title: www.cambridge.org/9780521553803

© Cambridge University Press 1997

First published 1997
First paperback printing 2010

*A catalogue record for this publication is available from the British Library*

*Library of Congress Cataloguing in Publication data*

Pippenger, Nicholas
Theories of computability / Nicholas Pippenger.
p. cm.
Includes bibliographical references and index.
ISBN 0-521-55380-6 (hc)
1. Machine theory. I. Title.
QA267.P553 1997
511.3 – dc20                                    96-44633
                                                CIP

ISBN 978-0-521-55380-3 Hardback
ISBN 978-0-521-15343-0 Paperback

# Contents

# Preface

The central theme of this book is computability, in that most of the questions
studied concern whether or not it is *possible* to perform some computation by
some particular means (rather than how hard or easy it might be to do so). For
this reason, I have reinterpreted many topics concerning formal languages as
questions of computability, and I have added material on the computability of
finite functions and relations that fits well within this framework (though it is
not traditionally presented in courses on computability). I have tried to promote
a broad view of computability, one that goes beyond the topics of simulations
among machine models and reductions from the Post correspondence problem.
On the other hand, I have excluded material that would naturally be regarded as
complexity theory, with the distinguishing criterion being whether the material
is essentially qualitative or quantitative. Thus, I made an exception for abstract
complexity theory, whose main conclusions are largely qualitative in character.

The methods of the book are mathematical. This means, first, that the
material is presented in terms of definitions, theorems, and proofs, in what is by
now the standard way throughout theoretical computer science. But more than
this, it means that I have tried to achieve the level of abstraction appropriate
in mathematics, with emphasis on the relationships among objects belonging
to broad classes, as well as on the detailed properties of specific examples.
I have tried to impose high standards for the mathematical significance and
elegance (at least in my view) of the topics treated; in particular, I have refrained
from including results whose sole claim to attention is their alleged relevance
to some other area of computer science. But of those results that pass the
mathematical threshold, I have tried to select those that have something to say
about the world of concrete computation, and to make these connections clear
for the reader whose background is computational or mathematical, but not
both.

It would be hard to characterize the results selected for inclusion in the book by any simple criterion, but I found a particular issue recurring frequently when choosing results. Two kinds of results can be identified in almost any mathematical discipline. They do not seem to have standardized names, and so I shall propose the names "structural" and "cautionary." It would be hopeless to attempt precise definitions, and so I shall try to epitomize the distinction with an example: the unique factorization of integers is a structural result, whereas the existence of number rings in which unique factorization fails is a cautionary result. Structural results show that the world (or at least the part being studied) is neater than one might expect, by exhibiting hidden simplicities. Most of the stones in the great structural edifices of mathematics fall into this category: structure theorems, normal forms, classifications, and so forth. Cautionary results show that the world is more complex than one might expect; it is here that the pathologies of examples and counterexamples are found. These results offer guidance to those who seek structural results, warning them away from impossible quests, but they also offer occasions to celebrate the richness and diversity of mathematical phenomena. Areas of mathematics differ in the relative emphasis they place on these two kinds of results, but I think that a balance between them is an important index of health in a mathematical discipline, and I have tried to reflect this attitude the choice of material for the book.

Chapter 1 treats the theory of finite functions and relations, starting with the Boolean (two-valued) case, and progressing to the general multi-valued case at the end. It includes a description of Post's Lattice (though not a proof of the classification), a proof of the finite-basis theorem, and a proof of the Galois correspondence for finite functions and relations.

Chapter 2 treats the regular languages, and establishes them as the meeting ground of numerous points of view: finite automata, regular expressions, and logical expressions. It includes a treatment of Eilenberg's varieties of languages, starting with the historically influential example provided by the variety of aperiodic languages.

Chapter 3 treats larger families of languages, largely by means of the grammars that generate them, starting with the regular languages and working up to the recursively enumerable languages. Following Nivat, rational transductions are used to classify languages into rational cones, and the notion of substitution is introduced. These tools provide some understanding of the central position occupied by the context-free languages in mathematical language theory.

Chapter 4 treats Turing's theory of computability in the form of recursive function theory, starting with the recursive functions and classifying other functions according to various reducibilities. The treatment is distinctive in that it is based on an axiomatic approach (which should be familiar after its use in the previous chapters), rather than on a machine model of computation. (Machine models are introduced for the purpose of establishing the equivalence of two axiomatic formulations, but their role is secondary.) In addition to the standard results, proofs are given for Rice's theorems on index sets, Friedberg's enumeration without repetition, the isomorphism of creative sets (Myhill) and universal functions (Blum), Arslanov's completeness criterion, and the Friedberg–Muchnik priority construction for incomparable recursively enumerable sets. Applications of the last result in Ramsey theory (Specker) and in the theory of 1-degrees (Young) are given. Finally, discussions (in terms of recursive function theory) of abstract complexity theory, prediction and inductive inference, and the computable real numbers are included.

As this book is written for those making their way to the frontier of research, proofs are given more fully than is customary in the literature (which is mostly written for those who have already arrived at the frontier). There are exercises of several types: mechanical tests of understanding of definitions and basic results (labelled (E) for "easy" or (M) for "moderate"), results that might have been presented in the text but are particularly instructive or provocative (labelled (H) for "hard," references to the literature are given), and finally open problems that will probably require significantly new ideas for their solution (labelled (U) for "unsolved").

I have tried to be thorough in attributing both specific results and important lines of thought throughout the book. Thus, at this point I should mention some books that have influenced me in a general or specific way. Minsky's [1967] engaging introduction to computability was my initiation into the area; it is still the book I would recommend to someone who wants a mathematically undemanding introduction to computability. Rogers [1967] was my introduction to recursive function theory, and I am struck by how much of the material of my Chapter 4 can be found there. (One thing that cannot be found there is the axiomatic approach I have used; Rogers develops the material from an unformalized intuitive notion of computability. Furthermore, Chapter 4 is the one chapter that does not attempt to bring the reader to the frontier of current research in its area: a researcher in recursive function theory must master the priority argument in its many variations, whereas I present it only in its simplest form as the climax of my development. For those who want to reach the frontier, I recommend Lerman [1983] and Soare [1987].) Berstel [1979], Eilenberg [1974/1976], and Pöschel and Kaluzhnin [1979] present more material on Chapters 3, 2, and 1, respectively.

Nicholas Pippenger

# 1

# Finite functions and relations

## 1.1. Stories

We shall begin by recounting some well-known stories from mathematics. We say "stories" because we are not concerned here with proofs, or even with precise statements. Rather, our purpose is twofold: to encourage the reader to view the term "computability" in a broader sense than the customary one and to show that many ideas that will figure prominently in later chapters have in fact old, and in some cases ancient, anticipations in mathematics.

Let us begin with a computational problem. You are given a machine that can perform the four arithmetic operations: addition, subtraction, multiplication, and division. You are asked to write a program that takes an input $x$ and delivers, after a finite sequence of such operations, the output $\sqrt{x}$. After some reflection, you remark that the task cannot be done: from the input 2, the given operations can produce only rational numbers; but $\sqrt{2}$ is irrational.

That $\sqrt{2}$ is irrational has been known from the time of Pythagoras (fifth century B.C.). The irrationality of $\sqrt{2}$ was expressed by the Greek geometers by saying that the diagonal of a square is incommensurable with the side. On the other hand, the Greeks (as represented in the writings of Euclid, third century B.C.) knew how to construct a square, and thus its diagonal on a given side, using "ruler and compass." Thus, although we have seen that $\sqrt{2}$ is not computable using rational operations, it *is* computable using what might be called ruler-and-compass operations.

Though ruler-and-compass operations are sufficient to construct $\sqrt{2}$, there are a number of other construction problems for which the Greeks sought ruler-and-compass solutions without success. One of these is the problem of "duplicating the cube," that is, given the side of a cube, constructing the side of a cube having twice the volume. If the original side is taken as 1, the problem is

1

to construct $\sqrt[3]{2}$. (The ruler-and-compass construction of $\sqrt{2}$ may be regarded as "duplicating the square.")

Another class of problems arises from the problem of constructing various regular polygons. The Greeks knew how to construct a regular 3-gon (equilateral triangle) and a regular 5-gon (pentagon), and they knew how to bisect an arbitrary given angle, all with ruler and compass. Thus, they could construct the regular polygons with $n = 2^k m \geq 3$ sides, where $k \geq 0$ is any natural number, and $m$ is any divisor of $3 \cdot 5 = 15$. But they were unable to find a ruler-and-compass construction for a regular 7-gon (heptagon), or to trisect an arbitrary given angle (which would have allowed them to construct a regular 9-gon, for example). For ruler-and-compass constructions, the construction of an angle is equivalent to the construction of its cosine as a straight line segment; thus, these problems are equivalent to those of constructing $\cos(2\pi/7)$, constructing $\cos(\vartheta/3)$ from $\cos \vartheta$, and constructing $\cos(2\pi/9)$, respectively.

Yet another class of problems is epitomized by that of "rectifying the circle." Here the problem is to construct a straight line segment whose length is the same as that of the circumference of a given circle. If the radius of the given circle is taken as 1, the problem is to construct $2\pi$. This problem is one of a class of problems that includes computing the area of a circle, the surface area of a sphere, and the volume of a sphere; Archimedes (third century B.C.) proved that these problems were equivalent (either all or none could be solved with ruler and compass), though he could not find a ruler-and-compass solution for any of them.

The resolution of these problems had to await the work of R. Descartes (in the 17th century) linking geometry and algebra, and the work of K. F. Gauss (at the end of the 18th century), who discovered the algebraic counterpart of the ruler-and-compass operations. Gauss's work began with the discovery (at the age of 18) that a regular 17-gon can be constructed with ruler and compass and culminated with a characterization of the $n$ for which a regular $n$-gon can be constructed. The characterization is: all $n = 2^k m \geq 3$, where $k \geq 0$ is any natural number and $m$ is any product of distinct prime factors of the form $2^{2^l} + 1$, for $l \geq 0$. The primes of this form are known as "Fermat primes"; P. Fermat conjectured that all numbers of this form are prime, but in fact 0, 1, 2, 3, and 4 are the only values of $l$ less than 22 that yield primes, and these are the only Fermat primes known. Thus, in addition to the 3-, 5-, and 17-gons, the regular 257- and 65537-gons can be constructed with ruler and compass!

To prove that his characterization was complete, Gauss had to determine what lengths of line segments could be constructed with ruler and compass. The answer is: those that can be computed using the rational operations (addition, subtraction, multiplication, and division) together with the extraction of square roots. These numbers are all solutions of algebraic equations with integer coefficients whose irreducible factors have degrees that are integral powers of 2. Thus ruler-and-compass construction can again be regarded as computation, if we add the operations of extracting square roots to the list of operations considered before.

Gauss showed that the regular 7- and 9-gons cannot be constructed with ruler and compass by showing that $\cos(2\pi/7)$ and $\cos(2\pi/9)$ are not the solutions of algebraic equations meeting the conditions previously mentioned. A similar analysis applies to $\sqrt[3]{2}$ and the duplication of the cube. In each case, however, the quantity in question *is* the solution of an algebraic equation with integral coefficients; but it is a cubic (degree 3) equation, rather than one with degree of a power of 2. Thus, $\cos(2\pi/7)$ satisfies the equation $8x^3 + 4x^2 - 4x - 1 = 0$, $\cos(\vartheta/3)$ satisfies $4x^3 - 3x - \cos\vartheta = 0$ (and thus, since $\cos(2\pi/3) = -1/2$, $\cos(2\pi/9)$ satisfies $8x^3 - 6x + 1 = 0$), and of course $\sqrt[3]{2}$ satisfies $x^3 - 2 = 0$.

The solution of algebraic equations also has a long history. The solution of linear and quadratic equations, using rational operations and square roots, goes back to the second millennium B.C. The solutions to cubic and quartic (degree 4) equations, using rational operations, square roots, and cube roots, were published by G. Cardano in 1545. (Here it is necessary to consider cube roots of complex numbers as well as real numbers, for while the real and imaginary parts of the square root of a complex number can be expressed in terms of square roots of real numbers, the same is not true for cube roots.) Thus, although $\sqrt[3]{2}$, $\cos(2\pi/7)$, and $\cos(2\pi/9)$ cannot be computed by rational operations and square roots, they can be computed if we again extend our list of operations to include cube roots (including complex cube roots) or, more generally, roots of all orders (the solution of all equations of the form $x^n - y = 0$ for integer $n \geq 2$ and complex $y$). The numbers and functions computable in this new sense are said to be "constructible by radicals," and the equations they satisfy are said to be "solvable by radicals."

After the solution of the cubic and quartic equations, it was natural to try to extend the success to quintic (degree 5) and higher equations. But almost three centuries passed before N. H. Abel showed in 1824 that the solution to the general quintic equation cannot be constructed from the coefficients by radicals. In 1832, E. Galois proved that certain specific quintic equations (for example, $x^5 - 6x + 3 = 0$) are not solvable by radicals. In fact, Galois gave a criterion for deciding whether an arbitrarily given algebraic equation with integer coefficients is solvable by radicals. Galois's argument established a pattern that has been fruitful in other areas of mathematics, and it will be worthwhile to describe it here.

If we start with the numbers 0 and 1 and perform a sequence of rational operations, we can obtain any rational number; we shall denote the set of rational numbers by $\mathbf{Q}$. If we add $i = \sqrt{-1}$ to the list of starting numbers, we obtain a larger set of numbers, which we shall denote $\mathbf{Q}(i)$. The sets $\mathbf{Q}$ and $\mathbf{Q}(i)$ are examples of "number fields," that is, sets of numbers containing 0 and 1 and closed under the rational operations; the smaller field $\mathbf{Q}$ is said to be a "subfield" of the larger field $\mathbf{Q}(i)$. The field $\mathbf{Q}(i)$ has only itself and $\mathbf{Q}$ as subfields, a situation that can be depicted thus:

$$\mathbf{Q}(i)$$
$$\uparrow \tag{1}$$
$$\mathbf{Q}$$

The field $\mathbf{Q}(i)$ is obtained from $\mathbf{Q}$ by adjoining $i$, which is a solution of the equation $x^2 + 1 = 0$, the other solution of which is $-i$. We can construct a one-to-one correspondence $\varrho$ between $\mathbf{Q}(i)$ and itself that exchanges the two elements $\pm i$, while fixing 0 and 1 and preserving the rational operations and, thus, fixing all of the elements of $\mathbf{Q}$. The identity map $\iota$ is the only other one-to-one correspondence of $\mathbf{Q}(i)$ to itself that fixes 0 and 1 and preserves the rational operations. The two maps $\varrho$ and $\iota$, restricted to the set $\{\pm i\}$, form a "permutation group," that is, a set of permutations that include the identity and are closed under composition and taking inverses; we shall denote this group $\{\varrho, \iota\}$. The set $\{\iota\}$ also forms a group, which is the only "subgroup" of $\{\varrho, \iota\}$. This situation can be depicted thus:

$$\{\varrho, \iota\}$$
$$\uparrow \tag{2}$$
$$\{\iota\}$$

The similarity between diagrams (1) and (2) is not accidental: Galois showed that under certain technical hypotheses, the picture of the subfields of a field obtained by adjoining the solutions of an equation to the rationals is the same as the picture of the subgroups of the group of permutations of the solutions that fix the rationals, but upside-down. (The "upside-down" qualification is not well illustrated by this example, since the pictures are too simple.) The solvability of the equation is then related to properties of the groups, which (being finite objects) are much easier to analyze.

The solutions of the equation $x^5 - 6x + 3 = 0$, though not constructible by radicals, do become computable if we extend our list of operations yet again, to include finding the solutions of all algebraic equations with previously computed coefficients. The numbers computable in this broader sense are called "algebraic numbers," and they include the rational numbers, the numbers constructible by ruler and compass, and the numbers constructible by radicals. It was not until 1844 that J. L. Liouville showed that there are numbers that are not algebraic (for example, $\sum_{n \geq 1} 2^{-n!}$); such numbers are called "transcendental numbers." In 1874, G. Cantor showed that in fact most real numbers are transcendental: he showed that the set of algebraic numbers is "countable" (can be put into one-to-one correspondence with the natural numbers), whereas the set of all real numbers is "uncountable" (cannot be put into such a one-to-one correspondence). At about the same time, in 1873, C. Hermite showed that $e$ (the base of natural logarithms) is transcendental; then in 1882, F. Lindemann showed that $\pi$ is transcendental. This implies, of course, that $\pi$ is not constructible by ruler and compass, thus finally settling the last of these famous Greek problems.

It is fitting that we began our account with the mathematics of the Greeks, for they have bequeathed to us much more than their concrete results. There is, first, their axiomatic and deductive approach, which long since has been a model for mathematics. Second, the precision of this approach made it possible for them to formulate open questions clearly and to preserve them for later generations to work on. (Knowledge may be the product of science, but ignorance, in the form of open questions, is its raw material.) Finally, this precision made it possible for them to prove negative results, to the effect that certain problems could not be solved by certain means. Such negative results occupy prominent position in the theory of computability.

The foregoing account has also introduced some of the "structures" that will play important roles in later chapters. Diagrams (1) and (2) depict the simplest examples of structures called "lattices"; we shall meet many other lattices in our work, and will often illustrate them though similar diagrams. We have repeatedly seen sets of objects defined by including certain initial objects and closing under certain operations. By varying the universe of objects, the initial objects and the operations, we shall obtain various "closures"; we shall meet further number fields and groups, but we shall encounter many other closures as well. Finally, the curious correspondence of Galois, wherein one lattice is the same as another turned upside-down, will also recur for other pairs of lattices; such reciprocal correspondences are called "Galois connections," and they arise from relations called "polarities." The following section will present more background on these three structures.

Finally, many themes present in the foregoing account will be echoed in later chapters: the distinctions between rational and irrational, algebraic and transcendental, finite and infinite, countable and uncountable. Even some proof techniques will recur (though we have not described any of these in enough detail for this to be clear).

What we have recounted is geometry and algebra; but it may also be regarded as computability, in terms of finite sequences of operations from four successively longer lists (rational operations, ruler-and-compass constructions, constructions by radicals, and algebraic constructions). Indeed, we might go so far as to say that computability is the study of the consequences of imposing finiteness conditions. Of course, we cannot discover the essence of computability in such a superficial slogan: most of combinatorics, and much of many other parts of mathematics, arises from the imposition of finiteness conditions. But it will be instructive in later chapters to identify the roles that finiteness conditions play, and to consider their effect on the resulting theories.

The historical and technical background to the stories in this chapter can be found in two admirable books: Heath [1931] and Stewart [1988].

### *Exercises*

1. (E)  Show that the equation $p^2 = 2q^2$ has no solutions in integers.
2. (M)  Show that the equation $2q^2 = p^2 \pm 1$ has infinitely many solutions in integers, in particular, those given by the sequences $p_0, p_1, \ldots,$ and $q_0, q_1, \ldots,$ defined by $p_0 = q_0 = 1$, $p_{k+1} = p_k + 2q_k$, and $q_{k+1} = p_k + q_k$. Show that $\lim_{k \to \infty} p_k/q_k = \sqrt{2}$, and conclude that although $\sqrt{2}$ is not rational, it can be approximated arbitrarily closely by rationals.
3. (E)  Show how to duplicate the cube by means of ruler-and-compass operations, together with operation of constructing a parabola with given focus and directrix. (The parabola $y = x^2$, for example, has focus $(x, y) = (0, 1/4)$ and directrix $y = -1/4$.)
4. (E)  For which of the following values of $n$ is the regular $n$-gon constructible with ruler and compass: $2^{16} - 1$, $2^{32} - 1$, $2^{64} - 1$?
5. (M)  The Canadian dollar coin (the "loonie") is based on a regular 11-gon. Find a quintic equation with integral coefficients satisfied by $\cos(2\pi/11)$.

### 1.2. Three Basic Structures

In this section we shall give basic mathematical background for three structures mentioned in previous section: lattices, closures, and polarities. The reader may wish to skip this material now, and refer back to it later if it should be needed.

#### *1.2.1. Lattices*

A binary relation $\leq$ on a set $L$ will be called an *order* if it satisfies the following three conditions:

$O_1$  For any $x \in L$, $x \le x$.

$O_2$  For any $x, y \in L$, if $x \le y$ and $y \le x$, then $x = y$.

$O_3$  For any $x, y, z \in L$, if $x \le y$ and $y \le z$, then $x \le z$.

(These three conditions are sometimes expressed by saying that $\le$ is reflexive, asymmetric and transitive.) What we have called an "order" is sometimes called a "partial order" to emphasize that it does not necessarily possess the following additional property: for every $x, y \in L$, either $x \le y$ or $y \le x$. Most of the orders we shall deal with will not possess this additional property; those that do will be called *total* orders.

An order $\le$ will be called a *lattice* order if it satisfies the following two additional conditions:

$LO_1$  For any $x, y \in L$, there exists $z \in L$ such that $z \le x$, $z \le y$, and for any $w \in L$, if $w \le x$ and $w \le y$, then $w \le z$.

$LO_2$  For any $x, y \in L$, there exists $z \in L$ such that $x \le z$, $y \le z$, and for any $w \in L$, if $x \le w$ and $y \le w$, then $z \le w$.

The elements guaranteed by conditions $LO_3$ and $LO_4$ are unique; they are called the *infimum* and the *supremum* of $x$ and $y$, and denoted $x \sqcap y$ and $x \sqcup y$, respectively.

The binary operations $\sqcap$, $\sqcup$ in a lattice order satisfy the following eight conditions:

$LA_1$  For any $x \in L$, $x \sqcap x = x$.

$LA_2$  For any $x \in L$, $x \sqcup x = x$.

$LA_3$  For any $x, y \in L$, $x \sqcap y = y \sqcap x$.

$LA_4$  For any $x, y \in L$, $x \sqcup y = y \sqcup x$.

$LA_5$  For any $x, y, z \in L$, $x \sqcap (y \sqcap z) = (x \sqcap y) \sqcap z$.

$LA_6$  For any $x, y, z \in L$, $x \sqcup (y \sqcup z) = (x \sqcup y) \sqcup z$.

$LA_7$  For any $x, y \in L$, $x \sqcap (x \sqcup y) = x$.

$LA_8$  For any $x, y \in L$, $x \sqcup (x \sqcap y) = x$.

(These four pairs of conditions are sometimes expressed by saying that $\sqcap$ and $\sqcup$ are idempotent, commutative, associative, and absorptive.) Reciprocally, if the operations $\sqcap$, $\sqcup : L^2 \to L$ satisfy conditions $LA_1$ through $LA_8$, then the relation $\le$ defined by $x \le y \Leftrightarrow x \sqcap y = x$ (or equivalently by $x \le y \Leftrightarrow x \sqcup y = y$) is a lattice order. Such a pair of operations form what is called a *lattice algebra*. Lattice orders and lattice algebras are different mathematical embodiments of the same underlying concept.

A valuable observation about lattices is the "duality" principle: if $\leq$ is a lattice order, then so is the opposite relation $\geq$ defined by $x \geq y \Leftrightarrow y \leq x$; the corresponding lattice algebra is obtained by exchanging the roles of $\sqcap$ and $\sqcup$.

Most of the lattices we shall deal with possess an additional property: we can define the infimum and supremum for arbitrary sets of elements. If $X \subseteq L$ is any set of elements, we shall call an element $y \in L$ an infimum for $X$ (denoted $\prod X$) if (1) for any $x \in X$, $y \leq x$ and (2) for any $z \in L$ such that $z \leq x$ for any $x \in X$, $z \leq y$. Similarly, we define a supremum (denoted $\coprod X$) for $X$ by reversing all inequalities. A lattice is said to be *complete* if every set $X \subseteq L$ has an infimum and a supremum. In a complete lattice, there is always a unique minimum element $\prod L$, which we shall call "bottom" and denote $\perp$, and a unique maximum element $\coprod L$, which we shall call "top" and denote $\top$. We then have $\coprod \emptyset = \perp$ and $\prod \emptyset = \top$.

Perhaps the simplest example of a lattice is obtained by taking an arbitrary set $U$ (the "universe"), letting $L = \text{Pow}(U)$ (where $\text{Pow}(U)$ denotes the "power set" of $U$: the set of all subsets of $U$), and letting $\leq$ be the relation $\subseteq$ of set inclusion. The resulting lattice is indeed quite special; it is what is called a "Boolean algebra," and its properties will be studied in more detail later.

Another important example of a lattice is the *partition lattice*. If $U$ is an arbitrary set, a collection $\mathcal{P}$ of non-empty subsets of $U$ is called a *partition* of $U$ if its members are mutually exclusive (that is, if $A \cap B = \emptyset$ for any $A, B \in \mathcal{P}$ with $A \neq B$) and exhaustive (that is, if $\bigcup \mathcal{P} = U$). The members of a partition are called its *blocks*. The set of all partitions of $U$ will be denoted $\text{Part}(U)$. The binary relation $\leq$ defined on $\text{Part}(U)$ by $\mathcal{P} \leq \mathcal{Q} \Leftrightarrow \forall_{A \in \mathcal{P}} \exists_{B \in \mathcal{Q}} A \subseteq B$ is a complete lattice order; the smallest partition is the "discrete" partition with each element of $U$ in a separate block, whereas the largest partition is the "accrete" partition with all elements of $U$ in a single block. Partition lattices are quite general among lattices; in fact, they contain within them copies of all lattices. This is expressed precisely by a theorem of Whitman [1946], which says: if $(L, \sqcap, \sqcup)$ is any lattice algebra, there is a set $U$ and an injective map $\phi : L \to \text{Part}(U)$ such that, for all $x, y \in L$, $\phi(x \sqcap y) = \phi(x) \sqcap \phi(y)$ and $\phi(x \sqcup y) = \phi(x) \sqcup \phi(y)$ (here the symbols $\sqcap$ and $\sqcup$ on the left-hand sides denote operations in $L$, while on the right-hand sides they denote operations in $\text{Part}(U)$). (Whitman's proof yields an infinite $U$, and thus an uncountable $\text{Part}(U)$, even when $L$ is finite; Pudlák and Tůma [1980] have given a proof that yields finite $U$, and hence finite $\text{Part}(U)$, for finite $L$.)

Though lattices appeared during the 19th century in the work of Schröder and Dedekind, their pervasiveness among mathematical structures was only recognized more recently; Birkhoff [1948] is a standard reference.

### *1.2.2. Closures*

A collection $\mathcal{F} \subseteq \text{Pow}(U)$ will be called a *closure system* if it satisfies the following condition:

CS₁ If $\mathcal{G} \subseteq \mathcal{F}$ is any subcollection of the sets of $\mathcal{F}$, then the intersection $\bigcap \mathcal{G}$ of all of the sets appearing in $\mathcal{G}$ also appears in $\mathcal{F}$.

Since one possible choice of $\mathcal{G}$ is $\mathcal{F}$ itself, every closure system contains a unique smallest set $\bigcap \mathcal{F}$ (smallest under set inclusion). Another possible choice is $\mathcal{G} = \emptyset$, in which case it is natural to agree that $\bigcap \emptyset = U$; thus every closure system contains the universe as its unique largest set. The sets in $\mathcal{F}$ are called the *closed sets*.

Even if $\mathcal{D} \subseteq \text{Pow}(U)$ does not satisfy CS₁, it is possible to obtain from it a closure system $\mathcal{D}^* = \{\bigcap \mathcal{E} : \mathcal{E} \subseteq \mathcal{D}\}$ by adjoining to $\mathcal{D}$ all intersections of arbitrary subcollections of $\mathcal{D}$. If $\mathcal{D}^* = \mathcal{F}$, we say that $\mathcal{D}$ is a *basis* for the closure system $\mathcal{F}$, or that $\mathcal{F}$ is the closure system *generated* by $\mathcal{D}$.

If $\mathcal{F}$ is a closure system, we may define a map cl : $\text{Pow}(U) \rightarrow \text{Pow}(U)$ by $\text{cl}(A) = \bigcap\{F \in \mathcal{F} : A \subseteq \mathcal{F}\}$. (Thus $\text{cl}(A)$ is the smallest closed set containing $A$.) Then cl satisfies the following three conditions.

CM₁ $A \subseteq \text{cl}(A)$.
CM₂ $A \subseteq B$ implies $\text{cl}(A) \subseteq \text{cl}(B)$.
CM₃ $\text{cl}(\text{cl}(A)) = \text{cl}(A)$.

(These three conditions are sometimes expressed by saying that cl is non-deflationary, non-decreasing, and idempotent.) Reciprocally, if cl : $\text{Pow}(U) \rightarrow \text{Pow}(U)$ is any map satisfying conditions CM₁, CM₂, and CM₃, then the collection $\mathcal{F} = \{A \subseteq U : \text{cl}(A) = A\}$ is a closure system. Such a map is called a *closure map*, and $\text{cl}(A)$ is called the *closure* of $A$. Closure systems and closure maps are different mathematical embodiments of the same underlying concept. (The equivalence between closure systems and closure maps was described by Ward [1942].)

One source of closure systems is topology: a set of reals is closed if it contains all its limit points. Arbitrary intersections of closed sets of reals are again closed, so that the closed sets of reals form a closure system. But closure systems arising in topology possess an important additional property: finite unions of closed sets are again closed (including zero as a finite number, so that the empty set is closed). This property can also be expressed in terms of the closure map: $\text{cl}(A \cup B) = \text{cl}(A) \cup \text{cl}(B)$ (and $\text{cl}(\emptyset) = \emptyset$). Most of the closure systems we shall deal with will not possess this additional property; the closure systems that do will be called *topological*.

We shall now consider another way of specifying a closure system, namely, by imposing "closure conditions." A *closure condition* for $U$ is a pair $(B, b)$ with $B \subseteq U$ and $b \in U$. The set of all closure conditions for $U$ will be denoted $\text{Cond}(U)$.

A set $A$ *satisfies* the closure condition $(B, b)$ if $B \subseteq A$ implies $b \in A$. If $\mathcal{B}$ is any collection of closure conditions, we shall say that $A$ satisfies $\mathcal{B}$ if $A$ satisfies every $(B, b) \in \mathcal{B}$. The collection $\mathcal{F}$ of sets that satisfy $\mathcal{B}$ forms a closure system, which we shall call the closure system *engendered* by $\mathcal{B}$.

We shall say that a collection $\mathcal{A} \subseteq \text{Pow}(U)$ of subsets of $U$ *satisfies* $(B, b)$ if every set $A \in \mathcal{A}$ satisfies $(B, b)$. A collection $\mathcal{B}$ is a *closure criterion* if it is the collection of all closure conditions satisfied by some closure system $\mathcal{A}$; we then say that $\mathcal{B}$ is the closure criterion *associated* with $\mathcal{A}$.

Even if $\mathcal{B}$ is not a closure criterion, it is possible to obtain from it a closure criterion $\mathcal{B}^*$, namely, the closure criterion associated with the closure system engendered by $\mathcal{B}$. If $\mathcal{B}^* = \mathcal{C}$, we say that $\mathcal{B}$ is a basis for the closure criterion $\mathcal{C}$, or that $\mathcal{C}$ is generated by $\mathcal{B}$. Closure criteria are yet another mathematical embodiment of the notion of closure.

Most of the closure systems we shall deal with will possess a special property: they can be engendered by a collection $\mathcal{B}$ of closure conditions $(B, b)$ for which $B$ is finite. Such a closure system will be called *algebraic*.

The closure map of an algebraic closure system assumes a particularly simple form. If $\mathcal{B}$ is a collection of closure conditions $(B, b)$ with $B$ finite, define

$$\mathcal{B}(A) = A \cup \{b : \exists_{(B,b) \in \mathcal{B}} B \subseteq A\}$$

Thus $\mathcal{B}(A)$ contains the elements of $A$, together with the elements that can be deduced to belong to $\text{cl}(A)$ by the application of a single closure condition. Define $\mathcal{B}_0(A) = A$ and $\mathcal{B}_{i+1}(A) = \mathcal{B}(\mathcal{B}_i(A))$. Then $\mathcal{B}_i(A)$ contains the elements of $A$, together with the elements that can be deduced to belong to $\text{cl}(A)$ by the application of at most $i$ stages of applications of closure conditions. Finally, define $\mathcal{B}_\infty(A) = \bigcup_{i \geq 0} \mathcal{B}_i(A)$. Then we have

$$\text{cl}(A) = \mathcal{B}_\infty(A) \tag{1.2.1}$$

**Proof of Eq. (1.2.1).** Any element of $\mathcal{B}_\infty(A)$ must belong to $\mathcal{B}_i(A)$ for some $i$, and we have already seen that such an element must belong to $\text{cl}(A)$. Thus, $\mathcal{B}_\infty(A) \subseteq \text{cl}(A)$. It follows that $\mathcal{B}_\infty(A)$ is contained in any closed set containing $A$, and so to complete the proof it will suffice to show that $\mathcal{B}_\infty(A)$ is itself closed. To do this, it suffices to show that it satisfies each of the closure conditions $(B, b)$ in $\mathcal{B}$. Suppose that $B \subseteq \mathcal{B}_\infty$. Each of the finitely many elements of $B$ belongs to $\mathcal{B}_i$ for some $i$; by taking the largest of these values of $i$ we obtain $B \subseteq \mathcal{B}_i$. Then $b \in \mathcal{B}_{i+1}(A)$, and thus $b \in \mathcal{B}_\infty(A)$. □

Almost all algebraic systems provide examples of algebraic closure systems; here are some examples. Consider the collection of closure conditions

$$\mathcal{B} = \{(\{x, y\}, x + y), (\{x, y\}, x - y), (\{x, y\}, x \cdot y),$$
$$(\{x, z\}, x/z) : x, y, z \in \mathbf{C}, z \neq 0\}$$

where $\mathbf{C}$ denotes the field of complex numbers, and $+$, $-$, $\cdot$, and $/$ denote the usual arithmetic operations on such numbers. A set $F \subseteq \mathbf{C}$ satisfying these closure conditions is a number field, a subfield of the field $\mathbf{C}$.

Let $X$ be an arbitrary set, and let $\mathrm{Sym}(X)$ denote the set of all permutations on $X$, that is, the set of bijective maps from $X$ to itself. The set $\mathrm{Sym}(X)$ forms a group under the operation $\circ$ of composition. Consider the collection of closure conditions

$$\mathcal{B} = \{(\emptyset, \iota), (\{\varrho, \sigma\}, \varrho \circ \sigma), (\{\varrho\}, \varrho^{-1}) : \varrho, \sigma \in \mathrm{Sym}(X)\}$$

where $\iota$ denotes the identity permutation on $X$ and $\varrho^{-1}$ denotes the permutation inverse to $\varrho$. A set $G \subseteq \mathrm{Sym}(X)$ satisfying these closure conditions is a permutation group, a subgroup of $\mathrm{Sym}(X)$.

Finally, let $(L, \sqcap, \sqcup)$ be an arbitrary lattice algebra. Consider the collection of closure conditions

$$\mathcal{B} = \{(\{x, y\}, x \sqcap y), (\{x, y\}, x \sqcup y) : x, y \in L\}$$

A set $K \subseteq L$ satisfying these closure conditions gives rise to a lattice algebra $(K, \sqcap, \sqcup)$, a sublattice of $L$.

Closure systems provide an important source of complete lattices. Specifically, the closed sets in a closure system are endowed with a lattice order by set inclusion; infima (of pairs or arbitrary sets) are obtained by taking intersections; suprema are obtained by taking closures of unions. Thus, there is a lattice associated with each of the three examples just presented: the subfields of a field, the subgroups of a group, and the sublattices of a lattice all themselves form a lattice.

### 1.2.3. Polarities

Let $\approx$ be an arbitrary binary relation between two universes $V$ and $W$ (that is, an arbitrary subset of $V \times W$).

Such a relation will be called a *polarity* between $V$ and $W$. Define the map $v : V \to W$ by

$$v(A) = \{b \in W : \forall_{a \in A} a \approx b\}$$

and the map $w : W \to V$ by

$$w(B) = \{a \in V : \forall_{b \in B} a \approx b\}$$

Then $v$ and $w$ satisfy the following four conditions:

GC$_1$ For $X, Y \subseteq V$, if $X \subseteq Y$, then $v(X) \supseteq v(Y)$.
GC$_2$ For $X, Y \subseteq W$, if $X \subseteq Y$, then $w(X) \supseteq w(Y)$.
GC$_3$ For $A \subseteq V$, $w(v(A)) \supseteq A$.
GC$_4$ For $B \subseteq W$, $v(w(B)) \supseteq B$.

It is a consequence of these conditions that (1) $v = v \circ w \circ v$ and $w = w \circ v \circ w$, (2) $v \circ w$ is a closure map on $V$ and $w \circ v$ is a closure map on $W$, and (3) if $\mathcal{V} \subseteq \mathrm{Pow}(V)$ and $\mathcal{W} \subseteq \mathrm{Pow}(W)$ denote the closure systems corresponding to these closure maps, then $v$ (restricted to $\mathcal{V}$) and $w$ (restricted to $\mathcal{W}$) are inverse maps that establish an order-reversing isomorphism between the lattices $\mathcal{V}$ and $\mathcal{W}$.

Reciprocally, if $v$ and $w$ satisfy conditions GC$_1$ through GC$_4$, we may define from them a polarity $\approx$ by $a \approx b \Leftrightarrow a \in w(\{b\})$ (or equivalently, $a \approx b \Leftrightarrow b \in v(\{a\})$). A pair of maps satisfying conditions GC$_1$ through GC$_4$ is called a *Galois connection* (or "Galois correspondence"); polarities and Galois connections are different mathematical embodiment of the same underlying concept. (The equivalence between polarities and Galois connections was described by Everett [1944] and Ore [1944].)

The relationship between closure systems and closure criteria provides an example of a polarity. Let $U$ be an arbitrary set, let $V = \mathrm{Pow}(U)$ be the collection of subsets of $U$, and let $W = \mathrm{Cond}(U)$ be the collection of closure conditions for $U$. Define the polarity $\approx$ between $V$ and $W$ by $A \approx (B, b) \Leftrightarrow (B \subseteq A \Rightarrow b \in A)$. The the map $v$ assigns to any collection $\mathcal{A}$ of subsets of $U$ the closure criterion associated with the closure system generated by $\mathcal{A}$. The map $w$ assigns to any collection of closure conditions $\mathcal{B}$ the corresponding closure system associated with the closure criterion generated by $\mathcal{B}$. Then $\mathcal{V}$ is class of all closure systems, and $\mathcal{W}$ is the class of all closure criteria. The map $v \circ w$ takes any collection of subsets of $U$ into the closure system it generates, and the map $w \circ v$ takes any collection of closure conditions into the closure criterion it generates.

### Exercises

1. (E) Does every lattice contain a minimum element and a maximum element?

2. (M) Show that the infimum operation in a lattice is non-decreasing: for all $x, y, z \in L$, if $x \leq y$, then $x \sqcap z \leq y \sqcap z$. (This property extends to the right operand of $\sqcap$ by commutativity and to $\sqcup$ by duality.)

3. (M) Show that every lattice satisfies the "modular inequality": for all $x, y, z \in L$, if $x \leq z$, then $x \sqcup (y \sqcap z) \leq (x \sqcup y) \sqcap z$.

4. (E) A lattice is "modular" if it satisfies the modular equality: $x \sqcup (y \sqcap z) = (x \sqcup y) \sqcap z$. Give an example of a lattice that is not modular. (Hint: There is an example with five elements.)

5. (M) Show that the five-element lattice $N$ found in the preceding exercise is the only "forbidden sublattice" for modular lattices: a lattice is modular if and only if it does not contain a sublattice isomorphic to $N$.

6. (M) Give an example of a non-algebraic closure criterion for which Eq. (1.2.1) fails.

7. (H) Let $B_n$ denote the number of elements in the partition lattice Part($U$) over the universe $U = \{1, \ldots, n\}$. (a) Show that $B_{n+1} = \sum_{0 \leq k \leq n} \binom{n}{k} B_k$ for $n \geq 0$. (b) Show that the coefficient of $x^n$ in the power-series expansion of $e^{e^x - 1}$ is $B_n / n!$. (c) Show that $B_{n+1} = (1^n/0! + 2^n/1! + 3^n/2! + \cdots)/(1/0! + 1/1! + 1/2! + \cdots)$. (Parts (b) and (c) are due to E. T. Bell and G. Dobinski, respectively; see Rota [1964] for proofs and references.)

8. (M) Show that the conditions $CM_1$ through $CM_3$ are equivalent to the following single condition: $A \subseteq \mathrm{cl}(B)$ if and only if $\mathrm{cl}(A) \subseteq \mathrm{cl}(B)$.

9. (E) The closure criteria for a universe $U$ form a closure system for the universe Cond($U$). Give a set of closure conditions in Cond(Cond(U)) that engender this closure system.

10. (H) (a) Let $\alpha(n)$ denote the number of closure systems over the universe $U = \{1, \ldots, n\}$. Show that $\log_2 \alpha(n) \geq \binom{n}{\lfloor n/2 \rfloor}$. (Hint: If $\mathcal{G} \subseteq \mathrm{Pow}(U)$ is *downward-saturated*, that is, if $\mathcal{G}$ is such that $B \in \mathcal{G}$ and $A \subseteq B$ imply $A \in \mathcal{G}$, then $\mathcal{G} \cup \{U\}$ is a closure system.) (b) Let $\beta(n)$ denote the number of downward-saturated systems over $U = \{1, \ldots, n\}$. Show that for some constant $C$, $\log_2 \beta(n) \leq C\binom{n}{\lfloor n/2 \rfloor}$. (See Hansel [1966] for a proof with $C = \log_2 3$; see Korshunov [1981] for a much sharper result.) (c) Show that for some constant $C$, $\log_2 \alpha(n) \leq C\binom{n}{\lfloor n/2 \rfloor}$. (See Burosch *et al.* [1991] for a proof that, combined with part (b), yields $C = \sqrt{8} \log_2 3$; see Alekseev [1989] for a much sharper result.)

11. (H) Say that a collection of sets is a *chain* if it is totally ordered by the inclusion relation $\subseteq$. Say that a collection $\mathcal{G}$ of sets is *inductive* if, for every

chain $C \subseteq G$, we have $\bigcup C \in G$. Show that a closure system $G$ is algebraic if and only if it is inductive. (See Schmidt [1952].)

12. (M) Show that if $v$ and $w$ form a Galois connection, then either may be defined in terms of the other:

$$w(B) = \bigcap \{A \subseteq V : v(A) \supseteq B\}$$

and reciprocally.

### 1.3. Boolean Functions

Although our goal in this chapter is to study functions taking their arguments and values from any finite domain, we shall begin with the simplest interesting case, in which the domain has just two values. Most concepts applicable to the general case can be fully developed in this setting, but many phenomena occur more simply here than they do in general. We shall take the two values to be the natural numbers 0 and 1, and write $\mathbf{B} = \{0, 1\}$ for this domain.

An *n-adic Boolean function* is a map $f : \mathbf{B}^n \to \mathbf{B}$. Although it makes sense to speak of 0-adic functions (they are constant functions, and so there are just two of them), it will be convenient for technical reasons to avoid this case and assume that $n \geq 1$; 1-adic, 2-adic, ..., functions are often called *monadic*, *dyadic*, ..., functions.

There are just $2^n$ ways of assigning Boolean values to the $n$ arguments of an $n$-adic Boolean function. Thus, there are just $2^{2^n}$ possible $n$-adic Boolean functions, and each of these is described by a table that specifies its value for each of the $2^n$ assignments of values to the arguments. It may not be apparent how any of these functions can reasonably be regarded as "non-computable," since each can be computed by "table look-up," and so we shall begin by giving a concrete example of the sense of computability we have in mind.

Consider the dyadic functions "nand" (for "not and") and "excl" (for "exclusive or") defined by the following tables.

| $x\ y$ | nand$(x, y)$ | | $x\ y$ | excl$(x, y)$ |
|--------|--------------|---|--------|--------------|
| 0 0 | 1 | | 0 0 | 0 |
| 0 1 | 1 | | 0 1 | 1 |
| 1 0 | 1 | | 1 0 | 1 |
| 1 1 | 0 | | 1 1 | 0 |

It is possible to express excl by a formula in terms of nand:

$$\mathrm{excl}(x, y) = \mathrm{nand}(\mathrm{nand}(x, \mathrm{nand}(x, y)), \mathrm{nand}(\mathrm{nand}(x, y), y))$$

The validity of this formula can be verified by an exhaustive examination of cases. If we try to express nand in terms of excl, no similar formula presents itself, but how could we prove that none exists?

First, we must specify exactly what kind of formulas we will allow. The function to be expressed (in this case, nand) is to appear, with dummy variables as arguments, to the left of the "=" sign. The expression on the right-hand side is to be a finite combination of function applications, with all of the functions being from some class of allowed functions (in this case, the class contains just the function excl) and with each argument of each function being either another function application or one of the variables appearing on the left-hand side (in this case, $x$ and $y$). We do not allow explicit Boolean constants on the right-hand side, though of course we do allow that a subexpression might yield a constant value. (This style of definition corresponds roughly to the "arithmetic function statement" in the language Fortran, though adapted, of course, to the Boolean domain. It also corresponds in scope, though not in succinctness, to the computation of a Boolean function from other Boolean functions by a "combinational logic network" or "circuit," and this is perhaps a more familiar motivation in the Boolean case.)

We claim that it is always possible to determine, in a finite number of steps, whether a given Boolean function can be expressed in this way in terms of a given finite set of Boolean functions. We shall informally describe a procedure for doing this.

Suppose the $n$-adic function $f$ is to be expressed in terms of the $m$-adic function $g$. (For simplicity we suppose that there is just one function allowed on the right-hand side.) The idea is to construct the set $F$ of *all* $n$-adic functions that can be expressed in terms of $g$. We start by putting the "projection functions" defined by

$$\text{proj}_{n,i}(x_1, \ldots, x_n) = x_i$$

into $F$. (They can certainly be expressed, since the right-hand side might consist of a single variable.) Then we add to $F$ all functions that can be expressed by "composing" $g$ with $m$ functions $h_1, \ldots, h_m$ that already belong to $F$. (They can certainly be expressed, since the right-hand sides that express the functions $h_1, \ldots, h_m$ might appear as the arguments of an application of $g$ on the right-hand side.) We continue until no new functions can be added to $F$ in this way. (This must eventually happen, since there are only finitely many $n$-adic functions.) When we are done, $F$ contains all $n$-adic functions that can be expressed in terms of $g$ (this can be verified by a "structural induction" on the right-hand side of the expression), and we have only to check whether or not $f$ appears in $F$ to answer our original question.

In the example, we start by putting the two dyadic projection functions into $F$. At the next stage, we add the dyadic constant function 0 and the function excl. After this, no more functions can be added, and we conclude that nand, which does not appear in $F$, cannot be expressed in terms of excl.

If we want to know whether a *particular* function can be expressed in terms of a particular finite set of other function, the procedure we have described will, in principle, always yield an answer (the number of possibilities to be considered will always be finite, though it may be too large to handle in practice). In the next section we shall present a theory that allows such questions to be resolved much more efficiently and, more importantly, yields qualitative information that could not be established by examining any number of particular cases. Here is an example of such a qualitative conclusion. Suppose that we have an infinite sequence $f_0, f_1, f_2, \ldots$, of Boolean functions. Then there exists a natural number $k$ such that every function $f_i$ can be computed from the set $\{f_0, f_1, f_2, \ldots, f_k\}$. This is not at all obvious; it might seem that one could construct a sequence of more and more complicated Boolean functions, without ever being able to express all Boolean functions. Nevertheless, it follows from the theory presented in the next section.

## 1.4. Clones

Let $\mathcal{F}_n$ denote the set of all $n$-adic Boolean functions. Let $\mathcal{F} = \bigcup_{n \geq 1} \mathcal{F}_n$ denote the set of all Boolean functions.

Let $\mathcal{P} \subseteq \mathcal{F}$ be a class of Boolean functions. We set $\mathcal{P}_n = \mathcal{P} \cap \mathcal{F}_n$ (the $n$-adic functions in $\mathcal{P}$). We shall say that $\mathcal{P}$ is a *clone* if it satisfies the following six conditions:

$C_1$  The monadic "identity function" $\mathrm{id}(x) = x$ belongs to $\mathcal{P}$.

$C_2$  For every $f \in \mathcal{P}_n$, the "cylindrification" $\mathrm{cyl}(f) \in \mathcal{F}_{n+1}$, defined by

$$\mathrm{cyl}(f)(x_1, \ldots, x_n, x_{n+1}) = f(x_1, \ldots, x_n)$$

belongs to $\mathcal{P}$.

$C_3$  For every $f \in \mathcal{P}_n$, the "diagonalization" $\mathrm{diag}(f) \in \mathcal{F}_{n-1}$, defined by

$$\mathrm{diag}(f)(x_1, \ldots, x_{n-1}) = f(x_1, \ldots, x_{n-1}, x_{n-1})$$

belongs to $\mathcal{P}$. (If $f$ is monadic, we shall take $\mathrm{diag}(f) = f$.)

$C_4$  For every $f \in \mathcal{P}_n$, the "rotation" $\mathrm{rot}(f) \in \mathcal{F}_n$, defined by

$$\mathrm{rot}(f)(x_1, x_2, \ldots, x_{n-1}, x_n) = f(x_2, x_3, \ldots, x_n, x_1)$$

belongs to $\mathcal{P}$. (If $f$ is monadic, we shall take $\mathrm{rot}(f) = f$.)

C$_5$ For every $f \in \mathcal{P}_n$, the "transposition" trans$(f) \in \mathcal{F}_n$, defined by

$$\text{trans}(f)(x_1, x_2, \ldots, x_{n-1}, x_n) = f(x_1, x_2, \ldots, x_n, x_{n-1})$$

belongs to $\mathcal{P}$. (If $f$ is monadic, we shall take trans$(f) = f$.)

C$_6$ For every $f \in \mathcal{P}_n$ and $g \in \mathcal{P}_m$, their "composition" comp$(f, g) \in \mathcal{F}_{n+m-1}$, defined by

$$\text{comp}(f, g)(x_1, \ldots, x_{n+m-1}) = f(x_1, \ldots, x_{n-1}, g(x_n, \ldots, x_{n+m-1}))$$

belongs to $\mathcal{P}$.

This list of conditions is rather long, though each condition is quite simple. We have chosen this list, which is due to Maltsev [1966], to emphasize the analogy with a similar list that will be given later for relations. A much shorter characterization of clones is given by the following two conditions:

C$'_1$ For each $n \geq m \geq 1$, $\mathcal{P}_n$ contains the "projection function" $\text{proj}_{n,m}$, defined by

$$\text{proj}_{n,m}(x_1, \ldots, x_n) = x_m$$

C$'_2$ For each $n, m \geq 1$, each $f \in \mathcal{P}_n$ and each $g_1, \ldots, g_n \in \mathcal{P}_m$, $\mathcal{P}_m$ contains the composite function $h = f \circ (g_1, \ldots, g_n)$ defined by

$$h(x_1, \ldots, x_m) = f(g_1(x_1, \ldots, x_m), \ldots, g_n(x_1, \ldots, x_m))$$

It is straightforward, though lengthy, to show that a class of Boolean functions forms a clone if and only if it satisfies conditions C$'_1$ and C$'_2$. A key step is to show that any permutation of arguments can be obtained through a sequence of rotations and transpositions. A few words concerning the origin of the terms "projection," "cylindrification," and "diagonalization" may be helpful. The first two arise from concrete analogies with geometry: one can easily visualize the projection of a three-dimensional figure onto a two-dimensional coordinate plane, for example, or the cylindrification of a two-dimensional figure into a three-dimensional one. The term "diagonalization" is most easily understood in terms of matrices: if the entry $M_{i,j}$ of a square matrix $M$ is regarded as a function of the row and column indices $i$ and $j$, then the entries $M_{k,k}$ obtained by substituting the same value for both arguments appear on the main diagonal.

The conditions defining clones are algebraic closure conditions, thus the clones constitute a closure system with universe $\mathcal{F}$. There is a smallest clone, which is the intersection of all clones; we shall denote it $\mathcal{I}$. From conditions C$'_1$ and C$'_2$ it is easy to see that $\mathcal{I}$ comprises exactly the projection functions. If

$\mathcal{A} \subseteq \mathcal{F}$ is any set of Boolean functions, there is a smallest clone containing all of the functions in $\mathcal{A}$; this is the clone generated by $\mathcal{A}$, and we denote it $\langle \mathcal{A} \rangle$. If $\mathcal{A} = \{f_1, \ldots, f_k\}$ is a finite set, we may write $\langle f_1, \ldots, f_k \rangle$ for $\langle \mathcal{A} \rangle$, and refer to $f_1, \ldots, f_k$ as generators of $\langle \mathcal{A} \rangle$. For $k = 0$ we have $\langle \rangle = \mathcal{I}$.

There is also a largest clone, namely, $\mathcal{F}$. Furthermore, the clones form a lattice under set inclusion; this lattice is called Post's Lattice (see Post [1920, 1941]), and we shall now proceed to describe it.

This description is facilitated by an important property of Post's Lattice called "duality." Although the domain of Boolean functions contains two elements, nothing in the closure conditions assigns any particular role to either of these elements. Thus, the entire theory we are developing, and in particular Post's Lattice, remains unchanged if we interchange the roles of 0 and 1. This process assigns to each Boolean function $f$ another function, which we call the *dual* of $f$ and denote by $\tilde{f}$, defined by

$$\tilde{f}(x_1, \ldots, x_k) = \overline{f(\overline{x_1}, \ldots, \overline{x_k})}$$

(Here the overlining denotes Boolean complementation, which interchanges the roles of 0 and 1.) If we take the dual of each function in a clone $\mathcal{P}$, we obtain another clone, which we call the dual of $\mathcal{P}$ and denote $\tilde{\mathcal{P}}$.

Duality imparts a bilateral symmetry to Post's Lattice. We shall regard this as a left–right symmetry, in which clones that are their own duals appear in a medial plane, and every other clone on one side of this plane is accompanied by its mirror-image on the other side. (We shall use the terms "up" and "down" to refer to the ordering of clones by set inclusion, so that $\mathcal{F}$ is the top of the lattice and $\mathcal{I}$ is the bottom.) We point out that there is a difference between saying that a clone $\mathcal{P}$ is "self-dual" (that is, that $\mathcal{P} = \tilde{\mathcal{P}}$) and saying that it consists entirely of self-dual functions (that is, functions $f$ such that $f = \tilde{f}$).

We shall say that a clone $\mathcal{P}$ is "covered" by another clone $\mathcal{P}'$ if $\mathcal{P} \subseteq \mathcal{P}'$ and, if $\mathcal{Q}$ is a clone such that $\mathcal{P} \subseteq \mathcal{Q} \subseteq \mathcal{P}'$, then either $\mathcal{Q} = \mathcal{P}$ or $\mathcal{Q} = \mathcal{P}'$. We may indicate this in diagrams by an upward arrow from $\mathcal{P}$ to $\mathcal{P}'$. To keep the diagrams clear, however, we shall not indicate all coverings in this way; those that we do not indicate with arrows will be described in the accompanying text.

The clones all have names that are fairly standardized, but some curious idiosyncrasies are due to the fact that Post dealt with what he called "iterative classes" rather than clones (he did not require the presence of the projection functions, or closure under cylindrification), so that some of the classes to which he gave names are missing from from the description given here.

There are two ways to describe any clone. One is to construct it "from the bottom up," by giving a set of functions that generate it (in which case adding more functions yields a larger clone). The other is to construct it "from the top down," by giving a set of constraints that all its constituent functions satisfy (in which case adding more constraints yields a smaller clone).

When listing generators, we shall write "0" and "1" for monadic constant functions (as well as for Boolean values), and write "neg" for the monadic "negation" (or complement) function. We shall say that a function is "quasi-monadic" if it has at most one essential argument (that is, argument on which its value actually depends). We shall say that a function $f$ is "monotone" if $x_1 \leq y_1, \ldots, x_n \leq y_n$ imply $f(x_1, \ldots, x_n) \leq f(y_1, \ldots, y_n)$. We shall say that a function $f$ is "0-preserving" if $f(0, \ldots, 0) = 0$, "1-preserving" if $f(1, \ldots, 1) = 1$, and "bi-preserving" if it is both 0-preserving and 1-preserving.

There are six clones that consist entirely of quasi-monadic functions. Four of these contain only monotone quasi-monadic functions, as follows:

Here $O_1 = \mathcal{I}$ comprises the bi-preserving quasi-monadic functions (equivalently, the self-dual monotone quasi-monadic functions), $O_6$ is generated by 0 and comprises the 0-preserving quasi-monadic functions, $O_5$ is the dual of $O_6$, and $O_8$ is generated by 0 and 1 and comprises all monotone quasi-monadic functions. Two more clones contain non-monotone quasi-monadic functions, as follows:

Here $O_4$ is generated by neg and comprises all self-dual quasi-monadic functions; $O_9$ is generated by neg and either constant function and comprises all quasi-monadic functions. In addition to the coverings shown in the preceding diagrams, $O_9$ covers $O_8$ and $O_4$ covers $O_1$.

We shall say that a function is "quasi-symmetric" if it is invariant under all permutations of its essential arguments. We shall say that a function is "conjunctive" if it is either constant or the conjunction (the "and") of its essential arguments. We shall say that a function is "disjunctive" if it is either constant or the disjunction (the "or") of its essential arguments. We shall say that a function is "linear" if it is either the sum modulo 2 (the "parity") of its essential arguments, or the negation of this sum.

We shall write "conj," "disj," and "par" for the dyadic conjunction, dyadic disjunction, and triadic sum modulo 2 (the function par is chosen to be triadic rather than dyadic so that, having an odd number of essential arguments, it will be self-dual).

There are 13 clones that consist entirely of quasi-symmetric functions (in addition to those that contain only quasi-monadic functions). Four of these consist entirely of conjunctive functions, as follows:

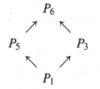

Here $P_1$ is generated by conj and comprises all bi-preserving conjunctive functions; $P_5$ is generated by conj and 0 and comprises all 0-preserving conjunctive functions; $P_3$ is generated by conj and 1 and comprises all 1-preserving conjunctive functions; and $P_6$ is generated by conj, 0, and 1 and comprises all conjunctive functions. In addition to the coverings shown in the preceding diagram, $P_6$, $P_5$, $P_3$, and $P_1$ cover $O_8$, $O_5$, $O_6$, and $O_1$, respectively.

Four clones consist entirely of disjunctive functions (in addition to those that contain only quasi-monadic functions). The situation for disjunction is dual to that for conjunction, with disj replacing conj and $S_i$ replacing $P_i$.

Five clones consist entirely of linear functions (in addition to those that contain only quasi-monadic functions), as follows:

Here $L_4$ is generated by par and comprises all bi-preserving linear functions (equivalently, all linear functions that satisfy any two of the three constraints: self-dual, 0-preserving, and 1-preserving); $L_3$ is generated by par and 0 and comprises all 0-preserving linear functions; $L_5$ is generated by par and neg and comprises all self-dual linear functions; $L_2$ is the dual of $L_3$; and $L_1$ is generated by par, 0, and 1 (equivalently, by par and any two of the three functions: neg, 0, and 1) and comprises all linear functions. In addition to the coverings shown in the preceding diagram, $L_1$, $L_2$, $L_5$, $L_3$, and $L_4$ cover $O_9$, $O_5$, $O_4$, $O_6$, and $O_1$, respectively.

We shall write "maj" for the triadic majority function, which, having an odd number of arguments, is self-dual.

There are three clones that consist entirely of self-dual functions (in addition to those that contain only linear functions), as follows:

$$D_3$$
$$\uparrow$$
$$D_1$$
$$\uparrow$$
$$D_2$$

Here $D_2$ is generated by maj and comprises the monotone self-dual functions; $D_1$ is generated by maj and par (equivalently, by maj ∘ neg, the triadic majority function with one argument negated) and comprises the bi-preserving self-dual functions; and $D_3$ is generated by maj, par, 0, and 1 (equivalently, by maj, par and neg, or by neg ∘ maj, the negation of the triadic majority function) and comprises all self-dual functions. In addition to the coverings shown in the preceding diagram, $D_3$, $D_1$, and $D_2$ cover $L_5$, $L_4$, and $O_1$, respectively.

Thus far we have developed our description from the bottom up; we shall now switch to working from the top down.

At the top of the picture, we have four clones as follows:

$$C_1$$
$$\nearrow \quad \nwarrow$$
$$C_2 \qquad C_3$$
$$\nwarrow \quad \nearrow$$
$$C_4$$

Here $C_1 = \mathcal{F}$, whereas $C_2$, $C_3$, and $C_4$ are obtained from $C_1$ by restricting the functions to be 0-preserving, 1-preserving, and bi-preserving, respectively. The clone $C_4$ is generated by par, conj, and disj, whereas $C_2$, $C_3$, and $C_1$ are generated by these functions together with 0, 1, or both.

In addition to the coverings shown in the preceding diagram, $C_1$ covers $D_3$ and $L_1$; $C_2$ and $C_3$ cover $L_2$ and $L_3$, respectively; and $C_4$ covers $D_1$.

If we further restrict the functions to be monotone, we obtain four additional clones as follows:

$$A_1$$
$$\nearrow \quad \nwarrow$$
$$A_2 \qquad A_3$$
$$\nwarrow \quad \nearrow$$
$$A_4$$

Here $A_1$ comprises all monotone functions, whereas $A_2$, $A_3$, and $A_4$ are obtained from $A_1$ by restricting the functions to be 0-preserving, 1-preserving, and bi-preserving, respectively. The clone $A_4$ is generated by conj and disj, whereas $A_2$, $A_3$, and $A_1$ are generated by these functions together with 0, 1, or both. In addition to the coverings shown in the preceding diagram, $A_1$, $A_2$, $A_3$, and $A_4$ are covered by $C_1$, $C_2$, $C_3$, and $C_4$, respectively; $A_1$ covers $P_6$ and $S_6$; and $A_2$ and $A_3$ cover $P_5$ and $S_5$, respectively.

At last we come to the most interesting part of the picture. We shall write "thresh$_{k,m}$" for the $m$-adic function that assumes the value 1 when at least $k$ of its arguments assume the value 1. (Thus, disj = thresh$_{1,2}$, conj = thresh$_{2,2}$, and maj = thresh$_{2,3}$.)

We shall say that a function $f$ is "doubly 0-preserving" if, given any two assignments $x_1^1, \ldots, x_n^1$ and $x_1^2, \ldots, x_n^2$ such that $f(x_1^1, \ldots, x_n^1) = f(x_1^2, \ldots, x_n^2)$ = 1, there exists a $j$ in the range $1 \leq j \leq n$ such that $x_j^1 = x_j^2 = 1$. We may generalize this definition by saying that a function $f$ is "$m$-tuply 0-preserving" (for $m \geq 1$) if, given any $m$ assignments $x_1^1, \ldots, x_n^1, \ldots, x_1^m, \ldots, x_n^m$ such that $f(x_1^1, \ldots, x_n^1) = \cdots = f(x_1^m, \ldots, x_n^m) = 1$, there exists a $j$ in the range $1 \leq j \leq n$ such that $x_j^1 = \cdots = x_j^m = 1$. (Here "singly 0-preserving" reduces to "0-preserving.") Finally, we shall say that a function is "infinitely 0-preserving" if it is $m$-tuply 0-preserving for all $m \geq 1$.

For each $m = 2, 3, \ldots, \infty$, there are four clones consisting entirely of $m$-tuply 0-preserving functions, as follows:

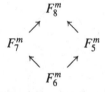

Here $F_8^m$ comprises all $m$-tuply 0-preserving functions; $F_7^m$ is obtained by restricting the functions to be monotone; $F_5^m$ is obtained by restricting the functions to be 1-preserving; and $F_6^m$ is obtained by restricting the functions to be monotone and 1-preserving. For $2 \leq m < \infty$, $F_8^m$ is generated by thresh$_{m,m+1}$ and conj ∘ disj; $F_7^m$ is generated by thresh$_{m,m+1}$, conj ∘ disj and 0; $F_6^m$ is generated by thresh$_{m,m+1}$ and conj ∘ disj ∘ neg; and $F_7^m$ is generated by thresh$_{m,m+1}$, conj ∘ disj ∘ neg and 0. The clones $F_8^m$, $F_5^m$, $F_7^m$, and $F_6^m$, cover $F_8^{m+1}$, $F_5^{m+1}$, $F_7^{m+1}$, and $F_6^{m+1}$, respectively, and these four sequences of clones descend to their intersections $F_8^\infty$, $F_5^\infty$, $F_7^\infty$, and $F_6^\infty$, respectively. The clone $F_6^\infty$ is generated by conj ∘ disj; $F_7^\infty$ is generated by conj ∘ disj and 0; $F_6^\infty$ is generated by conj ∘ disj ∘ neg; and $F_7^\infty$ is generated by conj ∘ disj ∘ neg and 0. In addition to these coverings, $C_3$ and $C_4$ cover $F_8^2$ and $F_5^2$, respectively; $A_3$ and $A_4$ cover $F_7^2$ and $F_6^2$, respectively; $F_6^2$ covers $D_2$; and $F_7^\infty$ and $F_6^\infty$ cover $P_3$ and $P_1$, respectively.

Finally, we may define "doubly 1-preserving," "$m$-tuply 1-preserving," and "infinitely 1-preserving." The situation for multiple 1-preservation is dual to that for 0-preservation, with $F_{i-4}^m$ replacing $F_i^m$.

This completes our "anatomy" of Post's Lattice, which contains eight infinite families of clones (the multiply 0- and 1-preserving families), together with finitely many other "sporadic" clones. This description was worked out by Post [1920, 1941]; the results were announced in 1920, but the details were not published until 1941. It is said (see Gavrilov [1984]) that Post's original derivation of the classification filled about a thousand pages; his published version takes about a hundred pages. A somewhat streamlined, but still lengthy, account is given by Yablonski, Gavrilov, and Kudryavtsev [1966, 1970]. Recently Ugolnikov [1988] has compressed a complete proof of the classification into just a dozen pages.

Many non-obvious facts about clones can be determined by inspection of the lattice. For example, since there are no infinite ascending chains (though there are infinite descending chains) every infinite set of functions can be generated from a finite subset (this is the example given at the end of the preceding section). Furthermore, since there are no infinite antichains (families of mutually incomparable clones), any infinite sequence of functions contains one that can be generated from one other.

A proof that Post's Lattice is as we have described it would be too lengthy to present here, but we shall at least indicate the overall structure of such a proof. The proof divides into two parts. The first part begins by giving, for each of the clones we have listed, two descriptions: one in terms of generators and the other in terms of constraints. It then includes for each clone in the list a lemma to the effect that any function meeting all of the constraints describing the clone can be expressed in terms of the generators describing the clone. At this point one knows that there are at least as many clones as appear in our list. The second part of the proof establishes that there are no others. Each of the clones in our list covers only finitely many other clones in the list. The second part includes a proof for each covering clone that any clone that satisfies all of its constraints, but that does not satisfy all of the constraints of the covered clones, includes a set of generators for the covering clone. In the following section we shall give a proof of one of the main consequences of the classification: the "Finite-Basis Theorem," which states that every Boolean clone is generated by a finite set of functions.

### Exercises

1. (E) What problem would arise in the definition of a clone if we allowed 0-adic functions?

2. (E) There are 16 dyadic Boolean functions. Which clone does each of them generate?
3. (E) (a) What clones contain both 0 and 1? (b) What clones contain neg?
4. (M) Show that if a clone comprising only monotone and self-dual functions contains a non-projection function, then it contains maj.
5. (M) Show that the clone of all monotone and self-dual functions is generated by maj.

## 1.5. The Finite-Basis Theorem

In this section we shall prove that every Boolean clone is generated by a finite set of functions. This result was first obtained as a corollary of Post's classification of the Boolean clones. More recent work by Gavrilov [1984] and Marchenkov [1984] has produced proofs of the Finite-Basis Theorem that take about ten pages. Our proof is a further simplification of Marchenkov's.

We shall say that a $n$-adic Boolean function $f$ (with $n \geq 3$) is a *rejection function* if $f(x_1, \ldots, x_n) = c$ whenever all, or all but one, of the arguments $x_1$, $\ldots, x_n$ assume the value $c \in \mathbf{B}$. The following proposition, which derives from the work of Baker and Pixley [1975], is the key to the Finite-Basis Theorem.

***Proposition 1.5.1.*** *If a Boolean clone $\mathcal{P}$ contains a rejection function, then $\mathcal{P}$ has a finite basis.*

For the proof of Proposition 1.5.1, we shall need some lemmas. The first of these requires us to consider "partial" Boolean functions. A *$n$-adic Boolean partial function* is a map $f : D \to \mathbf{B}$, where $D \subseteq \mathbf{B}^n$ is a set called the *domain* of $f$ and denoted $\mathrm{dom}(f) = D$. We shall call $f$ a *$p$-point* function if $\mathrm{dom}(f)$ has cardinality $p$. We shall call $f$ a *total* function if $\mathrm{dom}(f) = \mathbf{B}^n$. If $f$ and $g$ are $n$-adic Boolean partial functions, we shall say that $f$ is a *restriction* of $g$, or that $g$ is an *extension* of $f$, if (1) $\mathrm{dom}(f) \subseteq \mathrm{dom}(g)$ and (2) $f(x_1, \ldots, x_n) = g(x_1, \ldots, x_n)$ for all $(x_1, \ldots, x_n) \in \mathrm{dom}(f)$. If a partial Boolean function $f$ has an extension $g$ that belongs to a clone $\mathcal{P}$, we shall say that $f$ *extends into* $\mathcal{P}$ *(via $g$)*.

*Lemma 1.5.2.* Suppose the Boolean clone $\mathcal{P}$ contains a $(d + 1)$-adic rejection function $r$. For $d \leq p \leq 2^n$, if every $d$-point restriction of the $n$-adic total function $f$ extends into $\mathcal{P}$, then every $p$-point restriction of $f$ does also.

**Proof.** We proceed by induction on $p - d$. The basis $p = d$ is trivial, and so suppose that $p \geq d + 1$. Let $g$ be a $p$-point restriction of $f$. Let $g_1, \ldots, g_{d+1}$

be $(p-1)$-point restrictions of $g$ (and thus of $f$) obtained by deleting $d+1$ distinct points from dom$(g)$. By inductive hypothesis, the functions $g_1, \ldots, g_{d+1}$ extend into $\mathcal{P}$ via total functions $h_1, \ldots, h_{d+1}$. Then $g$ extends into $\mathcal{P}$ via $h = r \circ (h_1, \ldots, h_{d+1})$. $\square$

**Corollary 1.5.3.** *Suppose the Boolean clone $\mathcal{P}$ contains a $(d+1)$-adic rejection function $r$. If every $d$-point restriction of the $n$-adic total function $f$ extends into $\mathcal{P}$, then $f$ itself belongs to $\mathcal{P}$.*

**Proof.** We take $p = 2^n$ in Lemma 1.5.2. $\square$

*Lemma 1.5.4.* Suppose the Boolean clone $\mathcal{P}$ contains a $(d + 1)$-adic rejection function $r$. If every $2^d$-adic diagonalization of the $n$-adic function $f$ belongs to $\mathcal{P}$, then $f$ itself belongs to $\mathcal{P}$.

**Proof.** By Corollary 1.5.3, it will suffice to show that every $d$-point restriction $g$ of $f$ extends into $\mathcal{P}$. Since dom$(g)$ contains just $d$ rows (points), it contains at most $2^d$ distinct columns (argument indices). For $1 \le i \le n$, let $j_i$ denote the smallest argument index $j$ such that argument $j$ is equivalent to argument $i$. Define the diagonalization $h$ of $f$ by

$$h(x_1, \ldots, x_n) = f(x_{j_1}, \ldots, x_{j_n}).$$

Since $h$ depends essentially on, at most, $2^d$ arguments, $h$ belongs to $\mathcal{P}$ by hypothesis. Since $g$ agrees with $h$ on dom$(g)$, $g$ extends into $\mathcal{P}$ via $h$. $\square$

**Proof of Proposition 1.5.1.** We shall show that the finite set $\mathcal{P} \cap \mathcal{F}_{2^d}$ generates $\mathcal{P}$. We clearly have $\langle \mathcal{P} \cap \mathcal{F}_{2^d} \rangle \subseteq \mathcal{P}$, and so it will suffice to show that $\mathcal{P} \subseteq \langle \mathcal{P} \cap \mathcal{F}_{2^d} \rangle$. First, we have $r \in \langle \mathcal{P} \cap \mathcal{F}_{2^d} \rangle$, since $d+1 \le 2^d$. Thus, if $f$ belongs to $\mathcal{P}$, all of its $2^d$-adic diagonalizations belong to $\langle \mathcal{P} \cap \mathcal{F}_{2^d} \rangle$, and thus so does $f$. $\square$

We are now ready to begin the analysis leading to the Finite-Basis Theorem. The following lemma give the simplest case.

*Lemma 1.5.5.* If a clone contains only quasi-monadic functions, then it has a finite basis.

**Proof.** There are only four essentially different quasi-monadic functions. $\square$

Next we need the notion of the "Zhegalkin polynomial" of a Boolean function. The set **B** may be regarded as a field of two elements (usually denoted $GF(2)$), with the conjunction "conj" playing the role of multiplication and "excl" playing the role of addition. For $I \subseteq \{1, \ldots, n\}$, we shall write the "monomial" $\prod_{i \in I} x_i$ for the product of the appropriate arguments, and for $\mathcal{I} \subseteq \mathrm{Pow}(\{1, \ldots, n\})$, we shall write the "polynomial" $\sum_{I \in \mathcal{I}} \prod_{i \in I} x_i$ sum of the appropriate monomials. Each such polynomial represents an $n$-adic Boolean function, and distinct polynomials represent distinct functions (as can be seen by considering a monomial of minimum degree in the difference (that is, sum) of two polynomials). Since there are $2^{2^n}$ sets $\mathcal{I} \subseteq \mathrm{Pow}(\{1, \ldots, n\})$ and $2^{2^n}$ $n$-adic Boolean functions, this establishes a one-to-one correspondence between polynomials and functions. The polynomial corresponding to the function $f$ is called the *Zhegalkin polynomial* of $f$ (after Zhegalkin [1927, 1928]), and will be denoted $Z(f)$. A function $f$ will be called *linear* if all of the monomials in $Z(f)$ have degree at most 1; thus, a linear function has the form

$$f(x_1, \ldots, x_n) = \sum_{j \in J} x_j + c$$

for some $J \subseteq \{1, \ldots, n\}$ and $c \in \mathbf{B}$. (Since a constant term $c = 1$ is allowed, some would prefer to call these functions "affine," reserving the name linear for the case $c = 0$; but our usage is the more common one in the literature on Boolean functions.)

*Lemma 1.5.6.* If a clone contains only linear functions, and contains a non-quasi-monadic function, then it contains the function $\mathrm{par}(x, y, z) = x + y + z$.

**Proof.** Let $f$ be a non-quasi-monadic linear function. We may assume that $f$ depends essentially on all of its $n$ arguments, where $n \geq 2$ and, thus, that it has the form $f(x_1, \ldots, x_n) = x_1 + \cdots + x_n + c$. We may assume that $c = 0$ by transferring attention, if necessary, to the function $g(x_1, \ldots, x_{2n-1}) = f(x_1, \ldots, x_{n-1}, f(x_n, \ldots, x_{2n-1}))$. And we may assume that $n$ is odd (and thus that $n \geq 3$) by transferring attention, if necessary, in the same way. Then identifying all of the arguments $x_3, \ldots, x_n$ yields the function par.     □

*Lemma 1.5.7.* If a clone contains only linear functions, then it has a finite basis.

**Proof.** If the clone $\mathcal{P}$ contains only quasi-monadic functions, then we are done by Lemma 1.5.5, so we may assume by Lemma 1.5.6 that it contains the function par. We shall show that $\mathcal{P}$ is generated by $\{\mathrm{par}\} \cup \mathcal{P}_1$. Let $f$ be a function in $\mathcal{P}$, and let $g$ be the function in $\mathcal{P}_1$ obtained from $f$ by identifying all arguments.

The function $f$ is characterized by the number $n$ of arguments it depends on and the constant term $c$. If $n$ is odd, then we can obtain the function $\text{par}_n(x_1, \ldots, x_n) = \sum_{1 \le j \le n} x_j$ by repeated composition of $\text{par}_3 = \text{par}$ with itself. We then have $g(x) = x + c$, so that $f = g \circ \text{par}_n$. If $n$ is even, then we can obtain the function $\text{par}_{n+1}$ by repeated composition of $\text{par}_3$ with itself. We then have $g(x) = c$, so that $f(x_1, \ldots, x_n) = \text{par}_{n+1}(x_1, \ldots, x_n, g(x_n))$. □

**Lemma 1.5.8.** If a clone contains a non-linear function, then it contains a dyadic or triadic non-linear function.

**Proof.** Let $f$ be a non-linear function such that every diagonal of $f$ is linear. Let $X = \prod_{i \in I} x_i$ be a non-linear term of minimum degree $d \ge 2$ in the Zhegalkin polynomial of $f(x_1, \ldots, x_n)$. If $X$ has degree 3 or more, then identifying two of the arguments appearing in $X$ results in a non-linear diagonal of $f$, a contradiction. Thus, there are just two arguments in $X$. If there are two or more arguments not appearing in $X$, then identifying any two again results in a non-linear diagonal, a contradiction. Thus, there is at most one argument not in $X$, and there are at most three arguments in all. □

**Lemma 1.5.9.** Suppose that the clone $\mathcal{P}$ contains a triadic non-linear function $f$, but no dyadic non-linear function. Then $\mathcal{P}$ contains the triadic majority function.

**Proof.** First we shall show that $f(x, y, z) = \text{maj}(x, y, z) + g(x, y, z)$, where $g$ is a linear function. Let $k$ be the number of quadratic terms in $Z(f)$. If $k = 0$, the there must be a cubic term in $Z(f)$ (since $f$ is non-linear), and any diagonal of $f$ is non-linear, a contradiction. If $k = 1$ or $k = 2$, then there is one pair of similar arguments (with respect to quadratic terms) and two pairs of dissimilar arguments. If there is a cubic term, then identifying the similar pair yields a non-linear diagonal, whereas if there is no cubic term, then identifying a dissimilar pair yields a non-linear diagonal, in either case a contradiction. Thus, we have $k = 3$. If there is a cubic term, we again obtain a non-linear diagonal by identifying any two arguments, a contradiction. Thus, we have all three quadratic terms and no cubic term. These are precisely the non-linear terms in $Z(\text{maj})$, and so $f$ is the sum of maj and a linear function $g$.

Now consider the number $l$ of arguments appearing as terms of degree 1 in $Z(g)$. If $l$ is odd, then identifying all three arguments in $f$ yields a monadic constant function, and substituting this constant for any argument of $f$ yields a dyadic non-linear function, a contradiction. Thus $l$ is even. Now consider the constant term $c$ in $Z(g)$. If $c = 1$, then identifying all three arguments in

$f$ yields the monadic negation function, and composing $f$ with this function changes the constant term to 0 while leaving the rest of $Z(f)$ unchanged. Thus, we may assume that $c = 0$.

Now if $l = 0$, then $g(x, y, z) = 0$ and $f(x, y, z) = \text{maj}(x, y, z)$, and so we are done. If $l = 2$, then $g(x, y, z) = x + y$ (say), and so $f(x, y, z) = \text{maj}(x, y, \bar{z})$. Then $f(x, y, f(x, y, z)) = \text{maj}(x, y, z)$, and again we are done. $\square$

**Lemma 1.5.10.** If a clone $\mathcal{P}$ contains a dyadic non-linear function $f$, then it contains either the dyadic disjunction or the dyadic conjunction.

**Proof.** We observe that both the hypothesis and conclusion of the lemma are invariant under dualization. Since $f$ is dyadic and non-linear, we have $f(x, y) = \text{conj}(x, y) + g(x, y)$, where $g$ is a linear function. Consider the number $l$ of arguments appearing as terms of degree 1 in $Z(g)$.

If $l = 0$, then $f(x, y) = \text{conj}(x, y) + c$ for some constant $c \in \mathbf{B}$. If $c = 0$, then $f(x, y) = \text{conj}(x, y)$, and we are done. If $c = 1$, then diagonalizing $f$ yields the monadic negation function, and composing $f$ with this function changes the constant term to 0 while leaving the rest of $Z(f)$ unchanged, so again we are done.

If $l = 1$, then we have $f(x, y) = \text{conj}(x, y) + x + c$ (say). If $c = 1$, then the dual $\tilde{f}$ has $\tilde{l} = 1$ and $\tilde{c} = 0$. Thus, we may assume that $c = 0$, so that $f(x, y) = \text{conj}(x, \bar{y})$. Then $f(x, f(x, y)) = \text{conj}(x, y)$, and again we are done.

Finally, if $l = 2$, then the dual $\tilde{f}$ has $\tilde{l} = 0$, and again we are done. $\square$

If a function $f$ is monotone, we can write it as

$$f(x_1, \dots, x_n) = \bigvee_{I \in \mathcal{I}} \bigwedge_{i \in I} x_i,$$

where each minterm $\bigwedge_{i \in I} x_i$ contains a minimal set of arguments that, by simultaneously assuming the value 1, suffice to force $f$ to assume the value 1. This representation of $f$ will be denoted $D(f)$. A function is disjunctive if it is monotone and each minterm in $D(f)$ has degree at most 1. If an $n$-adic function $f$ is not monotone, then there is an argument $x_i$ and a sequence of $n-1$ constants $c_1, \dots, c_{i-1}, c_{i+1}, \dots, c_n \in \mathbf{B}$ such that $f(c_1, \dots, c_{i-1}, x_i, c_{i+1}, \dots, c_n) = \overline{x_i}$.

**Lemma 1.5.11.** If a clone $\mathcal{P}$ contains only disjunctive functions, then it has a finite basis.

**Proof.** If $\mathcal{P}$ contains only quasi-monadic functions, then it has a finite basis by Lemma 1.5.5. Thus, assume that $\mathcal{P}$ contains a non-quasi-monadic function $f(x_1, \ldots, x_n) = \bigvee_{1 \le i \le n} x_i \vee c$, with $c \in \mathbf{B}$. Since $f$ is not quasi-monadic, we must have $c = 0$, so that $f(x_1, \ldots, x_n) = \bigvee_{1 \le i \le n} x_i$, with $n \ge 2$. Then we have $f(x, y, \ldots, y) = \mathrm{disj}(x, y)$, and we can obtain any non-quasi-monadic disjunctive function by repeated composition of disj with itself. Since there are only finitely many essentially different quasi-monadic functions, we are done. $\square$

*Lemma 1.5.12.* If a clone $\mathcal{P}$ contains the dyadic function disj and a non-disjunctive function $f$, then $\mathcal{P}$ contains the triadic function $\mathrm{hook}(x, y, z) = \mathrm{disj}(x, \mathrm{conj}(y, z))$.

**Proof.** First, suppose that $f$ is monotone. Let $X = \bigwedge_{i \in I} x_i$ be a minterm of maximum degree $d$ in $D(f)$. Since $f$ is not disjunctive, $d \ge 2$. Furthermore, every other minterm in $D(f)$ must contain some argument not appearing in $X$. Thus, if we let $g(x, y, z)$ denote the function obtained by substituting $z$ for one argument appearing in $X$, $y$ for all other arguments appearing in $X$, and $x$ for all arguments not appearing in $X$, then we have $\mathrm{disj}(x, g(x, y, z)) = \mathrm{hook}(x, y, z)$.

Next suppose that $f$ is not monotone. We may assume that $f(0, \ldots, 0, 1, \ldots, 1, z) = \bar{z}$. Define $g(x, y, z) = f(x, \ldots, x, y, \ldots, y, z)$ (with as many $x$'s as 0's and $y$'s as 1's). First, suppose $g(0, 0, 0) = 0$. Then, if we let $h(x, y, z) = \mathrm{disj}(x, g(x, \mathrm{disj}(y, z), z))$, we have $h(x, y, z) = \mathrm{hook}(x, y, \bar{z})$, and $h(x, y, h(x, y, z)) = \mathrm{hook}(x, y, z)$. Next suppose that $g(0, 0, 0) = 1$. Then $g(0, z, z) = \bar{z}$, and so if we let

$$h(x, y, z) = \mathrm{disj}(x, g(x, \mathrm{disj}(g(x, y, y), z), \mathrm{disj}(g(x, y, y), z)))$$

then we have $h(x, y, z) = \mathrm{hook}(x, y, \bar{z})$, as before. $\square$

*Lemma 1.5.13.* If a clone $\mathcal{P}$ contains the triadic function hook and a function $f$ that is not infinitely 1-preserving, then $\mathcal{P}$ contains a rejection function.

**Proof.** Suppose that

$$f(c_{1,1}, \ldots, c_{1,n}) = 0$$
$$\vdots$$
$$f(c_{m,1}, \ldots, c_{m,n}) = 0$$

where no column $c_{1,i}, \ldots, c_{m,i}$ consists entirely of 0's. By replicating rows if necessary, we may assume that $m \ge 3$. We shall show that $\mathcal{P}$ contains the $m$-adic function $\mathrm{thresh}_{2,m}(x_1, \ldots, x_m) = \bigvee_{1 \le i < j \le m} \mathrm{conj}(x_i, x_j)$, which is a rejection function. It will suffice to show that $\mathcal{P}$ contains an $m$-adic function $g$ satisfying

$$g(0, \ldots, 0) = 0$$

and

$$g(1, 0, \ldots, \ldots, 0) = 0$$
$$g(0, 1, \ldots, \ldots, 0) = 0$$
$$\vdots$$
$$g(0, 0, \ldots, \ldots, 1) = 0$$

since then we can add the terms of thresh$_{2,m}$ by repeated composition with hook. Indeed, it will suffice to show that $\mathcal{P}$ contains an $m$-adic function $h$ satisfying

$$h(1, 0, \ldots, \ldots, 0) = 0$$
$$h(0, 1, \ldots, \ldots, 0) = 0$$
$$\vdots$$
$$h(0, 0, \ldots, \ldots, 1) = 0,$$

for then we may set $g(x_1, x_2, \ldots, x_m) = h(\text{disj}(h(x_1, x_2, \ldots, x_m), x_1), x_2, \ldots, x_m)$, where disj is obtained by identifying the last two arguments of hook. But if we define the $m$-adic functions $p_1, \ldots, p_n$ by

$$p_j(x_1, \ldots, x_m) = \bigvee_{1 \leq i \leq m} \text{conj}(c_{i,j}, x_i)$$

for $1 \leq j \leq n$, then each function $p_j$ belongs to $\mathcal{P}$ (since each disjunction contains at least one argument). Thus, we may set $h = f \circ (p_1, \ldots, p_m)$. $\quad\square$

We are finally ready for the main result of this section.

**Theorem 1.5.14.** *Every Boolean clone has a finite basis.*

**Proof.** Let $\mathcal{P}$ be a Boolean clone. If $\mathcal{P}$ contains only linear functions, we are done by Lemma 1.5.7. Suppose then that $\mathcal{P}$ contains a non-linear function. If $\mathcal{P}$ contains no dyadic non-linear function, then by Lemma 1.5.8, it contains a triadic non-linear function, so by Lemma 1.5.9, it contains a rejection function, and we are done by Proposition 1.5.1. If $\mathcal{P}$ does contain a dyadic non-linear function, then by Lemma 1.5.10, it contains the dyadic disjunction function or the dyadic conjunction function. If transferring attention to the dual clone $\tilde{\mathcal{P}}$ is necessary, we may assume that it contains the dyadic disjunction function.

If $\mathcal{P}$ contains only disjunctive functions, then we are done by Lemma 1.5.11. Suppose then that $\mathcal{P}$ also contains a non-disjunctive function. Then by Lemma 1.5.12, $\mathcal{P}$ contains the triadic function hook. If $\mathcal{P}$ also contains a function that is not infinitely 1-preserving, then by Lemma 1.5.13, it contains a rejection function, and we are done by Proposition 1.5.1. Suppose then that $\mathcal{P}$ contains only infinitely 1-preserving functions. Every such function $f$ can be written as

$$f(x_1, \ldots, x_n) = \mathrm{disj}(x_i, f(x_1, \ldots, x_{i-1}, 0, x_{i+1}, \ldots, x_n))$$

for some $1 \leq i \leq n$. We shall say that the function $g$ defined by

$$g(x_1, \ldots, x_{n-1}) = f(x_1, \ldots, x_{i-1}, x_i, \ldots, x_{n-1})$$

is a *companion* to $f$. The set $\mathcal{Q}$ of all companions of functions in $\mathcal{P}$ itself forms a clone. The clone $\mathcal{Q}$ contains the dyadic disjunction function (the companion of the triadic disjunction function) and the dyadic conjunction function (the companion of the triadic function hook). Thus $\mathcal{Q}$ contains the triadic majority function, which is a rejection function, and so by Proposition 1.5.1, $\mathcal{Q}$ has a finite basis, say $g_1, \ldots, g_k$. Then the functions $f_1, \ldots, f_k$ defined by

$$f_i(x_1, \ldots, x_{m+1}) = \mathrm{disj}(x_1, g_i(x_2, \ldots, x_{m+1}))$$

(so that $g_i$ is a companion of $f_i$) form a finite basis for $\mathcal{P}$.　　　□

The fact that every Boolean clone is finitely generated has a remarkable analogue. Consider a finite set $F$ of Boolean functions that generate the clone of all Boolean functions, say, $F = \{\mathrm{conj}, \mathrm{disj}, \mathrm{neg}\}$. Among these functions there are certain *identities* that are always valid, for example De Morgan's Law: $\mathrm{neg}(\mathrm{conj}(x, y)) = \mathrm{disj}(\mathrm{neg}(x), \mathrm{neg}(y))$. It is not hard to see that all such valid identities can be deduced from a finite set of such identities using the properties of equality (reflexivity, symmetry, and transitivity) and the principle that equals substituted into equals yield equals. (One way to see this is to take a set of identities that suffice to reduce any expression to a canonical form.) This circumstance is expressed by saying that the identities for $F$ are *finitely based*. It is also not hard to see that the property of being finitely based depends only on the clone generated, and not on the particular set of generators. (Roughly speaking, an identity involving one set of generators can be transformed into another identity involving another set of generators in such a way that a deduction of the second identity can be transformed back into a deduction of the first.) Lyndon [1951] showed the remarkable fact that the identities for all Boolean clones are finitely based. Lyndon's proof followed

a case-by-case consideration of Post's Lattice; a more unified proof (but one
depending on deeper algebraic facts) has been given by Berman [1980].

### Exercise

1. (M) Say that a Boolean function $f$ is a *reduct* of a function $g$ if $f$ can be
   obtained from $g$ by (optional) permutation of arguments and (obligatory)
   diagonalization. Say that a set $F$ of Boolean functions *irreducibly* generates
   a clone $\mathcal{P}$ if (1) $F$ generates $\mathcal{P}$, and (2) no set obtained from $F$ by replacing one of its functions by all of its reducts generates $\mathcal{P}$. Enumerate all
   sets of Boolean functions that irreducibly generate the clone of all Boolean
   functions. (See Shestopal [1961, 1966].)

## 1.6. Boolean Relations

We shall now develop a theory of Boolean relations analogous to the theory
of Boolean functions developed in the preceding two sections. Since Boolean
relations can be put into one-to-one correspondence with Boolean functions by
taking "characteristic functions," it may seem that there is little to be gained from
an independent theory of Boolean relations. The use of characteristic functions,
however, entails breaking the symmetry between the Boolean values 0 and 1;
the theory we shall develop will preserve this symmetry, while introducing an
asymmetry between relations and their complements.

An *m-ary Boolean relation* is a set $R \subseteq \mathbf{B}^m$ of Boolean $m$-tuples. For
reasons that will become clear later, we shall regard these $m$-tuples as columns
rather than rows. Again we shall assume that $m \geq 1$; 1-ary, 2-ary, $\ldots$, relations
are often called *unary, binary,* $\ldots$, relations.

Our theory of relations will be based on a notion of computability that
arises from expressing relations in terms of other relations using formulas, but
the formulas we consider will be different from those we used for functions.
Consider the binary relation "bi" and the ternary relation "tri" defined as follows.

$$\text{bi} = \left\{ \begin{pmatrix} 1 \\ 0 \end{pmatrix}, \begin{pmatrix} 0 \\ 1 \end{pmatrix} \right\} \qquad \text{tri} = \left\{ \begin{pmatrix} 1 \\ 0 \\ 0 \end{pmatrix}, \begin{pmatrix} 0 \\ 1 \\ 0 \end{pmatrix}, \begin{pmatrix} 0 \\ 0 \\ 1 \end{pmatrix} \right\}$$

It is possible to express bi by a formula in terms of tri as follows.

$$\text{bi}\begin{pmatrix} x \\ y \end{pmatrix} := \text{tri}\begin{pmatrix} x \\ y \\ z \end{pmatrix}, \ \text{tri}\begin{pmatrix} z \\ z \\ u \end{pmatrix}$$

The kind of formulas we are considering is as follows. The relation to be expressed (in this case, bi) is to appear, with dummy variables as arguments, to the left of the ":−" sign. The expression on the right-hand side is to be a finite sequence of relation instances separated by commas, and it represents the conjunction (the logical "and") of these relation instances. All of the relations are to be from some class of allowed relations (in this case, the class contains just the relation tri), and each argument must be either (1) one of the dummy variables appearing on the left-hand side (in this case, $x$ and $y$) or a "projection variable" appearing only on the right-hand side (in this case, $z$ and $u$). The projection variables are understood to be existentially quantified, so that the right-hand side holds if and only if there exists an assignment of Boolean values to the projection variables for which each of the relation instances holds. Again we do not allow explicit Boolean constants. (This style of definition corresponds roughly to that in the language Prolog, but with only variables allowed as terms, and with the arguments in columns rather than rows.)

In the preceding example, the second instance of tri can only hold if $z$ assumes the value 0 and $u$ assumes the value 1. This forces $z$ to behave like the constant 0 in the first instance of tri, which in turn behaves like bi when its third argument is 0. If we try to express tri in terms of bi, no similar formula presents itself, and again we are led to seek a proof that none exists.

We claim that it is always possible to determine, in a finite number of steps, whether a given Boolean relation can be expressed in this way in terms of a given finite set of Boolean relations. We shall informally describe a procedure for doing this.

Suppose that an $m$-ary relation $R$ is to be expressed in terms of an $n$-ary relation $S$. (For simplicity we suppose that there is just one relation allowed on the right-hand side.) We would like to consider all possible right-hand sides that could be used to define an $m$-ary relation, but it is not immediately clear that we can confine our attention to a finite set, since there might be many instances of $S$ with various combinations of dummy and projection variables. There are just $m$ dummy variables, and our first step is to obtain an upper bound to the number of projection variables. If a right-hand side can be satisfied by some assignment of Boolean values to the projection variables, then the satisfying values can be expressed as Boolean functions of the dummy variables. If the same Boolean function serves for two projection variables, then they may be replaced by a single projection variable without affecting the validity of the expression. Thus, if an $m$-ary relation is expressible, it is expressible with a right-hand side that contains at most $p = 2^{2^m}$ projection variables, since there are just this many $m$-adic Boolean functions. Thus, there are at most $q = (m + p)^n$ instances of the $n$-ary relation $S$ that might appear in such a right-hand side. Since the relation expressed is not affected by the order or repetition of instances on the right-hand side, there are at most $2^q$ right-hand sides that need be considered. In principle, we could construct the set of all $m$-ary relations that can be expressed in terms of $S$, then check whether or not $R$ appears in this set. (In practice, the procedure we have described would involve too many expressions to be carried out, even in the simplest cases.)

In the next section we shall work out a theory of "co-clones" of Boolean relations in exact analogy to the theory of clones of Boolean functions. Indeed, we shall see that the two theories, though involving quite different modes of expression, are in a certain sense equivalent.

## 1.7. Co-Clones

Let $\mathcal{R}_m$ denote the set of all $m$-ary Boolean relations. Let $\mathcal{R} = \bigcup_{m \geq 1} \mathcal{R}_m$ denote the set of all Boolean relations.

Let $\mathcal{Q} \subseteq \mathcal{R}$ be a class of Boolean relations. We set $\mathcal{Q}_m = \mathcal{Q} \cap \mathcal{R}_m$ (the $m$-ary relations in $\mathcal{Q}$). We shall say that $\mathcal{Q}$ is a *co-clone* if it satisfies the following six conditions:

CC$_1$  The binary equality relation $\mathrm{eq}\binom{x}{y}$ $\iff$ $x = y$ belongs to $\mathcal{Q}$.

CC$_2$  For every $R \in \mathcal{Q}_m$, the cylindrification $\mathrm{cyl}(R) \in \mathcal{R}_{m+1}$, defined by

$$
\mathrm{cyl}(R) \begin{pmatrix} x_1 \\ \vdots \\ x_m \\ x_{m+1} \end{pmatrix} \iff R \begin{pmatrix} x_1 \\ \vdots \\ x_m \end{pmatrix}
$$

belongs to $\mathcal{Q}$.

CC$_3$  For every $R \in \mathcal{Q}_m$, the rotation $\mathrm{rot}(R) \in \mathcal{R}_m$, defined by

$$
\mathrm{rot}(R) \begin{pmatrix} x_1 \\ x_2 \\ \vdots \\ x_{m-1} \\ x_m \end{pmatrix} \iff R \begin{pmatrix} x_2 \\ x_3 \\ \vdots \\ x_m \\ x_1 \end{pmatrix}
$$

belongs to $\mathcal{Q}$. (If $R$ is unary, we shall take $\mathrm{rot}(R) = R$.)

CC$_4$ For every $R \in \mathcal{Q}_m$, the transposition $\mathrm{trans}(R) \in \mathcal{R}_m$, defined by

$$\mathrm{trans}(R) \begin{pmatrix} x_1 \\ x_2 \\ \vdots \\ x_{m-1} \\ x_m \end{pmatrix} \iff R \begin{pmatrix} x_1 \\ x_2 \\ \vdots \\ x_m \\ x_{m-1} \end{pmatrix}$$

belongs to $\mathcal{Q}$. (If $R$ is unary, we shall take $\mathrm{trans}(R) = R$.)

CC$_5$ For every $R \in \mathcal{Q}_m$, the projection $\mathrm{proj}(R) \in \mathcal{R}_{m-1}$, defined by

$$\mathrm{proj}(R) \begin{pmatrix} x_1 \\ \vdots \\ x_{m-1} \end{pmatrix} \iff \exists_y \begin{pmatrix} x_1 \\ \vdots \\ x_{m-1} \\ y \end{pmatrix}$$

belongs to $\mathcal{Q}$. (If $R$ is unary, we shall take $\mathrm{proj}(R) = R$.)

CC$_6$ For every $R, S \in \mathcal{Q}_m$, the intersection $R \cap S$ belongs to $\mathcal{Q}$.

The first four conditions are quite similar to analogous conditions for clones. The last two, however, display a clear asymmetry between relations and their complements: co-clones need not be closed under universal quantification or under taking unions. (The use of the term *projection* for both a kind of function and an operation on relations is somewhat confusing, but well entrenched, as both usages are supported by the same geometric analogy.)

As a consequence of these conditions, co-clones satisfy a number of further closure conditions. First, co-clones contain the "full" $m$-ary relation $\mathbf{B}^m$ for each $m \geq 1$. To see this, observe that $\mathrm{proj(eq)}$ is the full unary relation, and that all others can be obtained from this by cylindrification. Second, co-clones are closed under taking Cartesian products: if a co-clone $\mathcal{Q}$ contains an $l$-ary relation $R$ and an $m$-ary relation $S$, then it also contains the $(l+m)$-ary relation $R \times S$. To see this, observe that by cylindrification and permutations of the rows (using rotations and transpositions), we can obtain from $R$ an $(l+m)$-ary relation $R'$ such that

$$R' \begin{pmatrix} x_1 \\ \vdots \\ x_{l+m} \end{pmatrix} \iff R \begin{pmatrix} x_1 \\ \vdots \\ x_l \end{pmatrix}$$

Similarly, we can obtain from $S$ an $(l+m)$-ary relation $S'$ such that

$$S' \begin{pmatrix} x_1 \\ \vdots \\ x_{l+m} \end{pmatrix} \iff S \begin{pmatrix} x_{l+1} \\ \vdots \\ x_{l+m} \end{pmatrix}$$

We then obtain $R \times S = R' \cap S'$. Finally, co-clones are closed under diagonalization: if a co-clone contains an $m$-ary relation $R$, where $m \geq 2$, then it also contains the $(m - 1)$-ary relation diag($R$), defined by

$$\text{diag}(R) \begin{pmatrix} x_1 \\ \vdots \\ x_{m-1} \end{pmatrix} \iff R \begin{pmatrix} x_1 \\ \vdots \\ x_{m-1} \\ x_{m-1} \end{pmatrix}$$

To see this, observe that by cylindrification and permutation of the rows we can obtain from eq an $m$-ary relation that holds if and only if its last two arguments are equal. By intersecting this relation with $R$ and then projecting out the last argument, we obtain diag($R$).

The conditions defining co-clones are algebraic closure conditions; the co-clones constitute a closure system with universe $\mathcal{R}$. There is a smallest co-clone, which we shall denote $\mathcal{J}$; it comprises just those relations obtained from full relations $\mathbf{B}^m$ by imposing any number of equality conditions $x_i = x_j$ $(1 \leq i, j \leq m)$ on the coordinates. If $\mathcal{A} \subseteq \mathcal{R}$ is any set of Boolean relations, there is a smallest co-clone containing all of the relations in $\mathcal{A}$; this is the closure of $\mathcal{A}$, or the co-clone generated by $\mathcal{A}$, and we denote it $\langle \mathcal{A} \rangle$. If $\mathcal{A} = \{R_1, \ldots, R_l\}$ is a finite set, we may write $\langle R_1, \ldots, R_l \rangle$ for $\langle \mathcal{A} \rangle$, and refer to $R_1, \ldots, R_l$ as generators of $\langle \mathcal{A} \rangle$.

Just as $\mathcal{J}$ is the smallest co-clone, so $\mathcal{R}$ is the largest. Furthermore, the co-clones form a lattice under set inclusion; we could work out its structure as we did for Post's Lattice, but it would soon become clear that a miracle has occurred: the lattice of co-clones is isomorphic to the lattice of clones, but upside-down! The remainder of this section is devoted to the explanation of this miracle.

The first step is to set up an appropriate polarity. Let $f$ be an $n$-adic Boolean function, and let $R$ be an $m$-ary Boolean relation. If $M$ is an $m \times n$ Boolean matrix, we shall write $M \prec R$ if every column of $M$ belongs to $R$. We shall write $f(M)$ for the column

$$\begin{pmatrix} f(M_{1,1}, \ldots, M_{1,n}) \\ \vdots \\ f(M_{m,1}, \ldots, M_{m,n}) \end{pmatrix}$$

obtained by applying $f$ to each row of $M$. Finally, we shall write $f \approx R$, and say that $f$ *preserves* $R$, if, for every $m \times n$ Boolean matrix $M$, $M \prec R$ implies $f(M) \prec R$. The relation $\approx$ is a polarity between $\mathcal{F}$ and $\mathcal{R}$. (It should now be clear why we put the arguments of functions in rows, but the arguments of relations in columns.)

Let $\mathcal{P}$ be a class of Boolean functions (not necessarily a clone). We shall write $\mathcal{P} \approx \mathcal{R}$ if $f \approx R$ for all $f \in \mathcal{P}$. We shall denote by $\text{Inv}(\mathcal{P})$ the set of all relations $R$ such that $\mathcal{P} \approx \mathcal{R}$. We call $\text{Inv}(\mathcal{P})$ the set of "invariants" of $\mathcal{P}$. Let $\mathcal{Q}$ be a class of Boolean relations (not necessarily a co-clone). We shall write $f \approx \mathcal{Q}$ if $f \approx R$ for all $R \in \mathcal{Q}$. We shall denote by $\text{Pol}(\mathcal{Q})$ the set of all functions $f$ such that $f \approx \mathcal{Q}$. We call $\text{Pol}(\mathcal{Q})$ the set of "polymorphisms" of $\mathcal{Q}$.

**Theorem 1.7.1 (Geiger [1968]; Bodnarchuk et al.[1969]).** *(a) If $\mathcal{P}$ is any class of Boolean functions, then $\text{Inv}(\mathcal{P})$ is a co-clone; if $\mathcal{P}$ is a clone, then $\text{Pol}(\text{Inv}(\mathcal{P}))$ $= \mathcal{P}$. (b) If $\mathcal{Q}$ is any class of Boolean relations, then $\text{Pol}(\mathcal{Q})$ is a clone of Boolean functions; if $\mathcal{Q}$ is a co-clone, then $\text{Inv}(\text{Pol}(\mathcal{Q})) = \mathcal{Q}$.*

The proof will depend on several lemmas.

*Lemma 1.7.2.* If $\mathcal{P}$ is a clone and $g \notin \mathcal{P}$, then there exists $R \in \text{Inv}(\mathcal{P})$ such that $g \not\approx R$.

**Proof.** Suppose that $g$ is $n$-adic, and let $f_1, \ldots, f_q$ be the $n$-adic functions in $\mathcal{P}$. Let $R$ be a $2^n$-ary relation containing $q$ columns, each one containing the $2^n$ values of one of the functions $f_p$ ($1 \leq p \leq q$), with the positions of the columns being indexed by the $2^n$ rows in $\mathbf{B}^n$ (the domain of $f_p$) in some consistent way.

First, we claim that $g \not\approx R$. The relation $R$ contains $n$ columns $M^{(1)}, \ldots, M^{(n)}$ corresponding to the projection functions $\text{proj}_{n,1}, \ldots, \text{proj}_{n,n}$. (The clone $\mathcal{P}$ contains all projection functions.) Let $M$ be the $2^n \times n$ matrix whose columns are $M^{(1)}, \ldots, M^{(n)}$. Then $M \prec R$. But if $f(M) \prec R$, we would have $g \in \mathcal{P}$, a contradiction. Thus, $g \not\approx R$.

It remains to be shown that $R \in \text{Inv}(\mathcal{P})$, that is, that $\mathcal{P} \approx \mathcal{R}$. Suppose that $f \in \mathcal{P}$ is $m$-adic, and that $M \prec R$ is a $2^n \times m$ Boolean matrix. The columns $M^{(1)}, \ldots, M^{(m)}$ correspond to functions $h_1, \ldots, h_m \in \mathcal{P}$. Since $\mathcal{P}$ is a clone, we have $f \circ (h_1, \ldots, h_m) \in \mathcal{P}$. But $f(M)$ is the column corresponding to $f \circ (h_1, \ldots, h_m)$, and so $f(M) \prec R$. Thus, $R \in \text{Inv}(\mathcal{P})$. $\square$

To state the next lemma, we shall need to introduce "partial" functions. A $n$-adic Boolean partial function is a map $f: D \to \mathbf{B}$, where $D \subseteq \mathbf{B}^n$ is a set called the *domain* of $f$ and denoted $\text{dom}(f) = D$. We shall call $f$ a *total* function if $\text{dom}(f) = \mathbf{B}^n$. If $f$ and $g$ are $n$-adic Boolean partial functions, we shall say that $f$ is a *restriction* of $g$, or that $g$ is an *extension* of $f$, if (1) $\text{dom}(f) \subseteq \text{dom}(g)$ and (2) $f(x_1, \ldots, x_n) = g(x_1, \ldots, x_n)$ for all $(x_1, \ldots, x_n) \in \text{dom}(f)$. If $R$ is an $m$-ary Boolean relation, we shall write $f \approx R$ to mean that, for every $m \times n$ Boolean matrix $M$, if $M \prec R$ and every row of $M$ belongs to $\mathrm{dom}(f)$, then $f(M) \prec R$.

*Lemma 1.7.3.* If $Q$ is a co-clone and if $f$ is an $n$-adic Boolean partial function such that $f \approx Q$, then there exists a total extension $g$ of $f$ such that $g \approx Q$.

**Proof.** Let $(y_1, \ldots, y_n)$ be a row not in the domain of $f$. We shall consider an extension $f_c$ of $f$, with $\mathrm{dom}(f_c) = \mathrm{dom}(f) \cup \{(y_1, \ldots, y_n)\}$ and defined by

$$f_c(x_1, \ldots, x_n) = \begin{cases} c, & \text{if } (x_1, \ldots, x_n) = (y_1, \ldots, y_n) \\ f(x_1, \ldots, x_n), & \text{otherwise} \end{cases}$$

We shall show that for some choice of $c \in \mathbf{B}$ we have $f_c \approx Q$. We may then continue in this way, adding rows to the domain of $f$, until we arrive at a total extension $g$ of $f$ with $g \approx Q$.

Suppose then, to obtain a contradiction, that for each $c \in \mathbf{B}$ we have $f_c \not\approx Q$. Then for each $c \in \mathbf{B}$ there is an $R_c \in Q$ such that $f_c \not\approx R_c$. We may suppose that each relation $R_c$ has the smallest possible number $m_c$ of rows among those in $Q$ such that $f_c \not\approx R_c$.

For each $c \in \mathbf{B}$, there is an $m_c \times n$ Boolean matrix $M_c$ such that $M_c \prec R_c$ but $f_c(M_c) \not\prec R_c$. The $m_c$ rows of $M_c$ must be distinct, for if not, we could use permutations of rows and diagonalization to obtain from $R_c$ a relation $R_c' \in Q$ with fewer rows such that $f_c \not\approx R_c'$. Furthermore, $(y_1, \ldots, y_n)$ must be a row of each $M_c$, for if not, $f(M_c) \prec R_c$ would imply $f_c(M_c) \prec R_c$, a contradiction. Using a permutation of the rows of $R_c$ if necessary, we may assume that this row is the last ($m_c$-th) row.

Let $M$ be the $(m_0 + m_1) \times n$ Boolean matrix

$$\begin{pmatrix} M_0 \\ M_1 \end{pmatrix}$$

obtained by putting $M_0$ atop $M_1$. Then $M \prec R$, where the Cartesian product $R = R_0 \times R_1$ belongs to $Q$, but $f_0(M) \not\prec R$ and $f_1(M) \not\prec R$.

Let $L$ be the $(m_0 + m_1 - 1) \times n$ Boolean matrix obtained from $M$ by deleting the $m_0$-th row (which duplicates the last row). Then $L \prec Q$, where $Q$ is obtained from $R$ using permutations of rows and diagonalization and, therefore, also belongs to $Q$, but $f_0(L) \not\prec Q$ and $f_1(L) \not\prec Q$.

Let $K$ be the $(m_0 + m_1 - 2) \times n$ Boolean matrix obtained from $L$ by deleting the last row, which is $(y_1, \ldots, y_n)$. Then $K \prec P$, where $P$ is the relation obtained from $Q$ by projecting out the last row, so that $P \in Q$. Thus we have

$f(K) \prec P$. Since $P$ is the projection of $Q$, there exists $c \in \mathbf{B}$ such that

$$\begin{pmatrix} f(K) \\ c \end{pmatrix} \in Q$$

But this implies $f_c(L) \prec Q$, a contradiction. □

*Lemma 1.7.4.* If $Q$ is a co-clone and $S \notin Q$, then there exists $g \in \mathrm{Pol}(Q)$ such that $g \not\approx S$.

**Proof.** It will suffice to construct a partial function $f \approx Q$ such that $f \not\approx S$, for then Lemma 1.7.3 will yield a total extension $g$ of $f$ such that $g \approx Q$, while maintaining $g \not\approx S$.

We may assume that all of the rows of $S$ are distinct, for if not, we may obtain $S$ using permutations of rows, cylindrifications and intersections with cylindrifications of the equality relation from a relation $S' \notin Q$ satisfying this condition, and such that $f \approx S'$ if and only if $f \approx S$.

Suppose that $S$ is $m$-ary, and let $T_1, \ldots, T_q$ be all of the $m$-ary relations $T_p$ ($1 \le p \le q$) in $Q$ such that $T_p \supseteq S$. Then the relation $T = T_1 \cap \cdots \cap T_q$ is also an $m$-ary relation in $Q$ such that $T \supseteq S$, and it is the smallest such relation (has the smallest number of columns) among the relations $T_p$ ($1 \le p \le q$).

Suppose that $S$ contains $n$ columns $S^{(1)}, \ldots, S^{(n)}$, and let $M$ be the $m \times n$ Boolean matrix whose columns are $S^{(1)}, \ldots, S^{(n)}$. Let $u$ be a column in $T \setminus S$, and define the $n$-adic partial function $f$ whose domain is the set of rows of $M$ and whose values are given by $f(M) = u$. Then $f \not\approx S$.

It remains to show that $f \approx Q$. Suppose, to obtain a contradiction, that $f \not\approx R$ for some $R \in Q$. We may assume that $R$ has the smallest possible number of rows among relations $R'$ such that $f \not\approx R'$ and $R' \in Q$.

There must be a Boolean matrix $L$ such that $L \prec R$ but $f(L) \not\prec R$. The rows of $L$ must be distinct, for if not, we could use permutations of rows and diagonalization to obtain from $R$ a relation $R'$ with fewer rows such that $f \not\approx R'$ and $R' \in Q$. Furthermore, every row of $L$ must be a row of $M$, since $f(L) \not\prec R$ implies that every row of $L$ belongs to $\mathrm{dom}(f)$. Thus, using permutations of rows and cylindrification, we obtain from $R$ an $m$-ary relation in $Q$ that contains all of the columns of $M$ but not $u$. This contradicts the selection of the column $u$ as being contained in every $m$-ary relation of $Q$ that contains every column of $M$. □

**Proof of Theorem 1.7.1.** (a) That $\mathrm{Inv}(\mathcal{P})$ is a co-clone is verified by checking conditions $CC_1$ through $CC_6$. By condition $GC_3$ for the Galois connection corresponding to the polarity $\approx$, we have $\mathrm{Pol}(\mathrm{Inv}(\mathcal{P})) \supseteq \mathcal{P}$; the reverse inclusion follows from Lemma 1.7.2. (b) That Pol($\mathcal{Q}$) is a clone is verified by checking conditions $C_1'$ and $C_2'$. By condition $GC_4$ for the Galois connection corresponding to the polarity $\approx$, we have Inv(Pol($\mathcal{Q}$)) $\supseteq \mathcal{Q}$; the reverse inclusion follows from Lemma 1.7.4.                                                                    □

It follows that there is a one-to-one correspondence between clones and co-clones, with Inv taking a clone into the corresponding co-clone, and Pol effecting the inverse transformation. The correspondence reverses the order within the lattices: by conditions $GC_1$ and $GC_2$ for the Galois connection corresponding to the polarity $\approx$, we have $\mathcal{P} \subseteq \mathcal{P}'$ if and only if Inv($\mathcal{P}'$) $\subseteq$ Inv($\mathcal{P}$), and $\mathcal{Q} \subseteq \mathcal{Q}'$ if and only if Pol($\mathcal{Q}'$) $\subseteq$ Pol($\mathcal{Q}$). Thus, the lattice of co-clones is the same as the lattice of clones, but upside-down.

In our discussion of Post's Lattice, we described clones in two ways: using generators and using "constraints." We can now see that each relation can be interpreted as a constraint, namely, the constraint that is satisfied by the functions that preserve the given relation. Certain constraints figured prominently in our description of Post's Lattice, and we shall now interpret each of these as a relation. A function is 0-preserving if and only if it preserves the unary relation $\{0\}$ and, dually, a function is 1-preserving if and only if it preserves the unary relation $\{1\}$. A function is self-dual if and only if it preserves the binary relation $\left\{ \binom{x}{y} : x = \bar{y} \right\}$. A function is monotone if and only if it preserves the binary relation $\left\{ \binom{x}{y} : x \leq y \right\}$ (or equivalently, preserves its dual). A function is quasi-monadic if and only if it preserves the ternary relation

$$\left\{ \begin{pmatrix} x \\ y \\ z \end{pmatrix} : x = y \quad \text{or} \quad y = z \right\}$$

A function is linear if and only if it preserves the quaternary relation

$$\left\{ \begin{pmatrix} w \\ x \\ y \\ z \end{pmatrix} : \text{excl}\,(w, x) = \text{excl}\,(y, z) \right\}$$

A function is conjunctive if and only if it preserves the ternary relation

$$\mathbf{B}^3 \setminus \left\{ \begin{pmatrix} 1 \\ 0 \\ 1 \end{pmatrix} \right\}$$

(and dually for disjunctive). Finally, a function is $m$-tuply 0-preserving if and only if it preserves the $m$-ary relation

$$\mathbf{B}^m \setminus \left\{ \begin{pmatrix} 0 \\ \vdots \\ 0 \end{pmatrix} \right\}$$

(and dually for $m$-tuply 1-preserving).

A clone of functions satisfying more than one, but finitely many, of these constraints preserves the Cartesian product of the corresponding relations. The clones $F_1^\infty, \ldots, F_8^\infty$, which satisfy infinitely many of these constraints, cannot be characterized by preservation of a single relation; the corresponding co-clones are not generated by any finite set of relations.

## *Exercises*

1. (E) Prove that the ternary relation tri does not belong to the co-clone generated by the binary relation bi.

2. (M) Prove that the ternary relation tri generates the co-clone $\mathcal{R}$ of all relations.

3. (M) (a) Which co-clones are closed under finite unions? (b) Which are closed under complements?

4. (H) If a co-clone is finitely generated, then it is generated by a single relation. Say that the *degree* $\deg(\mathcal{Q})$ of a co-clone $\mathcal{Q}$ is the smallest $m$ such that $\mathcal{Q}$ is generated by an $m$-ary relation, if $\mathcal{Q}$ is finitely generated, and $\infty$ otherwise. Determine the degrees of all the co-clones of Boolean relations. (See Blokhina [1970].)

## 1.8. Finite Functions and Relations

This section explores the prospects for generalizing the theory of Boolean functions and relations to domains with more than two elements. To this end we shall consider a fixed natural number $k \geq 2$ and let $\mathbf{B}_k = \{0, 1, \ldots, k-1\}$ be a standard domain with $k$ elements. We shall refer to $\mathbf{B}_k$ as the *k-ean* domain (so "2-ean" is a synonym for "Boolean"), and speak of "$k$-ean functions" and "$k$-ean relations."

One encouraging observation is that Theorem 1.7.1 applies to $k$-ean functions and relations; indeed, the proof we have given hardly requires more change than replacing some occurrences of "2" by "$k$." Thus, we know that the lattice of $k$-ean clones is isomorphic to the dual of the lattice of $k$-ean co-clones.

We could try to work out the lattice of $k$-ean clones in the same way as Post's Lattice, but the attempt soon leads to a seemingly patternless proliferation of cases. That such an attempt is, in fact, doomed to failure was observed by Yanov and Muchnik [1959]; they showed that, whereas Post's Lattice contains only countably many clones, there are uncountably many $k$-ean clones for $k \geq 3$ (and thus uncountably many co-clones as well). The proof for $k = 3$ is based on the following lemma (the generalization to $k \geq 3$ is easy).

*Lemma 1.8.1.* For $n \geq 1$, let $f_n$ denote the $n$-adic 3-ean function that assumes the value 0 if exactly one of its arguments is 1 and the remaining $n - 1$ arguments are 0, and assumes the value 2 otherwise. For $m \geq 1$, let $R_m$ denote the $m$-ary 3-ean relation that holds if and only if either (1) exactly one of its arguments is 1 and the remaining $m - 1$ arguments are 0, or (2) at least one of its arguments is 2. Then, $f_n \approx R_m$ if and only if $n \neq m$.

**Proof.** If $n = m$, we consider the $n \times n$ 3-ean matrix $M$ such that $M_{p,q} = 1$ if $p = q$, and $M_{p,q} = 0$ otherwise. Then $M \prec R_n$, but $f_n(M) \not\prec R_n$.

If $n \neq m$, we let $M$ be an arbitrary $m \times n$ 3-ean matrix and consider two cases. If any entry of $M$ is 2, then an entry of $f_n(M)$ is also 2, and thus $f_n(M) \prec R_m$. Suppose, on the other hand, that every entry of $M$ is either 0 or 1. If $M \prec R_m$, then every column of $M$ contains exactly one 1. Since $n \neq m$, it follows that there exists a row of $M$ that does not contain exactly one 1. This implies that some entry of $f_n(M)$ is 2, and so again $f_n(M) \prec R_m$.                              □

For each $I \subseteq \{1, 2, \ldots\}$, let $\mathcal{P}_I$ denote the 3-ean clone generated by $\{f_n : n \in I\}$. Then we have $f_n \in \mathcal{P}_I$ if and only if $n \in I$; for if $n \notin I$, then every generator of $\mathcal{P}_I$ preserves $R_n$, whence every function in $\mathcal{P}_I$ preserves $R_n$, whence $f_n \notin \mathcal{P}_I$. Thus, for any $I, J \subseteq \{1, 2, \ldots\}$ with $I \neq J$, we have $\mathcal{P}_I \neq \mathcal{P}_J$, and since there are uncountably many subsets of $\{1, 2, \ldots\}$, there are uncountably many 3-ean clones.

Since there are uncountably many $k$-ean clones for $k \geq 3$, it is clear that the $k$-ean clones cannot all be finitely generated (since there are only countably many finite subsets of the countable set of finite functions). Analogously, Murskiĭ [1965] has shown that there is a finitely generated 3-ean clone whose identities are not finitely based, which shows that the result of Lyndon [1951] also cannot be generalized to $k \geq 3$.

In light of these examples, much research on $k$-ean clones and co-clones has taken the form of showing that various properties of Boolean clones that are manifest by inspection of Post's Lattice are also true in the $k$-ean case for $k \geq 3$. We shall mention some examples of this phenomenon.

First, although Post's Lattice contains infinitely many clones, there are only finitely many maximal incomplete clones, that is, clones covered by the complete clone $C_1$. (These are often called simply "maximal," or "precomplete," clones.) These clones are $C_2$ (0-preserving), $C_3$ (1-preserving), $A_1$ (monotone), $D_3$ (self-dual), and $L_1$ (linear); they are significant because they provide a "completeness criterion" for a set of generators: a set of functions generates $C_1$ (all Boolean functions) if and only if, for each of the five precomplete clones, it contains at least one function outside that clone.

In the early 1950s, Yablonskiĭ [1954] enumerated all the 3-ean precomplete clones; there are 18 of them. Butler [1960] and Kuznetsov [1961] independently proved that for every $k$ there are only finitely many precomplete clones, and Rosenberg [1970] has given an explicit description of them. The proof of finiteness depends on the following remarkable proposition, which is due to Słupecki [1939] and Butler [1960]. Say that a $k$-ean function is *essential* if it is not quasi-monadic and it assumes $k$ distinct values.

**Proposition 1.8.2.** *For $k \geq 3$, a $k$-ean clone that contains all monadic functions and contains at least one essential function contains all $k$-ean functions.*

At the other end of Post's Lattice, there are seven clones that cover the trivial clone $O_1$: $O_6$ (generated by 0), $O_5$ (generated by 1), $O_4$ (generated by neg), $P_1$ (generated by conj), $S_1$ (generated by disj), $L_4$ (generated by par), and $D_2$ (generated by maj). These generators provide a completeness criterion for the co-clone of all Boolean relations. It is known that even for $k \geq 3$, the number of minimal non-trivial clones remains finite; see Rosenberg [1983]. For $k = 3$, a complete list has been given by Csákány [1983]. For $k \geq 4$, only a broad classification is known; the proof of finiteness depends on the following proposition, which is implicit in the work of Świerczkowski [1960].

**Proposition 1.8.3.** *Suppose that $f$ is an $n$-adic $k$-ean function with $n > k > 2$ and that every function obtained from $f$ by diagonalization is a projection. Then $f$ is a projection.*

**Proof.** Say that a pair $\{i, j\}$ of indices in the range $1 \leq i < j \leq n$ is *introvert* if

$$f(x_1, \ldots, x_{i-1}, y, x_{i+1}, \ldots, x_{j-1}, y, x_{j+1}, \ldots, x_n) = y$$

and that it is *extravert* (more specifically, that it is *h-extravert*) if

$$f(x_1, \ldots, x_{i-1}, y, x_{i+1}, \ldots, x_{j-1}, y, x_{j+1}, \ldots, x_n) = x_h$$

for some $h \notin \{i, j\}$. Since every function obtained from $f$ by diagonalization is a projection, every pair is either introvert or extravert.

At least one pair must be extravert. To see this, note that $n \geq 4$ (since $n > k > 2$). If the pairs $\{1, 2\}$ and $\{3, 4\}$ are both introvert, we obtain the contradiction

$$0 = f(0, 0, 1, 1, \ldots, 1) = 1$$

Thus, one of these pairs must be extravert. By permuting the arguments if necessary, we may assume that the pair $\{2, 3\}$ is 1-extravert.

We shall show that every pair $\{i, j\}$ in the range $2 \leq i < j \leq n$ is 1-extravert. For if not, we obtain the contradiction

$$0 = f(0, 1, \ldots, 1) = 1$$

To complete the proof that $f$ is the projection $f(x_1, \ldots, x_n) = x_1$, it remains to show that

$$f(y, x_2, \ldots, x_{j-1}, y, x_{j+1}, \ldots, x_n) = y$$

(that is, that the pair $\{1, j\}$ is introvert) for every $j$ in the range $2 \leq j \leq n$. But if not, we obtain the contradiction

$$0 = f(0, 1, \ldots, 1, 0, 1, \ldots, 1) = 1$$

(where 0's appear in the first and $j$-th positions).                    $\square$

The self-dual Boolean functions can be generalized to the $k$-ean functions $f$ that are invariant under conjugation by all permutations of the $k$ values, so that $f = g^{-1} \circ f \circ (g, \ldots, g)$ for any permutation $g : \mathbf{B}_k \rightarrow \mathbf{B}_k$. Such functions are called *homogeneous*. There are just eight clones that contain only self-dual Boolean functions: $D_1, D_2, D_3, L_1, L_4, L_5, O_1,$ and $O_4$. For each $k \geq 3$, there are still only finitely many $k$-ean clones containing only homogeneous functions, and they have been completely described by Marchenkov [1981].

Finally, for any $k \geq 2$ one can define the "quasi-monadic" functions as those that depend essentially on at most one argument. Since there are only finitely many monadic functions for each $k$, there are only finitely many clones in the sublattice between the trivial clone and the quasi-monadic clone. Burle [1967] has shown that there are also only finitely many clones in the sublattice between the quasi-monadic clone and the complete clone; in fact, there are exactly $k + 1$ such clones (including the top and bottom of this sublattice), and they form a totally ordered chain. This result has been generalized in two directions: if the clone generated by the monadic functions is replaced by the clone generated by the non-invertible monadic functions (that is, the monadic functions that do not assume all $k$ values), there are still only finitely many larger clones, and they have been completely classified by Denham [1994]. Alternatively, if the clone generated by the monadic functions is replaced by the clone generated by the invertible monadic functions (that is, the permutations), there are again only finitely many larger clones, and they have been completely classified by Haddad and Rosenberg [1994] (see Denham [1994] for a correction in the cases $k = 2, 3,$ or 4).

### Exercises

1. (M) Say that a function $f$ is a *reduct* of a function $g$ if $f$ can be obtained from $g$ by (optional) permutation of arguments and (obligatory) diagonalization. Say that a set $F$ of $k$-ean functions is *irreducibly* generates a clone $\mathcal{P}$ if (a) $F$ generates $\mathcal{P}$ and (b) no set obtained from $F$ by replacing one of its functions by all of its reducts generates $\mathcal{P}$. Show that the $k$-ean clone $\mathcal{F}$ of all $k$-ean functions is irreducibly generated by only finitely many sets of functions. (Hint: Use the fact that there are only finitely many precomplete clones.)

2. (H) Show that there are uncountably many $k$-ean clones that contain all $k$ constant functions. (See Ágoston, Demetrovics, and Hannak [1983].)

3. (H) (a) Show that if $k \geq 5$, then "all monadic functions" can be replaced by "all permutations" in Proposition 1.8.2. (b) Give examples to show that this replacement cannot be made if $k = 2, 3,$ or 4. (See Salomaa [1963].)

# 2

## Finite automata and their languages

### 2.1. Sequential Functions and Relations

Imagine a "machine" that receives a sequence $x_1, x_2, x_3, \ldots$, of "input symbols" from some finite set (say, $\mathbf{B}_k$), and produces a sequence $y_1, y_2, y_3, \ldots$, of corresponding "output symbols" from the same set. We think of the subscripts on these sequences as indexing successive moments in time: at time 1, the machine receives input symbol $x_1$ and produces the output symbol $y_1$, then at time 2, it receives $x_2$ and produces $y_2$, and so forth. We shall assume that the output symbol produced at any time depends only on the input symbols received at that time and earlier times. This assumption allows us to represent the behavior of the machine in terms of a function $f$ such that $f(x_1) = y_1$, $f(x_1, x_2) = y_2$, and so forth. The domain of the function $f$ is the set $\bigcup_{n \geq 1} \mathbf{B}_k^n$ of all sequences of one or more symbols from $\mathbf{B}_k$, and $f$ yields values in $\mathbf{B}_k$. The notation $f(x_1, \ldots, x_n) = y_n$ suggests that $f$ can take one, two, or more arguments; but it will be more convenient to regard $f$ as always taking a single argument, which is the sequence $x_1, \ldots, x_n$. To emphasize this point of view, we shall omit the commas separating the terms in these sequences and write

$$f(x_1) = y_1$$

$$f(x_1 x_2) = y_2$$

$$\vdots$$

$$f(x_1 x_2 \cdots x_n) = y_n$$

This will pave the way for the introduction later of functions that take several arguments, each of which is a sequence of this type.

If $A$ is any set, it will be convenient to write $A^+$ for the set $\bigcup_{n \geq 1} A^n$ of sequences of one or more elements from $A$; we shall call such sequences *words* over the *alphabet* $A$, and a word from $A^n$ will be said to have *length* $n$. Elements of the alphabet $A$ will be called *letters*, and a word of length $n$ will have $n$ *occurrences* of letters. It will also be convenient to introduce an *empty* word $\varepsilon$ of length 0, and to write $A^* = \{\varepsilon\} \cup A^+ = \bigcup_{n \geq 0} A^n$ for the set of sequences of zero or more elements from $A$.

A map $f : A^+ \to B$ will be called a *sequential function* from $A$ to $B$. Note that we say "from $A$ to $B$" and not "from $A^+$ to $B$." The reason is that, if $g$ is a sequential function from $B$ to $C$, it makes sense to define the *composition* $g \circ f$ to be a sequential function from $A$ to $C$ given by

$$(g \circ f)(x_1 \cdots x_n) = g(f(x_1) \cdots f(x_1 \cdots x_n))$$

We then have the usual condition that composition is possible if and only if the "domain" ("from" set) and "co-domain" ("to" set) match. Note also that there is no ambiguity in using the symbol "$\circ$" for this new operation: if two sequential functions can be composed as sequential functions, they cannot be composed as ordinary functions. If $A = B = \mathbf{B}_k$, we shall speak of a $k$-ean sequential function.

Throughout this chapter we will be dealing with words over *finite* alphabets, such as $\mathbf{B}_1 = \{0\}$, $\mathbf{B}_2 = \{0, 1\}$, and so forth. The way we have set things up, $\varepsilon$ is a word over every alphabet, 000 is a word over each of the alphabets $\mathbf{B}_1, \mathbf{B}_2, \ldots$, and so forth. In fact, we shall regard all words as being over some fixed infinite alphabet, say, $\mathbf{N} = \{0, 1, 2, \ldots\}$, and regard $\mathbf{B}_k^+$ and $\mathbf{B}_k^*$ as subsets of this universal set of words. (An alternative would be to say that a word comprises an alphabet together with a sequence of letters from that alphabet; we would then need maps that change the alphabets of words without changing any of their occurrences of letters.)

Thus far our formulation is applicable to all machines that (1) have a finite input and output alphabet, (2) are "causal" (the output depends only on the "past," not the "future"), and (3) are "deterministic" (the output is completely and univocally determined by the input). In this chapter we shall be particularly interested in machines that satisfy an additional condition: their behavior exhibits only finitely many "states."

The notion of *state* is introduced to answer the following question: what do you need to know about the past inputs to be able to predict the response of the machine to future inputs? If $x = x_1 \cdots x_n$ and $y = y_1 \cdots y_m$ are words over the alphabet $A$, we shall write $x \cdot y$ (or sometimes just $xy$) to denote the *concatenation* $x_1 \cdots x_n y_1 \cdots y_m$ of $x$ and $y$. If $f : A^+ \to A$ is a sequential function and $x \in A^*$ is a word, we shall write $x^{-1}f$ for the sequential function defined by

$$(x^{-1}f)(y) = f(x \cdot y)$$

If $f$ describes the behavior of a machine, then $x^{-1}f$ describes the behavior of this machine after it has received the initial word $x$. We shall call $x^{-1}f$ the *intrinsic state* reached by $f$ under $x$; for example, $f$ itself is the intrinsic state reached by $f$ under $\varepsilon$. We shall say that $f$ is *finite-state* if its set

$$\{x^{-1}f : x \in A^*\}$$

of intrinsic states is finite.

The notion of "intrinsic state", just defined, is due to Nerode [1958] (who introduced it in a slightly different context). We have used the qualification "intrinsic" to emphasize that we are not referring to any notion of physical or even mathematical state that might arise from the way in which the machine implements the behavior $f$. There might well be multiple physical states implementing a single intrinsic state (such physical states being indistinguishable from the behavior of the machine), as well as some physical states that do not correspond to any intrinsic state (such physical states being inaccessible under the considered inputs to the machine).

Thus far we have dealt with machines that receive a single input sequence, but it is straightforward to generalize the formulation to include machines that receive $m \geq 1$ such sequences $x^1 = x_1^1 \cdots x_n^1, \ldots, x^m = x_1^m \cdots x_n^m$ simultaneously and synchronously and produce an output sequence $y_1 \cdots y_n$. This leads us to the notion of an *$m$-adic $k$-ean sequential function* $f$ whose domain is $\bigcup_{n \geq 1} (\mathbf{B}_k^n)^m$ (the $m$ input words must have the same length), and which yields values in $\mathbf{B}_k$. We can then define the intrinsic states $(x^1, \ldots, x^m)^{-1}f$ for $(x^1, \ldots, x^m) \in \bigcup_{n \geq 0}(\mathbf{B}_k^n)^m$, and finite-state sequential functions as before. Among these sequential functions we find the "projection functions," defined by

$$\mathrm{proj}_{m,l}\left(x_1^1 \cdots x_n^1, \ldots, x_1^m \cdots x_n^m\right) = x_n^l$$

and the "composite function" $f \circ (g_1, \ldots, g_m)$. Thus, we can define clones of finite-state $k$-ean sequential functions by imposing closure conditions analogous to those used to define clones of Boolean functions. The resulting theory is not very satisfactory, however; for example, the clone of all finite-state Boolean sequential functions cannot be generated by any finite set of such functions.

This deficiency led Kudryavtsev [1965] to enlarge clones to what we shall call "super-clones" by imposing an additional closure condition, corresponding to a "feedback" operation. This operation takes an $m$-adic function (with $m \geq 2$) into an $(m-1)$-adic function by "feeding back" the output sequence as the last ($m$-th) input. (This operation is only well defined when the output is independent of the most recent symbol of the last input; thus feedback is only a partial operation, applicable to some but not all functions.) In the resulting theory, the super-clone of all finite-state Boolean (or even $k$-ean) sequential functions is generated by a finite set of such functions. But a new disappointment is in store: there are uncountably many precomplete super-clones, even in the Boolean case. Thus, there can be no simple criterion (analogous to Post's five conditions for Boolean functions) for completeness of sets of finite-state Boolean sequential functions. (For these and other results, mostly of a negative nature, see Dassow [1981].)

In the following sections we shall turn our attention from sequential functions to "sequential relations." A (unary) sequential relation over the alphabet $A$ is a subset $L \subseteq A^+$. Another name for a unary sequential relation is language, which fits well with the terms *alphabet*, *letter*, and *word* that we have already introduced: a language is just a set of words. (Much of the mathematical linguistics literature refers to languages that are sets of "sentences," which are sequences of words over a finite "lexicon." The use of language and word in these two ways often leads to confusion; we shall adhere to the convention that a language is a set of words.)

We may imagine a machine that receives a sequence of letters from $A$ and produces a sequence of affirmative or negative responses: affirmative responses whenever the word received thus far belongs to $L$, and negative responses whenever it does not. We then define $x^{-1}L$ by the condition

$$y \in x^{-1}L \iff x \cdot y \in L$$

define the intrinsic states of $L$ as the set

$$\{x^{-1}L : x \in A^*\}$$

and define a finite-state language to be one for which this set is finite.

For many purposes it is convenient to adopt a slightly broader framework, by allowing the empty word to be a member or non-member of a language. In this case, a language is a subset $L \subseteq A^*$. It might seem that such a minor difference in the framework could have no serious consequences, but in fact many parts of the theory can be made much more elegant by either allowing or disallowing the empty word. We shall usually choose the simpler path in each case, though of course every theorem can be adapted to the other situation by including enough special conditions in the statement and enough special cases in the proof.

The earliest work to identify the class of finite-state sequential functions is apparently that of McCulloch and Pitts [1943]. Their motivation was to provide a formalization of "neural nets," and their view of these as interconnections of "neurons" corresponds quite closely to the treatment of Kudryavtsev in terms of composition and feedback. Though historically earliest, this point of view is the least facile technically, and in later sections we shall use several other approaches to the same body of material. Before pursuing these other approaches, however, we shall again digress to present some mathematical background.

### Exercises

1. (M) Prove that there is no finite set of finite-state Boolean sequential functions that generate the clone of all finite-state Boolean sequential functions. (Hint: Consider functions that "count modulo $p$" for various primes $p$.)
2. (M) Give a finite set of finite-state Boolean sequential functions that generates the super-clone of finite-state Boolean sequential functions.

## 2.2. Two Basic Structures

In this section we shall give basic mathematical background for two structures that will play significant roles in this chapter: semigroups and Boolean algebras. The reader may wish to skip this material now and refer back to it later if it should be needed.

### 2.2.1. Semigroups

A *semigroup* $(S, \cdot)$ comprises a set $S$ (called the *carrier*), together with a binary operation $\cdot : S^2 \to S$ satisfying the following condition:

SG$_1$  For all $x, y, z \in S$, we have $x \cdot (y \cdot z) = (x \cdot y) \cdot z$.

(This condition is sometimes expressed by saying that the operation $\cdot$ is *associative*.) The condition SG$_1$ allows the wholesale elimination of parentheses from an expression involving only the semigroup operation: for example, the expression $w \cdot x \cdot y \cdot z$ yields the same value, no matter which of the five possible parenthesizations is used to evaluate it. We will often speak of the semigroup $S$, rather than the semigroup $(S, \cdot)$, when the operation is clear from context. We will also often indicate the operation by mere juxtaposition (as with multiplication in ordinary algebra), writing $xy$ instead of $x \cdot y$. Finally, if $k \geq 1$ we shall write $x^k$ for $x \cdots x$ ($k$ factors).

The set $A^+$ of non-empty words over an alphabet $A$ forms a semigroup when the operation is taken to be concatenation; it is called the *free* semigroup generated by $A$.

If $S$ is a semigroup, and $R \subseteq S$ is a subset such that $x \cdot y \in R$ for all $x, y \in R$ then $R$ is called a *subsemigroup* of $S$. The condition defining a subsemigroup is a closure condition, so that the subsemigroups of a semigroup $S$ form a lattice, with the empty semigroup as minimum and $S$ itself as maximum. If $Q \subseteq S$ is any set of elements, there is smallest subsemigroup of $S$ containing all of the elements of $Q$; this is called the subsemigroup generated by $Q$. A semigroup is called *cyclic* if it is generated by a single element.

An element $e \in S$ in a semigroup is called a *unit* (or identity, or *neutral element*) if, for all $x \in S$, we have $x \cdot e = x = e \cdot x$. If a semigroup contains a unit, then the unit is unique: if $e$ and $e'$ are units, then $e = e \cdot e' = e'$. A semigroup with a unit is called a *monoid*. A semigroup with just one element (which is necessarily a unit) will be called a unit semigroup. For a monoid $S$ and an element $x \in S$, we shall extend the notation $x^k$ to $k = 0$ by taking $x^0$ to be the unit.

The set $A^*$ of words over an alphabet $A$ forms a monoid when the operation is taken to be concatenation; it is called the free monoid generated by $A$, and the empty word $\varepsilon$ is its unit.

An element $z \in S$ in a semigroup is called a *zero* if, for all $x \in S$, we have $x \cdot z = z = z \cdot x$. If a semigroup contains a zero, then the zero is unique: if $z$ and $z'$ are zeroes, then $z = z \cdot z' = z'$.

Units and zeroes are special cases of an important class of elements called "idempotents." An element $p \in S$ in a semigroup is called an *idempotent* if $p = p \cdot p$. Every non-empty finite semigroup contains an idempotent element, as is shown by the following lemma.

*Lemma 2.2.1 (Frobenius [1895]).* Every finite cyclic semigroup contains a unique idempotent element.

**Proof.** Suppose $x$ generates the finite cyclic semigroup $S$. Then among the powers $x^1, x^2, \ldots, x^k, \ldots$, we must have $x^i = x^{i+j}$ for some $i, j \geq 1$ (since $S$ is finite). Suppose that in fact $x^i$ is the first element of this sequence to be duplicated later, and that $x^{i+j}$ is its first duplication. (The index $i$ is called the *threshold*, and $j$ is called the *period* of $S$.) Write $i = qj + r$ with $0 \leq r < j$. Then $x^{i+j-r} = x^{2(i+j-r)}$, since $i + j - r$ is greater than $i$, and exceeds its double by a multiple of $j$.

To see that this idempotent is unique, observe that if $y$ is an idempotent, then $y = y^2$ implies $y = y^k$ for all $k \geq 1$. Similarly, if $z$ is an idempotent, then $z = z^l$ for all $l \geq 1$. In particular, if $y = x^l$ and $z = x^k$ are both idempotents in $S$, then $y = y^k = (x^l)^k = (x^k)^l = z^l = z$.                                          □

If $S$ is a finite semigroup, the unique idempotent in the subsemigroup of $S$ generated by an element $x \in S$ will be denoted $x^\omega \in S$.

Recall that an *equivalence* on a set $U$ is a binary relation $\equiv\ \subseteq U^2$ satisfying the following three conditions.

$E_1$  For all $x \in U$, we have $x \equiv x$.

$E_2$  For all $x, y \in U$, if $x \equiv y$, then $y \equiv x$.

$E_3$  For all $x, y, z \in U$, if $x \equiv y$ and $y \equiv z$, then $x \equiv z$.

(These conditions are sometimes expressed by saying that $\equiv$ is "reflexive," "symmetric," and "transitive.") If $\mathcal{P} \in \mathrm{Part}(U)$ is a partition of $U$, then the relation $\equiv$ defined by $x \equiv y \iff \exists_{P \in \mathcal{P}}\, x, y \in P$ is an equivalence on $U$. Reciprocally, if $\equiv$ is an equivalence on $U$, the collection $\{\{x \in U : x \equiv y\} : y \in U\}$ is a partition of $U$. Partitions and equivalences are different mathematical embodiments of the same underlying concept.

If $S$ is a semigroup and $\equiv$ is an equivalence on $S$, we say that $\equiv$ is *right-invariant* if $x \equiv y$ implies $xz \equiv yz$ for all $x, y, z \in S$. We say that $\equiv$ is *left-invariant* if $x \equiv y$ implies $wx \equiv wy$ for all $w, x, y \in S$. We say that $\equiv$ is a *congruence* if it is both right- and left-invariant (or equivalently, if $w \equiv y$ and $x \equiv z$ imply $wx \equiv yz$ for all $w, x, y, z \in S$).

If $S$ is a semigroup and $\equiv$ is a congruence on $S$, there is a natural associative operation defined on the equivalence classes of $\equiv$ (that is, on the blocks of the partition corresponding to $\equiv$). If $X$ and $Y$ are equivalence classes, then the equivalence class containing $x \cdot y$ is independent of the choice of $x \in X$ and $y \in Y$; thus, we may denote it $X \cdot Y$ without ambiguity. We shall write $S/\equiv$ to denote the semigroup (called a *quotient semigroup*) defined in this way. The congruences of a semigroup $S$ form a lattice (a sublattice of the lattices of partitions on the set $S$), and, thus, so do the quotient semigroups of $S$.

A subset $I \subseteq S$ of elements of a semigroup $S$ is called an *ideal* if, for all $i \in I$ and $x \in S$, we have $ix \in I$ and $xi \in I$. If $I$ is an ideal, the equivalence $\equiv_I$ defined by $x \equiv_I y$ if and only if either (1) $x = y$ or (2) $x \in I$ and $y \in I$ is a congruence; thus, $S/\equiv_I$ is a quotient semigroup, which we shall also denote $S/I$.

If $(S, \cdot)$ and $(S', \cdot')$ are two semigroups, we shall denote by $S \times S'$, and call the *product* of $S$ and $S'$, the semigroup $(S'', \cdot'')$ with carrier the Cartesian product $S \times S'$ and with operation defined by $(x, x') \cdot'' (y, y') = (x \cdot y, x' \cdot' y')$. The product operation is not associative or commutative (the carriers of $S \times S'$ and $S' \times S$ are disjoint unless $S = S'$, for example), but they are essentially so. We shall say that two semigroups $(S, \cdot)$ and $(S', \cdot')$ are *isomorphic*, and write $S \approx S'$, if there is a bijection $f : S \to S'$ such that $f(x \cdot y) = f(x) \cdot' f(y)$ for all $x, y \in S$. Then we have the "associative law" $S \times (S' \times S'') \approx (S \times S') \times S''$ and the "commutative law" $S \times S' \approx S' \times S$, and a unit semigroup $E = \{e\}$ serves as a unit element for the product operation: $S \times E \approx S \approx E \times S$.

### 2.2.2. Boolean Algebras

A lattice algebra $(L, \sqcup, \sqcap)$ is said to be *distributive* if it satisfies the following two conditions.

$D_1$  For any $x, y, z \in L, x \sqcup (y \sqcap z) = (x \sqcup y) \sqcap (x \sqcup z)$.
$D_2$  For any $x, y, z \in L, x \sqcap (y \sqcup z) = (x \sqcap y) \sqcup (x \sqcap z)$.

In a distributive lattice algebra with a minimum element $\bot$ and a maximum element $\top$, an element $y$ is said to be a *complement* of an element $x$ if $y \sqcup x = \top$ and $y \sqcap x = \bot$. If an element $x$ has a complement $y$, then that complement is unique: for if we also have $y' \sqcup x = \top$ and $y' \sqcap x = \bot$, then we have $y = y \sqcap \top = y \sqcap (y' \sqcup x) = (y \sqcap y') \sqcup (y \sqcap x) = (y \sqcap y') \sqcup \bot = y \sqcap y'$, so that $y \leq y'$. A dual argument shows that $y' \leq y$, so that $y = y'$. A *Boolean algebra* is a distributive lattice algebra, with minimum and maximum, in which every element has a complement; we shall denote by $\bar{x}$ the complement of $x$.

If $U$ is any universe, the set $\mathrm{Pow}(U)$ forms a Boolean algebra with supremum, infimum, and complement given by the set-theoretic union, intersection, and complement. In the case in which $U$ contains a single element, $\mathrm{Pow}(U)$ contains just two elements, and the resulting Boolean algebra is isomorphic to the familiar Boolean algebra of truth values, or equivalently to the set **B** with supremum, infimum, and complement given by the Boolean functions of disjunction, conjunction, and negation, respectively.

Not every Boolean algebra is isomorphic to the set of all subsets of a universe, however. If we restrict attention to the elements of $\mathrm{Pow}(U)$ that are either finite or co-finite (that is, have complements that are finite), the resulting collection of elements is closed under unions, intersections, and complements, and thus forms a Boolean subalgebra of $\mathrm{Pow}(U)$. If $U$ is countably infinite, then this Boolean subalgebra is also countably infinite; thus, it cannot be isomorphic to the Boolean algebra $\mathrm{Pow}(V)$ for any $V$, since $\mathrm{Pow}(V)$ is always either finite or uncountably infinite. Tarski [1929] has given a characterization of Boolean algebras that are isomorphic to $\text{Pow}(U)$ for some $U$. Such algebras must be complete as lattices, but they must also satisfy an additional condition, which may be given in several equivalent forms (one of which, that they be "completely distributive," is a generalization of the distributive conditions $D_1$ and $D_2$).

If $L$ and $M$ are Boolean algebras, a map $h : L \to M$ will be called a *homomorphism* if it preserves the suprema, infima, and complements. Of particular interest are homomorphisms from a Boolean algebra $L$ to the two-element Boolean algebra $\mathbf{B}$; the set of such homomorphisms will be denoted $\text{Hom}(L)$. With each element $x \in L$ we can associate the subset $H(x) = \{h \in \text{Hom}(L) : h(x) = 1\}$ of $\text{Hom}(L)$. The collection $\{H(x) : x \in L\}$ of subsets of $\text{Hom}(L)$ is closed under unions, intersections, and complements and forms a Boolean subalgebra of $\text{Pow}(\text{Hom}(L))$ that is isomorphic to $L$. Thus, every Boolean algebra is isomorphic to a subalgebra of a Boolean algebra $\text{Pow}(U)$ for some $U$. This result is an embryonic form of the Stone representation theorem (see Stone [1936, 1937]); the full form of this theorem characterizes by means of topological conditions the collections that correspond to Boolean algebras in this way, and thus give a duality between Boolean algebras and certain topological spaces.

### Exercises

1. (M) Show that in a lattice algebra, the conditions $D_1$ and $D_2$ are equivalent to each other (so that either might be taken as characterizing distributive lattices) and to the following condition: for all $x, y, z \in L$, we have $(x \sqcup y) \sqcap z \leq (x \sqcap z) \sqcup y$.
2. (M) Show that every distributive lattice is modular.
3. (E) Give an example of a modular lattice that is not distributive. (Hint: There is an example with five elements.)

### 2.3. Finite Automata

In Section 2.1 we characterized the finite-state languages in terms of the input–output behavior of certain machines; in this section we shall look inside some of these machines and examine their internal structure. The main conclusion of this study, which occupies Section 2.3.1, is that finite machines with many diverse kinds of internal structure all define by their behavior precisely the class of finite-state languages. In Section 2.3.2 we shall study the closure of this class under various operations. In Section 2.3.3 we shall present two further characterizations of the finite-state languages.

### 2.3.1. Two Characterizations

In this section we shall introduce "non-deterministic" and "deterministic" finite automata, and our main result will be that these are equivalent as regards the languages they define. We shall regard languages as subsets of $A^*$, so that the empty word is allowed.

By a *non-deterministic finite automaton* over $A$ we shall mean a quintuple $M = (A, Q, I, J, R)$, where (1) $Q$ is a finite set of elements called states; (2) $I$ and $J$ are subsets of $Q$ whose elements are called the *initial* and *final* states, respectively; and (3) $R$ is a subset of $A \times Q \times Q$ called the *transition rule*. If $R$ is the transition rule of a non-deterministic finite automaton, we may define the *successor map* $S$ corresponding to $R$ by

$$S_a(q) = \{q' \in Q : (a, q, q') \in R\}$$

for all $a \in A$ and $q \in Q$. Reciprocally, if $S$ is such a successor map, we may recover the transition rule $R$ by

$$R = \{(a, q, q') \in A \times Q \times Q : q' \in S_a(q)\}$$

Thus we may specify a non-deterministic finite automaton by giving its successor map rather than its transition rule, if that is more convenient.

A *deterministic finite automaton* is a non-deterministic finite automaton $M = (A, Q, I, J, R)$ for which (1) $\#(I) = 1$ (there is a unique initial state) and (2) for every $a \in A$ and $q \in Q$, $\#(S_a(q)) = 1$ (for each letter, every state has a unique successor state). Roughly speaking, a deterministic finite automaton corresponds to a machine with finitely many states, whose state evolves deterministically in response to a word that is presented letter-by-letter; a non-deterministic finite automaton is a more general notion that lacks this deterministic interpretation, but possesses some redeeming mathematical advantages. All of the automata we shall deal with in this section will be finite, and so we shall omit the qualification "finite" when no confusion is possible.

We shall say that a non-deterministic automaton $M = (A, Q, I, J, R)$ *accepts* a word $x = x_1 \cdots x_n \in A^*$ if and only if there exists a sequence $q_0, \ldots, q_n \in Q$ of states such that (1) $q_0 \in I$, (2) $q_n \in J$, and (3) for all $m$ in the range $1 \le m \le n$, $(x_m, q_{m-1}, q_m) \in R$. Thus, a word is accepted by a non-deterministic automaton if and only if it is possible to start in an initial state, make a sequence of transitions corresponding to the successive letters of the word, and end in a final state. If $M$ is a non-deterministic automaton, we shall denote by Lang($M$) the set of all words accepted by $M$. We shall say that $M$ *recognizes* the language Lang($M$). We shall say that a language $L$ is *recognizable* if $L = \text{Lang}(M)$ for some non-deterministic finite automaton $M$.

We shall show later that the recognizable languages are exactly the finite-state languages, but first we shall prove the following theorem, which is the key to many of the proofs in this section.

**Theorem 2.3.1 (Rabin and Scott [1959]).** *If $L$ is recognizable, then $L = Lang$ $(M')$ for some deterministic finite automaton $M'$.*

**Proof.** Suppose that $L = \text{Lang}(M)$ for some non-deterministic automaton $M = (A, Q, I, J, R)$. We shall construct a deterministic automaton $M' = (A, Q', I', J', R')$ that recognizes the same language as $M$. The idea behind the construction is as follows. In the definition of a non-deterministic automaton accepting a word, there may be an ambiguity as to which initial state to start in, and for each letter of the word, there may be an ambiguity as to which member of the successor map to move to. We shall construct $M'$ so as to keep track of the *set* of states that $M$ might be in at any stage of its computation.

Set $Q' = \text{Pow}(Q)$, $I' = \{I\}$, and $J' = \{K \subseteq Q : K \cap J \neq \emptyset\}$. Finally, if $S$ is the successor map of $M$, set $S'_a(K) = \{\cup_{q \in K} S_a(q)\}$. This determines a transition rule $R'$. It is clear that $M' = (A, Q', I', J', R')$ is a deterministic automaton. It remains to prove that $\text{Lang}(M') = \text{Lang}(M)$.

We prove the following assertion by induction on $n$. Suppose we start $M'$ in its unique initial state, and proceed through the unique transitions corresponding to the word $x = x_1 \cdots x_n$. Then we end in the state of $M'$ that is the set of states in which we might end by starting $M$ in an initial state and proceeding through a sequence of transitions corresponding to the word $x$. The choice of $I'$ gives the basis for the induction, and the choice of $R'$ gives the inductive step. This assertion, together with the choice of $J'$, implies that $M'$ accepts $x$ if and only if $M$ accepts $x$, which in turn implies that $\text{Lang}(M') = \text{Lang}(M)$.     □

**Theorem 2.3.1'.** *A language is recognizable if and only if it is finite-state.*

**Proof.** Suppose that the language $L$ is recognized by the deterministic automaton $M = (A, Q, I, J, R)$, where $I = \{q_0\}$. For each state $q \in Q$, we define the deterministic automaton $M_q = (A, Q, \{q\}, J, R)$ and set $L_q = \text{Lang}(M_q)$. Then we can prove by induction on the length of $x$ that

$$x^{-1}L = L_{S_x(q_0)}$$

where $S$ is the successor map corresponding to the transition relation $R$. Since there are only finitely many languages $L_q$ ($q \in Q$), there are only finitely many languages $x^{-1}L$ ($x \in A^*$), and thus $L$ is finite-state.

Now suppose that $L$ is finite-state. Then the set $Q = \{x^{-1}L : x \in A^*\}$ is finite. Define $I = \{L\}$, $J = \{K \in Q : \varepsilon \in K\}$, and the successor map $S$ by $S_a(K) = \{a^{-1}K\}$. Then the deterministic automaton $(A, Q, I, J, R)$, where the transition relation $R$ corresponds to the successor map $S$, recognizes the language $L$. □

### 2.3.2. Closure Properties

The following two lemmas are good examples of how the equivalence of non-deterministic and deterministic automata can be used to simplify proofs.

If $x = x_1 \cdots x_n$, we shall let $\text{Rev}(x)$ (the "reversal" of $x$) denote the word $x_n \cdots x_1$. If $L$ is a language, we define

$$\text{Rev}(L) = \{\text{Rev}(x) : x \in L\}$$

*Lemma 2.3.2.* If $L$ is recognizable, then $\text{Rev}(L)$ is recognizable.

**Proof.** If $M = (A, Q, I, J, R)$ is a non-deterministic automaton that recognizes $L$, then $M' = (A, Q, J, I, R')$ is a non-deterministic automaton that recognizes $\text{Rev}(L)$, where $R' = \{(a, q, q') \in A \times Q \times Q : (a, q', q) \in R\}$. □

The preceding lemma exploited the symmetry of non-deterministic automata under "time reversal," which is not obviously present for deterministic automata. The following lemma exploits the ambiguity of non-deterministic automata as regards the transition corresponding to a letter, which is again not obviously present for deterministic automata.

If $x = x_1 \cdots x_n$ and $n \geq 1$, we shall let $\text{First}(x)$ denote $x_1$ and let $\text{Rest}(x)$ denote $x_2 \cdots x_n$. We shall say that a word $x$ is a *shuffle* of words $y$ and $z$ if (1) $x = y = z = \varepsilon$, or (2) $\text{First}(x) = \text{First}(y)$ and $\text{Rest}(x)$ is a shuffle of $\text{Rest}(y)$ and $z$, or (3) $\text{First}(x) = \text{First}(z)$ and $\text{Rest}(x)$ is a shuffle of $y$ and $\text{Rest}(z)$. We shall denote by $\text{Shuff}(y, z)$ the set of all words that are shuffles of $y$ and $z$. If $L$ and $L'$ are languages, we define

$$\text{Shuff}(L, L') = \{\text{Shuff}(y, z) : y \in L, z \in L'\}$$

*Lemma 2.3.3.* If $L$ and $L'$ are recognizable, then $\text{Shuff}(L, L')$ is recognizable.

**Proof.** Let $M = (A, Q, I, J, R)$ and $M' = (A, Q', I', J', R')$ be non-deterministic automata recognizing $L$ and $L'$, respectively. Set $Q'' = Q \times Q'$,

$I'' = I \times I'$, and $J'' = J \times J'$. Finally, set

$$S_a''((q, q')) = (S_a(q) \times \{q'\}) \cup (\{q\} \times S_a'(q'))$$

for every $a \in A$ and $(q, q') \in Q \times Q'$. Then $M'' = (A, Q'', I'', J'', R'')$ is a non-deterministic automaton recognizing Shuff($L, L'$). $\qquad\qquad\square$

The two preceding lemmas exploit the properties of non-deterministic automata; the following lemma exploits the properties of deterministic automata.

*Lemma 2.3.4.* If $L$ and $L'$ are recognizable, then (a) Compl($L$) $= A^* \setminus L$, (b) $L \cap L'$, and (c) $L \cup L'$ are recognizable.

**Proof.** (a) If $M = (A, Q, I, J, R)$ is a deterministic automaton recognizing $L$, then $M' = (A, Q, I, Q \setminus J, R)$ is a deterministic automaton recognizing Compl($L$). (b) If $M = (A, Q, I, J, R)$ is a deterministic automaton recognizing $L$ and $M' = (A, Q', I', J', R')$ is a deterministic automaton recognizing $L'$, then $M'' = (A, Q \times Q', I \times I', J \times J', R'')$ is an automaton recognizing $L \cap L'$, where

$$S_a''((q, q')) = S_a(q) \times S_a'(q')$$

for every $a \in A$ and $(q, q') \in Q \times Q'$. (c) This follows from (a) and (b) by De Morgan's Law: $L \cup L' = $ Compl(Compl($L$) $\cap$ Compl($L'$)). $\qquad\square$

The following simple lemma is useful in avoiding pitfalls in arguments involving the empty word.

*Lemma 2.3.5.* The language $L \cup \{\varepsilon\}$ is recognizable if and only if $L \setminus \{\varepsilon\}$ is recognizable.

**Proof.** Let $M = (A, Q, I, J, R)$ be a deterministic automaton recognizing $L$. Let $q_0$ be the unique state in $I$. Let $q_0'$ be a new state, not in $Q$, and set $Q' = Q \cup \{q_0'\}$ and $I' = \{q_0'\}$. Define

$$S_a'(q) = \begin{cases} S_a(q_0), & \text{if } q = q_0' \\ S_a(q), & \text{if } q \neq q_0' \end{cases}$$

for all $a \in A$ and $q \in Q'$. Then $M' = (A, Q', I', J \cup \{q_0'\}, R')$ and $M'' = (A, Q', I', J, R')$ are non-deterministic automata recognizing $L \cup \{\varepsilon\}$ and $L \setminus \{\varepsilon\}$, respectively. $\qquad\square$

If $L$ and $L'$ are languages, we define their concatenation by

$$L \cdot L' = \{y \cdot z : y \in L, z \in L'\}$$

As $\varepsilon$ is the identity element for concatenation of words, then $\{\varepsilon\}$ is the identity element for concatenation of languages.

**Lemma 2.3.6.** If $L$ and $L'$ are recognizable, then $L \cdot L'$ is recognizable.

**Proof.** We may write $L = L_0 \cup L_+$, where $L_0 \subseteq \{\varepsilon\}$ and $L_+ \subseteq A^+$, and similarly write $L' = L'_0 \cup L'_+$. By Lemma 2.3.5, both $L_+$ and $L'_+$ are recognizable. Since "$\cup$" distributes over "$\cdot$" we have

$$L \cdot L' = L_0 \cdot L'_0 \cup L_0 \cdot L'_+ \cup L_+ \cdot L'_0 \cup L_+ \cdot L'_+$$

The first three terms are obviously recognizable, so by Lemma 2.3.4(c) it suffices to show that $L_+ \cdot L'_+$ is recognizable.

To do this, we let $M = (A, Q, I, J, R)$ and $M' = (A, Q', I', J', R')$ be deterministic automata recognizing $L_+$ and $L'_+$, respectively. We may assume that $Q \cap Q' = \emptyset$. Let $q'_0$ be the unique state in $I'$. Define

$$S''_a(q) = \begin{cases} S_a(q), & \text{if } q \in Q \setminus J \\ S_a(q) \cup S'_a(q'_0), & \text{if } q \in J \\ S'_a(q), & \text{if } q \in Q' \end{cases}$$

for all $a \in A$ and $q \in Q \cup Q'$. Then $M'' = (A, Q \cup Q', I, J', R'')$ is a non-deterministic automaton recognizing $L_+ \cdot L'_+$. $\qquad\square$

If $L$ is a language, we define $L^0 = \{\varepsilon\}$, $L^1 = L$, and for $k \geq 1$, $L^{k+1} = L \cdot L^k$. We then define $L^* = \bigcup_{k \geq 0} L^k$ and $L^+ = \bigcup_{k \geq 1} L^k$.

**Lemma 2.3.7.** If $L$ is recognizable, then $L^*$ and $L^+$ are recognizable.

**Proof.** We may assume $L \subseteq A^+$, since deleting the empty word affects neither $L^*$ nor, by Lemma 2.3.5, the recognizability of $L$. Let $M = (A, Q, I, J, R)$ be a deterministic automaton recognizing $L$. Let $q_0$ be the unique state in $I$. Define

$$S'_a(q) = \begin{cases} S_a(q), & \text{if } q \in Q \setminus J \\ S_a(q) \cup S_a(q_0), & \text{if } q \in J \end{cases}$$

for all $a \in A$ and $q \in Q$. Then $M' = (A, Q, I, J, R')$ is a non-deterministic automaton recognizing $L^*$. The recognizability of $L^+$ now follows from Lemma 2.3.5.                                                                                    □

The interplay between non-deterministic and deterministic automata in these last four lemmas illustrates the power of Theorem 2.3.1.

### 2.3.3. Two Further Characterizations

We shall be concerned in this section with equivalences on the set $A^*$ of words over a finite alphabet $A$. Such an equivalence partitions $A^*$ into mutually exclusive and exhaustive sets called "equivalence classes." It is said to have *finite index* if the number of such equivalence classes is finite.

Let $L$ be a language over $A$. We shall define a relation $\simeq_L$ by $x \simeq_L y$ if and only if, for all $z \in A^*$, we have $xz \in L$ if and only if $yz \in L$. It is easy to see that $\simeq_L$ is a right-invariant equivalence.

***Proposition 2.3.8.*** *For every language L, the following three conditions are equivalent: (a) L is recognizable, (b) L is a union of equivalence classes of a right-invariant equivalence of finite index, and (c) the right-invariant equivalence $\simeq_L$ has finite index.*

**Proof.** To prove that (a) implies (b), suppose that $M = (A, Q, I, J, R)$ is a deterministic automaton that recognizes $L$. Extend the successor map $S_a(q)$ to $S_x(q)$ for $x \in A^*$ by $S_\varepsilon(q) = q$ and

$$S_{ay}(q) = \bigcup_{q' \in S_a(q)} S_y(q')$$

Define the relation $\equiv$ on $A^*$ by taking $x \equiv y$ if and only if $S_x(q_0) = S_y(q_0)$, where $q_0$ is the unique state in $I$. Clearly, $\equiv$ is an equivalence, and $x \equiv y$ implies $S_x(q_0) = S_y(q_0)$, which implies $S_{xz}(q_0) = S_{yz}(q_0)$, which in turn implies $xz \equiv yz$, and so $\equiv$ is right-invariant. The equivalence classes of $\equiv$ are the sets

$$C_q = \{x \in A^* : S_x(q_0) = \{q\}\}$$

so that $\equiv$ has finite index, and

$$L = \bigcup_{q \in J} C_q$$

To prove that (b) implies (c), suppose that $L$ is a union of equivalence classes of a right-invariant equivalence $\equiv$ of finite index. If $x \equiv y$, then for all $z \in A^*$, we have $xz \equiv yz$. Since $L$ is a union of equivalence classes, we have $xz \in L$ if and only if $yz \in L$. Thus, $x \equiv y$ implies $x \simeq_L y$. Since $\equiv$ is stronger than $\simeq_L$, the number of $\equiv$ equivalence classes is at least the number of $\simeq_L$ equivalence classes. Since the former is finite, so is the latter.

To prove that (c) implies (a), let $[x]$ denote the equivalence class of $\simeq_L$ containing $x \in A^*$. Define $Q = \{[x] : x \in A^*\}$, $I = \{[\varepsilon]\}$, and $J = \{[x] : x \in L\}$. Define $R$ by $S_a([x]) = \{[xa]\}$, which is coherent because $\simeq_L$ is right-invariant. It is easy to see that $M = (A, Q, I, J, R)$ is a deterministic automaton recognizing $L$. □

The construction in the last part of the proof of Proposition 2.3.8 associates with each recognizable language $L$ a deterministic finite automaton whose states are the equivalence classes of $\simeq_L$; this automaton will be called the *minimal automaton* of $L$, and will be denoted Min($L$). To explain the origin of this name, it will be convenient to introduce some further terminology.

Say that a deterministic automaton $M = (A, Q, I, J, R)$ is a *subautomaton* of a deterministic automaton $M' = (A, Q', I', J', R')$ if there is a one-to-one map $f$ of $Q$ into $Q'$ that preserves the structure of $M$ (that is, if $q \in I$ if and only if $f(q) \in I'$, $q \in J$ if and only if $f(q) \in J'$, and $(a, q, q') \in R$ if and only if $(a, f(q), f(q')) \in R'$). Say that two automata $M$ and $M'$ are *isomorphic* if there is a one-to-one correspondence $f$ between $Q$ and $Q'$ that preserves the structure of $M$ and whose inverse $f^{-1}$ preserves the structure of $M'$. It is easy to show that if $M$ and $M'$ are subautomata of each other, then they are isomorphic.

Say that a deterministic automaton $M = (A, Q, I, J, R)$ is a *quotient automaton* of a deterministic automaton $M' = (A, Q', I', J', R')$ if there is a map $f$ of $Q'$ onto $Q$ that preserves the structure of $M'$. It is easy to show that if $M$ and $M'$ are quotient automata of each other, then they are isomorphic.

Say that a state $q$ in a deterministic automaton $M$ is *accessible* if there is a word $x \in A^*$ such that $S_x(q_0) = \{q\}$, where $q_0$ is the unique initial state of $M$. Say that a deterministic automaton $M$ is accessible if all of its states are accessible. Every deterministic automaton $M$ has an accessible subautomaton Acc($M$), which is unique to within isomorphism.

Say that two states $q$ and $q'$ in a deterministic automaton $M$ are *distinguishable* if there is a word $x \in A^*$ such that $S_x(q) \in J$ unless and only unless $S_x(q') \in J$. Say that a deterministic automaton $M$ is *distinguishable* if each pair of distinct states is distinguishable. Every accessible automaton $M$ has a distinguishable quotient automaton Dist($M$), which is unique to within isomorphism.

Say that a deterministic automaton $M$ *covers* a deterministic automaton $M'$ if $M'$ is a quotient automaton of a subautomaton of $M$. (Note that covering is a transitive relation.) Then for any deterministic automaton $M$, $\mathrm{Min}(\mathrm{Lang}(M))$ is isomorphic to $\mathrm{Dist}(\mathrm{Acc}(M))$, and thus that $M$ covers $\mathrm{Min}(\mathrm{Lang}(M))$. This is the sense in which $\mathrm{Min}(L)$ is minimal for $L$.

Let $L$ be a language over $A$. We shall define a relation $\cong_L$ by $x \cong_L y$ if and only if, for all $w, z \in A^*$, we have $wxz \in L$ if and only if $wyz \in L$. It is easy to see that $\cong_L$ is a congruence on $A^*$ and that $x \cong_L y$ implies $x \simeq_L y$.

**Proposition 2.3.9.** *For every language $L$, the following three conditions are equivalent: (a) $L$ is recognizable, (b) $L$ is a union of equivalence classes of a congruence of finite index, and (c) the congruence $\cong_L$ has finite index.*

**Proof.** The proof that (a) implies (b) is similar to that for Proposition 2.3.8, but we define two words $x$ and $y$ to be equivalent if $S_x(q) = S_y(q)$ for all $q \in Q$, rather than just for the initial state $q = q_0$. The proofs of the remaining parts follow from Proposition 2.3.8 and the fact that $\cong_L$ is stronger than $\simeq_L$.    □

Since $\cong_L$ is a congruence on $A^*$ for any language $L \subseteq A^*$, there exists a quotient monoid $A^* / \cong_L$, which will be called the *syntactic* monoid of $L$ and which will be denoted $\mathrm{Syn}(L)$. The map $f : A^* \to \mathrm{Syn}(L)$ that assigns to each word in $A^*$ its equivalence class in $\mathrm{Syn}(L)$ is a homomorphism: we have $h(x \cdot y) = h(x) \cdot h(y)$. This homomorphism will be called the *canonical* homomorphism for $L$. This terminology yields the following paraphrase of Proposition 2.3.9.

**Proposition 2.3.9'.** *For every language $L \subseteq A^*$, the following three conditions are equivalent: (a) $L$ is recognizable; (b) there exists a finite monoid $M$, a homomorphism $g : A^* \to M$ and a subset $X \subseteq M$ such that $L = g^{-1}(X)$; and (c) the monoid $\mathrm{Syn}(L)$ is finite.*

Propositions 2.3.8 and 2.3.9 are due to J. Myhill (see Rabin and Scott [1959]) and Nerode [1958].

## Exercises

1. (E) What can go wrong if $M$ is a non-deterministic automaton in the proof of Lemma 2.3.4(a)? What about Lemma 2.3.4(b)?
2. (E) What can go wrong if we do not separate the treatment of the empty word in the proof of Lemma 2.3.6? What about Lemma 2.3.7?

3. (M) If $M$ is a non-deterministic automaton, let $\text{Det}(M)$ denote the deterministic automaton obtained by the construction of Theorem 2.3.1. If $M$ is a non-deterministic automaton, let $\text{Rev}(M)$ denote the non-deterministic obtained by the construction of Lemma 2.3.2. Say that an automaton $M$ is *minimized* if it is isomorphic to $\text{Min}(\text{Lang}(M))$. (a) Show that if $M$ is an accessible automaton, then $\text{Acc}(\text{Det}(\text{Rev}(M)))$ is a minimized automaton (which accepts the language $\text{Rev}(\text{Lang}(M))$). (b) Conclude that if $M$ is any non-deterministic automaton, then $\text{Acc}(\text{Det}(\text{Rev}(\text{Acc}(\text{Det}(\text{Rev}(M))))))$ is a minimized automaton (which accepts $\text{Lang}(M)$).

4. (M) Define a *generalized* non-deterministic automaton to be like a non-deterministic automaton, but with the transition rule $R$ being a finite subset of $A^* \times Q \times Q$, rather than $A \times Q \times Q$. Say that a generalized non-deterministic automaton accepts a word $x \in A^*$ if and only if there exists a sequence $q_0, \ldots, q_n \in Q$ of states and a sequence $y_1, \ldots, y_n \in A^*$ of words such that (1) $q_0 \in I$, (2) $q_n \in J$, (3) $x = y_1 \cdot \cdots \cdot y_n$, and (4) for $0 \leq m \leq n - 1$, $(y_m, q_m, q_{m+1}) \in R$. (Note that $n$ may be less than, equal to, or greater than the length of $x$.) Show that if $L$ is the set of words accepted by a generalized non-deterministic automaton, then $L$ is recognizable. (Exercise care with triples of the form $(\varepsilon, q, q')$ in $R$.)

5. (M) ("Pumping Lemma" for recognizable languages.) Let $L$ be recognizable. Show that there exists a natural number $n$ such that every word $w \in L$ with length at least $n$ can be written as $w = xyz$, with the length of $y$ at least 1, such that for all natural numbers $k$, $xy^k z \in L$ (where $y^k$ denotes the $k$-fold concatenation of $y$ with itself).

6. (M) ("Metric" characterization for recognizable languages.) Given two words $x$ and $y$ over a finite alphabet $A$, define the *distance* $d(x, y)$ between $x$ and $y$ to be the reciprocal of the smallest possible finite index of a congruence $\cong$ on $A^*$ such that $x \not\cong y$ (or to be zero if there is no such congruence of finite index). (a) Show that $d$ is a *metric* on $A^*$; that is, show that (i) $d(x, y) \geq 0$ and $d(x, y) = 0$ if and only if $x = y$, (ii) $d(x, y) = d(y, x)$, and (iii) $d(x, z) \leq d(x, y) + d(y, z)$. (Indeed, the "triangle inequality" (iii) holds in the stronger form $d(x, z) \leq \max\{d(x, y), d(y, z)\}$.) (b) Show that $L \subseteq A^*$ is recognizable if and only if there exists a real number $\varepsilon > 0$ such that

$$\min_{x \in L, y \notin L} d(x, y) \geq \varepsilon$$

## 2.4. Regular Expressions

In this section, we present an algebraic formalism that provides yet another characterization of the recognizable languages. The principal objects in this formalism are algebraic expressions called "regular expressions." Because of this characterization, the recognizable languages are often referred to as the "regular languages." We define *regular expressions* recursively by the following conditions:

1. The expression $O$ is a regular expression.
2. The expression $I$ is a regular expression.
3. For every $a \in \mathbf{N}$, the expression $a$ is a regular expression.
4. If $F$ and $G$ are regular expressions, then $(F \cup G)$ is a regular expression.
5. If $F$ and $G$ are regular expressions, then $(F \cdot G)$ is a regular expression.
6. If $F$ is a regular expression, then $F^*$ is a regular expression.

It is to be understood that nothing is a regular expression unless it is so by virtue of conditions (1) through (6). The regular expressions in conditions (1), (2), and (3) will be called *primitive*; those in conditions (4), (5), and (6) will be called *unions, concatenations*, and *asterations*, respectively. We shall often omit the parentheses indicated in conditions (4) and (5), with the convention that asteration takes precedence over concatenation, and concatenation takes precedence over union. With every regular expression $E$, we may associate a language $\mathrm{Lang}(E)$ by the following rules:

1. $\mathrm{Lang}(O) = \emptyset$.
2. $\mathrm{Lang}(I) = \{\varepsilon\}$.
3. $\mathrm{Lang}(a) = \{a\}$.
4. $\mathrm{Lang}(F \cup G) = \mathrm{Lang}(F) \cup \mathrm{Lang}(G)$.
5. $\mathrm{Lang}(F \cdot G) = \mathrm{Lang}(F) \cdot \mathrm{Lang}(G)$.
6. $\mathrm{Lang}(F^*) = \mathrm{Lang}(F)^*$.

These rules may be taken as a definition of $\mathrm{Lang}(E)$ by "structural induction" on the regular expression $E$. We have defined $\mathrm{Lang}(E)$ as a set of words over the infinite alphabet $\mathbf{N}$, but it is also a set of words over any finite alphabet that includes all of the letters that appear as subexpressions of $E$. A regular expression does not completely specify the finite alphabet that is appropriate, and if it matters it must be specified explicitly. Our main result in this section is the following.

**Theorem 2.4.1 (Kleene [1956]).** *A language $L$ is recognizable if and only if $L = \mathrm{Lang}(E)$ for some regular expression $E$.*

There are two things to prove here: that every recognizable language is described by a regular expression, and that every regular expression describes a recognizable language.

Kleene's proof of the first used induction, essentially on the number of states of a non-deterministic finite automaton recognizing the language. The proof begins by numbering the states, and the resulting regular expression depends strongly on the particular numbering chosen. We shall give a different proof, due to Eilenberg [1973], which has the merit of producing a "canonical" regular expression (at least up to the associativity and commutativity of the union operation).

Our proof will proceed by decomposing a recognizable language into simpler languages by means of the operations allowed in regular expressions. Since our hypothesis is that the language is recognizable, we shall refer to languages by the minimal deterministic automata recognizing them. In order to prove that our decomposition procedure terminates, we shall need a measure of the "complexity" of a deterministic finite automaton. The most obvious candidate is simply the number of states, but unfortunately this is not always reduced by our decomposition procedure. Thus, we shall begin by describing a more subtle complexity measure.

We shall say that a state $q$ of a deterministic finite automaton $M$ is *quick* if some final state of $M$ is accessible from $q$, and we shall say that $q$ is *dead* otherwise. Dead states are indistinguishable, and so a minimal automaton has at most one dead state. We shall say that a transition $(a, q, q')$ in $M$ is quick if the state $q'$ that it leads into it is quick, and we shall say that $(a, q, q')$ is dead otherwise. We shall adopt as our measure of the complexity of a deterministic finite automaton $M$ the number of quick transitions in $M$. The operations used to minimize an automaton (deleting inaccessible states and identifying indistinguishable states) cannot increase the number of quick transitions, and thus we may replace a deterministic automaton by the corresponding minimal automaton at any time without increasing the complexity. We shall adopt as our measure of the complexity of a recognizable language $L$ the complexity of the minimal automaton recognizing $L$ (which is the minimum of the complexities of all deterministic automata recognizing $L$).

We shall say that a recognizable language $L$ is unitary if $\mathrm{Min}(L)$ has exactly one final state. A unitary language is not empty. Suppose that $L$ is any recognizable language and that $M = (A, Q, I, J, R)$ is its minimal automaton. For each final state $j \in J$, define the automaton $M_j = (A, Q, I, \{j\}, R)$ and the recognizable language $L_j = \mathrm{Lang}(M_j)$. Since the operations used to minimize an automaton cannot increase the number of final states, the language $L_j$ is unitary. Thus, we can decompose any recognizable language $L$ into a finite number of unitary languages

$$L = \bigcup_{j \in J} L_j$$

in a canonical way, and each of these languages has complexity no greater than that of $L$. If $J$ is empty, then the language $L$ is described by the regular expression $O$. It remains to consider the decomposition of unitary languages.

We shall say that a word $x$ is a *prefix* of a word $y$, and write $x \prec y$, if there is a word $z$ such that $xz = y$. We shall say that a language $L$ is *prefix-free* if no word in $L$ is a prefix of another word in $L$, that is, if $x, y \in L$ and $x \prec y$ imply $x = y$. If a prefix-free language contains the empty word, then it contains only the empty word. A prefix-free language that does not contain the empty word will be called a *proper* prefix-free language. A prefix-free language $L$ is either empty or unitary, since all transitions of $\text{Min}(L)$ out of a final state must be dead, and thus all final states are indistinguishable. In fact, we can characterize prefix-free languages as those for which all transitions of the minimal automaton out of final states are dead.

We shall say that a language $L$ is *monoidal* if (1) it is closed under concatenation, that is, if $x, y \in L$ imply $xy \in L$ and (2) it contains the empty word. (Thus a monoidal language is one that forms a submonoid of the free monoid on its alphabet.) A monoidal language $L$ is unitary, since any final state in $\text{Min}(L)$ is indistinguishable from the initial state. In fact, we can characterize monoidal languages as those for which the initial state of the minimal automaton is the unique final state.

If $L$ is any unitary language, then we may decompose $L$ as

$$L = P \cdot Q, \tag{2.4.1}$$

where $P$ is non-empty and prefix-free and $Q$ is monoidal. Indeed, if $M = (A, Q, \{i\}, \{j\}, R)$ is the minimal automaton of $L$, then we may take $P$ to be the language recognized by the automaton obtained from $M$ by making all transitions out of $j$ dead (adding a dead state, if necessary), and we may take $Q$ to be the language recognized by the automaton $(A, Q, \{j\}, \{j\}, R)$. Furthermore, the decomposition (2.4.1) is unique. To see this, we observe that since the monoidal language $Q$ contains the empty word, $P$ must be a subset of $L$, and must contain all words of $L$ that have no shorter prefix in $L$. On the other hand, the prefix-free language $P$ cannot contain any word of $L$ that does have a shorter prefix in $L$. Thus, $P$ is uniquely determined by $L$. Similarly $Q$ must comprise all and only the words $y$ such that $x \in L$ implies $xy \in L$, and thus is also uniquely determined by $L$. Thus we decompose a unitary language $L$ as a product of a non-empty prefix-free language $P$ and a monoidal language $Q$ in a canonical way, and both of these languages have complexity no greater than that of $L$. It remains to consider the decomposition of non-empty prefix-free languages and monoidal languages.

If $L$ is any monoidal language, then either $L$ contains only the empty word, in which case $L$ is described by the regular expression $I$, or we may decompose $L$ as

$$L = R^* \qquad (2.4.2)$$

where $R$ is a non-empty prefix-free language. Indeed, if $M$ is the minimal automaton of $L$, then we may take $R$ to be the language recognized by the automaton obtained from $M$ by splitting the unique initial and final state into two states, one initial but not final, the other final but not initial, with transition out of the former being as before, and transitions out of the latter being dead (adding a dead state, if necessary). Furthermore, the decomposition (2.4.2) is unique. To see this, we observe that since $L$ is monoidal and contains a non-empty word, the language $L'$ obtained from $L$ by deleting the empty word is unitary, and thus can be decomposed uniquely as $L' = P \cdot Q$, where $P$ is non-empty and prefix-free and $Q$ is monoidal. We then see that $R$ must comprise all and only the words of $P$, so that it is uniquely determined by $L$. Thus, we may express a monoidal language $L$ that contains a non-empty word as the asterate of a non-empty prefix-free language $R$ in a canonical way, and $R$ has complexity no greater than that of $L$. It remains to consider the decomposition of non-empty prefix free languages.

Let $L$ be any non-empty prefix-free language. If $L$ contains the empty word, then it contains only the empty word, and thus it is described by the regular expression $I$. If $L$ does not contain the empty word, then every word of $L$ contains a last letter, and thus $L$ may be decomposed in a canonical way as

$$L = \bigcup_{a \in A} (La^{-1}) \cdot \{a\}$$

where $La^{-1}$ is the language comprising the words $x$ such that $xa \in L$. Each language $\{a\}$ is described by the regular expression $a$, so it remains to consider the languages $La^{-1}$. Since $L$ is a non-empty prefix that does not contain the empty word, $M = \text{Min}(L)$ contains a unique final state $j$ that is distinct from the initial state, and all transitions out of $j$ are dead. The language $La^{-1}$ is thus recognized by the automaton $M'$ obtained from $M$ by (1) making $j$ a non-final state (so that it becomes a dead state) and (2) making those states $q$ such that $(a, q, j)$ is a transition in $M$ final states. If $M'$ has no final states, then $La^{-1}$ is empty and is described by the regular expression $O$. Otherwise, at least one transition $(a, q, j)$ that was quick in $M$ is dead in $M'$. Furthermore, no transition that was dead in $M$ is quick in $M'$. Thus the language $La^{-1}$, if it is not empty, has complexity strictly less than that of $L$.

Since we have decomposed an arbitrary recognizable language by means
of the regular operations (union, concatenation, and asteration) into primitive
regular languages (described by the regular expressions $O$, $I$, and $a \in \mathbf{N}$) and
recognizable languages of strictly smaller complexity, an obvious induction
shows that every recognizable language is described by a regular expression.

We now turn to the converse proposition: that every regular expression describes a recognizable language. We have, in fact, already proved this, since the
languages described by the expressions $O$, $I$, and $a \in \mathbf{N}$ are recognizable, and
the recognizable languages are closed under union, concatenation, and asteration (Lemmas 2.3.4(c), 2.3.6, and 2.3.7 in Section 2.3). Thus, the converse
is proved by a structural induction on the regular expression. We shall now
present another proof, due in slightly different forms to Brzozowski [1964]
and Conway [1971], which is based on an interesting "differential calculus of
regular expressions." (For yet another proof, see McNaughton and Yamada
[1960].)

If $L$ is a language, we shall define $\iota(L) = L \cap \{\varepsilon\}$, that is, $\{\varepsilon\}$ if $\varepsilon \in L$
and $\emptyset$ if $\varepsilon \notin L$. We shall also define $\iota(E)$ for any regular expression $E$ by the
following rules:

1. $\iota(O) = O$.
2. $\iota(I) = I$.
3. $\iota(a) = O$.
4. $\iota(F \cup G) = \iota(F) \cup \iota(G)$.
5. $\iota(F \cdot G) = \iota(F) \cdot \iota(G)$.
6. $\iota(F^*) = I$.

We then have, by a simple structural induction on $E$, that $\mathrm{Lang}(\iota(E)) =$
$\iota(\mathrm{Lang}(E))$.

If $L$ is a language and $a \in \mathbf{N}$ is a letter, we define $a^{-1}L = \{x : ax \in L\}$ as
before. We shall also define $a^{-1}E$ for any regular expression $E$ by the following
rules:

1. $a^{-1}O = O$.
2. $a^{-1}I = O$.
3. $a^{-1}b = I$ if $a = b$, and $a^{-1}b = O$ if $a \neq b$.
4. $a^{-1}(F \cup G) = a^{-1}F \cup a^{-1}G$.
5. $a^{-1}(F \cdot G) = (a^{-1}F) \cdot G \cup \iota(F) \cdot (a^{-1}G)$.
6. $a^{-1}(F^*) = (a^{-1}F) \cdot F^*$.

We then have, by a simple structural induction on $E$, that $\mathrm{Lang}(a^{-1}E) =$
$a^{-1}\mathrm{Lang}(E)$. The rules for the operation $E \mapsto a^{-1}E$ are similar to those for

the operation $E \mapsto (\partial/\partial a)E$ in calculus, where $O$ and $I$ correspond to the constants 0 and 1, $a$ and $b$ correspond to independent variables, and $F \cup G$, $F \cdot G$, and $F^*$ correspond to $F + G$, $FG$, and $1/(1 - F)$, respectively. (The correspondence is not exact, however: union is not invertible, and concatenation is not commutative, for example.) For this reason, what we have denoted $a^{-1}E$ is sometimes written $\partial_a$ or $D_a$.

If $L$ is a language and $x = x_1 \cdots x_n$ is a word, then we have $x^{-1}L = x_n^{-1} \cdots x_1^{-1}L$, with the special case $\varepsilon^{-1}L = L$. This suggests that we define $x^{-1}E$ for a regular expression $E$ by $x^{-1}E = x_n^{-1} \cdots x_1^{-1}E$, with the special case $\varepsilon^{-1}E = E$. Since a language $L \subseteq A^*$ is finite-state, and therefore recognizable, if it has only finitely many intrinsic states $x^{-1}L$ (as $x$ runs through all words over $A$), we can show that the language described by the regular expression $E$ is recognizable by showing that it has only finitely many intrinsic states $x^{-1}\text{Lang}(E) = \text{Lang}(x^{-1}E)$ (again as $x$ runs through all words). To do this we shall generalize the notion of "quotient" still further.

If $K$ and $L$ are languages, we define $K^{-1}L = \bigcup_{x \in K} x^{-1}L$. We shall also define $D^{-1}E$ for any regular expressions $D$ and $E$ by the following rules:

1. $D^{-1}O = O$.
2. $D^{-1}I = \iota(D)$.
3. $D^{-1}a = \iota(D)a \cup \iota(a^{-1}D)$.
4. $D^{-1}(F \cup G) = D^{-1}F \cup D^{-1}G$.
5. $D^{-1}(F \cdot G) = (D^{-1}F) \cdot G \cup (F^{-1}D)^{-1}G$.
6. $D^{-1}(F^*) = \iota(D) \cup ((F^*)^{-1}D)^{-1}F) \cdot F^*$.

We then have, by simple structural induction on $E$ as before, that $\text{Lang}(D^{-1}E) = \text{Lang}(D)^{-1}\text{Lang}(E)$. We can then prove that $\text{Lang}(D^{-1}E)$ assumes only finitely many values as $D$ ranges over all regular expressions. If $E$ is of the form $O$, $I$, or $a \in \mathbf{N}$, then this finite number is 1, 2, or 4, respectively. If $E$ is of the form $F \cup G$, $F \cdot G$, or $F^*$, then this finite number is at most $fg$, $fg$, or $2f$, respectively, where $f$ and $g$ are the numbers of values assumed by $\text{Lang}(D^{-1}F)$ and $\text{Lang}(D^{-1}G)$, respectively, as $D$ ranges over all regular expressions. Since for every word $x \in A^*$, there is a regular expression $D_x$ that describes the language $\{x\}$, we conclude that $x^{-1}\text{Lang}(E) = \text{Lang}(D_x^{-1}E)$ assumes only finitely many values as $x$ ranges over all words, and thus that every regular expression describes a recognizable language.

We have developed regular expressions based on the three operations: union, concatenation, and asteration. These operations form a minimal set, in the sense that excluding any one of them restricts the class of languages that can be defined. For some purposes it is convenient to work with a larger set, and the most frequently added operation is complementation (with respect to the set of all words over a specified alphabet). When complementation is added, intersection can be performed as well, by using union and complementation with De Morgan's Law. Regular expressions in which complementation and intersection are allowed as operations are called *extended* regular expressions. We have seen that the recognizable languages are also closed under the operations of reversal and shuffle, and so these might also be added without expanding the class of languages that can be defined, though these are less commonly encountered in connection with recognizable languages.

We have confined our attention in this section to the use of regular expressions to define languages. They can, however, also be developed abstractly as an algebraic system in their own right, with algebraic identities corresponding to equalities among the languages they describe. This point of view is brought to the fore by Conway [1971].

In investigating the identities satisfied by any algebraic objects, it is natural to ask if they are *finitely based*; that is, if there is a finite set of identities from which all others may be derived by substitution of equals in equals, together with the reflexive, symmetric, and transitive laws of equality.

Let us begin by omitting the operation of asteration from regular expressions, and consider the following identities:

$R_1$  $a \cup (b \cup c) = (a \cup b) \cup c$.
$R_2$  $a \cup b = b \cup a$.
$R_3$  $a \cup O = a = O \cup a$.
$R_4$  $a \cup a = a$.
$R_5$  $a(bc) = (ab)c$.
$R_6$  $Ia = a = aI$.
$R_7$  $Oa = O = aO$.
$R_8$  $a(b \cup c) = ab \cup ac$ and $(a \cup b)c = ac \cup bc$.

It is not hard to see that identities $R_1$ through $R_8$ provide a basis for the derivation of all identities among regular expressions not involving asteration (see Exercise 5 to follow). Thus any problems of axiomatizing identities among regular expressions must arise from the presence of asteration.

In seeking a basis for the identities involving asteration, the following appear as natural candidates:

$S_1$  $(a \cup b)^* = (a^*b)^*a^*$.
$S_2$  $(ab)^* = I \cup a(ba)^*b$.
$S_3$  $(a^*)^* = a^*$.
$S_{4,n}$  $a^* = (a^n)^*(I \cup a \cup \cdots \cup a^{n-1})$.

The identities $S_{4,n}$ form an infinite family, in which the expressions "$a^n$" and "$a^{n-1}$" are, of course, abbreviations for expressions involving $a$ but not $n$. This infinite family inspired the first proof that there is no finite basis for the identities among regular expressions; this proof (see Redko [1964a, 1964b] and Conway [1971]) involves showing that when $n$ is prime, $S_{4,n}$ cannot be derived from any set of identities that do not somehow involve the prime $n$ in their construction. The conclusion then follows from the fact that there are infinitely many primes. This negative result sent the quest in two different directions: (1) for an infinite set of identities that form a basis and (2) for a finite set of axioms that allow the identities to be deduced with the help of some additional rules of inference.

Since the set of *all* identities among regular expressions is countably infinite, an infinite basis is only interesting if it possesses some further striking property. While this last condition is, of course, a matter of taste, a strong claim to success in this direction can be made by the work of Krob [1991], who supplements $R_1$ through $R_8$, $S_1$, and $S_2$ with an infinite family of identities that can be regarded as the generalizations of $S_{4,n}$ from the cyclic group on $n$ elements to the symmetric group on $n$ elements.

In the second direction, the earliest work was that of Salomaa [1966], who observed that it is easy to give an axiomatization of the property "$a$ does not contain the empty word," then showed how to axiomatize the identities among regular expressions with a finite set of identities and the rule of inference: "if $b$ does not contain the empty word, then from $a = ab \cup c$ deduce $a = cb^*$." Boffa [1990], using the work of Krob [1991], has shown that this rule of inference may be simplified to "if $b$ does not contain the empty word, then from $a = ab \cup I$ deduce $a = b^*$."

A different sort of axiomatization is obtained by confining the propositions to identities, but considering *implications* among identities as well as "absolute" identities. (Thus, for example, $ab = ba$ implies $(a \cup b)^* = a^*b^*$.) From an algebraic point of view, this leads to a theory that is almost as well understood as the theories of identities alone; see Selman [1972]. In this setting, Kozen [1994] has given a finite set of axioms that suffice to deduce all implications among regular expressions. Finally, we should mention that Boffa [1995], again using the work of Krob [1991], has shown that identities involving asteration can be deduced from axioms that seem to capture the essence of asteration (in the same way that $R_1$ through $R_8$ capture the essence of union and concatenation). In this system, the additional rules are (1) $a^*a^* = a^*$, (2) $a^* \geq a \cup I$, and (3) from $bb = b$ and $b \geq a \cup I$, deduce $b \geq a^*$. (In these rules, an inequality $b \geq a$ is an abbreviation for the identity $b = b \cup a$.) These rules then simply say that $a^*$ is the unique smallest idempotent (with respect to concatenation) that is at least as large as $a \cup I$.

### *Exercises*

1. (E) What languages can be defined by regular expressions without asteration (and without complementation)?
2. (M) Give an example of a recognizable language that cannot be defined by a regular expression without nested asteration (and without complementation).
3. (H) Give, for every $k \geq 0$, an example of a recognizable language that cannot be defined by a regular expression without asteration nested to depth $k$ (and without complementation). (See Eggan [1963] and Dejean and Schützenberger [1966].)
4. (U) Prove or disprove: Every recognizable language can be defined by an extended regular expression without nested asteration.
5. (M) Show that identities $R_1$ through $R_8$ provide a basis for the derivation of all identities among regular expressions not involving asteration. (Hint: Show that they allow all languages expressible without asteration to be expressed in a canonical form.)

## 2.5. Logical Expressions

This section presents yet another formalism that describes all and only the recognizable languages. In contrast with the regular expressions presented in the preceding section, which were quite algebraic in character, the formalism we present now has a distinctly logical character, and we shall call its principal objects "logical expressions." In this section it will be convenient to disallow the empty word and, thus, to regard a language over an alphabet $A$ as a subset of $A^+$ (rather than $A^*$).

A *logical expression* is an expression built up from "atomic expressions" using "logical connectives" and "logical quantifiers" in the usual way. Let us consider a fixed finite alphabet $A \subseteq \mathbf{N}$. We shall introduce two types of *variables*: *individual* variables (for which we shall use lower-case italic letters such as $r$, $s$, $s_1$, $s_2$, and so forth), and *set* variables (for which we shall use upper-case italic letters such as $R$, $S$, $S_1$, $S_2$, and so forth). We shall think of individual variables as ranging over the positions (from $N = \{1, \ldots, n\}$) of a word $x_1 \cdots x_n \in A^+$, and think of set variables as ranging over subsets (from $\text{Pow}(N)$) of positions. Atomic expressions will be of the following three kinds:

1. An *occurrence assertion*, $a \propto r$, where $a \in A$ and $r$ is an individual variable.
2. An *arithmetic comparison*, $r < s$, $r = s$ or $r > s$, where $r$ and $s$ are individual variables.
3. A *membership assertion*, $r \in R$, where $r$ is an individual variable and $R$ is a set variable.

We think of an occurrence assertion $a \propto r$ as asserting that "the letter $a$ occurs at position $r$" (that is, that $x_r = a$). The other kinds of atomic expressions have their customary interpretations. Logical connectives will be of the following three kinds:

1. A *conjunction*, $\phi \wedge \psi$, where $\phi$ and $\psi$ are logical expressions.
2. A *disjunction*, $\phi \vee \psi$, where $\phi$ and $\psi$ are logical expressions.
3. A *negation*, $\neg\phi$, where $\phi$ is a logical expression.

We shall interpret these as representing "and," "or," and "not" in the usual way. We shall also feel free to use other connectives, such as "implication" $\Rightarrow$ and "equivalence" $\Leftrightarrow$, which can be defined in terms of the ones we have adopted. Logical quantifiers will be of the following two kinds:

1. An *existential quantification*, $\exists_r \phi(r)$ or $\exists_R \phi(R)$, where $r$ or $R$ is an individual or set variable, respectively.
2. A *universal quantification*, $\forall_r \phi(r)$ or $\forall_R \phi(R)$, where $r$ or $R$ is an individual or set variable, respectively.

We shall interpret these as representing "there exists" and "for all" in the usual way. Formalizing this interpretation completely would require discussing the rules for "free" and "bound" variables; these rules harbor some subtleties, but nothing we do here will depend on any of these subtleties, and we shall not make the rules explicit here. With these interpretations we may assign a truth value ("true" or "false") to a given logical expression $\phi$ with respect to a given word $x$, provided any variables that are free in $\phi$ (that is, appear in atomic expressions without being bound by quantifiers) are assigned specific values of the appropriate type (that is, values in $N$ for individual variables and values in Pow($N$) for set variables). If $\phi$ is *closed* (that is, if $\phi$ contains no free variables), then we may speak of $\phi$ "holding" or "not holding" for $x$; we write $x \models \phi$ to indicate that $\phi$ holds for $x$. If $\phi$ is any closed logical expression, we shall write Lang($\phi$) for the set of all non-empty words $x \in A^+$ such that $x \models \phi$.

Our main result is the following.

**Theorem 2.5.1 (Büchi [1960]).** *A language $L$ is recognizable if and only if $L = Lang(\phi)$ for some closed logical expression $\phi$.*

There are two things to prove here: that every recognizable language is described by a logical expression and that every logical expression describes a recognizable language.

To prove the first part, let $L$ be a recognizable language and let $M = (A, Q, I, J, R)$ be a deterministic finite automaton recognizing $L$. Let $\{\varrho_1, \ldots, \varrho_m\} = R$ be the set of transitions of $M$. We begin by introducing a set variable $U_l$ for each transition $\varrho_l$ (where $1 \leq l \leq m$). Our expression $\phi$ will then have the form

$$\phi = \exists_{U_1} \cdots \exists_{U_l} \, \psi(U_1, \ldots, U_m)$$

Before describing the expression $\psi(U_1, \ldots, U_m)$, let us explain the intended interpretation of the variables $U_1, \ldots, U_m$. The computation of $M$ for input $x = x_1 \cdots x_n$ may be described by the sequence $\varrho^{(1)}, \ldots, \varrho^{(n)}$ of transitions, where $\varrho^{(i)}$ is the transition made for the occurrence $x_i$. We shall interpret $U_l$ as the set of positions $i$ such that $\varrho^{(i)} = \varrho_l$, and we shall construct the expression $\psi$ so that $\psi(U_1, \ldots, U_m)$ holds precisely when $U_1, \ldots, U_m$ are consistent with this interpretation and $M$ accepts the word $x$.

The formula $\psi(U_1, \ldots, U_m)$ will be constructed as the conjunction of five subexpressions,

$$\psi = \psi_1 \wedge \psi_2 \wedge \psi_3 \wedge \psi_4 \wedge \psi_5$$

where we have suppressed the indication of the free variables $U_1, \ldots, U_m$ common to all these expressions.

The expression $\psi_1$ asserts that one and only one transition is made at each position of the word,

$$\psi_1(U_1, \ldots, U_m) = \forall_r \left( \bigvee_{1 \leq l \leq m} (r \in U_l) \wedge \bigwedge_{1 \leq k < l \leq m} (\neg r \in U_k \vee \neg r \in U_l) \right)$$

Let At($a$) denote the set $\{l : \varrho_l \in \{a\} \times Q \times Q\}$ of indices of transitions compatible with occurrences of the letter $a$. The expression $\psi_2$ asserts that the transition made at each position is compatible with the letter that occurs at that position,

$$\psi_2(U_1, \ldots, U_m) = \forall_r \bigvee_{a \in A} \left( (a \propto r) \wedge \bigvee_{l \in \text{At}(a)} (r \in U_l) \right)$$

Let Out($q$) denote the set $\{l : \varrho_l \in A \times \{q\} \times Q\}$ of indices of transitions out of the state $q$. Let first($r$) denote the expression $\neg\exists_s (s < r)$, which asserts that $r$ is the first position (that is, $r = 1$). The expression $\psi_3$ asserts that the first transition is out of an initial state,

$$\psi_3(U_1, \ldots, U_m) = \forall_r \left( \text{first}(r) \Rightarrow \bigvee_{i \in I} \bigvee_{l \in \text{Out}(i)} (r \in U_l) \right)$$

Let $\text{In}(q)$ denote the set $\{l : \varrho_l \in A \times Q \times \{q\}\}$ of indices of transitions into the state $q$. Let $\text{last}(r)$ denote the expression $\neg \exists_s (s > r)$, which asserts that $r$ is the last position (that is, $r = n$). The expression $\psi_4$ asserts that the last transition is into a final state,

$$\psi_4(U_1, \ldots, U_m) = \forall_r \left( \text{last}(r) \Rightarrow \bigvee_{j \in J} \bigvee_{l \in \text{In}(i)} (r \in U_l) \right)$$

Let $\text{next}(r, s)$ denote the expression $r < s \wedge \neg \exists_t r < t \wedge t < s$, which asserts that $s$ is the next position after $r$ (that is, that $s = r + 1$). The expression $\psi_5$ asserts that in each successive pair of transitions, the first transition is into the state that the second transition is out of,

$$\psi_5(U_1, \ldots, U_m) = \forall_r \forall_s \left( \text{next}(r, s) \Rightarrow \bigvee_{q \in Q} \bigvee_{k \in \text{In}(q)} \bigvee_{l \in \text{Out}(q)} (r \in U_k \wedge s \in U_l) \right)$$

The conjunction of these five subexpressions $\psi_1, \ldots, \psi_5$ asserts that $U_1, \ldots, U_m$ are consistent with their interpretation as sets of positions at which the various transitions occur in a computation by $M$ accepting $x$. Thus the expression $\phi$ asserts that $x$ belongs to the language $L$ recognized by $M$. This completes the proof that every recognizable language is described by a closed logical expression.

We now turn to the converse proposition: that every closed logical expression describes a recognizable language. The proof that we give follows that of Ladner [1977], and uses a technique (a "model-theoretic game") developed by Fraïssé [1954] and Ehrenfeucht [1961].

We begin with an important observation about logical expressions. We shall say that a logical expression is in *prenex* form if it has the form $Q_1 \cdots Q_k \psi$, where each $Q_j$ ($1 \le j \le k$) is an existential or universal quantification and $\psi$ contains no quantifications. An expression in prenex form thus begins with a prefix of quantifiers, followed by a *nexus* of atomic expressions and logical connectives. Every logical expression is equivalent to one in prenex form; to prove this it suffices to show how to "move" quantifiers that are "inside" a logical connective to the "outside." For negation, we have the equivalence

$$\neg Q \psi \iff Q' \neg \psi$$

where $Q'$ is the quantifier dual to $Q$ (that is, $Q'$ is universal or existential according as $Q$ is existential or universal, respectively). For conjunction, we have the equivalence

$$(P_1 \cdots P_j \, \phi) \wedge (Q_1 \cdots Q_k \, \psi) \iff P_1 \cdots P_j Q'_1 \cdots Q'_k \, (\phi \wedge \psi')$$

where $Q'_1, \ldots, Q'_k$ and $\psi'$ are obtained from $Q_1, \ldots, Q_k$ and $\psi$ by systematically renaming the variables to be disjoint from those appearing in $P_1, \ldots, P_j$ and $\phi$. An analogous equivalence holds for disjunction. Thus, it will suffice to show that every closed logical expression in prenex form describes a recognizable language.

The proof will be presented in an anthropomorphized form, in terms of a "game" between two players, whom we shall refer to as the "identifier" and the "distinguisher." The game is played with respect to two words, $x$ and $y$, over an alphabet $A$, and for a number $k \geq 0$ of "rounds." We shall speak of the "$(x, y, k)$-game" when we wish to emphasize the values of these parameters.

The $(x, y, k)$-game is played in $k$ rounds, each of which consists of a move by the distinguisher followed by a response by the identifier. The distinguisher moves by (1) selecting one of the two words, $x$ or $y$, (2) electing to make either an "individual" move or a "set" move, and (3) in the case of an individual move, "marking" a single position in the selected word, and in the case of a set move, marking a set of positions in the selected word. The identifier responds by (1) considering the word opposite to that selected by the distinguisher, (2) agreeing to make the same kind of move (individual or set) as the distinguisher, and (3) in the case of an individual move, marking a single position in the opposite word, and in the case of a set move, marking a set of positions in the opposite word. The distinguisher may change the selection of $x$ or $y$ from round to round, and the identifier is always bound to respond in the opposite word in each round. We shall assume that the marks made in different rounds can be distinguished from each other (that is, that they include the number of the round in which they were made), but that all of the marks made within a single round are indistinguishable (so that, in particular, there is no record of which player marked $x$ and which player marked $y$). After the completion of $k$ rounds, the game is adjudicated in the following way. Let $V_1, \ldots, V_k$ be the positions or sets of positions marked in $x$ in rounds $1, \ldots, k$, respectively, and let $W_1, \ldots, W_k$ be the corresponding positions or sets of positions marked in $y$. We shall say that the identifier "wins" the game if (1) whenever $V_j$ (and therefore also $W_j$) is an individual move, the letter of $x$ at $V_j$ is the same as the letter of $y$ at $W_j$, (2) whenever $V_i$ and $V_j$ (and therefore also $W_i$ and $W_j$) are both individual moves, we have $V_i < V_j$, $V_i = V_j$, or $V_i > V_j$ according as $W_i < W_j$, $W_i = W_j$, or $W_i > W_j$, respectively, and (3) whenever $V_i$ (and therefore also $W_i$) is an individual move while $V_j$ (and therefore $W_j$) is a set move, we have $V_i \in V_j$ if and only if $W_i \in W_j$. The distinguisher "wins" if and only if the identifier does not win. (We agree that if $k = 0$, then the identifier wins.)

For any $x, y \in A^+$ and any $k \geq 0$, the $(x, y, k)$-game is a two-person zero-sum finite game with perfect information, so that either the identifier can force a win against any play by the distinguisher, or the distinguisher can force a win against any play by the identifier. We shall write $x \approx_k y$ to mean that the identifier can force a win in the $(x, y, k)$-game. The relevance of the model-theoretic game to logical expressions is shown by the following lemma.

*Lemma 2.5.2.* If $\phi$ is a closed logical expression in prenex form with $k$ quantifiers and if $x \approx_k y$, then $x \models \phi$ if and only if $y \models \phi$.

**Proof.** Suppose that $x \models \phi$, but not $y \models \phi$. We shall give a strategy whereby the distinguisher can win the $(x, y, k)$-game. Suppose that $\phi$ is the expression $Q_1 \cdots Q_k \psi$. For the first round, there are two cases, depending on whether $Q_1$ is an existential or universal quantification. If $Q_1$ is an existential quantification of an individual variable $r$ (or a set variable $R$), the distinguisher choses a particular value $v$ (or $V$) of $r$ (or $R$) that makes the expression $Q_2 \cdots Q_k \psi$ true for $x$ when $v$ (or $V$) is substituted for $r$ (or $R$), and marks the corresponding position (or set of positions) in $x$. The identifier then responds by marking a position (or set of positions) in $y$, which corresponds to a value $w$ (or $W$) that makes $Q_2 \cdots Q_k \psi$ false for $y$ when $w$ (or $W$) is substituted for $r$ (or $R$). If, on the other hand, $Q_1$ is a universal quantification of an individual variable $r$ (or a set variable $R$), the distinguisher choses a particular value $v$ (or $V$) of $r$ (or $R$) that makes the expression $Q_2 \cdots Q_k \psi$ false for $y$ when $v$ (or $V$) is substituted for $r$ (or $R$), and marks the corresponding position (or set of positions) in $y$. The identifier then responds by marking a position (or set of positions) in $x$, which corresponds to a value $w$ (or $W$) that makes $Q_2 \cdots Q_k \psi$ true for $x$ when $w$ (or $W$) is substituted for $r$ (or $R$). Play continues in this way for $k$ rounds, after which we have a sequence of marks in $x$ that make $\psi$ true and a sequence of marks in $y$ that make $\psi$ false. Since $\psi$ contains only logical connectives and atomic expressions, it follows that there must be an atomic expression that has a different truth value for the marks in $x$ than for the marks in $y$, and thus that the distinguisher wins. □

We can now carry out the proof of the converse simultaneously for all closed logical expressions in prenex form with $k$ quantifiers, by showing that $\approx_k$ is a right-invariant equivalence of finite index. Lemma 2.5.2 implies that for any

closed logical expression $\phi$ in prenex form with $k$ quantifiers, Lang($\phi$) is a
union of equivalence classes of the equivalence $\approx_k$, and thus by Proposition
2.3.8 is recognizable.

*Lemma 2.5.3.* For every $k \geq 0$, the relation $\approx_k$ is an equivalence.

**Proof.** Reflexivity and symmetry are trivial, and so we must prove transitivity:
if $x \approx_k y$ and $y \approx_k z$, then $x \approx_k z$. Let $S$ be a strategy whereby the identifier
wins the $(x, y, k)$-game, and let $T$ be a strategy whereby the identifier wins the
$(y, z, k)$-game. We shall describe a strategy whereby the identifier wins the
$(x, z, k)$-game. If the distinguisher begins by marking the position $v$ (or set of
positions $V$) in $x$, then the identifier consults the strategy $S$ to find a position $u$
(or set of positions $U$) that wins in the $(x, y, k)$-game if the distinguisher begins
by marking $x$ with $v$ (or $V$) in that game. The identifier then consults the strategy
$T$ to find a position $w$ (or set of positions $W$) that wins in the $(y, z, k)$-game if
the distinguisher begins by marking $y$ with $u$ (or $U$) in that game. The identifier
then responds by marking $z$ with $w$ (or $W$) in the $(x, z, k)$-game. If, on the other
hand, the distinguisher begins by marking the position $v$ (or set of positions $V$)
in $z$, then the identifier consults the strategy $T$ to find a position $u$ (or set of
positions $U$) that wins in the $(y, z, k)$-game if the distinguisher begins $z$ with $v$
(or $V$) in that game. The identifier then consults the strategy $S$ to find a position
$w$ (or set of positions $W$) that wins in the $(x, y, k)$-game if the distinguisher
begins by marking $y$ with $u$ (or $U$) in that game. The identifier then responds by
marking $x$ with $w$ (or $W$) in the $(x, z, k)$-game. Play continues in this way for $k$
rounds, after which the identifier has won the $(x, y, k)$- and $(y, z, k)$-games that
have been played according to the strategies $S$ and $T$. Since the criteria for the
identifier winning consist of logical equivalences, it follows from the transitivity
of logical equivalence that the identifier has also won the $(x, z, k)$-game.    □

*Lemma 2.5.4.* For every $k \geq 0$, the equivalence $\approx_k$ is right-invariant.

**Proof.** We must prove that if $x \approx_k y$, then $xa \approx_k ya$, where $x, y \in A^+$ and
$a \in A$. Let $S$ be a strategy whereby the identifier can win the $(x, y, k)$-game. We
shall describe a strategy whereby the identifier can win the $(xa, ya, k)$-game.
In each round, the identifier is confronted with a move by the distinguisher that
is a position or set of positions in $xa$ or $ya$. If this move is a position in the $x$
of $xa$ or $y$ of $ya$, the identifier consults the strategy $S$ for a winning response in
the $y$ of $ya$ or $x$ of $xa$, respectively. If this move is the last position of $a$ in $xa$ or
$ya$, the identifier responds with the last position of $a$ in $ya$ or $xa$, respectively.
If this move is a set $V$ of positions in $xa$ or $ya$, the identifier responds with a set

$W$ of positions, determined as follows, in $ya$ or $xa$, respectively. To determine the positions of $y$ in $ya$ or $x$ in $xa$ to be included in $W$, the identifier consults the strategy $S$ for a winning response to the set of positions of $V$ that are in the $x$ of $xa$ or $y$ of $ya$; the last position of $a$ in $ya$ or $xa$ is included in $W$ if and only if the last position of $a$ in $xa$ or $ya$ belongs to $V$. After $k$ rounds, the identifier will have won the $(x, y, k)$-game that has been played according to the strategy $S$ (the distinguisher may have "passed" during some rounds of this game by playing the last position of $xa$ or $ya$, but this only means that the identifier wins a game with fewer rounds). This, together with the equivalence of the marks at the last positions of $xa$ and $ya$, implies that the identifier has also won the $(xa, ya, k)$-game. □

*Lemma 2.5.5.* For every $k \geq 0$, the equivalence $\approx_k$ has finite index.

**Proof.** Let us consider the situations that can arise in the $(x, y, k)$-game after $l$ rounds have been played, for $0 \leq l \leq k$.

After $k$ rounds, at most $k$ individual moves and at most $k$ set moves have been made in the word $x$, with counterparts made in the word $y$. We are ready to adjudicate the situation, and the outcome of the adjudication depends only on the truth values of the atomic expressions for the moves made in $x$ and $y$. There are at most $ck$ occurrence assertions, where $c$ is the cardinality of the alphabet $A$. There are at most $3k^2$ arithmetic comparisons, and at most $k^2$ membership assertions. Thus to adjudicate the game, all we need to know about the marks made in $x$ and $y$ is which one of the at most $p = 2^{ck+4k^2}$ assignments of truth values to these atomic expression applies for the marks made in each of these words. Furthermore, the identifier will surely win if this information is the same for both $x$ and $y$. We shall refer to this information for $x$ as the "$k$-signature" of the marks made in $x$, and similarly for $y$.

After $k - 1$ rounds, all we need to know about the marks made in $x$ and $y$, in order to determine which player can force a win, is which of the at most $2^p$ subsets of the $k$-signatures of the marks made in $x$ the identifier can arrive at, given that the distinguisher plays in $y$, and which of the at most $2^p$ subsets of the $k$-signatures for the marks made in $y$ the identifier can arrive at, given that the distinguisher plays in $x$. Furthermore, the identifier will surely win if this information is the same for both $x$ and $y$. We shall call this information for $x$ the "$(k - 1)$-signature" of the marks made in $x$, and similarly for $y$.

Proceeding backward in this way, we see that there are at most

$$q = 2^{2^{2^{\cdot^{\cdot^{2^p}}}}} \left.\right\} k+1$$

"0-signatures" such that after 0 rounds, all we need to know about the marks made in $x$ and $y$ is which of these 0-signatures applies to $x$ and $y$. Furthermore, the identifier will surely win if this information is the same for both $x$ and $y$. But after 0 rounds, no marks have yet been made, and so the 0-signatures of $x$ and $y$ are completely determined by the words $x$ and $y$ themselves. This means that whether or not $x \approx_k y$ holds is completely determined by which of the at most $q$ 0-signatures applies to each of $x$ and $y$, which implies that the index of $\approx_k$ is at most $q$.                                                                    $\square$

Lemmas 2.5.3, 2.5.4, and 2.5.5 together complete the proof that every closed logical expression describes a recognizable language. Note that the direct and converse parts of Theorem 2.5.1 together show that every closed logical formula is equivalent to one in which all set variables are existentially quantified by the "outermost" quantifiers of the expression. It is by no means obvious that this should be so, and we know of no proof of this fact that is significantly more direct than the one given in this entire section.

### Exercises

1. (E) Give a closed logical expression in prenex form equivalent to the expression $(\exists_r 0 \propto r) \iff (\exists_r 1 \propto r)$.
2. (M) Show that every recognizable language $L$ is $L = \mathrm{Lang}(\phi)$ for some closed logical expression of the form $\exists_U \psi(U)$, where $\psi(U)$ contains quantifications only of individual variables (that is, every closed logical formula is equivalent to one with only a single, existentially quantified set variable).

### 2.6. Aperiodic Languages

In this section we shall study a property of recognizable languages called *aperiodicity*. This property has the remarkable feature of being characterizable in several different ways, of which we shall examine three: in terms of extended regular expressions, in terms of logical expressions, and in terms of syntactic monoids.

An extended regular expression will be called *star-free* if the only operations that occur in it are the Boolean operations (union, intersection, and complement) and concatenation; no asterations are allowed. A logical expression will be called *first-order* if the only variables that are quantified are individual variables; no set variables are allowed. A monoid $M$ will be called *aperiodic* if there exists a natural number $k \geq 1$ such that, for every $x \in M$, we have $x^k = x^{k+1}$.

For an example of these concepts, consider the simplest monoid that is not aperiodic, the monoid $M_2 = \{0, 1\}$ with the operation of addition modulo 2.

(For consistency, we shall continue to denote the operation by "·" or juxtaposition, so that $00 = 11 = 0$ and $01 = 10 = 1$.) This monoid is not aperiodic, since we have $1^k \neq 1^{k+1}$ for all $k$. The language $L_2 \subseteq \{0, 1\}^*$ comprising all words containing an odd number of 1's has $M_2$ as its syntactic monoid. We can easily write a regular expression for $L_2$, for example,

$$L_2 = \mathrm{Lang}(0^*10^*(10^*10^*)^*)$$

but no expression without asteration comes to mind, even if intersection and complementation are allowed. Similarly, we can easily write a logical expression for $L_2$ (viewed as a subset of $\{0, 1\}^+$) but no expression without set variables comes to mind. Our main result in this section shows that this example illustrates a general phenomenon.

**Theorem 2.6.1.** *For any recognizable language $L \subseteq A^*$, the following three conditions are equivalent: (i) $Syn(L)$ is aperiodic, (ii) $L = Lang(E)$ for some star-free extended regular expression $E$, and (iii) $L \cap A^+ = Lang(\phi)$ for some first-order closed logical expression $\phi$.*

The equivalence of conditions (i) and (ii) was shown by Schützenberger [1965], and the equivalence of (iii) with the others was shown by McNaughton and Papert [1971]. We shall prove the successive implications

$$\text{(i)} \Longrightarrow \text{(ii)} \Longrightarrow \text{(iii)} \Longrightarrow \text{(i)}$$

Our first part, the proof that (i) implies (ii), follows the proof of Schützenberger [1965]. Suppose $f : A^* \to M$, where $M = Syn(L)$ is finite and aperiodic, and $L = f^{-1}(X)$ for some $X \subseteq M$. We proceed by induction on the size of $M$.

If $X$ is empty, so is $L$, and we are done. If $X$ contains more than one element, we may express $L$ as a finite union,

$$L = \bigcup_{x \in X} f^{-1}(x)$$

and transfer attention to the languages $f^{-1}(x)$. Thus, we may assume that $X$ contains a single element $x$, so that $L = f^{-1}(x)$.

Define $F(x)$ (the "forbidden factors for $x$") to be the set of $y \in M$ such that $x \notin MyM$. Then $x \notin F(x)$, and $F(x)$ is an ideal. If $F(x)$ contains more than one element, we can form the quotient $M/F(x)$ and consider the canonical homomorphism $g : M \to M/F(x)$. Then we have $L = (f \circ g)^{-1}(g(x))$ and, since $M/F(x)$ has fewer elements that $M$, the result follows by inductive hypothesis. Thus, we may assume that $F(x)$ contains at most one element. We shall deal separately with two cases: first the case in which $F(x)$ contains one element, and then the case in which $F(x)$ is empty. In each case, our strategy for the induction will be to express the language $L = f^{-1}(x)$ in terms of simple languages and languages $f^{-1}(y)$, where $F(y)$ contains more elements than $F(x)$. These languages $f^{-1}(y)$ can be expressed without a star since if $F(x)$ is empty, then $F(y)$ contains an element, while if $F(x)$ contains an element, then $F(y)$ contains at least two elements, so that $M/F(y)$ contains fewer elements than $M$, and the result follows by inductive hypothesis.

Suppose first that $F(x)$ contains one element. Since $F(x)$ is an ideal, the unique element of $F(x)$ is a zero, say, $z$. We shall deal separately with two subcases: first the subcase in which $x$ is the unit $e$ of the monoid $M$, and then the case in which it is not.

Suppose first that $x = e$. We claim that

$$F(e) = M \setminus e \qquad (2.6.1)$$

Suppose that $w \notin F(e)$, so that $e = pwq$. We shall show that $w = e$. We have $w = wpwq$. Iterating gives $w = (wp)^k wq^k$ and taking $k$ such that $q^k = q^{k+1}$ gives $w = wq$. Similarly, $w = pwqw$ gives $w = pw$. Thus $w = pw = pwq = e$. This proves Eq. (2.6.1).

Equation (2.6.1) implies $M = \{z, e\}$ with the usual multiplicative structure: $ee = e$ and $zz = ze = ez = z$. Then $L$ is the set of words not containing any letter $a$ such that $f(a) = z$, and is easily expressed without a star.

Suppose then that $x \neq e$. We claim that

$$\{x\} = (xM \cap Mx) \setminus F(x) \qquad (2.6.2)$$

That $x$ belongs to the right side is clear. To see the reverse inclusion, suppose that $y \in (xM \cap Mx) \setminus F(x)$. We shall show that $y = x$. Since $y \in xM$ we have $y = xq$, and since $y \notin F(x)$ we have $x = rys$. Thus, $y = xq = rysq$, iterating gives $y = r^k y(sq)^k$, and taking $k$ such that $r^k = r^{k+1}$ gives $y = ry$. Similarly, $y \in Mx$ gives $y = ys$. Thus, $y = ry = rys = x$. This proves Eq. (2.6.2).

Equation (2.6.2) implies

$$L = (f^{-1}(xM) \cap f^{-1}(Mx)) \setminus f^{-1}(F(x)) \qquad (2.6.3)$$

We shall obtain a star-free expression for each of the three reflections in this equation.

First we look at $f^{-1}(F(x)) = f^{-1}(z)$. Let $A_z$ be the set of letters $a$ such that $f(a) = z$. Let $C$ be the set of triples $(a, y, b) \in A \times M \times A$ such that $f(a)yf(b) = z$ but $f(a)y \neq z$, $yf(b) \neq z$, and $y \neq z$. Then $f^{-1}(z)$ is the union of ($\alpha$) the language of all words containing a letter from $A_z$ (which is easily expressed without the star) and ($\beta$) the union $L_2$ over all $(a, y, b) \in C$ of the language of all words containing a word of the language $af^{-1}(y)b$. Every word in ($\alpha$) or ($\beta$) is clearly in $f^{-1}(z)$. To see the converse, suppose that $f(w) = z$, and consider a shortest subword $v$ of $w$ such that $f(v) = z$. The word $v$ is not empty, since $f(\varepsilon) = e \neq z$. If $v$ is of length one, then $w$ is contained in ($\alpha$). If $v$ has length of at least two, then $v = aub$, where $a$, $u$, and $b$ are in $A$, $A^*$, and $A$, respectively. Taking $y = f(u)$, we see that $(a, y, b) \in C$ (using the minimality of $v$) and thus that $w$ is in ($\beta$). Since the language of words containing a word of $af^{-1}(y)b$ can be expressed without the star if $f^{-1}(y)$ can, we can complete the argument by showing that $F(y)$ contains more than one element and applying the inductive hypothesis.

We now show that $F(y)$ contains more than one element. We have $z \in F(y)$, and so suppose for a contradiction that $F(y) = \{z\}$. Then $f(a)y \notin F(y)$, so that we can write $y = pf(a)yq$. Iterating gives $y = (pf(a))^k yq^k$, and taking $k$ such that $(pf(a))^k = (pf(a))^{k+1}$ gives $y = pf(a)y$. Similarly, from $yf(b) \notin F(y)$ we obtain $y = yf(b)q$ for some $q$. Thus $y = pf(a)y = pf(a)yf(b)q = pzq = z$, a contradiction. This completes the star-free expression for $f^{-1}(F(x)) = f^{-1}(z)$.

Now we look at $f^{-1}(xM)$. Because we have a star-free expression for $f^{-1}(z)$, it suffices to obtain one for a language $K$ such that $f^{-1}(xM \setminus z) \subseteq K \subseteq f^{-1}(xM)$, since then we will have $f^{-1}(xM) = K \cup f^{-1}(z)$. Let $B$ be the set of pairs $(y, a) \in M \times A$ such that $yf(a) \in xM \setminus z$ (so that, in particular, $y \neq z$) but $y \notin xM$. Then we may take $K$ to be the union over all $(y, a) \in B$ of the language of all words containing a word of the language $f^{-1}(y)a$. Every word of $K$ is clearly in $f^{-1}(xM)$. To see the reverse inclusion, let $w$ be a word of $f^{-1}(xM \setminus z)$ and consider a shortest subword $v$ of $w$ such that $f(v) \in xM \setminus z$. The word $v$ cannot be empty, since then we would have $f(v) = e \in xM$, whereas we have seen that $F(e) = M \setminus e$, and so $e \notin xM$. Thus, we may write $v = ua$, where $u$ and $a$ are in $A^*$ and $A$, respectively. Taking $y = f(u)$, we see that $(y, a) \in B$ (using the minimality of $v$) and thus that $w \in K$. Since the language of words containing a word of the language $f^{-1}(y)a$ can be expressed without the star if $f^{-1}(y)$ can, we can complete the argument by showing that $F(y)$ contains more than one element and applying the inductive hypothesis.

We now show that $F(y)$ contains more than one element. We have $z \in F(y)$, and so suppose for a contradiction that $F(y) = \{z\}$. Then $x \notin F(y)$ gives $y = pxq$. Since $yf(a) \in xM \setminus \{z\}$, we have $yf(a) \neq z$, so that $yf(a) \notin F(x) = \{z\}$ gives $x = ryf(a)s$. Thus, $y = pxq = pryf(a)sq$. Iterating gives $y = (pr)^k y(f(a)sq)^k$, and taking $k$ such that $(f(a)sq)^k = (f(a)sq)^{k+1}$ gives

$y = yf(a)sq = xsq$. Thus, $y \in xM$, a contradiction. This completes the star-free expression for $f^{-1}(xM)$. A similar argument gives a star-free expression for $f^{-1}(Mx)$, which completes the construction for the case in which $F(x)$ contains one element.

Suppose then that $F(x)$ is empty. In this case Eq. (2.6.2) gives

$$L = f^{-1}(xM) \cap f^{-1}(Mx) \tag{2.6.4}$$

We shall show that these two reflections in this equation have star-free expressions.

If $x = e$, then $L$ is the full language $A^*$, which is easily expressed without the star as the complement of the empty language. Thus, we may suppose that $x \neq e$.

First we look at $f^{-1}(xM)$. Let $B$ be the set of pairs $(y, a) \in M \times A$ such that $yf(a) \in xM$ but $y \notin xM$. Then $f^{-1}(xM)$ is the language $K$ formed by the union over all $(y, a) \in B$ of the language of all words containing a word of the language $f^{-1}(y)a$. Every word of $K$ is clearly in $f^{-1}(xM)$. To see the converse, let $w$ be a word of $f^{-1}(xM)$ and consider a shortest subword $v$ of $w$ such that $f(v) \in xM$. The word $v$ cannot be empty, since then we would have $f(v) = e \in xM$, whereas we have seen that $F(e) = M \setminus e$, and so $e \notin xM$. Thus, we may write $v = ua$, where $u$ and $a$ are in $A^*$ and $A$, respectively. Taking $y = f(u)$, we see that $(y, a) \in B$ (using the minimality of $v$) and thus that $w \in K$. Since the language of words containing a word of the language $f^{-1}(y)a$ can be expressed without the star if $f^{-1}(y)$ can, we can complete the argument by showing that $F(y)$ contains at least one element.

We now show that $F(y)$ contains at least one element. Suppose for a contradiction that $F(y) = \emptyset$. Then $x \notin F(y)$ gives $y = pxq$. Since $yf(a) \notin F(x) = \emptyset$, we also have $x = ryf(a)s$. As shown, these imply $y = yf(a)sq = xsq$. Thus, $y \in xM$, a contradiction. This completes the star-free expression for $f^{-1}(xM)$. A similar argument gives a star-free expression for $f^{-1}(Mx)$, which completes the construction for the case in which $F(x)$ is empty, and thus completes the proof of the implication (i) $\Longrightarrow$ (ii).

We now turn to the proof that (ii) $\Longrightarrow$ (iii). Our proof follows Ladner [1977], who attributes the construction to A. R. Meyer and L. J. Stockmeyer.

Let $E$ be a star-free extended regular expression such that $\text{Lang}(E) \subseteq A^+$. We shall associate with $E$ a first-order logical expression $\phi_E(i, j)$ with two free variables $i$ and $j$ such that $\phi_E(i, j)$ holds for $x_1 \cdots x_n$ if and only if the subword $x_i \cdots x_j$ belongs to $\text{Lang}(E)$. We shall arrange that $\phi_E$ is false unless $i \leq j$. We shall construct $\phi_E$ by structural induction on $E$. The first-order closed expression

$$\psi = \exists_i \exists_j (\text{first}(i) \wedge \text{last}(j) \wedge \phi_E(i, j))$$

then holds for $x$ if and only if $x \in \text{Lang}(E)$. (The subexpressions $\text{first}(i)$ and $\text{last}(j)$ are as defined in Section 2.5.)

If $E = O$, we take $\phi_E(i, j)$ to be any false expression, say, $(i = j) \wedge \neg(i = j)$. If $E = a \in A$, we take $\phi_E(i, j) = (i = j \wedge a \propto i)$. If $E = F \cup G$, we take $\phi_E(i, j) = \phi_F(i, j) \vee \phi_G(i, j)$. If $E = \neg F$, we take $\phi_E(i, j) = (i \leq j) \wedge \neg\phi_F(i, j)$. Finally, if $E = F \cdot G$, we take $\phi_E(i, j) = \exists_r \exists_s (\text{next}(r, s) \wedge \phi_F(i, r) \wedge \phi_G(s, j))$. (The subexpression $\text{next}(r, s)$ is as defined in Section 2.5.) This completes the construction of the expression $\phi_E(i, j)$. We may then prove by structural induction on $E$ that $\phi_E(i, j)$ has the property described in the preceding paragraph, which completes the proof of the implication (ii) $\Longrightarrow$ (iii).

Finally we turn to the proof that (iii) $\Longrightarrow$ (i). Our proof again follows Ladner [1977].

Just as we defined first-order logical expressions by excluding set variables, we may define a first-order model-theoretic game by excluding set moves. When played for $k$ rounds on the words $x, y \in A^+$, we shall call this the *first-order* $(x, y, k)$-game. We shall write $x \sim_k y$ to mean that the identifier can force a win in the first-order $(x, y, k)$-game. Exactly as in Lemma 2.5.2, we have: if $\phi$ is a first-order closed logical expression in prenex form with $k$ quantifiers, and if $x \sim_k y$, then $x \models \phi$ if and only if $y \models \phi$. And exactly as in Lemmas 2.5.3 and 2.5.4, we have that $\sim_k$ is a right-invariant equivalence.

We shall show that for every $k \geq 1$ there exists an $l$ such that for every word $x$, we have $x^l \sim_k x^{l+1}$. Since $\sim_k$ is a refinement of the syntactic equivalence for any language defined by an $k$-quantifier formula, this will show that every such language is aperiodic.

We take $l = 2^k - 1$, and proceed by induction on $k$. If $k = 1$, the game is played with $x$ and $x^2$. However the distinguisher moves, the identifier responds with a move at a corresponding position of an instance of $x$ in the other word and wins. Suppose then that $k \geq 2$, and set $m = 2^{k-1} - 1$. Write $x^l = x^m \cdot x \cdot x^m$ and $x^{l+1} = x^m \cdot x \cdot x \cdot x^m$. If the distinguisher moves in one of the first two parts of either word, the identifier responds with a move at a corresponding position in the other word and resolves to move at corresponding positions of these four parts in all future rounds. For future moves in the remaining parts, the inductive hypothesis gives the identifier a winning strategy. If the initial move of the distinguisher is in one of the last two parts of either word, a reversal of this strategy allows the identifier to win. This completes the proof of the implication (iii) $\Longrightarrow$ (i), and thus of Theorem 2.6.1.

The aperiodic regular languages have been classified more finely by Cohen and Brzozowski [1971] according to their "dot-depth"; the *dot-depth* of an aperiodic language $L$ is the smallest possible depth to which the concatenation operation can be nested (in alternation with Boolean operations) in any star-free extended regular expression describing $L$. This definition partitions the aperiodic languages into a hierarchy according to their dot-depth, but it is not at all obvious whether or not this hierarchy is infinite (that is, whether or not there exist aperiodic languages of arbitrarily large dot-depth). Brzozowski and Knast [1978] proved that the hierarchy is indeed infinite by dealing directly with star-free regular expressions. Thomas [1982, 1984] has characterized this hierarchy in terms of the "quantifier-depth" of first-order logical expressions, and has used this characterization to give a simpler proof that the hierarchy is infinite.

### Exercise

1. (E) Characterize the aperiodic regular languages over an alphabet with just one letter.

## 2.7. Varieties

This section presents the most satisfying connection between languages and their syntactic monoids, by giving a one-to-one correspondence between "varieties" of recognizable languages and varieties of finite monoids.

Let $\mathcal{L}$ be a class of languages. We shall say that $\mathcal{L}$ is a *variety* (of languages) if it satisfies the following three conditions:

VL$_1$  If $L \in \mathcal{L}$, $L \subseteq A^*$ and $w \in A^*$, then $w^{-1}L, Lw^{-1} \in \mathcal{L}$.

VL$_2$  If $L \in \mathcal{L}$, $L \subseteq B^*$ and $h : A^* \rightarrow B^*$ is a homomorphism, then $h^{-1}(L) \in \mathcal{L}$.

VL$_3$  If $L, L' \in \mathcal{L}$ and $L, L' \subseteq A^*$, then Compl($L$), $L \cup L', L \cap L' \in \mathcal{L}$.

Conditions VL$_1$, VL$_1$, and VL$_1$ are sometimes expressed by saying that varieties of languages are closed under left and right quotients, homomorphic reflections, and Boolean operations, respectively. Since the notion of a variety is defined in terms of closure conditions, if $\mathcal{L}$ is a class of languages, there is a smallest variety of languages that includes $\mathcal{L}$, which is called the variety generated by $\mathcal{L}$ and denoted Var($\mathcal{L}$).

Let $\mathcal{C}$ be a class of finite monoids. We shall say that $\mathcal{C}$ is a variety (of monoids) if it satisfies the following three conditions:

VM$_1$  If $C$ is a submonoid of $C'$ and $C' \in \mathcal{C}$, then $C \in \mathcal{C}$.

VM$_2$  If $C$ is a quotient monoid of $C'$ and $C' \in \mathcal{C}$, then $C \in \mathcal{C}$.

VM$_3$  If $C, C' \in \mathcal{C}$, then $C \times C' \in \mathcal{C}$.

Since the notion of a variety is defined in terms of closure operations, if $\mathcal{C}$ is a class of monoids, there is a smallest variety of monoids that includes $\mathcal{C}$, which is called the variety generated by $C$ and denoted Var($C$). (We caution the reader that the term variety is used somewhat differently in universal algebra, where closure under "infinite products" is also required. The present definition is more appropriate for the study of recognizable languages, for which the syntactic monoids are all finite.)

We shall say that a monoid $C$ is covered by a monoid $C'$, and write $C \prec C'$, if $C$ is isomorphic to a quotient monoid of a submonoid of $C'$. The relation $\prec$ is reflexive and transitive, and if $C$ and $C'$ are finite monoids, and $C \prec C'$ and $C' \prec C$, then $C \approx C'$. We observe that conditions VM$_1$ and VM$_2$ together imply that if $C \prec C'$ and $C' \in \mathcal{C}$, then $C \in \mathcal{C}$.

We have defined the syntactic monoid Syn($L$) for a language $L$, which is a subset of a free monoid $A^*$. It is possible, however, to use essentially the same definition for a subset $Y$ of elements of an arbitrary monoid $C$.

Let $C$ be a monoid, and let $Y \subseteq C$ be a set of elements of $C$. For any $x, y \in X$, we shall write $x \cong_Y y$, and say that $x$ and $y$ are *syntactically equivalent modulo Y* if, for all $w, z \in X$, we have $wxz \in Y$ if and only if $wyz \in Y$. We observe that $\cong_Y$ is a congruence. Thus, the equivalence classes of $\cong_Y$ form a quotient monoid of $C$, which we shall denote $C//Y$, and there is a canonical homomorphism $f : C \to C//Y$ of $C$ onto $C//Y$. We observe that if $L$ is a language over the finite alphabet $A$, then Syn($L$) = $A^*//L$.

If $C$ is a monoid, we shall say that a set $Y$ of its elements is *rigid* if, for all $x, y \in X$, $x \cong_Y y$ implies $x = y$. This is equivalent to saying that the canonical homomorphism $f : C \to C//Y$ is injective, which in turn is equivalent to saying that $C \approx C//Y$. We shall say that a monoid is syntactic if it has a rigid set of elements. We observe that our two uses of the adjective syntactic are consistent, in the sense that a finite monoid $C$ is syntactic if and only if $C \approx$ Syn($L$) for some language $L$. For if $f : A^* \to$ Syn($L$) is the canonical homomorphism, then $f(L)$ is a rigid set in Syn($L$), and so any monoid isomorphic to Syn($L$) also has a rigid set, and thus is syntactic. Conversely, if $C$ is syntactic and $Y$ is rigid in $C$, take $A = X$, extend the identity map $i : A \to X$ to a homomorphism $i$ from $A^*$ onto $C$, and note that $C \approx$ Syn($i^{-1}(Y)$).

To state the main result of this section, we shall need two further notations. If $\mathcal{C}$ is a class of monoids, let $\lambda(\mathcal{C})$ denote the set of all languages $L$ such that Syn($L$) $\in \mathcal{C}$. If $\mathcal{L}$ is a class of languages, let $\mu(\mathcal{L})$ denote the set of all syntactic monoids Syn($L$) of languages $L$ in $\mathcal{L}$.

**Theorem 2.7.1 (Eilenberg [1973]).** *Let $\mathcal{C}$ be a variety of monoids and let $\mathcal{L}$ be a variety of languages. (a) The set $\lambda(\mathcal{C})$ is a variety of languages. (b) Var($\mu(\lambda(\mathcal{C}))$) $= \mathcal{C}$. (c) $\lambda($Var($\mu(\mathcal{L})$)$) = \mathcal{L}$.*

The proof of part (a) is an immediate consequence of the following lemma.

*Lemma 2.7.2.* Let $L$ and $L'$ be recognizable languages over $B$, let $w$ be a word over $B$, and let $h$ be a homomorphism from $A^*$ to $B^*$. (a) $\mathrm{Syn}(w^{-1}L)$, $\mathrm{Syn}(Lw^{-1})$, $\mathrm{Syn}(h^{-1}(L)) \prec \mathrm{Syn}(L)$. (b) $\mathrm{Syn}(\mathrm{Compl}(L)) = \mathrm{Syn}(L)$. (c) $\mathrm{Syn}(L \cup L')$, $\mathrm{Syn}(L \cap L') \prec \mathrm{Syn}(L) \times \mathrm{Syn}(L')$.

**Proof.** (a) We consider the left quotient; the right quotient and the homomorphic reflection are analogous. The relation $\cong_{w^{-1}L}$ is implied by $\cong_L$. Thus, each equivalence class of the former comprises one or more equivalence classes of the latter. The classes of the latter that arise in this way form a submonoid of $\mathrm{Syn}(L)$, and $\mathrm{Syn}(w^{-1}L)$ is a quotient monoid of this submonoid. (b) This part is immediate from the definition. (c) We consider the union; the intersection is analogous. The relation $\cong_{L \cup L'}$ is implied by the conjunction of $\cong_L$ and $\cong_{L'}$. Thus, each equivalence class of the former relation comprises one or more ordered pairs of equivalence classes of the latter relations. The ordered pairs that arise in this way form a submonoid of $\mathrm{Syn}(L) \times \mathrm{Syn}(L')$, and $\mathrm{Syn}(L \cup L')$ is a quotient monoid of this submonoid.                                                    ☐

The proof of part (b) is an immediate consequence of the following lemma.

*Lemma 2.7.3.* Let $C$ and $C'$ be varieties of finite monoids. If every syntactic monoid in $C$ belongs to $C'$, then $C \subseteq C'$.

**Proof.** Suppose that the monoid $C$ belongs to $C$. For each $x \in X$, form the syntactic monoid $C_x = C//\{x\}$, and let $f_x : C \to C_x$ be the canonical homomorphism. Since $C$ is closed under taking quotient monoids, each $C_x$ belongs to $C$. Since every syntactic monoid in $C$ belongs to $C'$, each $C_x$ also belongs to $C'$. Since $C'$ is closed under taking products, the finite product $D = \prod_{x \in X} C_x$ belongs to $C'$. The homomorphisms $f_x$ combine to form a homomorphism $f : C \to D$ that agrees with $f_x$ when projected on the factor $C_x$. This homomorphism is one-to-one, since if $f(x) = f(y)$, we have $f_x(x) = f_x(y)$, or equivalently $x \cong_{\{x\}} y$, and this implies $x = y$, since $\{x\}$ is rigid in $C_x$. Thus, $C$ is a submonoid of $D$. Since $C'$ is closed under taking submonoids, $C$ belongs to $C'$.   ☐

The proof of part (c) will depend on the following two lemmas.

*Lemma 2.7.4.* Let $C$ be a class of monoids. If $C \in \mathrm{Var}(C)$, then

$$C \prec C_1 \times \cdots \times C_k$$

for some $C_1, \ldots, C_k \in C$.

**Proof.** Recall that if $C \prec D$ and $C' \prec D'$, then

$$C \times C' \prec D \times D'$$

This, together with the transitivity of $\prec$, implies that if $C$ and $C'$ satisfy the conclusion of the lemma, then so does $C \times C'$. Since any monoid in $\text{Var}(\mathcal{C})$ can be obtained from monoids in $\mathcal{C}$ by a finite sequence of applications of conditions $\text{VM}_1$ through $\text{VM}_3$ in the definition of a variety of monoids, the lemma follows by induction on the length of this sequence. □

*Lemma 2.7.5.* Let $L$ be a recognizable language over an alphabet $A$, let $f : A^* \to \text{Syn}(L)$ be the canonical homomorphism from $A^*$ onto $\text{Syn}(L)$, and let $u$ be an element of $\text{Syn}(L)$. Then $f^{-1}(u) \in \text{Var}(L)$.

**Proof.** Since $f$ is onto, we have $u = f(x)$ for some $x \in A^*$, so that it will suffice to show that $f^{-1}(f(x)) \in \text{Var}(L)$. We observe that $f^{-1}(f(x))$ is just the $\cong_L$ equivalence class of $x$, which we shall denote $[\![x]\!]$. For any $y \in A^*$, define

$$R_y = \{(w, z) \in A^* \times A^* : wyz \in L\}.$$

Then we have $x \cong_L y$ if and only if $R_x = R_y$. We also have $(w, z) \in R_x$ if and only if $x \in w^{-1}Lz^{-1}$. Thus,

$$[\![x]\!] = \left( \bigcap_{(w,z) \in R_x} w^{-1}Lz^{-1} \right) \cap \left( \bigcap_{(w,z) \notin R_x} \text{Compl}(w^{-1}Lz^{-1}) \right).$$

The language $w^{-1}Lz^{-1}$ depends only on the $\cong_L$ equivalence classes of $w$ and $z$. Since $L$ is recognizable, there are only finitely many such equivalence classes, so that the intersection just displayed is finite. Since $\text{Var}(L)$ contains $L$ and is closed under left and right quotients and Boolean operations, $[\![x]\!] \in \text{Var}(L)$. □

**Proof of Theorem 2.7.1(c).** Suppose that $L_1, \ldots, L_k \in \mathcal{L}$, and that

$$\text{Syn}(L) \in \text{Var}(\text{Syn}(L_1), \ldots, \text{Syn}(L_k))$$

We shall show that $L \in \text{Var}(L_1, \ldots, L_k)$. By Lemma 2.7.4, we may assume

$$\text{Syn}(L) \prec \text{Syn}(L_1) \times \cdots \times \text{Syn}(L_k) \qquad (2.7.1)$$

Suppose that $A$ is the alphabet of $L$, and let $h : A^* \to \text{Syn}(L)$ be the canonical homomorphism. Then $L = h^{-1}(Y)$ for some set $Y$ in $\text{Syn}(L)$. By virtue of the covering Eq. (2.7.1), there is a homomorphism $g$ of $A^*$ into $C = \text{Syn}(L_1) \times \cdots \times \text{Syn}(L_k)$, and a set $Z$ in $C$ such that $L = g^{-1}(Z)$. We have

$$L = \bigcup_{z \in Z} g^{-1}(z)$$

Since $C$, and therefore $Z$, is finite, and since $\text{Var}(L_1, \ldots, L_k)$ is closed under taking finite unions, it will suffice to show that $g^{-1}(z) \in \text{Var}(L_1, \ldots, L_k)$. Let $z = (z_1, \ldots, z_k)$, where $z_j \in \text{Syn}(L_j)$. We have

$$g^{-1}(z) = \bigcap_{1 \leq j \leq k} g^{-1}(Z_j),$$

where $Z_j = \{(y_1, \ldots, y_k) \in C : y_j = z_j\}$. Since $\text{Var}(L_1, \ldots, L_k)$ is closed under taking finite intersections, it will suffice to show that $g^{-1}(Z_j) \in \text{Var}(L_j)$. Suppose that $A_j$ is the alphabet of $L_j$, and let $f_j : A_j^* \to \text{Syn}(L_j)$ be the canonical homomorphism. The homomorphisms $f_j$ combine to form a homomorphism $f : A_1^* \times \cdots \times A_k^* \to C$ that agrees with $f_j$ when projected on the factor $\text{Syn}(L_j)$. Since the homomorphism $f$ is onto, there exists a homomorphism $d : A^* \to A_1^* \times \cdots \times A_k^*$ such that $g = d \circ f$. Thus, $g^{-1}(Z_j) = d^{-1}(f^{-1}(Z_j)) = d_j^{-1}(f_j^{-1}(z_j))$, where $d_j$ denotes the component of $d$ in the factor $A_j^*$. By Lemma 2.7.5, $f_j(z_j) \in \text{Var}(L_j)$. Since $\text{Var}(L_j)$ is closed under taking homomorphic reflections, $d_j^{-1}(f_j^{-1}(z_j)) \in \text{Var}(L_j)$, which completes the proof.                                                                          □

The aperiodic monoids described in the preceding section provide a central example of a variety of monoids. This example is unusual in that there are natural characterizations of the corresponding variety of languages in other terms (star-free regular expressions and first-order logical expressions). For most varieties the monoids themselves provide the most satisfactory characterization. This circumstance has led to a flowering of interest in varieties of finite monoids, semigroups, and other algebraic structures; see Pin [1995] for a survey. By defining an appropriate class of objects, the "pseudoidentities," it is possible to establish a polarity between finite monoids (or semigroups) and pseudoidentities in such a way that the closed sets of monoids arising from the Galois connection is precisely the varieties; this gives a convenient way of describing many varieties (see Eilenberg and Schützenberger [1976], Reiterman [1982], and Pippenger [1997]).

### *Exercise*

1. (H) Say that a monoid $X$ is idempotent if $x = x^2$ for every $x \in X$. Let $A$ be a fixed finite alphabet. Show that there is a finite monoid $C$ such that every language $L$ over $A$ that has an idempotent syntactic monoid $\text{Syn}(L)$ has $\text{Syn}(L) \prec C$. (See McLean [1954].)

## 2.8. Extras

In this section we shall present three additional topics concerning finite automata. The first of these is the relationship between finite automata and numbers.

### 2.8.1. Finite Automata and Numbers

Thus far we have regarded the inputs to finite automata as sequences of letters forming words. One common use of such sequences is to encode numbers, and we shall now study the consequences of interpreting words in this way. If $x = x_1 \cdots x_n$ is a word over the alphabet $\mathbf{B}_k = \{0, \ldots, k-1\}$ we shall write $\text{val}_k(x) = \sum_{1 \le i \le n} x_i k^{n-i}$ for the natural number represented by the word $x$ to the base $k$, if $k \ge 2$, and write $\text{val}_k(x)$ for the length of $x$ if $k = 1$. (In either case we take $\text{val}_k(\varepsilon) = 0$.) Let $\mathbf{N} = \{0, 1, \ldots\}$ denote the set of natural numbers. If $R \subseteq \mathbf{N}$ is a set of natural numbers, we shall write $\text{codes}_k(R)$ for the set of all words $x \in \mathbf{B}_k^*$ such that $\text{val}_k(x) \in R$. We observe that if a word $x$ belongs to $\text{codes}_k(R)$ for $k \ge 2$, so do all words obtained by prefixing 0's to $x$.

We shall write $\mathcal{S}_k$ for the collection of all sets $R \subseteq \mathbf{N}$ such that the language $\text{codes}_k(R)$ is recognizable. We shall say that a set $R \subseteq \mathbf{N}$ is *ultimately periodic* if there exist natural numbers $t \ge 0$ (the "threshold") and $p \ge 1$ (the "period") such that, for all $n \ge t$, we have $n \in R$ if and only if $n + p \in R$.

*Lemma 2.8.1.* If $R \subseteq \mathbf{N}$, we have $R \in \mathcal{S}_1$ if and only if $R$ is ultimately periodic.

The proof is trivial and will be omitted.

*Lemma 2.8.2.* For all $k \ge 2$, we have $\mathcal{S}_k \supseteq \mathcal{S}_1$.

**Proof.** Suppose that $R \in \mathcal{S}_1$, so that $R$ is ultimately periodic. We must show that $\text{codes}_k(R)$ is recognizable. For a natural number $n \ge t$ (where $t$ is the threshold of $R$), we can determine whether $n \in R$ from the remainder $r$ left upon dividing $n$ by $p$ (the period of $R$). The remainder $r_k(x, p)$ left upon dividing $\text{val}_k(x)$ by $p$ can be maintained by a finite automaton using the formulas $r_k(\varepsilon, p) = 0$ and $r_k(xa, p) = kr_k(x, p) + a \pmod{p}$. Finally, the natural numbers $n < t$ can be handled as special cases. $\quad\square$

For $k \ge 2$, $\mathcal{S}_k$ contains sets that are not ultimately periodic: the set $\{k^m : m \ge 0\}$ of perfect powers of $k$, for example. We shall describe the relationship that these additional sets hold to one another for different values of $k \ge 2$.

Say that a natural number $k \geq 2$ is *radical* if $k$ is not a perfect power of another natural number $l \geq 2$; that is, if $k = l^m$ implies $m = 1$. Every number $k \geq 2$ can be expressed uniquely in the form $k = l^m$, where $l$ is radical (the "radical" of $k$) and $m \geq 1$ (the "exponent" of $k$). We shall say that two numbers $k, l \geq 2$ are *dependent* if they have the same radical, and are *independent* otherwise.

**Lemma 2.8.3.** If $k, l \geq 2$ are dependent, then $S_k = S_l$.

**Proof.** It will suffice to show that

$$S_k = S_j \tag{2.8.1}$$

where $j$ is the radical of $k = j^m$, for the same argument will show that $S_l = S_j$. But Eq. (2.8.1) follows by recoding each letter in $\mathbf{B}_k$ as a word of $m$ letters in $\mathbf{B}_j$ and *vice versa*.                                                                                    □

**Theorem 2.8.4 (Cobham [1969]).** *If $k, l \geq 2$ are independent, then $S_k \cap S_l = S_1$.*

The proof of this theorem will not be given here; it is intricate, even after considerable simplification by G. Hansel (see Perrin [1990]). See also Semenov [1977] for an extensive generalization.

Theorem 2.8.4 shows that the sets $S_k$ for the radicals $k \geq 2$ are like the petals of a sunflower, meeting each other only in the center $S_1$.

We shall now turn from sets of natural numbers to real numbers. For $R \subseteq \mathbf{N}$ and $p \geq 2$ we shall write $\mathrm{real}_p(R)$ for the real number $\sum_{n \in R} p^{-n}$. For $R_1 \subseteq \cdots \subseteq R_{p-1} \subseteq \mathbf{N}$, we shall write $\mathrm{real}_p(R_1, \ldots, R_{p-1})$ for the sum $\mathrm{real}_p(R_1) + \cdots + \mathrm{real}_p(R_{p-1})$. (For most real numbers $\xi$ in the interval $0 \leq \xi < 1$, there is a unique list $R_1 \subseteq \cdots \subseteq R_{p-1}$ such that $\xi = \mathrm{real}_p(R_1, \ldots, R_{p-1})$; the exception is when $\xi$ is a positive rational with a perfect power of $p$ as denominator, in which case there are two such lists.)

For $k \geq 1$ and $p \geq 2$, we shall write $\mathbf{T}_{k,p}$ for the set of real numbers

$$\{\mathrm{real}_p(R_1, \ldots, R_{p-1}) : R_1 \subseteq \cdots \subseteq R_{p-1} \quad \text{and} \quad R_1, \ldots, R_{p-1} \in S_k\}$$

**Lemma 2.8.5.** For $p \geq 2$, $\mathbf{T}_{1,p}$ is the set of rational numbers $\xi$ in the range $0 \leq \xi < 1$.

The proof is trivial and will be omitted.

**Theorem 2.8.6 (Loxton and van der Poorten [1988]).** *For $k, p \geq 2$, the numbers in $\mathbf{T}_{k,p}$ are each either rational or transcendental.*

The proof of this theorem will not be given here; it extends in spirit and technique a theorem of Mahler [1929] to the effect that the number $\eta = \sum_{m \geq 0} 2^{-2^m}$

($\eta$ = 0.1101000100000001 . . . in base 2), among other special numbers, is transcendental.

### Exercises

1. (M) Say that a set $R \subseteq \mathbf{N}$ has *many large gaps* if there exists a real number $\delta > 0$ such that, for infinitely many $m$, there is no element $n \in R$ in the range $m \le n \le (1 + \delta)m$. Say that $R$ has *only small gaps* if there exists a natural number $d$ such that, for all $m$, there is an element $n \in R$ in the range $m \le n \le m + d$. (a) Suppose $R \in \mathcal{S}_k$, for some $k \ge 2$. Show that either $R$ has many large gaps or $R$ has only small gaps. (b) Conclude that the set $\{n^2 : n \in \mathbf{N}\}$ of perfect squares does not belong to $\mathcal{S}_k$ for any $k$.

2. (U) Prove or disprove: if $p, q \ge 2$ are independent, then $\mathbf{T}_{2,p} \cap \mathbf{T}_{2,q} = \mathbf{T}_{2,1}$.

### 2.8.2. Variations on Finite Automata

Before taking up our next topic, we shall survey some of the ways in which the notion of a deterministic or non-deterministic finite automaton has been extended. In most cases, finite automata of the extended type still define only finite-state languages (thus providing evidence of the naturalness and robustness of this class of languages).

We may look upon the difference between deterministic and non-deterministic automata in the following way. For a given input word, the state of a deterministic automaton evolves in a predetermined way. In contrast, we may regard the state of a non-deterministic automaton as being manipulated by an external agent who is attempting to solve the "puzzle" of guiding the automaton from an initial state to a final state through transitions compatible with the input word. The words accepted by the automaton are precisely those for which this puzzle has a "solution." We can obtain a broader class of automata by replacing this puzzle with a two-person competitive game of perfect information.

We shall call the two players E (Ego, "there Exists") and A (Alter, "for All"). Given the input word and the automaton, E chooses the starting state from the set of initial states. For each letter of the input word, two consecutive transitions will be made; the first is chosen by A, the second is chosen by E, and both must be compatible with the corresponding input letter. We shall say that E wins if the last state of the sequence belongs to the set of final states, and that A wins otherwise. Since this is a finite two-person zero-sum game with perfect information, either E or A must have a winning strategy. We shall say that the automaton accepts those words for which E has a winning strategy and that it recognizes the language comprising just those words. An automaton of this type will be called an *alternating* automaton (though it is defined by the same data $M = (A, Q, I, J, R)$ as a non-deterministic automaton, and only the definitions of acceptance and recognition have changed). It is clear that every language recognized by a non-deterministic finite automaton is also recognized by an alternating finite automaton (just add states and transitions so that A has only one possible move in any situation). Conversely, any language recognized by an alternating finite automaton is also recognized by a deterministic finite automaton (though possibly only by one with many more states), and thus alternating finite automata recognize only the finite-state languages. (The proof depends on the fact that a monotone Boolean function can be put into "conjunctive (or disjunctive) normal form" and on the fact that (for a given number of arguments) there are only a finite number of such functions.) Alternating automata (both finite automata and those of more general kinds) were introduced by Chandra, Kozen, and Stockmeyer [1981].

Let us return to deterministic automata for the moment. We have regarded such automata as receiving the successive letters of the input word from left to right (though, in fact, the same class of languages is defined if they receive the letters from right to left). We may obtain a broader class of automata by giving the automaton itself a measure of control over the order in which it receives the letters, even allowing it to revisit letters that it has received before. The most convenient way to do this is to imagine that the input word is written on a "tape," with one letter in each "cell" of the tape. We may then imagine an automaton that can move left or right (or perhaps remain stationary) as it makes each transition, can sense the extremities of the word (so that it does not "fall off the end"), and can "announce" its decision to accept the word at any time. With appropriate formalization of this intuitive idea, we obtain the notion of a *two-way* finite automaton (with the old notion being referred to as a *one-way* finite automaton when necessary). It is clear that every language recognized by a one-way finite automaton is also recognized by a two-way finite automaton (just move right with each transition, announcing the decision upon reaching the right end). Conversely, every language that is recognized by a two-way finite automaton is also recognized by a one-way finite automaton (though possibly only by one with many more states), and thus two-way finite automata recognize only the finite-state languages. This equivalence was discovered by Rabin and Scott [1959] and Shepherdson [1959]. One can in fact combine this extension with the preceding one and define "two-way non-deterministic" and "two-way alternating" finite automata; still only the finite-state languages are recognized (see Chandra, Kozen and Stockmeyer [1981]).

Let us return to two-way deterministic automata for the moment. We may obtain a broader class of automata by providing the automaton with a "pebble" that it can use to keep track of cells on the input tape. We may imagine that the automaton can "carry" the pebble with it as it moves from cell to cell, or "put down" the pebble on the cell it is currently visiting (in which case the pebble will remain at this cell until the automaton returns to the cell and "picks up" the pebble) and that it can sense the presence or absence of the pebble at the cell it is currently visiting. With appropriate formalization of this intuitive idea, we obtain the notion of a *one-pebble* finite automaton (with the old notion being referred to as a *zero-pebble* finite automaton when necessary). It is clear that every language recognized by a zero-pebble finite automaton is also recognized by a one-pebble finite automaton (just carry the pebble at all times). Conversely, every language that is recognized by a one-pebble finite automaton is also recognized by a zero-pebble finite automaton (though possibly only by one with many more states), and thus one-pebble finite automata recognize only the finite-state languages. This equivalence was discovered by Blum and Hewitt [1967]. One can, in fact, combine this extension with the preceding ones and define "one-pebble non-deterministic" and "one-pebble alternating" finite automata; still only the finite-state languages are recognized (see Goralčik, Goralčiková, and Koubek [1991]).

One can go still further and define "two-pebble" finite automata, and so forth; these automata, however, recognize non-finite-state languages. For example, a deterministic two-pebble finite automaton can recognize the set Pal $= \{x \in$ $\mathbf{B}^* : x = \text{Rev}(x)\}$ of "palindromes": it simply starts a pebble at each end, shuttles back and forth between them, verifying the matching of letters and moving them toward each other, and accepts if the pebbles meet at the center without any mismatches having occurred. On the other hand, Pal is non-finite-state: every word of the form $x = 0^n 1$ give rise to a distinct intrinsic state $x^{-1}$Pal, since it contains $0^n$, but does not contain $0^m$ for any $m \neq n$.

### 2.8.3. *Finite Automata on Arrays*

We come now to our second additional topic: finite automata with two-dimensional rectangular input "arrays" in place of the one-dimensional tapes just considered. Let us assume for simplicity that the input alphabet is $\mathbf{B}$, and consider $m \times n$ arrays with $m, n \geq 1$. For example,

$$
\begin{matrix}
1111 \\
1000 \\
1011 \\
1000 \\
1111
\end{matrix}
$$

is a $5 \times 4$ array. We shall consider a deterministic four-way finite automaton that can move left, right, up, or down (or perhaps remain stationary) as it makes each transition and can sense the boundaries of the array (so that it does not "fall off the edge"). We shall consider the problem of recognizing the language Conn, comprising all two-dimensional rectangular arrays with all the 1's for a single connected region (counting vertical and horizontal adjacencies as connected, but not diagonal adjacencies).

**Theorem 2.8.7 (Blum and Hewitt [1967]).**    *The two-dimensional language Conn can be recognized by a deterministic four-way one-pebble automaton.*

The proof, which will only be sketched here, is based on the following criterion. An array belongs to Conn if and only if it satisfies the following three conditions:

1. The rows that contain one or more 1's form a consecutive interval of rows.
2. In any consecutive pair of rows that both contain one or more 1's, some occurrence of 1 in the first is adjacent vertically to (in the same column as) some occurrence of 1 in the second.
3. Among the 1's in any row that contains two or more 1's, each successive pair belongs to the same connected region of 1's.

The first two conditions are easily checked, even by a deterministic four-way finite automaton without a pebble. For the third condition, the automaton uses the pebble to check that each successive pair of 1's in a row are connected, even when they are not adjacent. To do this, it leaves the pebble to mark its place on the "shore" of an "island" of 1's while it explores this shore, searching for the succeeding 1 in the same row. If it finds it while following the shore, it follows that the two occurrences of 1 are connected; if it returns to the place where it left the pebble before finding the succeeding 1 in the same row, it follows that they are not connected.

### Exercises

1. (E) Show that a deterministic two-dimensional four-way one-pebble finite automaton can recognize the set of arrays that are (a) square (that is $n \times n$ for some $n \geq 1$), (b) odd-sided (that is, $n \times n$ with $n$ odd), and (c) have a 1 at their center.
2. (H) Show that no deterministic two-dimensional four-way zero-pebble finite automaton can recognize the set of arrays described in the preceding

exercise, and thus that a single pebble helps a two-dimensional automaton. (See Blum and Hewitt [1967].)

3. (U) Prove or disprove: No deterministic four-way zero-pebble finite automaton can recognize the two-dimensional language Conn.

### 2.8.4. Finite Automata in Mazes

Our final additional topic concerns automata in "mazes." A *maze* is just a finite set of cells, in two dimensions, that are connected in the sense of the previous section: they need not be "simply connected" (there may be "holes"), but they all form a single component, so that an automaton can move from any cell of the maze to any other through its orthogonal moves. We shall not assume that there are any input letters written on the cells, but we shall assume that an automaton can sense the boundaries, which may be complicated (there will always be an "outer" boundary, and there may be any finite number of "inner" boundaries for the holes). The task we shall set the automaton is now merely to "search" the maze: to visit every cell of the maze, no matter what cell it is started from. We do not require that the automaton "know" when it has completed its task; it may go into an infinite loop, so long as its trajectory (including the initial non-periodic portion) includes every cell.

All automata will be deterministic and four-way, and we shall classify them according to the number of pebbles they use. Mazes, on the other hand, will be classified according to the number of holes they contain. The earliest result in this setting is due to Döpp [1971]: there exists a zero-pebble automaton that searches every zero-hole (that is, simply connected) maze. This result is simply a formalization of the ancient algorithm: keep one hand against the wall when moving vertically, while sweeping each row encountered. (If it is required that the automaton halt after visiting each cell at least once, then a zero-pebble automaton cannot search every zero-hole maze; see Bull and Hemmerling [1990].)

Although it seems intuitively obvious that no finite automaton can search all mazes with holes, it was not until 1978 that a proof was published by Budach [1978]. The proof uses several general propositions concerning automata in mazes, together with an ingenious construction based on a case analysis, and the maze constructed may have any number of holes. Müller [1979] modified the case analysis so that the maze always has at most two holes. It is not known whether there is always a maze with at most one hole.

Since zero-pebble automata cannot search every maze, it is natural to ask what can be accomplished by automata with pebbles. Blum and Kozen [1978] showed that a finite two-pebble automaton can search every maze, irrespective of the number of holes. This left open the question of what can be accomplished with one pebble. The answer is quite interesting: for every fixed number $k$ of holes, there is a finite one-pebble automaton that searches all $k$-hole mazes (irrespective of how complicated they are in respects other than number of holes); see Hemmerling and Kriegel [1984]. On the other hand, no finite one-pebble automaton can search every maze (irrespective of the number of holes); see Hoffmann [1981]. For a survey of results on automata in mazes, see Kudryavtsev, Ushchumlich, and Kilibarda [1993].

## *Exercises*

1. (H) Define finite automata in three-dimensional mazes, and show that no finite zero-pebble automaton can search every three-dimensional maze. (See Budach [1978] and Blum and Sakoda [1977] for two much stronger results.)
2. (U) Prove or disprove: No finite automaton can search every one-hole two-dimensional maze.

# 3

# Grammars and their languages

## 3.1. Grammars

In Chapter 2, we began our study of languages by examining one particular class of languages, the finite-state languages, from several points of view: finite automata, regular expressions, logical expressions, *etc.* In this chapter, we shall continue our study of languages by using one particular formalism, "grammars," to describe several classes of languages: "enumerable," "context-free," "linear," finite-state, *etc.* Whereas in most of the preceding chapter the finite-state languages were the largest class of languages we studied, and the tools we used (such as varieties) allowed us to delineate various subclasses of the finite-state languages, in this chapter the finite-state languages will be the smallest class of languages we study. The formalism of grammars leads us to adopt the enumerable languages as the largest class we study, and the tools we use (such as "rational cones") will allow us to delineate various subclasses of the enumerable languages, including the finite-state languages.

As in Chapter 2, we shall study languages that are subsets of a free monoid $A^*$, where $A$ is a finite alphabet that is a subset of a fixed countably infinite alphabet, say, the natural numbers $\mathbf{N}$. In this way we shall always have access to alphabets larger than or disjoint from a given alphabet, while maintaining a concrete framework for the discussion. We shall speak of classes of such languages, and there is one condition we shall always want to hold. We shall say that two languages $L \subseteq A^*$ and $L' \subseteq A'^*$ are *copies* (of each other) if there is a bijection between the alphabets $A$ and $A'$ that induces a bijection between the languages $L$ and $L'$. If two languages are copies, they differ only by the particular letters chosen to represent them, and for many purposes we will not want to distinguish between them. We shall say that a class of languages is a *family* of languages if it is closed under taking copies (always with respect to

99

the fixed countable alphabet **N**). Thus, the question of whether or not a language $L$ belongs to a family $\mathcal{F}$ of languages depends only on the structure of $L$, and not on the particular alphabet used to represent it.

A *grammar* is a quadruple $G = (A, B, s, P)$ where (1) $A$ is a finite alphabet of objects called *letters*, (2) $B$ is a finite alphabet of objects called *symbols*, (3) $s \in B$ is a distinguished symbol called the *starting* symbol, and (4) $P \subseteq B^+ \times (A \cup B)^*$ is a finite set of pairs $(v, w)$ called *productions*, where each production comprises a *pattern* $v \in B^+$ and a *replacement* $w \in (A \cup B)^*$. The letters and symbols of $A \cup B$ will be referred to collectively as *marks*. A grammar has this in common with a finite automaton: it is a finite object. Thus, if we agree to take all letters from a fixed countably infinite alphabet of letters, and to take all symbols from a fixed countably infinite alphabet of symbols, then there are just countably many grammars.

We shall now associate with every grammar $G = (A, B, s, P)$ a language $\text{Lang}(G) \subseteq A^*$ over the alphabet $A$ as follows. For $u, z \in (A \cup B)^*$, write $u \rightarrow_G z$, and say that $u$ *produces* $z$ (according to $G$), if there exist $x, y \in (A \cup B)^*$ and $(v, w) \in P$ such that $u = xvy$ and $z = xwy$. Thus, $u$ produces $z$ if $z$ can be obtained from $u$ by replacing some occurrence of the pattern $v$ of some production $(v, w)$ by the corresponding replacement $w$. Write $u \Rightarrow_G z$, and say that $u$ *derives* $z$ (according to $G$) if either $u = z$ or there exist $k \geq 1$ and a sequence $x_0, x_1, \ldots, x_k \in (A \cup B)^*$ such that $u = x_0$, $z = x_k$, and $x_{j-1} \rightarrow_G x_j$ for $1 \leq j \leq k$. Thus, $u$ derives $z$ if $z$ can be obtained from $u$ by applying a sequence of zero or more productions. The sequence $x_0, x_1, \ldots, x_k$ will be called a *derivation* of $z$ from $u$ (according to $G$). If $G = (A, B, s, P)$, we shall define the language $\text{Lang}(G)$ by

$$\text{Lang}(G) = \{z \in A^* : s \Rightarrow_G z\}$$

Thus, $z$ belongs to $\text{Lang}(G)$ if and only if there exists a derivation of $z$ from the starting symbol $s$ (according to $G$). This is similar to the condition defining membership in $\text{Lang}(M)$ for a non-deterministic finite automaton $M$, but with this difference: whereas the computation of an automaton on an input word $z$ is no longer (in transitions) than $z$ (in letters), a derivation of a word $z$ according to a grammar may be much longer (in productions) than $z$ (in letters), and there is, in general, no way to tell whether or not such a derivation exists by checking a finite number of cases.

A language $L \subseteq A^*$ is *enumerable* (or "recursively enumerable" or "semide-cidable") if $L = \text{Lang}(G)$ for some grammar $G = (A, B, s, P)$. It is clear that the enumerable languages form a family of languages, which we shall denote $\mathcal{E}$. The enumerable languages form the broadest family of languages we shall study in this chapter. They appear, in fact, to be the broadest family of languages whose words can be systematically generated by effective procedures. It is obvious that there are languages that are not enumerable (there are uncountably many languages, but only countably many grammars). Nevertheless, when we prove in Section 3.5 that a *particular* language is not enumerable, this result will have great significance, for it asserts in effect that a particular language surpasses in its subtlety the generative capabilities of effective procedures.

A grammar $G = (A, B, s, P)$ will be called *context-free* if $P \subseteq B \times (A \cup B)^*$ (that is, if the pattern of each production consists of a single symbol). A language $L \subseteq A^*$ will be called context-free if $L = \text{Lang}(G)$ for some context-free grammar $G$. It is clear that the context-free languages form a family of languages, which we shall denote $\mathcal{K}$. The context-free languages are the most extensively studied family of languages, incomparably more tractable than the enumerable languages, yet incomparably richer than the finite-state languages. Evidence of both the tractability and richness will be presented in Sections 3.3 and 3.4.

A context-free grammar $G = (A, B, s, P)$ will be called *linear* if $P \subseteq B \times (A^* \cup A^*BA^*)$ (that is, if the replacement of each production contains at most one symbol). A language $L \subseteq A^*$ will be called linear if $L = \text{Lang}(G)$ for some linear grammar $G$. It is clear that the linear languages form a family of languages, which we shall denote $\mathcal{L}$. A linear grammar $G = (A, B, s, P)$ will be called *right-linear* (respectively, *left-linear*) if $P \subseteq B \times (A^* \cup A^*B)$ (respectively, $P \subseteq B \times (A^* \cup BA^*)$). We shall see in Section 3.2 that the languages generated by the right- and left-linear grammars are precisely the finite-state languages studied in Chapter 2. The family of linear languages contains far more than the finite-state languages, and it contains in miniature many of the features of the family of context-free languages. We shall see in Sections 3.7 and 3.8, however, some important differences between these families, and most such differences go to show that the class of linear languages is not nearly as "nice" as the family of context-free languages.

The families of languages just introduced were all defined by placing various restrictions on grammars, which serve as a common generating mechanism for all of them. In Section 3.6 we shall see another framework, that of rational cones, into which they may all be put, and which allows them to be studied independently of the generative machinery of grammars. Indeed, this new framework is based on closure conditions, and thus it puts the whole theory of languages in the same setting that we have seen so often in Chapters 1 and 2.

## 3.2. Linear Languages

In the course of this chapter, various classes of languages will be defined by placing various restrictions on grammars. In most cases, there will be a range of successively weaker or stronger restrictions that results in the same class of generated languages. It will be useful to recognize these equivalences, since they will allow us to make strong assumptions about languages we are given as hypotheses, but require us to prove only weak conditions on languages we produce as conclusions. We begin our study with an example of this phenomenon.

Recall that a grammar $G = (A, B, s, P)$ is right-linear if $P \subseteq B \times (A^* \cup A^* B)$ (that is, if every production has a pattern that consists of just one symbol and a replacement that contains at most one symbol, which must be the rightmost mark if present).

**Proposition 3.2.1.** *Every language generated by a right-linear grammar is generated by a right-linear grammar $G = (A, B, s, P)$ in which $P \subseteq B \times (\{\varepsilon\} \cup AB)$ (that is, every production has a replacement that is either empty or consists of a single letter followed by a single symbol).*

The grammar promised by Proposition 3.2.1 will be obtained as the culmination of a series of transformations. Let us write $A^- = A^0 \cup A^1 = \{\varepsilon\} \cup A$ for the language comprising the words containing at most one occurrence of a letter from $A$. Then the condition defining a right-linear grammar may be written $P \subseteq B \times A^* B^-$. Our first transformation will reduce this to $P \subseteq B \times A^- B^-$.

If $(c, a_1 \cdots a_k b)$ is a production, where $k \geq 2$, we may alter the grammar containing it by (1) deleting this production, (2) adding to the alphabet of symbols $k-1$ new symbols $b_1, \ldots, b_{k-1}$, and (3) adding to the set of productions $k$ new productions $(c, a_1 b_1), (b_1, a_2 b_2), \ldots, (b_{k-2}, a_{k-1} b_{k-1})$, and $(b_{k-1}, a_k b)$. If $(c, a_1 \cdots a_k)$ is a production, where $k \geq 2$, we may alter the grammar in a similar way, but with the last of the new productions being $(b_{k-1}, a_k)$. These alterations leave the language generated by the grammar unchanged, but reduce by one the number of productions of the form $B \times A^2 A^* B$ (that is, with two or more letters in the replacement). After performing these alterations whenever possible, we will arrive at a grammar for which $P \subseteq B \times A^- B^-$ or, equivalently, $P \subseteq B \times (\{\varepsilon\} \cup A \cup B \cup AB)$. Our next transformation will reduce this to $P \subseteq B \times (\{\varepsilon\} \cup B \cup AB)$.

Suppose that our grammar contains a symbol $e$ such that $(e, \varepsilon)$ is a production (if there is no such symbol, add a new symbol $e$ to the alphabet of symbols and add the new production $(e, \varepsilon)$ to the set of productions). If $(b, a)$ is a production, we may alter the grammar by (1) deleting this production and (2) adding the new production $(b, ae)$. This alteration leaves the language generated by the grammar unchanged, but reduces by one the number of productions of the form $B \times A$. (And of course it does not introduce any productions of the form $B \times A^2 A^* B$.) After performing this alteration whenever possible, we will arrive at a grammar for which $P \subseteq B \times (\{\varepsilon\} \cup B \cup AB)$. Our final transformation will reduce this to $P \subseteq B \times (\{\varepsilon\} \cup AB)$.

Let us define a closure system on the class $\text{Pow}(B \times (A \cup B)^*)$ of sets of productions (for given letter and symbol alphabets) by saying that a set of productions is *closed* if it contains the production $(b, w)$ whenever it contains the productions $(b, c)$ and $(c, w)$. Every finite set of productions in $B \times (\{\varepsilon\} \cup B \cup AB)$ generates a closed set of productions, which is also finite since it is also contained in $B \times (\{\varepsilon\} \cup B \cup AB)$. If we replace the set of productions of our grammar by its closure, the language generated by the grammar is unaffected. If from the resulting grammar we delete all productions in $B \times B$ (that is, of the form $(b, c)$), the language generated by the grammar is still unaffected, and the resulting grammar has $P \subseteq B \times (\{\varepsilon\} \cup AB)$. This completes the proof of Proposition 3.2.1.

**Theorem 3.2.2.** *A language is generated by a right-linear grammar if and only if it is regular.*

**Proof.** Suppose that $L$ is generated by the right-linear grammar $G = (A, B, s, P)$. We may assume that $G$ satisfies the conclusion of Proposition 3.2.1. We define a non-deterministic finite automaton $M = (A, Q, I, J, R)$ by taking $Q = B$, $I = \{s\}$, $J = \{b : (b, \varepsilon) \in P\}$, and $R = \{(a, b, c) : (b, ac) \in P\}$. We can then prove by induction on the length of $x \in A^*$ that $x \in \text{Lang}(G)$ if and only if $x \in \text{Lang}(M)$.

Conversely, suppose that $L$ is accepted by the deterministic finite automaton $M = (A, Q, \{i\}, J, R)$. We define a right-linear grammar $G = (A, B, s, P)$ by taking $B = Q$, $s = i$, and $P = \{(q, \varepsilon) : q \in J\} \cup \{(q, aq') : (a, q, q') \in R\}$. We can again then prove by induction on the length of $x \in A^*$ that $x \in \text{Lang}(G)$ if and only if $x \in \text{Lang}(M)$. $\quad\square$

If $G = (A, B, s, P)$ is any grammar, we may define $\text{Rev}(G)$ (the *reversal* of $G$) to be $(A, B, s, \text{Rev}(P))$, where

$$\text{Rev}(P) = \{(\text{Rev}(v), \text{Rev}(w)) : (v, w) \in P\}$$

If the grammar $G$ generates the language $L$, then $\text{Rev}(G)$ generates $\text{Rev}(L)$.

We shall say that a grammar $G = (A, B, s, P)$ is left-linear if $P \subseteq B \times (A^* \cup BA^*)$ (that is, if every production has a pattern that consists of just one symbol and a replacement that contains at most one symbol, which must be the leftmost mark if present). The conditions defining right- and left-linear grammars are mirror-images: $G$ is right-linear if and only if $\text{Rev}(G)$ is left-linear, and *vice* *versa.* We then have that a language $L$ is generated by a left-linear grammar $G$ if and only if $\mathrm{Rev}(L)$ is generated by a right-linear grammar $\mathrm{Rev}(G)$, if and only if $\mathrm{Rev}(L)$ is regular (by Theorem 3.2.2), if and only if $L$ is regular (by Lemma 2.3.2). Thus, the left-linear grammars, like the right-linear grammars, generate all and only the regular languages.

It is often desirable to show that some particular language is not regular. In Chapter 2 we have done this by exhibiting infinitely many distinct intrinsic states of the language. We shall now present another tool for showing that languages are not regular. Although not especially significant as regards regular languages, it serves as the prototype of a family of tools applicable to many other classes of languages. The tools of this family are called "pumping lemmas" (or "iteration lemmas").

*Lemma 3.2.3.* Let $L$ be regular. Then there exists a natural number $n$ such that every word $w \in L$ with length at least $n$ can be written as $w = xyz$, with the length of $y$ at least 1, such that for all natural numbers $k$, $xy^k z \in L$ (where $y^k$ denotes the $k$-fold concatenation of $y$ with itself).

**Proof.** Let $L$ be generated by the right-linear grammar $G = (A, B, s, P)$ satisfying the conclusion of Proposition 3.2.1. Take $n$ be the number of symbols in $B$, and let $w \in L$ have length at least $n$. In a deriviation of $w$ according to $G$, every word except the last contains exactly one symbol, and every application of a production except the last increases the number of letters by one. Thus, the number of words containing symbols is one more than the length of $w$ and, thus, is greater than the number of distinct symbols. It follows (by the pigeon-hole principle) that there exist two distinct words in the derivation that contain the same symbol, say, $xb$ and $xyb$ in the derivation

$$s \Rightarrow_G xb \Rightarrow_G xyb \Rightarrow_G xyz = w$$

where $y$ has length at least one. But then we also have

$$s \Rightarrow_G xb \Rightarrow_G xy^2 b \Rightarrow_G \cdots \Rightarrow_G xy^k z$$

so that $xy^k z \in L$ for all $k \geq 0$.                                      □

We observe that it is possible to strengthen this lemma so that $xy$ (or alternatively, $yz$) has length at most $n$. (This is because the pigeon-hole principle can be applied to *any* sufficiently long sequence of occurrences of symbols.) Thus, one can guarantee that the subword $y$ to be "pumped" is short and that it occurs near a chosen end of the word (that is, that $x$ or $y$ is short).

As an example, consider the language $\text{Sym}_1 = \{0^m 1^m : m \geq 0\}$, and take $m$ large enough that Lemma 3.2.3 applies to the word $w = 0^m 1^m$. The word $y$ cannot contain both 0's and 1's, for if it did, $xy^2z$ would contain a 1 preceding a 0, and thus could not belong to $\text{Sym}_1$. Thus, $y$ consists either of one or more 0's, or of one or more 1's. In either case, $xy^2z$ contains unequal numbers of 0's and 1's, and thus cannot belong to $\text{Sym}_1$. We conclude that $\text{Sym}_1$ is not regular.

Recall that a grammar $G = (A, B, s, P)$ is linear if $P \subseteq B \times A^* B^- A^*$ (that is, if every production has a pattern that consists of just one symbol and a replacement that contains at most one symbol). A language $L$ is linear if $L = \text{Lang}(G)$ for some linear grammar $G$. The family of linear languages will be denoted $\mathcal{L}$. Straightforward arguments show that the linear languages are closed under union. The situation with regard to concatenation and asteration will be considered later.

By transformations analogous to those used to prove Proposition 3.2.1, we obtain the following restricted form for linear grammars.

**Proposition 3.2.4.** *Every language generated by a linear grammar is generated by a linear grammar $G = (A, B, s, P)$ in which $P \subseteq B \times (\{\varepsilon\} \cup AB \cup BA)$.*

As an example, let $A = \{0, 1, \ldots, 2n - 1\}$ and let $h : A^* \to A^*$ be the homomorphism defined by $h(a) = a + n$ (modulo $2n$). Let $\text{Sym}_n \subseteq A^*$ be the language comprising the words $x\text{Rev}(h(x))$, where $x \in \{0, 1, \ldots, n-1\}^*$. The language $\text{Sym}_n$ consists of words $x$ over an $n$-letter alphabet followed by their transliterated reversals $\text{Rev}(h(x))$, where the transliteration makes the "center" of the combined word apparent. We have already seen that $\text{Sym}_1$ is not regular. Thus, since the regular languages are closed under homomorphic images, $\text{Sym}_n$ is not regular (since it has a copy of $\text{Sym}_1$ as an image). On the other hand, $\text{Sym}_n$ is linear, since it is generated by the grammar $(A, \{s\}, s, P)$, where

$$P = \{(s, \varepsilon)\} \cup \{(s, ash(a)) : a \in \{0, 1, \ldots, n - 1\}\}$$

Thus, the family of linear languages is strictly larger than the family of regular languages.

An argument similar to that used to prove Lemma 3.2.3 yields the following pumping lemma for linear languages.

**Lemma 3.2.5.** *Let $L$ be linear. Then there exists a natural number $n$ such that every word $u \in L$ with length at least $n$ can be written as $u = vwxyz$, with the length of $wy$ at least 1 and the length of $vwyz$ at most $n$, such that for all natural numbers $k$, $vw^k xy^k z \in L$.*

In contrast with the pumping lemma for regular languages, we now must pump two subwords ($w$ and $y$) simultaneously, but we can guarantee that both are short and that both are near their respective ends (that is, that $v$ and $z$ are also short).

As an example, consider the language $\mathrm{Sym}_1^2 = \mathrm{Sym}_1 \cdot \mathrm{Sym}_1$. Applying Lemma 3.2.5 to the word $u = 0^m 1^m 0^m 1^m$ for sufficiently large $m$, we find that $u = vwxyz$, where $v$ and $w$ are each subwords of the beginning $0^m$ and $y$ and $z$ are each subwords of the ending $1^m$. Since $0^p 1^m 0^m 1^q$ does not belong to $\mathrm{Sym}_1^2$ if $p < m$ or $q < m$, we conclude that $vxz \notin \mathrm{Sym}_1^2$ and, thus, that $\mathrm{Sym}_1^2$ is not linear. This shows that $\mathcal{L}$ is not closed under concatenation, and a similar argument shows that it is not closed under asteration.

As another example, let $\mathrm{Eq}_1 \subseteq \{0, 1\}^*$ be the language comprising the words that contain an equal number of 0's and 1's. Applying Lemma 3.2.5 to the word $u = 0^m 1^{2m} 0^m$ for sufficiently large $m$ yields a contradiction that shows that $\mathrm{Eq}_1$ is not linear.

As yet another example, let $\mathrm{Dyck}_1 \subseteq \{0, 1\}^*$ be the language comprising the words that contain an equal number of 0's and 1's, and in which every initial segment contains at least as many 0's as 1's. (The words in $\mathrm{Dyck}_1$ are those that become balanced sequences of parentheses when 0 is replaced by "(" and 1 is replaced by ")".) Again applying Lemma 3.2.5 to the word $u = 0^m 1^m 0^m 1^m$ for sufficiently large $m$ yields a contradiction that shows that $\mathrm{Dyck}_1$ is not linear.

The basic properties of right- and left-linear grammars were presented by Chomsky and Miller [1958], and those of linear grammars by Chomsky and Schützenberger [1963].

### Exercises

1. (E)  Show that $\mathcal{L}$ is closed under union.
2. (M)  Show that $\mathcal{L}$ is not closed under intersection (and thus is also not closed under complement).

## 3.3. Context-Free Languages

This section deals with one of the most studied classes of languages: the context-free languages. The original impetus for defining and studying the context-free languages came from attempts to use them as models for both natural and computer languages, though now it is clear that there are many important phenomena in both domains that they cannot capture. Their study has, however, led to the discovery of many remarkable mathematical properties that continue to support their position of importance in mathematical language theory (though these properties will not become apparent until later in this chapter).

Recall that a grammar $G = (A, B, s, P)$ is context-free if $P \subseteq B \times (A \cup B)^*$ (that is, if every production has exactly one symbol in its pattern). The name "context-free" arises from the fact that each production indicates how a symbol may be replaced, independently of the context in which it appears. We shall say that a language $L$ is context-free if $L = \text{Lang}(G)$ for some context-free grammar $G$. We shall denote by $\mathcal{K}$ the class of all context-free languages. Straightforward arguments show that the context-free languages are closed under union, concatenation, and asteration.

**Example 3.3.1.** Let $A = \{0, 1, 2, 3\}$, $B = \{i, j\}$, and

$$P = \{(i, \varepsilon), (i, ji), (j, 0i1), (j, 2i3)\}$$

The language generated by $G = (A, B, i, P)$ is denoted $\text{Dyck}_2$, the "Dyck language on two types of brackets." To understand the nature of this language, note that the first two productions allow an $i$ to be replaced by a sequence of zero or more $j$'s, while the last two productions allow a $j$ to be replaced by an $i$ between a "matching pair of brackets": the "left-bracket" 0 matches the "right-bracket" 1, while 2 matches 3. If we replace the starting symbol $i$ by $j$, the language generated by $G' = (A, B, j, P)$ is denoted $\text{Dyck}_2'$, the language of "Dyck primes" on two types of brackets. (The name "prime" and notation " $'$ " arise because every word in the Dyck language can be "factored" into a uniques "product" of zero or more Dyck primes.) If $n \geq 1$ is a positive integer, there is an obvious generalization of this definition to $\text{Dyck}_n$ and $\text{Dyck}_n'$ over the alphabet $A = \{0, 1, \ldots, 2n - 2, 2n - 1\}$ containing $n$ matching pairs of brackets. In particular, the languages $\text{Dyck}_1$ and $\text{Dyck}_1'$ give languages of matching parentheses. These languages are all context-free, but we have seen that even $\text{Dyck}_1$ is not linear. (The Dyck languages originate in the work of von Dyck [1882] on what has become "combinatorial group theory.")

**Example 3.3.2.** Let $A$ and $B$ be as in Example 3.3.1, but take $P = \{(i, \varepsilon), (i, 0i1), (i, 2i3)\}$. (The symbol $j$ now plays no role.) The language generated by $G = (A, B, i, P)$ is denoted $\text{Inv}_2$; its words have a symmetry under reversal similar to that of palindromes, except that the roles of the left-brackets 0 and 2 must also be exchanged with those of the right-brackets 1 and 3. If we replace the productions $(i, 0i1)$ and $(i, 2i3)$ by $(i, 0i0)$ and $(i, 1i1)$, we obtain the language of palindromes of even length over the alphabet $\{0, 1\}$, and with the addition of two obvious productions we can obtain the language $Pal_2$ of all palindromes over this alphabet. The generalization to $Inv_n$ and $Pal_n$ is obvious. These languages are all linear, but we have seen that even $Inv_1 = Sym_1$ is not regular.

**Example 3.3.3.** Let $A = \{0, 1, 2, 3\}$ and $B = \{i\}$, and take $P = \{(i, 0), (i, 1i2i3)\}$. Here the language Expr generated by $G = (A, B, i, P)$ encodes "binary trees" in the fashion of fully parenthesised expressions: 0 represents a leaf, 1 represents a left parenthesis, 2 represents an infix operator, and 3 represents a right parenthesis.

**Example 3.3.4.** Let $A = \{0, 2\}$ and $B = I = \{i\}$, and take $P = \{(i, 0), (i, 2ii)\}$. Here the language L generated by $G = (A, B, I, P)$ encodes binary trees more succinctly than Expr: the encoding is the "Polish notation" in which 0 represents a leaf and 2 represents a binary prefix operator. (Some definitions add the letter 1 to $A$ and the production $(i, 1i)$ to $P$, to cater for a unary prefix operator. One can add further prefix operators of any "arity," of course. The notation "L" and the adjective "Polish" derive from the name and the nationality of the logician Łukasiewicz.)

We begin by describing some simplifications that can be performed on context-free grammars without affecting the languages they generate. Let us say that a mark $c$ in a grammar $G = (A, B, s, P)$ is *accessible* if $s \Rightarrow_G xcy$ for some $x, y \in (A \cup B)^*$. If a mark is not accessible, then it cannot appear in the derivation of any word in Lang($G$), and thus it (and any productions involving it) can be discarded from the grammar without affecting the language generated. We can determine the set Acc($G$) of accessible marks as follows: Acc($G$) is the smallest set of marks that (1) contains the starting symbol $s$ and (2) contains all of the marks in the replacement $w$ of a production $(b, w)$ whenever it contains the pattern $b$.

Let us say that a mark $c$ is *terminable* in the grammar $G = (A, B, s, P)$ if $c \Rightarrow_G x$ for some $x \in A^*$. If a mark is not terminable, then it cannot appear in the derivation of any word in Lang($G$), and thus it (and any productions involving it) can be discarded from the grammar without affecting the language generated. We can determine the set Term($G$) of terminable marks as follows: Term($G$) is the smallest set of marks that (1) contains the letters in $A$ and (2) contains the pattern $b$ of a production $(b, w)$ whenever it contains all of the marks in the replacement $w$. We observe that after marks that are not both accessible and terminable have been removed from the grammar, we have Lang($G$) = Ø if and only if $P = Ø$. Thus, it is easy to check whether a context-free grammar generates the empty language.

Let us say that a symbol $b$ is *evanescent* in the grammar $G = (A, B, s, P)$ if $b \Rightarrow_G \varepsilon$. We can determine the set Evan($G$) of evanescent symbols as follows: Evan($G$) is the smallest set of symbols that contains the pattern $b$ of a production $(b, w)$ whenever it contains all of the marks in the replacement $w$. Clearly, we can add a production $(b, \varepsilon)$ to $P$ for every evanescent symbol $b$ without affecting the language generated by $G$. We observe that after all such productions have been added, we have $\varepsilon \in \text{Lang}(G)$ if and only if $(s, \varepsilon) \in P$. Thus, it is easy to check whether a context-free grammar generates the empty word.

Suppose that $G = (A, B, s, P)$ is a context-free grammar in which each symbol $b$ is evanescent if and only if $(b, \varepsilon) \in P$. The language generated by $G$ will not be affected if, for every production $(b, w) \in P$, we add to $P$ all productions obtained from $(b, w)$ by deleting from $w$ some set of occurrences of evanescent symbols. After these additions have been made, we may delete from $P$ all productions of the form $(b, \varepsilon)$ (except possibly the production $(s, \varepsilon)$, if it appears in $P$) without affecting the language generated by $G$. After these deletions have been made, we have a grammar with no production of the form $(b, \varepsilon)$ (except possibly $(s, \varepsilon)$) and in which no symbol is evanescent (except possibly $s$). In particular, if the language $L$ generated by $G$ is "$\varepsilon$-free" (that is, if $\varepsilon \notin \text{Lang}(G)$), then $G$ is $\varepsilon$-free (that is, contains no production of the form $(b, \varepsilon)$). Thus, the theory of context-free languages and grammars falls into two symmetrical parts: there are the $\varepsilon$-free languages, which are generated by the $\varepsilon$-free grammars, and for each of them there is a corresponding language obtained by adding $\varepsilon$, which is generated by a corresponding grammar obtained by adding the production $(s, \varepsilon)$. For this reason we may assume without any real loss of generality that a context-free language either contains or does not contain the empty word. We shall state the next proposition and theorem for $\varepsilon$-free grammars and languages, but they have obvious analogues for general context-free grammars and languages.

Let $G = (A, B, s, P)$ be an $\varepsilon$-free context-free grammar. We shall say that $G$ is in *Chomsky normal form* if $P \subseteq B \times (A \cup B^2)$ (that is, if every production has a replacement that consists of either exactly one letter or exactly two symbols). An argument similar to that used to prove Propositions 3.2.1 and 3.2.4 yields the following proposition.

**Proposition 3.3.1.** *Every $\varepsilon$-free context-free language is generated by a grammar in Chomsky normal form.*

Let $G = (A, B, s, P)$ be an $\varepsilon$-free context-free grammar. We shall say that $G$ is in *Greibach normal form* if $P \subseteq B \times AB^*$ (that is, if every production has a replacement that begins with a letter and contains no other letters).

The following theorem lies much deeper than Proposition 3.3.1, and it is the key to much of the theory of context-free languages.

**Theorem 3.3.2.** *Every $\varepsilon$-free context-free language is generated by a grammar in Greibach normal form.*

**Proof.** Let $G = (A, B, s, P)$ be an $\varepsilon$-free context-free grammar for which $P \subseteq B \times (A \cup B^2)$ (such as the grammar given by Proposition 3.3.1). We shall subject this grammar to a series of transformations in such a way that we always have $P \subseteq B \times (AB^* \cup B^+)$. Say that a production $(b, w)$ is "bad" if $w$ begins with a symbol. Our goal is to eliminate all bad productions, so that we are left with $P \subseteq B \times AB^*$.

Suppose that $b_1, \ldots, b_n$ are the symbols in $B$. We shall begin by adding $n$ new symbols $c_1, \ldots, c_n$ to $B$. We shall add productions later in such a way as to maintain the following condition: if $(c_i, w)$ is a production, then the first mark of $w$ is either a letter or a symbol $b_j$.

Say that a production $(b_i, w)$ is *forward-looking* if the first mark of $w$ is either a letter or a symbol $b_j$ with $j > i$. Our first goal will be to transform the grammar so that all productions $(b_i, w)$ are forward-looking.

Initially, we can claim that all productions $(b_i, w)$ with $i \leq 0$ are forward-looking (since there are no such productions). We shall achieve our goal in a sequence of $n$ steps: at the outset of the $m$-th step, we assume that all productions $(b_i, w)$ with $i < m$ are forward-looking, and we shall arrange that at the conclusion of the $m$-th step all productions $(b_i, w)$ with $i \leq m$ are forward-looking. Thus, at the conclusion of the $n$-th step we shall have achieved our first goal.

We shall accomplish the $m$-th step in two stages. Say that a production $(b_i, w)$ is *almost forward-looking* if the first mark of $w$ is either a letter or a symbol $b_j$ with $j \leq i$. We shall arrange that at the conclusion of the first stage, all productions $(b_m, w)$ are almost forward-looking (while maintaining the condition that all productions $(b_i, w)$ for $i < m$ are forward-looking).

To accomplish the task of the first stage, we must eliminate all productions $(b_m, w)$ that are not almost forward-looking. Say that a production $(b_m, w)$ is $k$-*clean* if the first mark of $w$ is either a letter or a symbol $b_j$ with $j > k$. Initially, we can claim that all productions $(b_m, w)$ are 0-clean. We shall accomplish the task of the first stage in a sequence of $m$ phases: at the outset of the $l$-th phase, we assume that all productions $(b_m, w)$ are $(l - 1)$-clean, and we shall arrange that at the conclusion of the $l$-th phase all such productions are $l$-clean. Thus, at the conclusion of the $l$-th phase we shall have accomplished the task of the first stage.

We now consider the $l$-th phase. Let $(b_m, b_l x)$ be a production that is not $l$-clean, and let $(b_l, y^{(1)}), \ldots, (b_l, y^{(p)})$ be all of the productions of the form $(b_l, w)$. Then the language generated will be unaffected if we (1) delete from $P$ the production $(b_m, b_l x)$ and (2) add to $P$ the productions $(b_m, y^{(1)} x), \ldots,$ $(b_m, y^{(p)} x)$. Furthermore, this alteration reduces by one the number of productions that are not $l$-clean (and does not violate any of the other conditions we are maintaining). Thus, by performing this alteration for every production that is not $l$-clean, we will eventually eliminate all such productions, and complete the $l$-th phase.

To accomplish the task of the second stage, we must eliminate all productions $(b_m, w)$ that are not forward-looking. By virtue of the first stage, such productions are almost forward-looking and, thus, must have $b_m$ as the first mark in $w$. Let $(b_m, b_m x^{(1)}), \ldots, (b_m, b_m x^{(p)})$ be all such productions. Let $(b_m, y^{(1)}), \ldots, (b_m, y^{(q)})$ be all other productions of the form $(b_m, w)$. These productions together imply that

$$b_m \Rightarrow_G \{y^{(1)}, \ldots, y^{(q)}\} \cdot \{x^{(1)}, \ldots, x^{(p)}\}^* \qquad (3.3.1)$$

If we (1) delete the productions $(b_m, b_m x^{(1)}), \ldots, (b_m, b_m x^{(p)})$ from $P$, (2) add the productions $(b_m, x^{(1)} c_m), \ldots, (b_m, x^{(p)} c_m)$ to $P$, (3) add the productions $(c_m, y^{(1)}), \ldots, (c_m, y^{(q)})$ to $P$, and (4) add the productions $(c_m, x^{(1)} c_m), \ldots,$ $(c_m, x^{(p)} c_m)$ to $P$, then the language generated will be unaffected, since we will have

$$c_m \Rightarrow_G \{y^{(1)}, \ldots, y^{(q)}\} \cdot \{x^{(1)}, \ldots, x^{(p)}\}^*$$

as well as Eq. (3.3.1), and the task of the second stage will be accomplished.

After achieving our first goal, every production $(b_i, w)$ is forward-looking. Say that a production $(b, w)$ is *left-terminal* if the first mark of $w$ is a letter. Our second goal will be to transform the grammar so that all productions $(b_i, w)$ are left-terminal.

Initially, we can claim that all productions $(b_i, w)$ with $i \geq n$ are left-terminal (since a production $(b_n, w)$ is left-terminal if it is forward-looking). We shall achieve our second goal in a sequence of $n - 1$ steps: at the outset of the $m$-th step, we assume that all productions $(b_i, w)$ with $i \geq n - m$ are left-terminal, and we shall arrange that at the conclusion of the $m$-th step, all productions $(b_i, w)$ with $i \geq n - 1 - m$ are left-terminal. Thus, at the conclusion of the $(n - 1)$-st step we shall have achieved our second goal.

To accomplish the task of the $m$-th step, we must eliminate all productions $(b_{n-m}, w)$ that are not left-terminal. By virtue of the first goal, such a production must be forward-looking and, thus, must be of the form $(b_{n-m}, b_j x)$ for some $j > n - m$. Let $(b_j, y^{(1)}), \ldots, (b_j, y^{(q)})$ be the productions of the form

$(b_j, w)$. By virtue of the previous steps, these productions are left-terminal. Thus, if we (1) delete the production $(b_{n-m}, b_j x)$ and (2) add the productions $(b_{n-m}, y^{(1)}x), \ldots, (b_{n-m}, y^{(q)}x)$, the language generated will be unaffected, but we will reduce by one the number of productions $(b_{n-m}, w)$ that are not left-terminal. Thus, by performing this alteration for every production $(b_{n-m}, w)$ that is not left-terminal, we shall accomplish the task of the $m$-th step.

After achieving our second goal, all productions $(b_i, w)$ are left-terminal. Our third goal will be to transform the grammar so that all productions $(c_i, w)$ are left-terminal. Let $(c_i, w)$ be such a production. By inspection of the process creating such productions, the first mark in $w$ must be either a letter or a symbol $b_j$. If the first mark is a letter, the production is left-terminal. Otherwise, it is of the form $(c_i, b_j x)$. Let $(b_j, y^{(1)}), \ldots, (b_j, y^{(q)})$ be the productions of the form $(b_j, w)$. By virtue of our second goal, these productions are left-terminal. Thus, if we (1) delete the production $(c_i, b_j x)$ and (2) add the productions $(c_i, y^{(1)}x), \ldots, (c_i, y^{(q)})$, the language generated will be unaffected, but we will reduce by one the number of productions $(c_i, w)$ that are not left-terminal. Thus, by performing this alteration for every production $(c_i, w)$ that is not left-terminal, we shall achieve our third goal. After achieving our third goal, every production is left-terminal, and the grammar is in the form promised by the theorem.                                                                          □

The proof of Theorem 3.3.2 (like others we have encountered in this chapter) gives us a definite procedure for converting a context-free grammar into one in Greibach normal form. (Scrutiny of this procedure reveals an essential similarity to the procedure for solving a system of linear equations over a field by Gaussian elimination.)

In a derivation of a word according to a grammar in Greibach normal form, each application of a production increases the number of letters in the resulting word by one. It follows that there are exactly as many applications in such a derivation as there are letters in the derived word. This effect of guaranteeing short derivations is one of the most important consequences of the Greibach normal form.

An argument similar to that used to prove Lemmas 3.2.3 and 3.2.5 yields the following pumping lemma for context-free languages.

*Lemma 3.3.3.* Let $L$ be context-free. Then there exists a natural number $n$ such that every word $u \in L$ with length at least $n$ can be written as $u = vwxyz$, with the length of $wy$ at least 1 and the length of $wxy$ at most $n$, such that for all natural numbers $k$, $vw^k xy^k z \in L$.

In contrast to the pumping lemma for linear languages, we can no longer guarantee that the subwords to be pumped are near the ends of the word, though we can guarantee that they are close to each other.

As an example, consider the language Trim $= \{0^m 1^m 2^m : m \geq 1\}$. Applying Lemma 3.3.3 to the word $u = 0^m 1^m 2^m$ for sufficiently large $m$, we find that $u = vwxyz$. Neither $w$ nor $y$ can contain more than one of the three distinct letters 0, 1, and 2, since otherwise $vw^2xy^2z$ would contain letters in the wrong order and, thus, would not belong to Trim. On the other hand, if $w$ and $y$ each contain only one of the three letters 0, 1, and 2, one of these letters does not occur in $wy$, while another one does (since $wy$ is not empty). It follows that $vxz$ does not contain equal numbers of occurrences of 0's, 1's, and 2's and, thus, does not belong to Trim. This contradiction shows that Trim is not context-free.

Since Trim is the intersection of the context-free languages $K = \{0^m 1^m 2^n : m, n \geq 1\}$ and $L = \{0^m 1^n 2^n : m, n \geq 1\}$, we see that $\mathcal{K}$ is not closed under intersections. Since it is closed under unions, it follows that it is also not closed under complementation (since if it were, it would also be closed under intersections, by De Morgan's Laws).

As another example, let $n$ be a positive integer, let $A = \{0, 1, \ldots, 2n - 1\}$, and let $f, g : A^* \to A^*$ be homomorphisms defined by $f(a) = a$ for $0 \leq a \leq n - 1$, $f(a) = \varepsilon$ for $n \leq a \leq 2n - 1$, $g(a) = \varepsilon$ for $0 \leq a \leq n - 1$, and $g(a) = a - n$ for $n \leq a \leq 2n - 1$. Define the language $\mathrm{Eq}_n \subseteq A$ by

$$\mathrm{Eq}_n = \{x \in A^* : f(x) = g(x)\}$$

The language $\mathrm{Eq}_1$ is context-free, though we have seen that it is not linear. Applying Lemma 3.3.3 to the word $u = 0^m 1^m 2^m 3^m \in \mathrm{Eq}_2$ for sufficiently large $m$, we find that $u = vwxyz$. Since the length of $wxy$ is at most $n$, we see that $wy$ cannot contain both 0's and 2's and also that it cannot contain both 1's and 3's. Since $wy$ is not empty, it follows that $vxz$ does not belong to $\mathrm{Eq}_2$. This contradiction shows that $\mathrm{Eq}_2$ is not context-free.

The general theory of context-free languages was founded by Chomsky [1956, 1959], who also proved Proposition 3.3.1. The Greibach normal form is due to Greibach [1965]. The pumping lemma for context-free languages is due to Bar-Hillel, Perlis, and Shamir [1961], and the fact that context-free languages are not closed under intersection is due to Scheinberg [1960].

### *Exercises*

1. (E) Show that every context-free language over an alphabet with just one letter is regular.

2. (M) Show that every $\varepsilon$-free context-free language is generated by a grammar $G = (A, B, s, P)$ in which $P \subseteq B \times (A \cup AB \cup AB^2)$.

3. (E) Show that a derivation of a word of length $n$ according to a grammar in Chomsky normal form has exactly $2n - 1$ applications of productions.

## 3.4. Ambiguity

If $G$ is a context-free grammar and $x \in \text{Lang}(G)$, there will, in general, be many derivations of $x$ according to $G$ corresponding to the applications of different productions and to different orders of applications of productions. The differences among order of application can be neglected to a certain extent. Say that a derivation is *left-most* if in every application $xby \to_G xwy$ of a production $(b, w)$, $x$ contains only letters (so that the occurrence of $b$ replaced by $w$ is the left-most occurrence of any symbol in $xby$). If $x \in \text{Lang}(G)$, then there is a left-most derivation of $x$ according to $G$, since the replacement of one occurrence of a symbol can affect neither the obligation nor the opportunity to replace another occurrence of that or another symbol. Thus, we can reduce the number of derivations we need to consider by focussing our attention on left-most derivations.

We shall say that a context-free grammar $G$ is *unambiguous* if every word in $\text{Lang}(G)$ has exactly one left-most derivation according to $G$. Roughly speaking, this means that $G$ provides a unique parsing for each word in $\text{Lang}(G)$. We shall say that a context-free language is *unambiguous* if it is generated by some unambiguous grammar; otherwise we shall say that it is *inherently ambiguous*.

The most appealing example of an inherently ambiguous context-free language is a close relative of the example that shows that the context-free languages are not closed under intersection. Let

$$K = \{0^m 1^m 2^n : m, n \geq 1\}$$

and

$$L = \{0^m 1^n 2^n : m, n \geq 1\}$$

The intersection

$$K \cap L = \{0^m 1^m 2^m : m \geq 1\}$$

is not context-free, as was shown in Section 3.3. But $K$ and $L$ are each context-free, and therefore so is their union $K \cup L$. We shall show, however, that $K \cup L$ is inherently ambiguous. Roughly speaking, we shall show that every context-free grammar for $K \cup L$ must provide at least two distinct left-most derivations for infinitely many words $0^m 1^m 2^m$ in $K \cap L$: one corresponding to the membership of the word in $K$ and another corresponding to the membership of the word in $L$. The remainder of this section will be devoted to making this assertion precise.

Let the context-free grammar $G$ generate the language Lang($G$), and let $s = u_0 \to_G \cdots \to_G u_n = x$ be a left-most derivation of a word $x \in L$ according to $G$. Let us define a closure system on the set of all occurrences of marks in words $u_0, \ldots, u_n$ of this derivation. Specifically, we shall say that a set of occurrences is closed if, whenever it contains the pattern of some application of a production, it also contains all of the occurrences of marks in the replacement (which are in the succeeding word of the derivation). If $o$ is an occurrence of some symbol in some word of the derivation, the occurrences in the closed set generated by $o$ will be called the *descendants* of $o$ in the derivation. The descendants of $o$ in the derived word $x$ will be called the *phrase subtended* by $o$ in the derivation. The phrases in a derivation have the following simple property: given any two phrases, either they are disjoint, or one of them is contained entirely within the other (that is, if they "overlap," then they are "nested"). Furthermore, all of the derivations corresponding to the same left-most derivation have the same phrases. Thus, our strategy for showing that $K \cup L$ is inherently ambiguous is as follows: for a grammar $G$ that generates $K \cup L$, we shall find two derivations of a word $0^i 1^i 2^i$ that contain phrases that overlap, without either being contained within the other. It will follow that the derivations correspond to different left-most derivations and thus that $G$ is ambiguous.

*Lemma 3.4.1.* For every context-free grammar $G$, there exists a natural number $n$ such that, if $u$ is any word in Lang($G$) in which at least $n$ consecutive occurrences of letters have been "painted," then $u$ can be written as $u = vwxyz$ in such a way that (1) either $w$ and $x$ each contain at least one painted occurrence or $x$ and $y$ each contain at least one painted occurrence, (2) $w$, $x$ and $y$ together contain at most $n$ painted occurrences, and (3) there exists a derivation

$$s \Rightarrow_G vbz \Rightarrow_G vwbyz \Rightarrow_G vwxyz = u$$

(Condition (3) implies that for every $k \geq 0$, $vw^k xy^k z$ belongs to Lang($G$) and has a derivation in which $w^k xy^k$ is a phrase.)

**Proof.** Let $G = (A, B, s, P)$, let $\beta$ denote the cardinality of $B$, and let $q$ denote the maximum number of marks in the replacement of any production. Take $n = q^{\beta+2}$.

Let $u \in \mathrm{Lang}(G)$ have at least $n$ consecutive occurrences of letters painted, and consider any derivation of $u$ according to $G$. Let us say that the "weight" of any occurrence of a symbol in this derivation is the number of painted occurrences of letters in the phrase it subtends. Take a walk from the initial occurrence of $s$ in the derivation, always passing from an occurrence to the mark in its replacement having maximum weight. The weight can fall by at most a factor of $q$ at each step of the walk. The walk terminates at an occurrence of a letter, having weight 1.

Let $\varrho$ be the first occurrence in this walk having weight at most $n$. Then $\varrho$ has weight at least $n/q = q^{\beta+1}$. In the remainder of the walk from $\varrho$, there must be at least $\beta + 1$ occurrences of symbols for which the weight falls at the step taken from that occurrence (including, perhaps, $\varrho$ itself). Thus, at least two of these, say, $\sigma$ followed later by $\tau$, must be occurrences of the same symbol, say, $b$. Let $x$ be the phrase subtended by $\tau$. Let $w$ be the occurrences preceding $x$ in the phrase subtended by $\sigma$, and let $y$ be the occurrences following $x$ in the phrase subtended by $\sigma$. Let $v$ be the occurrences preceding $w$ in $u$, and let $z$ be the occurrences following $y$ in $u$. It is easily verified that this factorization of $u$ satisfies the conditions of the lemma.                                    □

Now let $G$ be any context-free grammar for $K \cup L$ and let $n$ be the number given by Lemma 3.4.1. Let $j = n!$ and let $i = 3j$. We shall find two derivations for $0^i 1^i 2^i$ according to $G$ that have overlapping, but not nested, phrases.

**Proposition 3.4.2.** *There exists a derivation of $0^i 1^i 2^i$ according to $G$ that contains a phrase with at least one occurrence of $0$, at least $2j$ occurrences of $1$, and no occurrences of $2$.*

**Proof.** Apply Lemma 3.4.1 to the word $u = 0^{2j} 1^{2j} 2^{3j}$ in which that last $j$ occurrences of 2 have been painted. We shall show that in the resulting factorization $u = vwxyz$ we have, for some $m \geq 1$, that $w$ consists of $m$ occurrences of 0 and $y$ consists of $m$ occurrences of 1. Since $x$ contains at least one painted 1, all of the 1's in $y$ are painted, and since $y$ contains at most $n$ painted 1's, we have $m \leq n$. Thus $m$ divides $j = n!$, and by taking $k = 1 + j/m$ we obtain a derivation for $vw^k xy^k z = 0^i 1^i 2^i$ in which $w^k xy^k$ is a phrase. This phrase meets the conditions of the proposition: it contains an occurrence of 0 (since $w$ does), it contains at least $2j$ occurrences of 1 (since $xy$ contains all $j$ unpainted 1's and $y^{k-1}$ contains $j$ more 1's), and it contains no occurrence of 2 (since none of $w$, $x$, or $y$ does).

Consider the factorization $u = vwxyz$ given by Lemma 3.4.1. We observe that neither $w$ nor $y$ can contain occurrences of two distinct letters, for otherwise

$vw^2xy^2z$ would contain two distinct letters in the wrong order (that is, 10, 21, or 20). Thus, $w$ and $y$ each contain only occurrences of a single letter. Either $w$ or $y$ must contain occurrences of 1, since only 1's are painted, and either $w$ or $y$ contains at least one painted occurrence. The other must contain occurrences of 0 and must contain an equal number of such occurrences, since only in this way can $vw^kxy^kz$ remain in $K \cup L$ for all $k \geq 0$. □

**Corollary 3.4.3.** *There exists a derivation of $0^i1^i2^i$ according to $G$ that contains a phrase with at least one occurrence of 2, at least $2j$ occurrences of 1, and no occurrences of 0.*

**Proof.** This follows from Proposition 3.4.2 by considering $\text{Rev}(G)$ and $\text{Rev}(K \cup L) = h(K \cup L)$, where $h$ is the homomorphism defined by $h(a) = 3 - a$ that exchanges 0's and 2's. □

Proposition 3.4.2 and Corollary 3.4.3 together yield the desired derivations, since the phrases they refer to must overlap (they each contain at least $2j$ of the $3j$ occurrences of 1) but cannot be nested (since one contains a 0 but no 2, while the other contains a 2 but no 0). This completes the proof that $K \cup L$ is inherently ambiguous.

The first proof of the inherent ambiguity of a context-free language is due to Parikh [1966], who dealt with a slightly more complicated example. Lemma 3.4.1 is due to Ogden [1968].

### *Exercise*

1. (M) Show that the language $\{0^i1^i2^j3^j : i, j \geq 1\} \cup \{0^i1^j2^j3^i : i, j \geq 1\}$ is inherently ambiguous.

### 3.5. Enumerable Languages

We come now to the broadest class of languages generated by grammars. Recall that a language $L$ is *enumerable* if $L = \text{Lang}(G)$ for some grammar $G$. The enumerable languages form a family of languages, which will be denoted $\mathcal{E}$.

Straightforward arguments show that the enumerable languages are closed under union, concatenation, and asteration. The following four closure properties will also be important in our development.

*Lemma 3.5.1.* If $L$ is generated by $G = (A, C, s, P)$ and $h : A^* \to B^*$ is a homomorphism, then $h(L) = \{h(x) : x \in L\}$ is also enumerable.

**Proof.** We may suppose that $A \cap B = \emptyset$. Let $G' = (B, A \cup C, s, P')$, where

$$P' = P \cup \{(a, h(a)) : a \in A\}$$

Then $h(L)$ is generated by $G'$. □

*Lemma 3.5.2.* If $L$ is generated by $G = (A, B, s, P)$ and $L'$ is generated by $G' = (A, B', s', P')$, then $L \cap L'$ is also enumerable.

**Proof.** Let $\hat{G}$ denote the grammar obtained from $G$ by putting a caret "^" over every mark, so that $\hat{G}$ generates a language $\hat{L}$ over the alphabet $\hat{A}$. Similarly, let $\tilde{G}$ denote the grammar obtained from $G'$ by putting a tilde "~" over every mark. Construct the grammar $G'' = (A, B'', s'', P'')$ as follows. Let

$$B'' = \{s''\} \cup \hat{B} \cup \hat{A} \cup \tilde{B}' \cup \tilde{A}$$

and let

$$P'' = \{(s'', \hat{s}\tilde{s}')\} \cup \hat{P} \cup \tilde{P}' \cup \{(\hat{a}\tilde{a}', \tilde{a}'\hat{a}) : a, a' \in A\} \cup \{(\hat{a}\tilde{a}, a) : a \in A\}$$

Then $L \cap L'$ is generated by $G''$. □

*Lemma 3.5.3.* If $L$ is generated by $G = (A, B, s, P)$ and $L'$ is generated by $G' = (A', B', s', P')$, then Shuff$(L, L')$ is also enumerable.

**Proof.** Define $\hat{G}$ and $\tilde{G}'$ as in the proof of Lemma 3.5.2. Construct the grammar $G'' = (A'', B'', s'', P'')$ as follows. Let

$$A'' = A \cup A'$$
$$B'' = \{s''\} \cup \hat{B} \cup \hat{A} \cup \tilde{B}' \cup \tilde{A}$$

and

$$P'' = \{(s'', \hat{s}\tilde{s}')\} \cup \hat{P} \cup \tilde{P}' \cup \{(\hat{a}\tilde{a}', \tilde{a}'\hat{a}) : a, a' \in A\} \cup \{(\hat{a}, a) : a \in A\}$$
$$\cup \{(\tilde{a}', a') : a' \in A'\}$$

Then Shuff$(L, L')$ is generated by $G''$. □

*Lemma 3.5.4.* If $L$ is generated by $G = (B, C, s, P)$ and $h : A^* \to B^*$ is a homomorphism, then $h^{-1}(L) = \{x \in A^* : h(x) \in L\}$ is also enumerable.

**Proof.** We may suppose that $A \cap B = \emptyset$. By Lemma 3.5.3, the language Shuff$(A^*, L)$ is enumerable. Let $R \subseteq (A \cup B)^*$ be the regular language $\{ah(a) : a \in A\}^*$. By Lemma 3.5.2, the language $K = $ Shuff$(A^*, L) \cap R$ is enumerable. Define the homomorphism $g : (A \cup B)^* \to A^*$ by $g(a) = a$ for $a \in A$ and $g(b) = \varepsilon$ for $b \in B$. Then $h^{-1}(L) = g(K)$ is enumerable by Lemma 3.5.1. $\quad\square$

We shall need one more general tool for constructing enumerable languages. Let $f, g : A^* \to B^*$ be homomorphisms. We shall define Eq$(f, g)$ (the *equalizer* of $f$ and $g$) by

$$\text{Eq}(f, g) = \{x \in A^* : f(x) = g(x)\}$$

(Observe that the languages Eq$_n$ defined in Section 3.3 are instances of Eq$(f, g)$ for particular choices of $f$ and $g$.)

*Lemma 3.5.5.* If $f, g : A^* \to B^*$ are homomorphisms, then Eq$(f, g)$ is enumerable.

**Proof.** We first consider a special case. Let $B'$ be the disjoint union of two copies of $B$, with the letters of one copy painted pink, and the letters of the other copy painted blue. Let $f : B'^* \to B^*$ be the homomorphism that bleaches pink letters and erases blue letters, and let $g : B'^* \to B^*$ be the homomorphism that bleaches blue letters and erases pink letters. Let Twin$(B) \subseteq B'^*$ be the language Eq$(f, g)$. It is straightforward to construct a grammar generating Twin$(B)$: there are productions that allow symbols to be generated in matching pairs (one pink, the other blue), productions that allow two adjacent symbols (one pink, the other blue) to exchange places, and productions that allow symbols to be replaced by corresponding letters. Thus Twin$(B)$ is enumerable.

Now consider arbitrary homomorphisms $f, g : A^* \to B^*$. We may suppose that $A \cap B = \emptyset$. By Lemma 3.5.3, the language Shuff$(A^*, \text{Twin}(B))$ is enumerable. Let $f' : A^* \to B'^*$ be the homomorphism whose value is the value of $f$ painted pink, and let $g' : A^* \to B'^*$ be the homomorphism whose value is the value of $g$ painted blue. Let $R \subseteq (A \cup B')^*$ be the regular language $\{af'(a)g'(a) : a \in A\}^*$. Then by Lemma 3.5.2, the language $K = $ Shuff$(A^*, \text{Twin}(B)) \cap R$ is enumerable. Define the homomorphism $h : (A \cap B')^* \to A^*$ by $h(a) = a$ for $a \in A$ and $h(b) = \varepsilon$ for $b \in B'$. Then Eq$(f, g) = h(K)$ is enumerable by Lemma 3.5.1. $\quad\square$

The technique of "painting" letters used in the proof of Lemma 3.5.5 is, of course, equivalent to the technique of adding "diacritical marks," as in the proofs of Lemma 3.5.2 and 3.5.3. The painting metaphor, however, usually leads to more vivid descriptions of constructions and, thus, to more comprehensible proofs.

If $L \subseteq A^*$ is a language, we shall call the set $\{x \in A^* : x \notin L\}$ of words over $A$ not in $L$ the *complement* of $L$ over $A$, and denote it by $\mathrm{Compl}_A(L)$.

We shall say that a language $L \subseteq A^*$ is *decidable* if both $L$ and its complement $\mathrm{Compl}_A(L)$ are enumerable. If $L$ is a language over $A$, then it is also a language over any larger alphabet $A' \supseteq A$. Although $\mathrm{Compl}_A(L)$ depends on the alphabet $A$, the question as to whether $L$ is decidable does not: the languages $\mathrm{Compl}_A(L)$ and $\mathrm{Compl}_{A'}(L)$ differ by a language comprising all words that contain letters from $A' \setminus A$, and this language is regular.

The remainder of this section will be devoted to constructing a language that is enumerable but not decidable, thereby showing that $\mathcal{E}$ is not closed under complementation.

Let $A$ be a finite alphabet, let $c$ be a letter not in $A$, and let $A' = A \cup \{c\}$. Let $\mathrm{Rep}(A, c) \subseteq A'^*$ denote the language

$$\mathrm{Rep}(A, c) = \{(xc)^k x : x \in A^*, k \geq 0\}$$

Thus, a word in $\mathrm{Rep}(A, c)$ consists of one or more repetitions of a word $x$ over $A$, separated by the letter $c$.

*Lemma 3.5.6.* The language $\mathrm{Rep}(A, c)$ is enumerable.

**Proof.** Imagine that we may paint each letter of a word over $A'$ pink or blue, or both (making it violet), or neither (leaving it white). Let $A''$ (with four times as many letters as $A'$) denote the alphabet of these painted letters. Let $R$ be the regular language of over $A''$ comprising all and only the words in which letters except for the first occurrence of a version of $c$ and any preceding letters are painted pink, and all letters except for the last occurrence of a version of $c$ and all succeeding letters are painted blue. Let $f$ be the homomorphism that bleaches all pink letters and erases all letters that are not pink, and let $g$ be the homomorphism that bleaches all letters that are blue and erases all letters that are not blue. Then

$$\mathrm{Rep}(A, c) = R \cap \mathrm{Eq}(f, g)$$

Thus, the lemma follows from Lemmas 3.5.3 and 3.5.5.                    □

Let $A$ be a finite alphabet, and let $c$ and $d$ be letters not in $A$. Let $A'$ denote the alphabet $A \cup \{c, d\}$. Let $\mathrm{Decl}(A, c, d) \subseteq A'^*$ denote the language

$$\mathrm{Decl}(A, c, d) = \{x_1 c \cdots c x_k d y_1 c \cdots c y_l : x_1, \ldots, x_k, y_1, \ldots, y_l \in A^*,$$
$$\forall_{1 \leq j \leq l} \exists_{1 \leq i \leq k} y_j = x_i\}$$

Thus, a word in Decl($A, c, d$) consists of a sequence of zero or more subwords over $A$ separated by occurrences of $c$, followed by the letter $d$, followed by an additional sequence of zero or more subwords over $A$ separated by occurrences of $c$, with each subword after the $d$ matching one of the subwords preceding the $d$. (This language embodies the process of checking the identifiers used in the body of a program block against those declared at the head of the block, in a language such as Algol, in which identifiers must be declared before they are used.)

*Lemma 3.5.7.* The language Decl($A, c, d$) is enumerable.

**Proof.** Let $e$ be a letter not in $A'$, and let $A'' = A' \cup \{e\}$. Let $L = \mathrm{Rep}(A, e) \cdot \{d\} \cdot (A \cup \{c\})^*$. By Lemma 3.5.6 and closure under regular operations, $L$ is enumerable. By taking a homomorphic reflection of $L$, we may paint some of the occurrences of letters pink and others blue. By intersecting with a suitable regular language, we may ensure that the pink letters comprise zero or more complete subwords over $A$ and preceding the unique $d$ and that the blue letters comprise all the subwords over $A$ following the $d$. Let $L'$ denote the resulting language. Then

$$\mathrm{Decl}(A, c, d) = L' \cap \mathrm{Eq}(f, g)$$

where $f$ and $g$ are homomorphisms that bleach all letters that are pink and blue, respectively, and erase all letters that are blue and pink, respectively. Thus, the lemma follows from Lemmas 3.5.3 and 3.5.5. □

We shall want to encode grammars using words that can themselves be generated by grammars. We shall assume that all of the grammars we wish to encode have an alphabet of letters that is a subset of the infinite alphabet $\{a_0, a_1, \ldots\}$ and an alphabet of symbols that is a subset of the infinite alphabet $\{b_0, b_1, \ldots\}$. We shall encode all of these marks using just three letters, say, 0, 1, and 2. Specifically, we shall encode the letter $a_k$ by the word $10^k$ and the symbol $b_k$ by the word $20^k$. We shall encode a production $(v, w)$ by the word encoding the pattern $v$, followed by an occurrence of the letter 3, followed by the word encoding the replacement $w$. We shall set $P$ of productions by the words encoding the productions (in some order), separated by occurrences of the letter 4. We may take the encoding of $P$ as the encoding of the grammar $G = (A, B, s, P)$, where $A$ is the alphabet of letters occurring in productions in $P$, $B$ is the alphabet of symbols occurring in productions in $P$, and $s$ is taken to be the symbol $b_0$. We observe that every grammar using only the letters and symbols we have adopted can be encoded in this way, and that every grammar is equivalent (to within a renaming of the letters and symbols) to one of this form.

Let Gram $\subseteq \{0, 1, 2, 3, 4\}^*$ denote the language comprising all of the encodings of grammars as just described. The language Gram is regular.

We shall encode an application of a production $(v, w)$ to produce $xwy$ from $xvy$ by the word encoding the left context $x$, followed by an occurrence of the letter 5, followed by the word encoding the pattern $v$, followed by an occurrence of the letter 5, followed by the word encoding the replacement $w$, followed by an occurrence of the letter 5, followed by the word encoding the right context $y$. We shall encode a sequence of such applications by the words encoding the individual applications, separated by occurrences of the letter 6.

Let Seq $\subseteq \{0, 1, 2, 5, 6\}^*$ denote the language comprising all encodings of sequences of applications as just described. The language Seq is regular.

Let Deriv $\subseteq$ Gram $\cdot \{7\} \cdot$ Seq denote the language in which the sequence of applications encoded by the word following the occurrence of 7 forms a derivation according to the grammar encoded by the word preceding the occurrence of the letter 7. There are four conditions implicit in this definition: (1) the pattern of the first application is the starting symbol, and its left- and right-contexts are empty; (2) for each successive pair of applications, the left-context followed by the replacement followed by the right-context of the first application is equal to the left-context followed by the pattern followed by the right-context of the second application; (3) the left-context, replacement, and right-context of the last application consist entirely of letters; and (4) the pattern and replacement of each application match the pattern and replacement of some production of the grammar.

*Lemma 3.5.8.* The language Deriv is enumerable.

**Proof.** It will suffice to verify that the four languages comprising the words satisfying the four conditions just stated are each enumerable, since they may then be intersected with each other and the regular language Gram $\cdot \{7\} \cdot$ Seq to yield Deriv. The languages corresponding to conditions (1) and (3) are, in fact, regular. To check condition (2), we start with Gram $\cdot \{7\} \cdot$ Seq, and use a homomorphic reflection to paint some occurrences of letters pink, or blue, or both. By intersecting with a suitable regular language, we can check that the pink letters comprise the left-context, replacement, and right-context of every application except the last, separated by occurrences of the letter 6, and that the blue letters comprise the left-context, pattern, and right-context of every application except the first, separated by occurrences of the letter 6. We can then check condition (2) by intersecting with the language Eq($f$, $g$) for an appropriate choice of homomorphisms $f$ and $g$, then take a homomorphic image to bleach all letters. To check condition (4), we use a similar construction, except that we paint the pattern and replacement of each production in the grammar, and the pattern and replacement of each application in the sequence, with appropriate separators, then intersect with homomorphic reflection of Decl to check the condition and take a homomorphic image to bleach all letters. □

Let Prod $\subseteq$ Gram $\cdot$ {7} $\cdot$ {0, 1}* denote the language comprising all words for which the word encoded by the word following the 7 belongs to the language generated by the grammar encoded by the word preceding the 7.

**Proposition 3.5.9.** *The language Prod is enumerable.*

**Proof.** We start with the language Deriv. By taking a homomorphic reflection we paint some of the letters. By intersecting with a suitable regular language, we check that the painted letters comprise the encoding of the grammar, the occurrence of 7, and the left-context, replacement, and right-context of the last application of the sequence. Taking a homomorphic image that erases all unpainted letters yields Prod. □

The language Prod is over the alphabet {0, ..., 7}. Its definition involves grammars and languages with alphabets of the form $\{a_0, \ldots, a_k\}$ for any $k$. If we agree that the letters 0, ..., 7 "correspond" to the letters $a_0, \ldots, a_7$, then we can interpret words in Prod as assertions about languages and grammars including Prod itself and grammars defining it. This correspondence is embodied in a homomorphism $h : \{0, \ldots, 7\}^* \to \{0, 1\}^*$. Let Diag be the language comprising the words of the form $u7x$, where $u \in$ Gram and $h(u) = x$.

*Lemma 3.5.10.* The language Diag is enumerable.

**Proof.** The language Diag is defined as the intersection of a regular language with the equalizer of two homomorphisms. □

**Theorem 3.5.11.** *The complement of the language Prod is not enumerable.*

**Proof.** Suppose that the complement of Prod is enumerable. By intersecting with the enumerable language Diag, we conclude that the language Paradox, comprising all words of the form $u7x$ for which $u \in$ Gram, $h(u) = x$, and $x$ does not belong to the grammar encoded by $u$, is enumerable. Since Paradox is enumerable it is generated by some grammar $G$. Let $\hat{u}$ be a word encoding $G$ and let $\hat{x} = h(\hat{u})$. Then $\hat{u}7\hat{x} \in$ Diag. Furthermore, we have that $\hat{x}$ belongs to the language generated by the grammar encoded by $\hat{u}$ if and only if $\hat{u}7\hat{x} \in$ Prod if and only if $\hat{u}7\hat{x} \notin$ Paradox if and only if $\hat{x}$ does not belong to the language generated by the grammar encoded by $\hat{u}$. This contradiction completes the proof. □

The generation of enumerable languages by grammars was first described by Chomsky [1959], though the notion of enumerable set of other objects (natural numbers, for example) was by then well known (this will be discussed more fully in Chapter 4). The complement of the language Diag and the proof of Theorem 3.5.11 have many precursors in mathematics: the "paradox of the liar" (based on a statement that asserts its own falsehood), G. Cantor's diagonal argument (used to prove that the cardinality of Pow($U$) is strictly greater than that of $U$), B. Russell's paradox (based on the assumption that there exists a set that contains all and only those sets that do not contain themselves), and K. Gödel's theorem (based on a proposition that asserts its own unprovability).

The notions of enumerable and decidable languages developed in this section provide an important "meta-theoretic" tool for language theory. That is, they may be used to reflect the study of language theory as problems of language theory. In order to speak of the decidability or undecidability particular problem one must first express it as a language over a finite alphabet. A historically central problem of this sort is the "Post Correspondence Problem," which is to determine whether the equalizer Eq($f, g$) of two homomorphisms $f, g: A^* \to B^*$ is empty. Here a natural way to represent the homomorphisms is to give the values of $f(a)$ and $g(a)$ for all $a \in A$ as a sequence of words over $B$ separated by suitable delimiters. Post [1946] showed that the resulting language is undecidable; the instances in which Eq($f, g$) $\neq \emptyset$ are clearly enumerable, so that this means that the instances in which Eq($f, g$) $= \emptyset$ are *not* enumerable.

Using the Post Correspondence Problem as the point of departure, subsequent researchers have shown many natural problems concerning languages to be undecidable. In these problems, it is assumed that a recognizable language is represented by a regular or logical expression (or a right- or left-linear grammar), and that a linear, context-free, or enumerable language is represented by a grammar of the corresponding type.

It is easy to show using the procedures described in Chapter 2 that all of the most natural problems involving recognizable languages are decidable: one can determine whether a recognizable language is empty, finite, co-finite, or full, and of course one can solve the "membership problem," to determine whether a given word belongs to a given recognizable language.

For linear and context-free languages, the procedures given earlier in this chapter show that it is decidable to determine whether such a language is empty or finite, and to solve the membership problem, but Bar-Hillel, Perlis, and Shamir [1961] and Chomsky and Schützenberger [1963] have shown that it is undecidable to determine whether a context-free language is recognizable, co-finite or full, and Greibach [1966] has shown that it is undecidable to determine whether a context-free language is linear. It is undecidable whether a particular context-free grammar is ambiguous (as was shown independently by Cantor [1962], Floyd [1962] and Chomsky and Schützenberger [1963]), and whether a context-free language is inherently ambiguous (see Ginsburg and Ullian [1962]).

For enumerable languages, we are at the opposite extreme from the recognizable languages, and most natural questions are easily seen to be undecidable. This phenomenon is so sweeping that it can be established as an explicit "meta-theorem"; this will be presented as Rice's Theorem in the next chapter.

Language theory is, of course, not the only branch of mathematics to present decision problems, and the process of showing various classical problems to be undecidable took place in other areas as well. One of the most fruitful of these areas is that of the combinatorial "word problems" for presentations of various algebraic structures. Post [1947] inaugurated this line of work by showing the word problem for semigroups to be undecidable; the analogous result for groups was a long sought prize that eluded many efforts before being won by P. S. Novikov (see Stillwell [1982]). (The word problems for *commutative* semigroups and groups are decidable.)

Another class of structures whose word problems have been studied is that of lattices. Free lattices have a decidable word problem (see Whitman [1941]), as do free *distributive* lattices (which are in fact finite), but the word problem for free *modular* lattices on five or more generators is undecidable (see Freese [1980]).

No discussion of undecidability results would be complete without mention of problem of determining whether a multivariate polynomial with integer coefficients has a solution in integers (the problem of "Diophantine equations"). This was first posed (as a demand for an algorithm) by Hilbert [1901–1902] in his famous list of problems; it was 10th on his list of 23 problems, and thus became known simply as "Hilbert's Tenth Problem." By the time that a theory capable of proving undecidability results was developed (in the 1930s), the consensus seemed to be that Hilbert's Tenth Problem was undecidable; decisive progress was made by M. Davis, H. Putnam and J. Robinson in the 1950s, but it was not until 1970 that the final step in proving undecidability was taken by Yu. Matiyasevich (see Davis [1973]).

### Exercise

1. (U) Determine whether the word problem for the free modular lattice on four generators is decidable or undecidable. (The free modular lattices on

three or fewer generators are finite; for four generators the free modular lattice is known to be infinite, as was shown by Birkhoff [1948].)

### 3.6. Rational Cones

In this section we shall introduce a notion, that of rational cones, that allows all of the families of languages studied earlier in this chapter to be viewed from a new perspective.

We shall say that a family of languages is a *ray* if it satisfies the following condition:

> $RC_1$  $C$ is closed under homomorphic reflections: if $L \in C$, $L \subseteq B^*$ and $h : A^* \to B^*$ is a homomorphism, then $h^{-1}(L) \in C$.

We shall say that a ray $C$ is a *rational cylinder* if it satisfies the following additional condition:

> $RC_2$  $C$ is closed under intersections with regular languages: if $L, R \in A^*$, $L \in C$ and $R$ is regular, then $L \cap R \in C$.

We shall say that a rational cylinder $C$ is a *rational cone* if it satisfies the following additional condition:

> $RC_3$  $C$ is closed under homomorphic images: if $L \in C$, $L \subseteq A^*$ and $h : A^* \to B^*$ is a homomorphism, then $h(L) \in C$.

If a rational cone contains a language that contains a word, then by taking first the image and then the reflection under a homomorphism that erases everything, we obtain first the language containing only the empty word, then the language that contains all words over a given alphabet. From that language, any regular language over that alphabet can then be obtained by intersecting with an appropriate regular language. Thus, if a rational cone contains a non-empty language, it contains all regular languages. Some authors define rational cones so that they must contain a non-empty language and, thus, so that the regular languages form the smallest rational cone. This difference only adds or subtracts the empty cone and the cone comprising only the empty language, and it has no effect on the greater part of the theory.

Since rational cones are defined by closure conditions, there is a smallest rational cone Cone($C$), the rational cone generated by $C$, containing any given set $C$ of languages. If $C$ contains just a single language $L$, we shall write Cone($L$) rather than Cone($C$). A rational cone is called *principal* if it is generated by a single language.

**Proposition 3.6.1 (Engelfriet and Rozenberg [1980]).** *The enumerable languages $\mathcal{E}$ form a principal rational cone generated by $Eq_2$.*

**Proof.** That $\mathcal{E}$ is a rational cone follows from Lemmas 3.5.1, 3.5.2, and 3.5.4 together with the fact that regular languages are enumerable.

That $Eq_2$ belongs to $\mathcal{E}$ follows from Lemma 3.5.5. It remains to show that a rational cone containing $Eq_2$ includes $\mathcal{E}$. Since $Eq_n$ is the reflection of $Eq_2$ under the homomorphism defined by $h(a) = 10^a$ for $0 \le a < n$ and $h(a) = 32^{a-n}$ for $n \le a < 2n$, it will suffice to show that a rational cone containing $Eq_n$ for each $n \ge 2$ includes $\mathcal{E}$. The proof of Lemma 3.5.5 shows that such a cone contains all equalizers $Eq(f, g)$. Let $G = (A, B, s, P)$ be a grammar. Let $c$ be a mark not in $A \cup B$, and set $C = \{c\}$. We shall define an alphabet $D$ and two homomorphisms $f, g : D^* \to (A \cup B \cup C)^*$ as follows. The alphabet $D$ will have four parts: $D = D_\sigma \cup D_\pi \cup D_\kappa \cup D_\tau$. For each mark $d \in A \cup C$, $D_\tau$ will contain a letter $\tau_d$ with $f(\tau_d) = d$ and $g(\tau_d) = \varepsilon$. For each mark $d \in A \cup B \cup C$, $D_\kappa$ will contain a letter $\kappa_d$ with $f(\kappa_d) = g(\kappa_d) = d$. For each production $(v, w) \in P$, $D_\pi$ will contain a letter $\pi_{(v,w)}$ with $f(\pi_{(v,w)}) = v$ and $g(\pi_{(v,w)}) = w$. Finally, $D_\sigma$ will contain a letter $\sigma$ with $f(\sigma) = \varepsilon$ and $g(\sigma) = sc$. Then the language $Eq(f, g) \subseteq D^*$ belongs to any rational cone containing $Eq_n$ for all $n \ge 2$. Define the regular language $R$ by

$$R = D_\sigma \cdot (D_\pi \cup D_\kappa)^* \cdot \{\tau_a : a \in A\}^* \cdot \{\tau_c\}$$

Then the language $Eq(f, g) \cap R$ belongs to any rational cone containing $Eq_2$. Finally, define the homomorphism $h : D^* \to A^*$ by $h(\tau_a) = a$ for $a \in A$ and $h(d) = \varepsilon$ for $d \in D \setminus \{\tau_a : a \in A\}$. Then $Lang(G) = h(Eq(f, g) \cap R)$ belongs to any rational cone containing $Eq_n$ for all $n \ge 2$. $\qquad\square$

**Proposition 3.6.2.** *The context-free languages $\mathcal{K}$ form a principal rational cone generated by $Dyck_2$.*

**Proof.** We begin by proving that $\mathcal{K}$ is a rational cone. To prove condition $RC_3$, let $L$ be generated by the grammar $G = (A, C, s, P)$, and let $h : A^* \to B^*$ be a homomorphism. To obtain a grammar generating $h(L)$, we replace $A$ by $B$, replace $C$ by $C \cup A$ (we may assume that $C \cap A = \emptyset$), and add to $P$ all productions of the form $(a, h(a))$ for $a \in A$.

To prove condition $RC_2$, let $L$ be generated by the grammar $G = (A, B, s, P)$, and let $L'$ be accepted by the deterministic finite automaton $M = (A, Q, I, J, R)$ with successor map $S$ corresponding to $R$. Without loss of generality, we may assume that neither $L'$ nor $L$ contains $\varepsilon$. Furthermore, we may assume that $G$ is in Chomsky normal form, that is, that $P \subseteq B \times (A \cup B^2)$ (see Proposition 3.3.1). Construct a new grammar $G' = (A, B', s', P')$ as follows. Let $B' = \{s'\} \cup B \times Q \times Q$. We want to define $P'$ so that $(b, q, q') \Rightarrow_{G'} x \in A^*$ if and only if (i) $b \Rightarrow_G x$ and (ii) $S_x(q) = q'$. To do this we replace each production $(b, a) \in B \times A$ in $P$ by all productions $((b, q, q'), a)$ in $P'$ such that $S_a(q) = q'$. Furthermore, we replace each production $(b, cc') \in B \times B^2$ in $P$ by all productions $((b, q, q'), (c, q, r)(c', r, q'))$ in $P'$ such that $r \in Q$. Then if we add to $P'$ the productions $(s', (s, i, j))$, for all $i \in I$ and $j \in J$, we have $L \cap L' = \text{Lang}(G')$.

To prove condition $RC_1$, let $L$ be generated by the grammar $G = (B, C, s, P)$, and let $h : A^* \to B^*$ be a homomorphism. We may assume that $A \cap B = \emptyset$. Define the homomorphism $f : (A \cup B)^* \to A^*$ by $f(a) = a$ for $a \in A$ and $f(b) = \varepsilon$ for $b \in B$, and the homomorphism $g : (A \cup B)^* \to B^*$ by $g(a) = \varepsilon$ for $a \in A$ and $g(b) = b$ for $b \in B$. The language $g^{-1}(L)$ is generated by the grammar $G' = (A \cup B, C \cup \{e\}, s, P')$, where $e$ is a new symbol not in $C$, and $P'$ is obtained from $P$ by replacing each production $(c, y_1 \cdots y_k)$ by $(c, ey_1 \cdots ey_k e)$ and adding the productions $(e, \varepsilon)$ and $(e, ae)$ for $a \in A$. Thus, $g^{-1}(L) \in \mathcal{K}$.

The language $L' = \{ah(a) : a \in A\}^* \subseteq (A \cup B)^*$ is regular, and so by condition $RC_2$ we have $g^{-1}(L) \cap L' \in \mathcal{K}$. Thus, by condition $RC_1$, $f(g^{-1}(L) \cap L') \in \mathcal{K}$. But it is easy to see that $f(g^{-1}(L) \cap L') = h^{-1}(L)$, which completes the proof that $\mathcal{K}$ is a rational cone.

We have already seen that $\text{Dyck}_2$ is a context-free language. It remains to show that a rational cone containing $\text{Dyck}_2$ includes $\mathcal{K}$. Since $\text{Dyck}_n$ is the reflection of $\text{Dyck}_2$ under the homomorphism defined by $h(a) = 10^a$ for $0 \le a < n$ and $h(a) = 32^{a-n}$ for $n \le a < 2n$, it will suffice to show that a rational cone containing $\text{Dyck}_n$ for each $n \ge 2$ includes $\mathcal{K}$.

Let $L$ be generated by $G = (B, C, I, P)$. Let $n$ be the cardinality of $B \cup C$, where of course $B \cap C = \emptyset$. For clarity we shall denote the elements of $A = \{0, \ldots, 2n - 1\}$ by subscripted brackets: $[_a$ and $]_a$ for $a \in B \cup C$. We shall take $R = R_0 \cdot (R_1 \cup R_2)^*$, where $R_0$, $R_1$, and $R_2$ are finite languages defined as follows. Let $R_0 = \{[_c : c \in I\}$, let $R_1 = \{]_c[_{y_k} \cdots [_{y_1} : (c, y_1 \cdots y_k) \in P\}$, and let $R_2 = \{]_b : b \in B\}$. We shall define the homomorphism $h : A^* \to B^*$ by $h(]_b) = b$ for $b \in B$, $h(]_c) = \varepsilon$ for $c \in C$, and $h([_a) = \varepsilon$ for $a \in B \cup C$. It is now routine to verify that each word $w$ in $\text{Dyck}_n \cap R$ corresponds to a Polish encoding of a left-most derivation for $h(w)$, and that every left-most derivation for a word $x$ is encoded by a word in $\text{Dyck}_n \cap R \cap h^{-1}(x)$.                    $\square$

Proposition 3.6.2 is due in essence to Chomsky and Schützenberger [1963], though the notion of rational cone was not explicit at that time. Much work has been done on characterizing the context-free languages that generate the rational cone $\mathcal{K}$; see Beauquier [1979] and Beauquier and Gire [1987].

The following proposition, which we state without proof, is obtained by arguments similar to those given for Proposition 3.6.2.

**Proposition 3.6.3.** *The linear languages $\mathcal{K}$ form a principal rational cone generated by $Sym_2$.*

We now turn to an alternative characterization of rational cones. Let $A_1, \ldots, A_k$ be finite alphabets. A subset $K$ of $A_1^* \times \cdots \times A_k^*$ will be called a *k-ary relation* over $A_1, \ldots, A_k$. A language is, of course, a unary relation (that is, one with $k = 1$).

Let $A_1, \ldots, A_k$ be finite alphabets. A class $\mathcal{R}$ of relations over $A_1, \ldots, A_k$ will be called *regularly closed* if it satisfies the following six conditions:

RR$_1$  The empty relation $\emptyset$ belongs to $\mathcal{R}$.

RR$_2$  The relation $\{(\varepsilon, \ldots, \varepsilon)\}$ containing only the list of empty words belongs to $\mathcal{R}$.

RR$_3$  For each $1 \le j \le k$ and each letter $a \in A_j$, the language $\{(\varepsilon, \ldots, \varepsilon, a, \varepsilon, \ldots, \varepsilon)\}$ containing just one list with one letter in one position belongs to $\mathcal{R}$.

RR$_4$  If $K$ and $K'$ belong to $\mathcal{R}$, then $K \cup K'$ belongs to $\mathcal{R}$.

RR$_5$  If $K$ and $K'$ belong to $\mathcal{R}$, then $K \cdot K'$ belongs to $\mathcal{R}$.

RR$_6$  If $K$ belongs to $\mathcal{R}$, then $K^*$ belongs to $\mathcal{R}$.

In condition RR$_5$, we define

$$K \cdot K' = \{(x_1 \cdot x_1', \ldots, x_k \cdot x_k') : (x_1, \ldots, x_k) \in K, (x_1', \ldots, x_k') \in K'\}$$

and in condition RR$_6$ we define

$$K^* = \bigcup_{n \ge 0} K^n,$$

where $K^0 = \{(\varepsilon, \ldots, \varepsilon)\}$ and, for $n \ge 0$, $K^{n+1} = K^n \cdot K$. In the case of $k = 1$, these definitions reduce to those for languages.

It is natural to seek a characterization of $\mathcal{R}^*$ in terms of machines such as non-deterministic finite automata. Care must be used in doing this, however, since distinctions that are unimportant in the case of languages become important in the case of relations.

Define a *generalized k-ary* non-deterministic finite automaton to be a quintuple

$$M = ((A_1, \ldots, A_k), Q, I, J, R)$$

where the transition rule $R$ is a finite subset of $A_1^* \times A_k^* \times Q \times Q$. Say that a generalized $k$-ary non-deterministic finite automaton accepts a list $x = (x_1, \ldots, x_k)$ of words if and only if there exist a sequence $q_0, \ldots, q_n \in Q$ of states and a sequence $y_1, \ldots, y_n \in A_1^* \times \cdots \times A_k^*$ of lists of words such that (1) $q_0 \in I$, (2) $q_n \in J$, (3) $x = y_1 \cdot \cdots \cdot y_n$, and (4) for $0 \leq m \leq n - 1$, $(y_m, q_m, q_{m+1}) \in R$. If $M$ is a generalized $k$-ary non-deterministic finite automaton, the relation comprising the lists accepted by $M$ will be denoted Rel($M$). A $k$-ary relation $K$ is called a *rational relation* if $K = \text{Rel}(M)$ for some generalized $k$-ary non-deterministic finite automaton. Let $\mathcal{R}^*$ denote the class of rational relations.

**Proposition 3.6.4.** *The class $\mathcal{R}^*$ is regularly closed.*

**Proposition 3.6.5.** *If $\mathcal{R}$ is regularly closed, then $\mathcal{R}^* \subseteq \mathcal{R}$.*

Propositions 3.6.4 and 3.6.5, which will not be proved here, establish the rational relations as a generalization of the regular languages, which are the special case of unary relations. The formulation that we have presented is due to Elgot and Mezei [1965].

The extension of our formalism from languages to relations brings with it an important operation: composition.

Let $K \subseteq A_1^* \times \cdots \times A_k^*$ be a $k$-ary relation, and let $K' \subseteq B_1^* \times \cdots \times B_l^*$ be an $l$-ary relation. Suppose further that $A_k = B_1$. By the *composition* of $K$ and $K'$ we shall mean the $(k+l-2)$-ary relation $K \circ K' \subseteq A_1^* \times \cdots \times A_{k-1}^* \times B_2^* \times \cdots \times B_l^*$ defined by

$$K \circ K' = \{(x_1, \ldots, x_{k-1}, y_2, \ldots, y_l) : (x_1, \ldots, x_{k-1}, z) \in K$$
$$\text{and } (z, y_2, \ldots, y_l) \in K' \text{ for some } z \in A_k^* = B_1^*\}$$

**Theorem 3.6.6 (Elgot and Mezei [1965]).** *If $K$ and $K'$ are rational relations, and the last alphabet of $K$ equals the first alphabet of $K'$, then $K \circ K'$ is also a rational relation.*

**Proof.** A generalized non-deterministic finite automaton $M''$ accepting $K \circ K'$ can be constructed from generalized non-deterministic finite automata $M$ and $M'$ accepting $K$ and $K'$, respectively. In essence, $M''$ non-deterministically "guesses" the word $z$ and runs $M$ and $M'$ as "coroutines" to verify that $(x_1, \ldots, x_{k-1}, z) \in K$ and $(z, y_2, \ldots, y_l) \in K'$, respectively. $\square$

The operation of composition derives its name from the important special case $k = l = 2$, where it corresponds to composition of functions (when the relations involved are functional: for every $x_1 \in A_1^*$ there is a unique $x_2 \in A_2^*$ such that $(x_1, x_2) \in K$). Another important special case is $k = 2$ and $l = 1$, in which $K'$ is a language $L$. In this case, the composition $K \circ L$ is called the *transduction* of $L$ by $K$. If $K$ is rational, then $K \circ L$ is called a *rational transduction* of $L$.

Let $L$ and $L'$ be languages. We shall write "$L \leq_{rat} L'$" if $L$ is a rational transduction of $L'$. This suggestive notation is appropriate because the relation $\leq_{rat}$ is (1) reflexive (since the "identity relation" given by $\bigcup_{a \in A} (a, \varepsilon) \cdot (\varepsilon, a)^*$ is rational) and (2) transitive (by Theorem 3.6.6 and the associativity of composition). Thus, if we define $L \equiv_{rat} L'$ (read "$L$ is rationally equivalent to $L'$") to mean that $L \leq_{rat} L'$ and $L' \leq_{rat} L$, then the relation $\equiv_{rat}$ is an equivalence.

We shall say that a class $\mathcal{L}$ of languages is *saturated* if it is closed under rational transduction, that is, if $L \in \mathcal{L}$ and $L' \leq_{rat} L$ imply $L' \in \mathcal{L}$. The following theorem ties together rational cones and rational relations.

**Theorem 3.6.7 (Nivat [1968]).** *A language $L \subseteq B^*$ is a rational transduction of a language $L' \subseteq C^*$ if and only if there exist (1) a finite alphabet $A$, (2) a regular language $L'' \subseteq A^*$, and (3) two homomorphisms $f : A^* \to B^*$ and $g : A^* \to C^*$ such that*

$$L = f(g^{-1}(L') \cap L'') \tag{3.6.1}$$

**Proof.** To prove the "if" part, it will suffice to show that intersection with a regular language, homomorphic images and homomorphic reflections are each rational transductions, since then their composition in Eq. (3.6.1) will also be a rational transduction by Theorem 3.6.6. If $L'' \subseteq A^*$ is a regular language, then by replacing the primitive expressions $\{\varepsilon\}$ and $\{a\}$ in a regular expression for $L''$ by the expressions $\{(\varepsilon, \varepsilon)\}$ and $\{(a, \varepsilon)\} \cdot \{(\varepsilon, a)\}$, respectively, we obtain a regular expression for a rational relation $K$ such that $K \circ \hat{L} = L'' \cap \hat{L}$ for every language $\hat{L} \subseteq A^*$. If $f : A^* \to B^*$ is a homomorphism, then the regular expression $\{(f(a), a) : a \in A\}^*$ defines a rational relation $K$ such that $K \circ \hat{L} = f(\hat{L})$ for every language $\hat{L} \subseteq A^*$. Finally, if $g : A^* \to C^*$ is a homomorphism, then the regular expression $\{(a, g(a)) : a \in A\}^*$ defines a rational relation $K$ such that $K \circ \hat{L} = g^{-1}(\hat{L})$ for every language $\hat{L} \subseteq C^*$.

To prove the "only if" part, let $L = K \circ L'$, where $K$ is accepted by $M = (B, C, Q, I, J, R)$. Take $A = R \subseteq B^* \times C^* \times Q \times Q$. Let $L'' = L_0 \cap L_1 \cap L_2$, where $L_0 = \{(y, z, i, q) \in A : i \in I\} \cdot A^*$ (this describes sequences of transitions that begin in an initial state), $L_1 = \{(y, z, q, j) \in A : j \in J\} \cdot A^*$ (this describes sequences of transitions that end in a final state), and the language $L_2$ is the complement of the union, over all pairs $r' \neq r$ of distinct states in $Q$, of the languages $A^* \cdot \{(y, z, q, q') \in A : q' = r'\} \cdot \{(y, z, q, q') \in A : q = r\} \cdot A^*$

(this describes all sequences of transitions in which the state to which each transition arrives is the state from which its successor departs). Define $f$ and $g$ by $f((y, z, q, q')) = y$ and $g((y, z, q, q')) = z$. Then Eq. (3.6.1) is straightforward to verify. $\quad\square$

**Corollary 3.6.8.** *A class of languages is a rational cone if and only if it is saturated.*

**Proof.** If $\mathcal{L}$ is a rational cone, and thus is closed under the operations appearing in Eq. (3.6.1) then it is closed under rational transductions by Theorem 3.6.7 and, thus, is saturated. Conversely, if $\mathcal{L}$ is closed under rational transductions, then by taking two of the three elements $R$, $f$, and $g$ to be trivial ($R = A^*$, $f(x) = x$ or $g(x) = x$) we conclude that $\mathcal{L}$ is closed under the operations defining a rational cone. $\quad\square$

### Exercises

1. (M) Show that the rational relations are not closed under intersection (and thus are not closed under complement). (Hint: Consider the relations defined by the regular expressions $(2, 0)^*(\varepsilon, 1)^*$ and $(\varepsilon, 0)^*(2, 1)^*$.)
2. (H) Show that if $K$ and $L$ are languages over disjoint alphabets and if $K \cdot L \leq_{\text{rat}} \text{Eq}_1$, then either $K$ is recognizable or $L$ is recognizable. Observe that if $K = \{0^a 1^b : a \geq b \geq 0\}$ and $L = \{2^c 3^d : d \geq c \geq 0\}$, then $K \cdot L \leq_{\text{rat}} \text{Dyck}_1$. Conclude that $\text{Dyck}_1 \not\leq_{\text{rat}} \text{Eq}_1$. (See Latteux [1977].)
3. (H) Show that if $L \subseteq A^*$ is commutative (that is, if $wxyz \in L$ if and only if $wyxz \in L$, for all $w, x, y, z \in A^*$) and if $L \leq_{\text{rat}} \text{Dyck}_1$, then $L$ is recognizable. Conclude that $\text{Eq}_1 \not\leq_{\text{rat}} \text{Dyck}_1$. (See Latteux and Rozenberg [1984].)
4. (H) Say two languages are *rationally isomorphic* if one is a transduction of the other under a rational relation that is also a bijection. (a) Show that rational isomorphism is an equivalence relation. (b) Classify the recognizable languages with respect to rational isomorphism according to the number of words of various lengths that they contain. (See Maurer and Nivat [1980].)
5. (U) Prove or disprove: the intersection of two principal rational cones is itself principal.

### 3.7. Rational Cylinders and Rays

Recall that a ray is a family of languages closed under homomorphic reflections. A ray $\mathcal{R}$ is principal if there exists a language $K$ such that, for every language

$L \in \mathcal{R}$, there exists a homomorphism $h$ such that $L = h^{-1}(K)$. In this case, $K$ is said to be a generator of the ray $\mathcal{R}$. (Note that if $\mathcal{R}$ is a rational cone, it is also a ray, but a generator of the cone $\mathcal{R}$ is not necessarily a generator of the ray $\mathcal{R}$.) The ray generated by a language $K$ will be denoted Ray($K$).

If $h$ is a homomorphism, then $h^{-1}(K)$ contains the empty word if and only if $K$ contains the empty word. Thus, we shall always consider separately the cases in which a language does or does not contain the empty word. We shall state theorems for $\varepsilon$-free languages, but they have obvious analogues for languages that contain the empty word.

**Proposition 3.7.1.** *The family of $\varepsilon$-free context-free languages is a principal ray.*

The proof, which will not be given here, depends upon the Greibach normal form for context-free grammars. The resulting generator $K_0$ of the ray is called a "hardest context-free language," since any device for recognizing or parsing words from $K_0$ will serve to recognize or parse the words of any other $\varepsilon$-free context-free language after pre-processing these words by a homomorphism.

The quest for an analog of Proposition 3.7.1 for the linear languages does not reveal any obvious candidate; the following proposition, however, gives an infinite sequence that generates the ray of linear languages.

**Proposition 3.7.2.** *There exists a sequence $S_0, S_1, S_2, \ldots,$ of $\varepsilon$-free linear languages such that (1) for $n \geq 0$, $S_n$ belongs to $Ray(S_{n+1})$, and (2) the family of all $\varepsilon$-free linear languages is the union of the principal rays $Ray(S_n)$ for $n \in \mathbf{N}$.*

The proof is similar to that of Proposition 3.7.1, but is complicated by the absence of an analogue of the Greibach normal form for linear grammars.

Recall that a *rational cylinder* is a family of languages closed under homomorphic reflections and intersections with regular languages. A rational cylinder $C$ is principal if there exists a language $K$ such that, for every language $L \in C$, there exists a homomorphism $h$ such that $L = h^{-1}(K)$. In this case, $K$ is said to be a generator of the rational cylinder $\mathcal{R}$. The rational cylinder generated by a language $K$ will be denoted Cyl($K$).

That the linear languages do not form a principal ray is shown by the following theorem, which proves even more.

**Theorem 3.7.3.** *The family of $\varepsilon$-free linear languages is not a principal cylinder.*

The proof proceeds by showing that $S_{n^2}$ does not belong to the rational cylinder generated by $S_n$. The theorem then follows, for if $L_0$ were a generator of the rational cylinder $\mathcal{L}$, $L_0$ would have to appear in $\text{Cyl}(S_n)$ for some $n \geq 0$, by Proposition 3.7.2. We would then have $\mathcal{L} = \text{Cyl}(L_0) = \text{Cyl}(S_n)$, contradicting $S_{n^2} \notin \text{Cyl}(S_n)$.

Proposition 3.7.1 is due to Greibach [1973]. Proposition 3.7.2 and Theorem 3.7.3 are due to Boasson and Nivat [1977].

### Exercises

1. (E) Show that the family of $\varepsilon$-free regular languages is not a principal ray.
2. (E) Show that the family of $\varepsilon$-free enumerable languages is a principal ray.

### 3.8. Substitution

Let $P \subseteq A^*$ be a language over the finite alphabet $A$. Let $\mathcal{Q}$ be a family of languages. A $\mathcal{Q}$-*substitution* for $A$ is a map $f : A \to \mathcal{Q}$ that assigns a language $f(a)$ in $\mathcal{Q}$ to each letter $a$ in $A$. This map can be extended in an obvious way to a map $f : A^* \to \mathcal{Q}^*$, where $\mathcal{Q}^*$ is the smallest family of languages containing $\mathcal{Q}$ and closed under concatenation. We then define

$$f(P) = \bigcup_{x \in P} f(x)$$

to be the image of the language $P$ under the substitution $f$. Finally, if $\mathcal{P}$ is a family of languages, we define $\mathcal{P} \bowtie \mathcal{Q}$ to be the class of all languages $f(P)$, where $P$ runs through $\mathcal{P}$ and $f$ runs through all $\mathcal{Q}$-substitutions. It is easy to see that $\mathcal{P} \bowtie \mathcal{Q}$ is a family of languages, and that $\bowtie$ is an associative operation. The following key lemma was proved by Ginsburg and Spanier [1970].

*Lemma 3.8.1.* If $\mathcal{P}$ and $\mathcal{Q}$ are rational cones, then so is $\mathcal{P} \bowtie \mathcal{Q}$.

We shall say that a family of languages $\mathcal{P}$ is *closed under substitution* if $\mathcal{P} \bowtie \mathcal{P} \subseteq \mathcal{P}$. It is easy to verify that the recognizable languages $\mathcal{R}$, the context-free languages $\mathcal{K}$, and the enumerable languages $\mathcal{E}$ are all closed under substitution. If $\mathcal{P} \supseteq \mathcal{R}$ is a family of languages that is closed under substitution, then $\mathcal{P}$ is closed under union, concatenation, and asteration. Since the family $\mathcal{L}$ of linear languages is not closed under concatenation (or asteration), $\mathcal{L}$ is *not* closed under substitution.

If $\mathcal{P}$ is a family of languages, define $\mathcal{P}^{(n)}$ by $\mathcal{P}^{(1)} = \mathcal{P}$ and $\mathcal{P}^{(n+1)} = \mathcal{P} \bowtie \mathcal{P}^{(n)}$, and define $\mathcal{P}^{\bowtie}$ by

$$\mathcal{P}^{\bowtie} = \bigcup_{n \geq 1} \mathcal{P}^{(n)}$$

Then $\mathcal{P}^{\bowtie}$ is the *substitution closure* of $\mathcal{P}$, the smallest family of languages containing $\mathcal{P}$ and closed under substitution, and we have $\mathcal{P}^{\bowtie} = \mathcal{P}$ if and only if $\mathcal{P}$ is closed under substitution. If $\mathcal{P}$ is a rational cone, then by Lemma 3.8.1 so is each $\mathcal{P}^{(n)}$ and, thus, so is $\mathcal{P}^{\bowtie}$.

We shall now consider the substitution closure $\mathcal{L}^{\bowtie}$ of the linear languages. Since $\mathcal{L} \subset \mathcal{K}$, we have $\mathcal{L}^{\bowtie} \subseteq \mathcal{K}^{\bowtie} = \mathcal{K}$ and, thus,

$$\mathcal{L} \subseteq \mathcal{L}^{\bowtie} \subseteq \mathcal{K}$$

We have already seen that $\mathcal{L} \neq \mathcal{L}^{\bowtie}$; one of the main results of this section will be that $\mathcal{L}^{\bowtie} \neq \mathcal{K}$. Since, $\mathcal{K}$ is a principal cone, it will suffice to show that $\mathcal{L}^{\bowtie}$ is *not* a principal cone; this will give as an interesting byproduct the result that there are rational cones that are not principal.

To show that $\mathcal{L}^{\bowtie}$ is not a principal cone, it will suffice to show that the cones $\mathcal{P}^{(2^k)}$ form an infinite ascending sequence of cones: for if $\mathcal{L}^{\bowtie}$ were the cone generated by some languages $L$, then $L$ would appear in the cone $\mathcal{P}^{(2^k)}$ for some $k$; it would follow that $\mathcal{P}^{(2^k)} = \mathcal{L}^{\bowtie}$ and thus that $\mathcal{P}^{(2^k)}$ was closed under substitution, contradicting $\mathcal{P}^{(2^k)} \neq \mathcal{P}^{(2^{k+1})}$. This will also give the interesting byproduct that there are infinite ascending sequences of rational cones.

The inequality $\mathcal{P}^{(2^k)} \neq \mathcal{P}^{(2^{k+1})}$ will follow from the following proposition.

**Proposition 3.8.2.** *If the cone $\mathcal{P}$ is not closed under substitution, then neither is the cone $\mathcal{P} \bowtie \mathcal{P}$.*

Proposition 3.8.2 is a consequence of a central result concerning substitutions known as the Syntactic Lemma. To state this result we shall need to define a special type of substitution. If $P$ and $Q$ are languages over disjoint alphabets $A$ and $B$, we define $P \bowtie Q$ to be the language resulting from the substitution $f$ defined by $f(a) = aQ$ for all $a \in A$. (Thus a word in $P \bowtie Q$ is obtained by writing an arbitrary word of $Q$ after each letter in a word of $P$.) It is easy to see that if $\mathcal{P}$ is a family of languages, $\mathcal{Q}$ is a rational cone, $P \in \mathcal{P}$ and $Q \in \mathcal{Q}$, then $P \bowtie Q \in \mathcal{P} \bowtie \mathcal{Q}$.

*Lemma 3.8.3 (The "Syntactic Lemma").* Let $P$ and $Q$ be languages over disjoint alphabets, and let $\mathcal{P}$ and $\mathcal{Q}$ be rational cones. If $P \bowtie Q \in \mathcal{P} \bowtie \mathcal{Q}$, then either $P \in \mathcal{P}$ or $Q \in \mathcal{Q}$.

The Syntactic Lemma in this form is due to Beauquier [1981]; it was first proved under slightly stronger hypotheses by Greibach [1970]. We shall not prove it here, but shall proceed to the following corollary.

**Corollary 3.8.4.** *If $\mathcal{P}$ is a proper sub-cone of $\mathcal{P}'$ and $\mathcal{Q}$ is a proper sub-cone of $\mathcal{Q}'$, then $\mathcal{P} \bowtie \mathcal{Q}$ is a proper sub-cone of $\mathcal{P}' \bowtie \mathcal{Q}'$.*

**Proof.** Take $P \in \mathcal{P}' \setminus \mathcal{P}$ and $Q \in \mathcal{Q}' \setminus \mathcal{Q}$ in the Syntactic Lemma.                           □

Proposition 3.8.2 now follows from Corollary 3.8.3 by taking $\mathcal{P} = \mathcal{Q} = \mathcal{L}$ and $\mathcal{P}' = \mathcal{Q}' = \mathcal{L} \bowtie \mathcal{L}$.

The languages in the cone $\mathcal{L}^{\bowtie}$ are known as the "quasi-rational" languages, and by a great number of other names; see Yntema [1967], Nivat [1968], Brzozowski [1968], Ginsburg and Spanier [1968] and Gruska [1971a, 1971b]. The Syntactic Lemma grew out of earlier work by Greibach [1969] that dealt specifically with the substitution properties of linear languages, among others.

### *Exercise*

1. (E) Show that the conclusion "either $P \in \mathcal{P}$ or $Q \in \mathcal{Q}$" in the Syntactic Lemma cannot be strengthened to "$P \in \mathcal{P}$ and $Q \in \mathcal{Q}$."

### 3.9. Generating Functions

This section describes a connection between grammars and languages on one hand, and mathematical objects called "generating functions" on the other. The connection can be used to show that languages are not regular, or that context-free languages are inherently ambiguous, by means of arguments that deal only with the languages themselves, without any reference to derivations or grammars. A disadvantage of the method, however, is that it applies only in very special cases.

Let $L \subseteq A^*$ be any language over the finite alphabet $A$. We shall write $\ell(x)$ for the length of the word $x$. Define the formal power series

$$\Phi_L(\xi) = \sum_{x \in L} \xi^{\ell(x)} \tag{3.9.1}$$

where $\xi$ is an indeterminate. If $\alpha$ denotes the cardinality of $A$, then there are at most $\alpha^k$ words of length $k$ in $L$. Thus, the coefficient of $\xi^k$ in Eq. (3.9.1) is at most $\alpha^k$ (and it is non-negative, of course). It follows that, if $|\xi| < 1/\alpha$, then the sum in Eq. (3.9.1) is absolutely convergent; thus Eq. (3.9.1) defines $\Phi_L$ as an analytic function on at least the open disk $\{\xi : |\xi| < 1/\alpha\}$ in the complex plane **C**. The definition (3.9.1) thus assigns to each language $L$ an analytic function $\Phi_L$ that ignores much of the structure of the language $L$ (which particular words of a given length are in the language), keeping track only of the *number* of words of each length in the language. Nevertheless, $\Phi_L$ often contains significant language-theoretic information about $L$.

**Proposition 3.9.1.** *If $L$ is a regular language, then $\Phi_L$ is a rational function (that is, there are polynomials $P(\xi), Q(\xi) \in \mathbf{Z}[\xi]$ such that $\Phi_L(\xi) = P(\xi)/Q(\xi)$).*

Let $M = (A, Q, I, J, R)$ be a non-deterministic finite automaton. For every word $x$ in the language $\text{Lang}(M)$ recognized by $M$, there is at least one accepting computation by $M$ on $x$. Furthermore, if $\psi$ denotes the cardinality of $Q$, then there are at most $\psi^{1+\ell(X)}$ such accepting computations. Let $C_M(x)$ denote the number of accepting computations by $M$ on $x$, so that $1 \leq C_M(x) \leq \psi^{1+\ell(x)}$ if $x \in \text{Lang}(M)$, and $C_M(x) = 0$ otherwise. Define the formal power series

$$\Phi_M(\xi) = \sum_{x \in A^*} C_M(x)\, \xi^{\ell(x)} \tag{3.9.2}$$

Then Eq. (3.9.2) defines $\Phi_M$ as an analytic function on at least the open disk $\{\xi : |\xi| < 1/\alpha\psi\}$ in the complex plane $\mathbf{C}$. If $M$ is deterministic, then $M$ has just one accepting computation for every $x \in \text{Lang}(M)$, and thus we have $\Phi_{\text{Lang}(M)} = \Phi_M$. Since every regular language is recognized by a deterministic finite automaton, Proposition 3.9.1 is a corollary of the following lemma.

*Lemma 3.9.2.* If $M$ is a finite automaton, then $\Phi_M$ is a rational function.

**Proof.** Suppose that $M = (A, Q, I, J, R)$ and that $Q$ contains $\psi$ states. Let $U$ be a $\psi \times \psi$ matrix of natural numbers whose rows and columns are indexed by $Q$. We shall take the entry $U_{q,q'}$ to be the number of letters $a \in A$ such that $(a, q, q') \in R$. Then $U_{q,q'}$ is the number of computations by $M$ on words of length 1 that take $M$ from state $q$ to state $q'$. If $U^n$ is the $n$-th power of $U$ (under the usual product of matrices), then $(U^k)_{q,q'}$ is the number of computations on words of length $n$ that take $M$ from state $q$ to state $q'$. This holds for $n = 0$ if we take $U^0$ to be the $\psi \times \psi$ identity matrix Id. Now consider the matrix $\text{Id} - \xi U$, which is a $\psi \times \psi$ matrix whose entries are linear polynomials in $\xi$. When $\xi$ is sufficiently small, this matrix is close to the identity matrix Id and, thus, is non-singular. Thus, $\text{Id} - \xi U$ has an inverse $(\text{Id} - \xi U)^{-1}$, which is a $\psi \times \psi$ matrix whose entries are rational functions of $\xi$. We also have the power series expansion

$$(\text{Id} - \xi U)^{-1} = \sum_{n \geq 0} \xi^n U^n$$

Thus, $((\mathrm{Id} - \xi U)^{-1})_{q,q'}$ has a power series expansion in which the coefficient of $\xi^n$ is the number of computations by $M$ on words of length $n$ that take $M$ from state $q$ to state $q'$. If we let $V$ be a row vector indexed by $Q$, whose entries are 1's for states in $I$ and 0's otherwise, and let $W$ be a column vector indexed by $Q$, whose entries are 1's for states in $J$ and 0's otherwise, then we have

$$\Phi_M(\xi) = V(\mathrm{Id} - \xi U)^{-1}W$$

Since $\Phi_M(\xi)$ is a sum of entries in $(\mathrm{Id} - \xi U)^{-1}$, and these entries are rational functions of $\xi$, the proposition is proved.                                                $\Box$

As an example, consider the power series expansion

$$\frac{1}{\sqrt{1 - 4\xi^2}} = \sum_{n \geq 0} \binom{2n}{n} \xi^{2n}$$

The coefficient of $\xi^m$ in the right-hand side is the number of words $m$ in the language $\mathrm{Eq}_1 \subseteq \{0, 1\}^*$ comprising the words containing equal numbers of 0's and 1's. Thus, we have $\Phi_{\mathrm{Eq}_1}(\xi) = 1/\sqrt{1 - 4\xi^2}$. Since this is not a rational function of $\xi$, the language $\mathrm{Eq}_1$ is not regular. (Proposition 3.9.1 also explains in part why the regular languages are sometimes called the "rational" languages.)

Let us now turn to context-free languages. We begin by associating a generating function $\phi_G$ with a context-free grammar $G = (A, B, s, P)$ by

$$\Phi_G(\xi) = \sum_{x \in A^*} D_G(x) \xi^{\ell(x)} \tag{3.9.3}$$

where $D_G(x)$ is the number of left-most derivations of the word $x$ according to $G$. If $G$ is in Greibach normal form, and if $\psi$ denotes the cardinality of $P$, then there are at most $\ell(x)$ applications of productions in a derivation of $x$ and, thus, at most $\psi^\ell(x)$ left-most derivations. Thus, $1 \leq D_G(x) \leq \psi^\ell(x)$ for $x \in \mathrm{Lang}(G)$ and $D_G(x) = 0$ otherwise. It follows that Eq. (3.9.3) defines $\Phi_G$ to be an analytic function in at least the open disk $\{\xi : |\xi| < 1/\alpha\psi\}$ in the complex plane $\mathbf{C}$.

To proceed further, we must use the identity $\Phi_{\mathrm{Lang}(G)} = \Phi_G(\xi)$. This holds, however, only in the case where $G$ is unambiguous, so that there is a one-to-one correspondence between words in $\mathrm{Lang}(G)$ and left-most derivations according to $G$. This fact accounts for the qualification in the following proposition.

**Proposition 3.9.3.** *If $L$ is a context-free language with an unambiguous context-free grammar, then $\Phi_L$ is an algebraic function.*

Because of Proposition 3.9.3, the context-free languages are sometimes called "algebraic" languages. Proposition 3.9.3 is a consequence of the following lemma.

*Lemma 3.9.4.* For any context-free grammar $G$, $\Phi_G$ is an algebraic function (that is, $P(\xi, \Phi_G(\xi)) = 0$ for some polynomial $P(\xi, \eta) \in \mathbf{Z}[\xi, \eta]$ that is not identically zero).

The proof of Lemma 3.9.4 proceeds by associating with each symbol $b \in B$ of the grammar $G = (A, B, s, P)$ a generating function $\Phi_{G,b}(\xi) = \Phi_{G'}(\xi)$, where $G' = (A, B, b, P)$. We then have $\Phi_G(\xi) = \Phi_{G,s}(\xi)$. The generating functions $\Phi_{G,b}(\xi)$ for $b \in B$ satisfy a system of simultaneous algebraic equations as follows. Let $(b, w^{(1)}), \ldots, (b, w^{(l)})$ be all of the productions of the form $(b, w)$ in $P$. Let $i_k$ be the number of occurrences of letters in $w^{(k)}$, and let $j_k(c)$ be the number of occurrences of the symbol $c$ in $w^{(k)}$. Then we have

$$\Phi_{G,b}(\xi) = \sum_{1 \le k \le l} \xi^{i_k} \prod_{c \in B} \Phi_{G,c}(\xi)^{j_k(c)}$$

If $\beta$ denotes the cardinality of $B$, this gives $\beta$ equations in the $\beta + 1$ "unknowns" $\xi$ and $\Phi_{G,b}(\xi)$. Elimination of $\Phi_{G,b}(\xi)$ for $b \ne s$ yields one equations in $\xi$ and $\Phi_{G,s}(\xi) = \Phi_G(\xi)$, as desired. If $G$ is a linear grammar, the resulting system of equations is linear, which yields the following corollary.

*Corollary 3.9.5.* If $L$ is a linear language with an unambiguous linear grammar, then $\Phi_L$ is a rational function.

As an example consider the two languages

$$K = \{0\} \cdot \{1^n 0^{2n} : n \ge 1\}^* \cdot \{1\}^*$$

and

$$L = \{0^n 1^{2n} : n \ge 1\}^* \cdot \{0\}^*$$

They both have unambiguous context-free grammars, and so $\Phi_K$ and $\Phi_L$ are algebraic functions (in fact, they are rational functions). Their union $K \cup L$ is certainly a context-free language. If it had an unambiguous context-free grammar, then $\Phi_{K \cup L}$ would be an algebraic function. By the identity

$$\Phi_{K \cap L}(\xi) = \Phi_K(\xi) + \Phi_L(\xi) - \Phi_{K \cup L}(\xi)$$

this would imply that $\Phi_{K \cap L}$ is also an algebraic function. (The algebraic functions form a field, and thus are closed under addition and subtraction.) But $K \cap L$ is the language

$$K \cap L = \{0, 011, 0110000, 011000011111111, \ldots\}$$

which contains a single word of length $n$ when $n = 2^k - 1$ for some $k \geq 1$, and no words of other lengths. Thus

$$\Phi_{K \cap L}(\xi) = \sum_{k \geq 1} \xi^{2^k - 1} \tag{3.9.4}$$

That this is not an algebraic function follows from a result of Comtet [1964], to the effect that the coefficients in the power series expansion of an algebraic function satisfy a recurrence of fixed order with polynomial coefficients. Thus, if a sequence of consecutive coefficients of length greater than the order of the recurrence vanish, all further coefficients must also vanish, and the power series must reduce to a polynomial. Since Eq. (3.9.4) has arbitrarily long "lacunæ" of vanishing coefficients, but does not reduce to a polynomial, it is a transcendental function. Thus, $K \cup L$ is an inherently ambiguous language.

That regular languages have rational generating functions is implicit in the work of Chomsky and Miller [1958]. The analogous connection between unambiguous context-free languages and algebraic functions is due to Chomsky and Schützenberger [1963]. The use of this result to deal with questions of ambiguity is due to Flajolet [1987].

### Exercises

1. (M) Determine the generating function for the language $\text{Dyck}_1^* \subseteq \{0, 1\}^*$ (comprising the words in which parentheses are balanced after 0's are replaced by "(" and 1's by ")"); observe that it is not a rational function and conclude that $\text{Dyck}_1^*$ is not regular.

2. (E) Can properties of generating functions be used to prove that the language $\{0^i 1^i 2^j : i, j \geq 1\} \cup \{0^i 1^j 2^j : i, j \geq 1\}$ is inherently ambiguous?

# 4

## Computable functions and relations

### 4.1. Computability Theory

Our study of languages generated by grammars has brought us to the outermost boundary of what may reasonably be regarded as computable, in the form of the enumerable languages. This final chapter is devoted to a deeper study of this notion of computability. For the purposes of this study, it is less convenient to continue the study of languages than to return to a study of functions and relations, along the lines of our initial study of Boolean functions and relations.

An early goal of our study will be to define the notion of a "recursive cone" as a set of functions that contains certain initial functions and is closed under certain operations. This definition is analogous to that of a clone of finite functions, but differs in three main respects. First, the underlying domain from which functions take their arguments and return their values will be infinite; specifically, it will be the set natural numbers. Second, we shall not insist that functions be defined for all possible choices of values for their arguments; we shall allow them to be "partial" functions. Technically, this will be accomplished by adjoining to the domain a special value "$\perp$" (read "bottom") representing an "undefined" value. This value will be treated differently from the others (the "defined" values), so as to enforce the intended interpretation. Third, we shall add enough initial functions and closure operations to ensure that every recursive cone contains all of the computable functions. Thus, the theory presented in this chapter has the computable functions at its lowest level, as the common members of all of the recursive cones. The main objects of interest will be the principal recursive cones, obtained by adjoining a single function to this common intersection and closing under the "recursive operations."

The definition of "recursive cone" just alluded to stands in complete analogy to the notions of "clone of finite functions," "variety of languages," and "rational

141

cone" studied in previous chapters. It will be profitable to study the computable functions from another point of view as well, with the aid of a conceptual framework that is quite different from those we have employed thus far. This framework is established by defining a "reflexive class" to be a set of functions containing certain initial functions and closed under certain operations, but satisfying certain "universal properties" as well. Unlike closure operations, these universal properties are not "local," insisting that certain functions appear in the set when others do, but are "global" properties of the reflexive class as a whole. (It is this form of self-reference that gives reflexive classes their name.) Roughly speaking, the universal properties ensure that "programs" are finite objects (and thus can be represented by natural numbers) and that "terminating computations" are finite objects (by insisting that the distinction between function applications that are defined and those that are undefined corresponds to the distinction between computations that terminate after a finite number of steps and those that do not).

A later goal of our study will be to establish the equivalence between our two frameworks, by showing that principal recursive cones are in one-to-one correspondence with reflexive classes. It would be possible, of course, to ignore reflexive structures altogether, and to develop all our results in terms of recursive cones. There are two good reasons for embarking on this detour, however. First, to study computable functions exclusively from the viewpoint of recursive cones requires undertaking a considerable amount of tedious "programming" before one comes to interesting results. These interesting results follow immediately from the defining conditions for reflexive classes, however, thus allowing the tedious programming to be deferred to the proof of the equivalence between viewpoints. Second, the universal properties mentioned correspond directly to intuitively evident notions concerning computability; thus, the use of reflexive classes serves to indicate the role these notions play in the overall theory.

We conclude this section with two problems; we call them problems, rather than exercises, because of the vagueness of their formulation. Nevertheless, they have definite answers, which are invariant under all reasonable efforts at reformulation.

For each of the problems, we imagine that we have a computer $M$ that is capable of accepting instructions in the form of a finite sequence (or program) $\pi$ of symbols over a finite alphabet (we assume that it can recognize the end of the sequence), and of producing as output another sequence $M(\pi)$ of symbols over the same alphabet. We also assume that it can indicate (by "halting") that it has finished working. We shall not be more specific about the nature of its operation, beyond saying that it should be capable of executing an arbitrary sequence of definite instructions, without regard for the time that might be required for their execution, or for the space that might be required for the storage of intermediate results.

We might, for example, instruct it to "produce as output the sequence $x$, then halt." We assume there is some convention whereby the "parameter" $x$ can be an arbitrary sequence over the finite alphabet (so that, in particular, the machine can recognize the end of the parameter). In general, this sequence of instructions $\pi[x]$ will be longer than the output $M(\pi[x]) = x$ that it produces. On the other hand, it is easy to imagine a sequence of instructions that produces an output sequence longer than itself, for example, "list in lexicographic order all of the permutations of the sequence $x$, then halt." The first problem is the following.

**Problem 4.1.1.** *Is there a finite sequence $\pi$ of symbols that, when presented to M as instructions, causes M to produce the sequence $M(\pi) = \pi$ as output and then halt?*

The sequences of instructions just given eventually cause the machine to halt, but it is easy to imagine sequences that do not, for example, "print the infinite sequence '0101 $\cdots$', with the symbol '0' in positions $0, 2, \ldots$ and the symbol '1' in positions $1, 3, \ldots$." (where we assume that "0" and "1" are symbols of the alphabet). The second problem is the following.

**Problem 4.1.2.** *Is there a finite sequence $\pi[x]$ of symbols that, like the first example problem, includes an arbitrary finite sequence $x$ as a parameter and that, when presented to M as instructions, causes M to produce the symbol 0 as output and then halt if M eventually halts when presented with $x$ as input, and to produce the symbol 1 as output and then halt if M does not eventually halt when presented with $x$ as input?*

## 4.2. Recursive Partial Functions

In this section we shall characterize the recursive partial functions in several ways. We begin with some conventions concerning functions and partial functions generally.

The most important objects at the outset of our study will be "functions" and "partial functions." These will always be functions taking one or more natural numbers as arguments, and taking a natural number as value. Let $\mathbf{N} = \{0, 1, 2, \ldots\}$ denote the natural numbers. We shall denote by $\mathcal{G}_k$ the set of all functions $f : \mathbf{N}^k \to \mathbf{N}$ of $k$ arguments ($k$-adic functions), where $k \geq 1$. We set $\mathcal{G} = \cup_{1 \leq k < \infty} \mathcal{G}_k$.

We shall often need to work with functions that are not defined for all possible combinations of arguments (these are usually called "partial functions"). A convenient way to do this is to imagine that **N** contains, in addition to the natural numbers $0, 1, 2, \ldots$, an "undefined" element $\perp$, and to write $f(x_1, \ldots, x_k) = \perp$ if $f(x_1, \ldots, x_k)$ is undefined. We shall adopt the following convention for the composition of partial functions: a partial function is undefined if one or more of its arguments are undefined. (This means that there is no "lazy evaluation" in our notation.)

Formally, we set $\bar{\mathbf{N}} = \mathbf{N} \cup \{\perp\}$, and then define a $k$-adic *partial function* to be a map $f : \bar{\mathbf{N}}^k \to \bar{\mathbf{N}}$ satisfying the following condition: if $\perp \in \{x_1, \ldots, x_k\}$, then $f(x_1, \ldots, x_k) = \perp$. We shall let $\mathcal{F}_k$ denote the set of $k$-adic partial functions. We set $\mathcal{F} = \cup_{1 \leq k < \infty} \mathcal{F}_k$.

A *total function* is a partial function $f$ for which the condition $f(x_1, \ldots, x_k) = \perp$ only if $\perp \in \{x_1, \ldots, x_k\}$ holds. Clearly these "total functions" are in one-to-one correspondence with the functions defined earlier. It will be convenient to regard $\mathcal{G}_k$ and $\mathcal{G}$ as subsets of $\mathcal{F}_k$ and $\mathcal{F}$, respectively.

### 4.2.1. Reflexive Classes

Let $\mathcal{P} \subseteq \mathcal{F}$ be a set of partial functions. We set $\mathcal{Q} = \mathcal{P} \cap \mathcal{G}$ (the total functions in $\mathcal{P}$), and for each $k \geq 0$, we set $\mathcal{P}_k = \mathcal{P} \cap \mathcal{F}_k$ (the $k$-adic partial functions in $\mathcal{P}$) and $\mathcal{Q}_k = \mathcal{Q} \cap \mathcal{G}_k$ (the $k$-adic total functions in $\mathcal{P}$).

We shall say that $\mathcal{P}$ is a *reflexive class* if it satisfies the following seven conditions:

FC$_1$  $\mathcal{P}$ forms a clone (that is, $\mathcal{P}$ contains all projection functions and is closed under composition).

FC$_2$  $\mathcal{P}$ contains the monadic constant function zero, defined by $\text{zero}(x) = 0$.

FC$_3$  $\mathcal{P}$ contains the monadic successor function succ, defined by $\text{succ}(x) = x + 1$.

FC$_4$  $\mathcal{P}$ contains the dyadic pairing function pair, defined by

$$\text{pair}(x, y) = (x + 1) + (x + y + 1)(x + y)/2$$

FC$_5$  $\mathcal{P}$ contains the tetradic conditional function cond, defined by

$$\text{cond}(v, w, x, y) = \begin{cases} x, & \text{if } v = w \\ y, & \text{if } v \neq w \end{cases}$$

The foregoing conditions yield a variety of rather pedestrian functions. The remaining two give recursive function theory its distinctive character:

FC$_6$ $\mathcal{P}$ contains a monadic partial function $u$ satisfying the following condition. For each $k \geq 0$ and each function $f \in \mathcal{P}_k$, there is a number $\pi \in \mathbf{N}$ (called an "index" for $f$) such that

$$f(x_1, \ldots, x_k) = u_k(\pi, x_1, \ldots, x_k)$$

for all $x_1, \ldots, x_k \in \mathbf{N}$, where the partial function $u_k$ is defined by induction on $k$ as follows: $u_0 = u$ and

$$u_{k+1}(\pi, x_1, x_2, \ldots, x_{k+1}) = u_k(\mathrm{pair}(\pi, x_1), x_2, \ldots, x_{k+1})$$

for all $\pi, x_1, x_2, \ldots, x_{k+1} \in \mathbf{N}$. (It is sometimes helpful to think of $\pi$ as a program for $f$ and of the function $u$ as an "interpreter" for such programs.)

FC$_7$ $\mathcal{Q}$ contains a dyadic function $m$ satisfying the following two conditions. First, for all $\pi, t \in \mathbf{N}$, we have $0 \leq m(\pi, t) \leq m(\pi, t + 1) \leq 1$. (This condition says that $m$ assumes only the values 0 and 1, and that for each fixed $\pi$ it is "non-decreasing" in its second argument.) Second, for all $\pi \in \mathbf{N}$, $u(\pi) \in \mathbf{N}$ if and only if there exists $t \in \mathbf{N}$ such that $m(\pi, t) = 1$. (One may think of $m(\pi, t) = 1$ as signifying that "the execution of program $\pi$ halts in at most $t$ steps." As we shall see later, many alternative significations are also possible.)

It will be useful to define, for each $k \geq 0$, the function $m_k \in \mathcal{G}_{k+2}$ by induction on $k$ as follows: $m_0 = m$ and

$$m_{k+1}(\pi, x_1, x_2, \ldots, x_{k+1}, t) = m_k(\mathrm{pair}(\pi, x_1), x_2, \ldots, x_{k+1}, t)$$

for all $\pi, x_1, x_2, \ldots, x_{k+1}, t \in \mathbf{N}$. It is easy to see that, in fact, $u_k \in \mathcal{P}_{k+1}$ and $m_k \in \mathcal{Q}_{k+2}$.

The function pair assigns a distinct value $\mathrm{pair}(x, y)$ to each distinct ordered pair $(x, y)$ of natural numbers, and it does not assign the value 0 to any pair. Thus, if we define $\langle \rangle = 0$, $\langle x_1 \rangle = \mathrm{pair}(0, x_1)$, and, for $k \geq 2$, $\langle x_1, x_2, \ldots, x_k \rangle = \mathrm{pair}(\langle x_2, \ldots, x_k \rangle, x_1)$, then the resulting notation assigns a distinct value $\langle x_1, x_2, \ldots, x_k \rangle$ to each distinct finite list of zero or more natural numbers.

Since pair is a bijection from $\mathbf{N} \times \mathbf{N}$ to $\mathbf{N} \setminus \{0\}$, we can define monadic functions left and right by setting $\mathrm{left}(0) = \mathrm{right}(0) = 0$ and requiring that

$$\mathrm{left}(\mathrm{pair}(x, y)) = x \quad \text{and} \quad \mathrm{right}(\mathrm{pair}(x, y)) = y$$

for all $x, y \in \mathbf{N}$. We shall see later that these functions belong to $\mathcal{Q}$.

It will also be convenient to have a similar set of functions that does not treat the value 0 differently. We first define the monadic function pred by setting $\mathrm{pred}(0) = 0$ and then requiring that

$$\mathrm{pred}(\mathrm{succ}(x)) = x$$

for all $x \in \mathbf{N}$. Then we define the dyadic function bipair = pred $\circ$ pair in $\mathcal{Q}$, a bijection from $\mathbf{N} \times \mathbf{N}$ to $\mathbf{N}$. We also define the monadic functions bileft = left $\circ$ succ and biright = right $\circ$ succ. We shall see later that these functions also belong to $\mathcal{Q}$.

It will sometimes be helpful to have an explicit notation for projection functions and constant functions. We shall write $\mathrm{proj}_{k,j}$ for the $k$-adic function such that

$$\mathrm{proj}_{k,j}(x_1, \ldots, x_k) = x_j$$

and $\mathrm{const}_{k,n}$ for the $k$-adic function such that

$$\mathrm{const}_{k,n}(x_1, \ldots, x_k) = n$$

for all $x_1, \ldots, x_k \in \mathbf{N}$. Of course, all these functions belong to $\mathcal{Q}$.

Our definition of a reflexive class is based on the axiomatic treatments of Wagner [1969] and Strong [1968], together with a final condition suggested by the work of Blum [1967a]. We remark that it is not obvious that there is any class $\mathcal{P}$ that satisfies these conditions; we shall see later that there is.

*Lemma 4.2.1.* For every $k \geq 1$, $\mathcal{P}_k$ contains a function $\mathrm{undef}_k$ that is everywhere undefined: $\mathrm{undef}_k(x_1, \ldots, x_k) = \bot$ for all $x_1, \ldots, x_k \in \mathbf{N}^k$.

**Proof.** Applying FC$_1$ to the partial function $u_1 \in \mathcal{P}_2$, we define the partial function $v(x) = u_1(x, x)$ in $\mathcal{P}_1$. Using FC$_1$ and FC$_3$, we define the partial function $f(x) = \mathrm{succ}(v(x))$, also in $\mathcal{P}_1$, such that

$$f(x) = \mathrm{succ}(u_1(x, x)) \tag{4.2.1}$$

By FC$_6$, there is an index $\pi$ for $f$ such that

$$f(x) = u_1(\pi, x) \tag{4.2.2}$$

for all $x \in \mathbf{N}$.

We claim now that $f(\pi) = \bot$. For if $f(\pi) = c \in \mathbf{N}$, then we have $c = \mathrm{succ}(u_1(\pi, \pi))$ by Eq. (4.2.1) and $c = u_1(\pi, \pi)$ by Eq. (4.2.2), whence we have $c = \mathrm{succ}(c)$, a contradiction.

Taking $\mathrm{undef}_k = f \circ \mathrm{const}_{k,\pi}$ completes the proof.                    $\square$

The proof of Lemma 4.2.1, though simple, exhibits one of the fundamental techniques of recursive function theory: diagonalization. Here the function $u_1$, which takes two arguments, is given the same value for both. This is used to implement a "self-reference," when the function $f$ is given its own index $\pi$ as argument. We shall encounter this pattern many times.

It will sometimes be convenient to speak of 0-adic partial functions and to regard them as constituting a subset $\mathcal{F}_0$ of $\mathcal{F}$. Such partial functions, having no arguments, must either be constants in $\mathbf{N}$, or be always undefined; thus, they are in one-to-one correspondence with the elements of $\bar{\mathbf{N}}$. It is clear from conditions $FC_1$, $FC_2$, and $FC_3$, and Lemma 4.2.1, that all 0-adic partial functions belong to any reflexive class $\mathcal{P}$. Thus, we may speak of "indices" for such partial functions (that is, numbers $\pi$ such that $u_0(\pi) = u(\pi)$ takes on the appropriate value or is undefined), and regard them as constituting a subset $\mathcal{P}_0$ of $\mathcal{P}$.

Our first theorem shows that for every reflexive class $\mathcal{P}$, there is a monadic total function that is not in $\mathcal{P}$. Specifically, define

$$d(x) = \begin{cases} 0, & \text{if } u_1(x, x) = \perp \\ 1, & \text{if } u_1(x, x) \in \mathbf{N} \end{cases}$$

**Theorem 4.2.2.** *The function d is not in* $\mathcal{P}$.

**Proof.** Suppose, with an eye to contradiction, that $d \in \mathcal{P}$. Define the function

$$p(x) = \begin{cases} 0, & \text{if } d(x) = 0 \\ \perp, & \text{if } d(x) = 1 \end{cases}$$

We claim that $p \subset \mathcal{P}$. We shall prove this later, but take it for granted now.

Since $p \in \mathcal{P}_1$, there is by condition $FC_6$ an index $\pi$ for $p$ such that

$$p(x) = u_1(\pi, x) \tag{4.2.3}$$

We now ask the key question: is $p(\pi)$ equal to 0 or $\perp$?

If $p(\pi) = 0$, then $d(\pi) = 0$ (by the definition of $p$) and $u_1(\pi, \pi) = \perp$ (by the definition of $d$). But then Eq. (4.2.3) yields $p(\pi) = u_1(\pi, \pi) = \perp$, contradicting the assumption that $p(\pi) = 0$.

On the other hand, if $p(\pi) = \perp$, then $d(\pi) = 1$ (by the definition of $p$) and $u_1(\pi, \pi) \in \mathbf{N}$ (by the definition of $d$). But then Eq. (4.2.3) yields $p(\pi) = u_1(\pi, \pi) \in \mathbf{N}$, contradicting the assumption that $p(\pi) = \perp$.

Thus, either answer to the key question leads to a contradiction, refuting the supposition that $d \in \mathcal{P}$. It remains to prove the claim.

Using condition $FC_6$, let $\xi$ be an index for the function $zero_0$ and let $\eta$ be an index for the function $undef_0$ (whose existence is assured by Lemma 4.2.1).

The function $p$ can now be expressed as

$$p(x) = u_0(\text{cond}(d(x), 0, \xi, \eta))$$

Condition $FC_1$ together with the assumption that $d$ is in $\mathcal{P}$ prove that that $p$ is in $\mathcal{P}$.                                                                              □

The construction of the function $d$ may appear somewhat artificial, but Theorem 4.2.2 has the following very natural corollary, which may be viewed as answering the first of the two problems raised in Section 4.1. Define

$$\text{halt}(x) = \begin{cases} 0, & \text{if } u_0(x) = \bot \\ 1, & \text{if } u_0(x) \in \mathbf{N} \end{cases}$$

(This function is simply the characteristic function of the domain of $u_0$.)

**Corollary 4.2.3 (Turing [1936/1937]).** *The function halt is not in $\mathcal{P}$.*

**Proof.** Observe that, since $u_1(x, x) = u_0(\text{pair}(x, x))$, $d(x) = \text{halt}(\text{pair}(x, x))$ for all $x \in \mathbf{N}$. Thus if halt were in $\mathcal{P}$, then $d$ would also be in $\mathcal{P}$, and this would contradict Theorem 4.2.2.                                                              □

Corollary 4.2.3 shows that a fundamental question ("Does it halt?") about programs cannot be answered by a program that always halts. We might try to prove similar results for other questions about programs, including those that operate on data (compute functions in $\mathcal{P}_k$ for $k \geq 1$). There are infinitely many such questions ("Does it ever halt?"; "Does it always halt?"; "Is it constant?"; *etc.*). There is an amazingly simple theorem, that disposes of all such questions at once. It says, roughly speaking, that any non-trivial question about the behavior of programs cannot be answered by a program that always halts. Here, "non-trivial" means simply that "Yes" and "No" are both possible answers. By a question about the "behavior" of programs, we mean simply that question has the same answer for all programs that compute the same partial function.

Let $\mathcal{A} \subseteq \mathcal{P}_0$ be a class of 0-adic partial functions. We shall say that $\mathcal{A}$ is *non-trivial* if neither $\mathcal{A} = \emptyset$ nor $\mathcal{A} = \mathcal{P}_0$ holds. Given $\mathcal{A}$, we define the set $A$ to be the set of indices for functions in $\mathcal{A}$. We further define

$$a(x) = \begin{cases} 1, & \text{if } x \in A \\ 0, & \text{if } x \notin A \end{cases}$$

to be the characteristic function of the set $A$.

**Theorem 4.2.4 (Rice [1953]).** *If $\mathcal{A}$ is non-trivial, then the associated function $a$ does not belong to $\mathcal{Q}_1$.*

**Proof.** Suppose, with an eye to contradiction, that $a \in \mathcal{Q}_1$.

Assume, without loss of generality, that $undef_0 \notin \mathcal{A}$. To justify this, observe that if $undef_0 \in \mathcal{A}$, we may turn our attention to the complement $\mathcal{B} = \mathcal{P}_0 \setminus \mathcal{A}$. Since $\mathcal{A}$ is non-trivial, so is $\mathcal{B}$. The set of indices of functions in $\mathcal{B}$ is $B = \mathbf{N} \setminus A$. The characteristic function of $B$ is $b(x) = \text{cond}(a(x), 0, 1, 0)$; since $a$ is in $\mathcal{Q}$, so is $b$. But $undef_0 \notin \mathcal{B}$, and so the argument that follows applies with $\mathcal{B}$ in the place of $\mathcal{A}$.

Since $\mathcal{A}$ is non-trivial, there exists some $\alpha \in A$. Define $p$ by

$$p(x) = \begin{cases} u_0(\alpha), & \text{if } u_0(x) \in \mathbf{N} \\ \perp, & \text{if } u_0(x) = \perp \end{cases}$$

We have $p(x) = u_0(\text{const}_{1,\alpha}(u_0(x)))$, and so $p \in \mathcal{P}_1$.

Let $\pi$ be an index for $p$, and define $h$ by

$$h(x) = a(\text{pair}(\pi, x))$$

Since $a$ and pair are in $\mathcal{Q}$, so is $h$. We shall prove that $h = $ halt, contradicting Corollary 4.2.3, and thus refuting the supposition that $a \in \mathcal{Q}$.

To prove that $h(x) = \text{halt}(x)$ for all $x \in \mathbf{N}$, we consider two cases: $\text{halt}(x) = 0$ and $\text{halt}(x) = 1$. If $\text{halt}(x) = 0$, then $u_0(x) = \perp$ (by the definition of halt), so that $p(x) = \perp$ (by the definition of $p$). Since $p(x) = \perp$, $\text{pair}(\pi, x)$ is an index for $undef_0$. Since $undef_0 \notin \mathcal{A}$, $h(x) = a(\text{pair}(\pi, x)) = 0$. Thus, $h(x) = 0$ whenever $\text{halt}(x) = 0$.

On the other hand, if $\text{halt}(x) = 1$, then $u_0(x) \in \mathbf{N}$ (by the definition of halt), so that $p(x) = u_0(\alpha)$ (by the definition of $p$). Since $u_0(\text{pair}(\pi, x)) = p(x) = u_0(\alpha)$, $\text{pair}(\pi, x)$ and $\alpha$ are indices for the same function in $\mathcal{P}_0$, and since $\alpha \in A$, this function belongs to $\mathcal{A}$, so that $\text{pair}(\pi, x) \in A$ as well. Thus, $h(x) = a(\text{pair}(\pi, x)) = 1$, so that $h(x) = 1$ whenever $\text{halt}(x) = 1$. □

Although the possible questions one might ask about a function with no arguments may seem limited, this proof is easily extended to prove the following corollary.

**Corollary 4.2.5.** *For any $k \geq 0$, if $\mathcal{A} \subseteq \mathcal{P}_k$ and $\mathcal{A}$ is non-trivial, then the associated function $a$ does not belong to $\mathcal{Q}_1$.*

The proof follows the same lines as that of Theorem 4.2.4, with modifications only in notation.

The following theorem, one of the most beautiful gems of recursive function theory, will play an important role in what follows. It was called the "Recursion

Theorem" by its inventor (see Kleene [1938, Sec. 6]); it is also often called the "Fixed-Point Theorem."

**Theorem 4.2.6 (Kleene [1938]).** *For every* $f \in \mathcal{Q}_1$, *there exists* $n \in \mathbf{N}$ *such that*

$$u_0(f(n)) = u_0(n)$$

**Proof.** Define the function $a$ by

$$a(x) = u_0(u_1(x, x))$$

Then $a \in \mathcal{P}_1$. Let $\alpha$ be an index for $a$, so that

$$a(x) = u_1(\alpha, x) \tag{4.2.4}$$

for all $x \in \mathbf{N}$.

Let

$$b(x) = \mathrm{pair}(\alpha, x)$$

and

$$c(x) = f(b(x))$$

Then $b$, and hence also $c$, is in $\mathcal{Q}_1$. Let $\gamma$ be an index for $c$, so that

$$c(x) = u_1(\gamma, x) \tag{4.2.5}$$

for all $x \in \mathbf{N}$.

Take $n = b(\gamma)$. Then

$$
\begin{aligned}
u_0(f(n)) &= u_0(f(b(\gamma))) \\
&= u_0(c(\gamma)) \\
&= u_0(u_1(\gamma, \gamma)) \\
&= a(\gamma) \\
&= u_1(\alpha, \gamma) \\
&= u_0(\mathrm{pair}(\alpha, \gamma)) \\
&= u_0(b(\gamma)) \\
&= u_0(n)
\end{aligned}
$$

by the definition of $n$; the definition of $c$, Eq. (4.2.5); the definition of $a$; Eq. (4.2.4); the definition of $u_1$; the definition of $b$; and the definition of $n$ again. $\qquad\square$

The proof of the Recursion Theorem, like that of Rice's Theorem, is easily extended to yield a corollary for functions with any number of arguments.

**Corollary 4.2.7.** *For every $k \geq 0$ and every $f \in \mathcal{Q}_1$, there exists an $n \in \mathbf{N}$ such that*

$$u_k(f(n), x_1, \ldots, x_k) = u_k(n, x_1, \ldots, x_k)$$

*for all $x_1, \ldots, x_k \in \mathbf{N}$.*

The proof follows the same lines as that of Theorem 4.2.6, with modifications only in notation.

The Recursion Theorem yields an elegant solution to the second of the problems raised in Section 4.4.1; we shall show that there is an $n$ such that

$$u_0(n) = n \qquad (4.2.6)$$

Let id be the monadic identity function, so that

$$\mathrm{id}(x) = x$$

for all $x \in \mathbf{N}$. By condition $FC_1$, id $\in \mathcal{Q}_1$. Let $\iota$ be an index for id, so that

$$u_1(\iota, x) = x$$

for all $x \in \mathbf{N}$. If we define $f$ by

$$f(x) = \mathrm{pair}(\iota, x)$$

then $f \in \mathcal{Q}_1$, and by Theorem 4.2.6 there exists $n \in \mathbf{N}$ such that

$$u_0(f(n)) = u_0(n)$$

Thus, we have

$$
\begin{aligned}
u_0(n) &= u_0(f(n)) \\
&= u_0(\mathrm{pair}(\iota, n)) \\
&= u_1(\iota, n) \\
&= \mathrm{id}(n) \\
&= n
\end{aligned}
$$

which yields Eq. (4.2.6).

This application of the Recursion Theorem may seem a mere curiosity, but in fact it represents in abstract form an argument that is prominent in discussions of self-reproduction. It is due, in more concrete forms, to von Neumann [1966].

Conditions FC$_1$ through FC$_7$ tell us that every reflexive class contains certain basic functions. Lemma 4.2.1 tells us that it also contains certain other partial functions, the undefined functions, though this is not obvious from the definition. What other partial functions are contained in every reflexive class? We shall see that this question has a simple answer: the partial functions that can be computed by algorithms. We shall also see that these partial functions themselves form a reflexive class, which is therefore the "smallest" reflexive class.

Every reflexive class contains the successor function. What about its inverse, the predecessor function? We shall define this function by

$$\text{pred}(x) = \begin{cases} 0, & \text{if } x = 0 \\ x - 1, & \text{if } x \neq 0 \end{cases}$$

(The stipulation that $\text{pred}(0) = 0$ is convenient, because it makes pred a total function, but nothing in what follows would be different if we set $\text{pred}(0) = \bot$.) We can use cond to perform selection by cases, but how are we to get $x - 1$? We must construct it by the method that yields all of the natural numbers: starting with zero and repeatedly taking successors. Consider the definition

$$\text{pred}(x) = \begin{cases} 0, & \text{if } x = 0 \\ p(x, 0), & \text{if } x \neq 0 \end{cases} \tag{4.2.7}$$

Here we use the auxiliary partial function $p$ defined by

$$p(x, y) = \begin{cases} y, & \text{if } x = \text{succ}(y) \\ p(x, \text{succ}(y)), & \text{if } x \neq \text{succ}(y) \end{cases} \tag{4.2.8}$$

From Eq. (4.2.7) it is clear that pred is in $\mathcal{P}_1$ if $p$ is in $\mathcal{P}_2$. Equation (4.2.8) defines $p$ in terms of itself, as well as previously defined functions such as succ and cond. (Actually, Eq. (4.2.8) does not define $p$ uniquely, but only for those $x$ and $y$ such that $x \geq \text{succ}(y)$. We shall return to this point later; for now we merely observe that any partial function $p$ that satisfies Eq. (4.2.8) for all $x$ and $y$ will yield the function pred in Eq. (4.2.7), since Eq. (4.2.7) only refers to values $x \geq 1$ and $y = 0$, for which $p$ is uniquely defined by Eq. (4.2.8).) Our next task will be to show that such "recursive" definitions yield partial functions in $\mathcal{P}$.

We begin by replacing one of the occurrences of $p$ in Eq. (4.2.8) by $q$. The resulting definition is no longer recursive; it is merely a definition of one partial function in terms of another:

$$q(x, y) = \begin{cases} y, & \text{if } x = \text{succ}(y) \\ p(x, \text{succ}(y)), & \text{if } x \neq \text{succ}(y) \end{cases} \tag{4.2.9}$$

From Eq. (4.2.9) it is clear that $q$ is in $\mathcal{P}_2$ if $p$ is in $\mathcal{P}_2$. But more is true: there is a function $f$ in $\mathcal{Q}_1$ such that if $\pi$ is an index for $p$ then $f(\pi)$ is an index for $q$. To see this, we define the partial function $r$ by

$$r(\pi, x, y) = \begin{cases} y, & \text{if } x = \text{succ}(y) \\ u(\pi, x, \text{succ}(y)), & \text{if } x \neq \text{succ}(y) \end{cases}$$

We now have the index $\pi$ for $p$ appearing as an argument, rather than $p$ itself appearing on the right-hand side. The partial function $r$ is also in $\mathcal{P}$. Let $\varrho$ be an index for $r$. Then if we set $f(\pi) = \text{pair}(\varrho, \pi)$, we obtain the function $f$ we seek.

Let us now apply the Recursion Theorem (with $k = 2$ in Corollary 4.2.7) to the function $f$ just constructed, to obtain an $n \in \mathbf{N}$ such that $n$ and $f(n)$ index the same partial function. If the partial function indexed by $n$ is $p$, then the partial function indexed by $f(n)$ is $q$, as given by Eq. (4.2.9). The Recursion Theorem says that these two partial functions are the same, and so we have found a partial function $p$ that satisfies Eq. (4.2.8) for all $x$ and $y$. And since we have found an index $n$ for $p$, we have that $p$ is in $\mathcal{P}$. Finally, by Eq. (4.2.7), we have that pred is in $\mathcal{P}$.

In proving the existence of a partial function $p$ satisfying Eq. (4.2.8) we used a partial function $r$, which took, in addition to the arguments $x$ and $y$, an argument $\pi$ that was eventually an index for the partial function $p$. Thus, the Recursion Theorem allows us, when defining a partial function, to assume that we are given an index for the partial function we are defining as an additional argument. In programming languages that allow recursive programming, the identifier of the procedure being defined may be used in the body of the procedure definition in the same way as a "formal parameter" of the procedure. Though the name *recursive function* and the Recursion Theorem are older than the technique of recursive programming (see Dijkstra [1960] for an early account), the similarity of the names is quite appropriate.

We mentioned that there are many partial functions $p$ satisfying Eq. (4.2.8) for all $x$ and $y$. The Recursion Theorem has given us one, but which one? The statement of the Recursion Theorem does not tell us (though an analysis of its proof might). For the purpose of defining pred, it does not matter which function we get, but for other purposes it might, and so we shall consider the point further now.

Among all partial functions that satisfy Eq. (4.2.8) for all $x$ and $y$, there is one that is distinguished. It is the one that is defined for those $x$ and $y$ for which it must be in order to satisfy Eq. (4.2.8), but assumes the value $\bot$ for all other $x$ and $y$. Every other partial function that satisfies Eq. (4.2.8) can be obtained from this distinguished one by "extending" its domain with additional combinations of $x$

and $y$. (There may be many ways to assign a value for a particular combination, and adding one combination may force the addition of other combinations to maintain consistency with Eq. (4.2.8).) The distinguished partial function is therefore the "least defined" function satisfying Eq. (4.2.8), or the "greatest common restriction" of all partial functions satisfying Eq. (4.2.8).

It is possible to amend the Recursion Theorem so that it always gives this "least fixed-point," rather than just a "fixed-point," but its statement then becomes much more cumbersome. To avoid this, we shall sacrifice a bit of elegance and rely on a simple device that will allow us to conclude that the distinguished partial function $p$ satisfying Eq. (4.2.8) is in $\mathcal{P}$. The idea is to regard Eq. (4.2.8) as an algorithm for computing the value of $p$ for some combination of arguments. The result of the first step might yield this value (if $x = \mathrm{succ}(y)$) or it might call for the evaluation of $p$ for another combination of arguments, giving rise to a second step. The distinguished partial function is the one that is defined when this process terminates after a finite number of steps, but is undefined whenever the process continues indefinitely. To distinguish between these cases, we define an auxiliary partial function that counts the number of steps in the process. Specifically, define $t$ by

$$t(x, y) = \begin{cases} 1, & \text{if } x = \mathrm{succ}(y) \\ \mathrm{succ}(t(x, \mathrm{succ}(y))), & \text{if } x \neq \mathrm{succ}(y) \end{cases} \qquad (4.2.10)$$

It is easy to see that the partial function whose value is the number of steps when the process for $p$ terminates, and whose value is undefined when the process for $p$ is infinite, satisfies Eq. (4.2.10) for all $x$ and $y$. But in this case there is a unique such partial function. (It is easy to show that any attempt to define $t$ for an additional combination of $x$ and $y$ leads to an inconsistency with Eq. (4.2.10), by induction on the value assigned to the combination.) The argument that we used earlier for $p$ can be repeated for $t$, and the Recursion Theorem then tells us that the unique partial function $t$ satisfying Eq. (4.2.10) is in $\mathcal{P}$. If $p$ is any partial function satisfying Eq. (4.2.8), then by composing an appropriate projection function with $p$ and $t$, we obtain the distinguished partial function satisfying Eq. (4.2.8), and so this distinguished partial function is also in $\mathcal{P}$.

We have encountered some useful arguments for showing that partial functions belong to $\mathcal{P}$. We shall now present some conventions that are frequently used in the literature to specify such partial functions.

The first item is the "lambda notation." A function such as

$$\mathrm{cond} \circ (\mathrm{proj}_{2,1}, \mathrm{proj}_{2,2}, \mathrm{const}_{2,1}, \mathrm{const}_{2,0})$$

can be defined much more perspicuously by giving it a name (say, "eq") and using "dummy arguments" (say, $x$ and $y$):

$$eq(x, y) = \text{cond}(x, y, 1, 0)$$

The lambda notation is a device for using such dummy arguments without giving the function a name. In this example, the expression $\lambda(x, y).\text{cond}(x, y, 1, 0)$ represents the function eq; one might read the expression "that function whose value for $x$ and $y$ is $\text{cond}(x, y, 1, 0)$."

We have introduced the lambda notation as a way of representing partial functions of natural numbers, and that is the only use we shall make of it in this book. It becomes much more powerful, however, if "lambda expressions" are regarded as representing partial functions that take other lambda expressions as arguments. The resulting "lambda calculus," first formulated by Church [1941], is sufficiently rich to serve as an alternate foundation for all of recursive function theory. (In this formulation, everything is a lambda expression; in particular, the natural numbers are certain lambda expressions, and the successor function is a lambda expression that can be applied to these lambda expressions, and so forth.) The prospect of functions taking themselves (not merely indices for themselves) as arguments leads to foundational questions that have been resolved by D. Scott; the lambda calculus has been forged by D. Scott and C. Strachey into a tool of central importance to the semantics of programming languages (see Stoy [1977] for an account).

The second item is the notion of a "primitive recursive function." Define the class $C$ of total functions (where we shall write $C_k$ for $C \cap \mathcal{G}_k$) to be the smallest clone (the intersection of all clones) of functions that (1) contains the monadic functions zero and succ and (2) is closed under the following operation (called "definition by primitive recursion"): if $f \in C_{k-1}$ and $g \in C_{k+1}$, then $C_k$ contains the function $h$ defined by

$$h(x_1, \ldots, x_k)$$
$$= \begin{cases} f(x_2, \ldots, x_k), & \text{if } x_1 = 0 \\ g(\text{pred}(x_1), h(\text{pred}(x_1), x_2, \ldots, x_k), x_2, \ldots, x_k), & \text{if } x \neq 0 \end{cases}$$

The functions in $C$ are called "primitive recursive functions." It is not hard to show that pair and cond are primitive recursive functions, and so there is no need to mention them in the definition of $C$. The techniques used to show that pred belongs to every reflective class can be used to show that the primitive recursive functions are included in every reflexive class. (Definition by primitive recursion uniquely defines a total function, and the Recursion Theorem always gives an index for this function.)

The primitive recursive functions include many of the total functions that are computable by algorithms, but not by any means all of them. The following definition is a variant of one given by Ackermann [1928], who proved that the function defined is not primitive recursive. First define the primitive recursive function double by

$$\text{double}(x) = \begin{cases} 0, & \text{if } x = 0 \\ \text{succ}(\text{succ}(\text{double}(\text{pred}(x)))), & \text{if } x \neq 0 \end{cases}$$

Then define the function $A$ by the following "nested" recursive definition:

$$A(x, y) = \begin{cases} 2, & \text{if } y = 0 \\ \text{double}(y) & \text{if } y \neq 0 \text{ and } x = 0 \\ A(\text{pred}(x), A(x, \text{pred}(y))), & \text{if } x \neq 0 \text{ and } y \neq 0 \end{cases}$$

It is clear that this recursively defines a total function; indeed, this definition can be regarded as an algorithm for computing this function. Using the Recursion Theorem, one can show that this function belongs to every reflexive class. But, in a certain precise technical sense, it "grows faster than" any primitive recursive function.

The final item is the "mu notation" or "definition by minimalization." If $f$ is a total function of $k + 1$ arguments, we shall let $\mu(w).f(w, x_1, \ldots, x_k)$ denote that function of $x_1, \ldots, x_k$ whose value is the smallest natural number $w$ such that $f(w, x_1, \ldots, x_k) \neq 0$, if such a natural number exists, and is undefined, if no such natural number exists. If $f \in \mathcal{Q}_{k+1}$, then the techniques used can be used to show that $\mathcal{P}_{k+1}$ contains the auxiliary function $g$ that is the least defined partial function satisfying the recursive definition

$$g(w, x_1, \ldots, x_k) = \begin{cases} w & \text{if } f(w, x_1, \ldots, x_k) \neq 0 \\ g(\text{succ}(w), x_1, \ldots, x_k), & \text{if } f(w, x_1, \ldots, x_k) = 0 \end{cases}$$

Thus, $\mathcal{P}_k$ also contains $\mu(w).f(w, x_1, \ldots, x_k) = g(0, x_1, \ldots, x_k)$. It follows that $\mathcal{P}$ contains all partial functions defined by minimalization over total functions in $\mathcal{Q}$.

The operations of definition by primitive recursion and by minimalization are very comprehensive. Indeed, we shall see later that together they give all of the functions computable by algorithms.

### Exercises

1. (M) Prove that for each $k, l \geq 0$, $\mathcal{Q}_{k+1}$ contains a total function $\text{comp}_{k,l}$ such that if $f \in \mathcal{P}_k$ and $g_1, \ldots, g_k \in \mathcal{P}_l$, and if $a, b_1, \ldots, b_k$ are indices for $f, g_1, \ldots, g_k$, respectively, then $\text{comp}_{k,l}(a, b_1, \ldots, b_k)$ is an index for $f \circ (g_1, \ldots, g_k)$.

2. (E) Suppose that $\mathcal{P}$ is a reflexive class by virtue of $u$ and $m$, and also by virtue of $u'$ and $m'$. Show that there are total functions $g, g' \in \mathcal{Q}_1$ such that $u = u' \circ g$ and $u' = u \circ g'$. (Given any two programming languages (defined by interpreters), there exist computable translators between them. There is also a connection between $m$ and $m'$, which will be discussed later.)

3. (M) Show that every partial function in $\mathcal{P}$ has infinitely many distinct indices.

4. (M) Show that there is a function pad $\in \mathcal{Q}_2$ such that for every $\pi \in \mathbf{N}$, $\mathrm{pad}(\pi, 0), \mathrm{pad}(\pi, 1), \ldots$, are distinct indices for the partial function indexed by $\pi$.

5. (M) Show that there are two distinct programs that produce each other as output: there exist $n \neq m$ such that

$$u_0(n) = m \qquad \text{and} \qquad u_0(m) = n$$

6. (M) ("Parametrized Recursion Theorem") Prove that for every $k \geq 0$ and every $f \in \mathcal{Q}_2$, there is a $g \in \mathcal{Q}_1$ such that, for all $x \in \mathbf{N}$, $f(g(x), x)$ and $g(x)$ index the same function in $\mathcal{P}_k$.

7. (H) ("Double Recursion Theorem") Prove that for every $k \geq 0$ and every $f, f' \in \mathcal{Q}_2$, there exist $n, n' \in \mathbf{N}$ such that $f(n, n')$ indexes the same function as $n$ in $\mathcal{P}_k$, and $f'(n, n')$ indexes the same function as $n'$ in $\mathcal{P}_k$. (See Smullyan [1961].)

### 4.2.2. Register Machines

We shall now connect our postulational treatment of recursive function theory with the world of computation by machines and programs. (The machines and programs we shall use are similar to ones introduced by Shepherdson and Sturgis [1963].) A byproduct of this connection will be the explicit construction of a reflexive class of partial functions.

We shall begin by describing a class $\mathcal{M}$ of *machines*. Each machine will have some number $k \geq 0$ of *input registers*, some number $l \geq 0$ of *working registers*, one *output register*, and a *program* comprising some number $m \geq 1$ of *instructions*. (We have previously used the term "program" as an informal interpretation of the term "index," but in this section it will have a precise technical meaning.) The class of machines having $k$ input registers, $l$ working registers, and $m$ instructions will be denoted $\mathcal{M}_{k,l,m}$, and we set $\mathcal{M} = \cup_{k \geq 0, l \geq 0, m \geq 1} \mathcal{M}_{k,l,m}$.

An input register of a machine in $\mathcal{M}_{k,l,m}$ will be designated by an *address* from the set $\{1, \ldots, k\}$. A working register of such a machine will be designated by an address from the set $\{k + 1, \ldots, k + l\}$. The output register will be designated by the address $k + l + 1$. Thus, an arbitrary register is designated by an address from $[k + l + 1] = \{1, \ldots, k + l + 1\}$.

An instruction in the program of a machine in $\mathcal{M}_{k,l,m}$ will be designated by a *location* from the set $[m]$. Each instruction will be of one of four types. The first type has the form **halt**. The second type has the form **clear** $R$, where $R$ is an address. The third type has the form **incr** $R$, where $R$ is an address. The fourth type has the form **if** $R = R'$ **then** $L$ **else** $L'$, where $R$ and $R'$ are addresses and $L$ and $L'$ are locations.

Given a machine $M \in \mathcal{M}_{k,l,m}$, we shall associate with it a partial function $f_M \in \mathcal{F}_k$ (the partial function computed by $M$). Given $x_1, \ldots, x_k \in \mathbf{N}$, we determine the value of $f_M(x_1, \ldots, x_k)$ as follows. For $1 \leq j \leq k$, put $x_j$ into the input register with address $j$. For $k + 1 \leq j \leq k + l$, put 0 into the working register with address $j$, and put 0 into the output register. Execute the sequence of instructions defined as follows. The first instruction is the one with location 1. If the current instruction is of the form **halt**, then it is the last instruction in the sequence. If the current instruction is of form **clear** $R$, put 0 into the register with address $R$; the next instruction is the one with location one larger than that of the current instruction. If the current instruction is of form **incr** $R$, increase by one the number in the register with address $R$; the next instruction is the one with location one larger than that of the current instruction. If the current instruction is of the form **if** $R = R'$ **then** $L$ **else** $L'$, compare the numbers in the registers with addresses $R$ and $R'$; if they are equal, the next instruction is the one with location $L$; if they are unequal, the next instruction is the one with location $L'$. If this sequence ends (with an instruction of the form **halt**), the value of $f_M(x_1, \ldots, x_k)$ is the number in the output register at the end. If the sequence does not end, or if an instruction is executed that refers to an address outside the set $[k + l + 1]$ or a location outside the set $[m]$, then $f_M(x_1, \ldots, x_k)$ is undefined.

Define

$$\mathcal{P}^* = \{f_M : M \in \mathcal{M}\}$$

**Theorem 4.2.8.** *If $\mathcal{P}$ is any reflexive class, then $\mathcal{P}^* \subseteq \mathcal{P}$.*

**Proof.** Given a partial function $f \in \mathcal{P}^*$, let $M \in \mathcal{M}_{k,l,m}$ be a machine that computes $f$. Define a partial function $g_M \in \mathcal{F}_{k+l+2}$ as follows. Given $x_1, \ldots, x_{k+l+1}, y \in \mathbf{N}$, we determine the value of $g_M(x_1, \ldots, x_{k+l+1}, y)$ in the same way as $f_M(x_1, \ldots, x_k)$, except that we initially put $x_j$ into the register with address $j$ for $1 \leq j \leq k + l + 1$, and the first instruction is the one with location $y$. Clearly,

$$f(x_1, \ldots, x_k) = g_M(x_1, \ldots, x_k, \underbrace{0, \ldots, 0}_{l+1 \text{ 0's}}, 1)$$

and so it will suffice to show that $g_M \in \mathcal{P}$.

To do this, we write the following recursive definition for a partial function $g \in \mathcal{F}_{k+l+2}$:

$$g(x_1, \ldots, x_{k+l+1}, y) = \begin{cases} G_1, & \text{if } y = 1 \\ \cdots \\ G_m, & \text{if } y = m \\ \text{undef}_{k+l+2}, & \text{otherwise} \end{cases}$$

Here, each $G_n$ is defined as follows. If the instruction with location $j$ is of the form **halt**, then $G_j$ is $x_{k+l+1}$. If the instruction with location $j$ is of the form **clear** $R$, then $G_j$ is $g(x_1, \ldots, x_{R-1}, 0, x_{R+1}, \ldots, x_{k+l+1}, j+1)$. If the instruction with location $j$ is of the form **incr** $R$, then $G_j$ is $g(x_1, \ldots, x_{R-1}, \text{succ}(x_R), x_{R+1}, \ldots, x_{k+l+1}, j+1)$. If the instruction with location $j$ is of the form **if** $R = R'$ **then** $L$ **else** $L'$, then $G_j$ is $\text{cond}(x_R, x_{R'}, g(x_1, \ldots, x_{k+l+1}, L), g(x_1, \ldots, x_{k+l+1}, L'))$. It is clear that $g_M$ is the least defined partial function satisfying this recursive definition. On the other hand, this least defined function is in $\mathcal{P}$, by the argument of Section 4.2.1. □

Let $\mathcal{Q}^* = \mathcal{P}^* \cap \mathcal{G}$. We shall use subscripts on $\mathcal{P}^*$ and $\mathcal{Q}^*$ to indicate the number of arguments, as usual.

**Theorem 4.2.9.** *There exist $u^* \in \mathcal{P}_1^*$ and $m^* \in \mathcal{Q}_2^*$ such that $\mathcal{P}^*$ is a reflexive class by virtue of $u^*$ and $m^*$.*

**Proof.** That $\mathcal{P}^*$ satisfies conditions FC$_1$ through FC$_5$ is straightforward to verify: for conditions FC$_2$ through FC$_5$, it is a question of writing the program for a machine that computes the appropriate function; for condition FC$_1$, it is a question of combining programs (with appropriate modifications) to obtain a program for the composite partial function.

The crux of the proof, then, is the construction of the partial function $u^*$ and the function $m^*$. To do this, it is necessary to do some more programming.

Given a machine $M \in \mathcal{M}_{k,l,m}$ with instructions $I_1, \ldots, I_m$, we shall associate with it a natural number $\#M = \langle\langle k, l, m\rangle, \langle\#I_1, \ldots, \#I_m\rangle\rangle$, where the number $\#I_n$ associated with the instruction $I_n$ is determined as follows. If $I_n$ is of the form **halt**, then $\#I_n = \langle 1 \rangle$. If $I_n$ is of the form **clear** $R$, then $\#I_n = \langle 2, R \rangle$. If $I_n$ is of the form **incr** $R$, then $\#I_n = \langle 3, R \rangle$. If $I_n$ is of the form **if** $R = R'$

**then** $L$ **else** $L'$, then $\#I_n = \langle 4, R, R', L, L' \rangle$. In this way a natural number is associated with each machine, and it is clear that $M$ is uniquely determined by $\#M$.

To define $u^*$ and $m^*$, we must associate indices with partial functions. The most important indices will be of the form $\langle x_j, \ldots, x_1, \#M \rangle$ where $\#M$ is associated with a machine $M \in \mathcal{M}_{k,l,m}, x_1, \ldots, x_j \in \mathbf{N}$, and $j \le k$. All natural numbers not of this form will be regarded as indices for the partial functions undef.

We now define $u^*(\pi)$ to be $f_M(x_1, \ldots, x_k)$ if $\pi = \langle x_k, \ldots, x_1, \#M \rangle$, where $\#M$ is associated with a machine $M \in \mathcal{M}_{k,l,m}$, and to be $\perp$ otherwise. It is a straightforward (though tedious) exercise to write a program that implements this definition, thus showing that $u^*$ belongs to $\mathcal{P}^*$ and satisfies condition $FC_6$. (After some preliminary manipulations, this program performs a step-by-step "simulation" of the execution of the program of the machine $M$.)

Finally, we define $m^*(\pi, t)$ to be 1 if the step-by-step simulation described in the definition of $u^*$ ends after at most $t$ steps, and to be 0 otherwise. It is again a straightforward programming exercise to show that $m^*$ belongs to $\mathcal{Q}^*$ and satisfies $FC_7$.                                                                      □

At this point we have shown that $\mathcal{P}^*$ is a reflexive class, and since $\mathcal{P}^* \subseteq \mathcal{P}$ for any other reflexive class $\mathcal{P}$, $\mathcal{P}^*$ is the smallest reflexive class. In view of its definition in terms of machines and programs, it seems justified to regard $\mathcal{P}^*$ as the class of partial functions that are computable by algorithms; any lingering doubts about whether we would get the same class for a different notion of machine or program should be cleared up by the proof of Theorem 4.2.9, since the step-by-step simulation mentioned there could carried out for any other precisely defined classes of machines and programs.

It is common to exploit this situation by asserting that a partial function is in $\mathcal{P}^*$ whenever a precise algorithm for computing it has been described, even if that algorithm is not expressed in terms of the machines and programs used here. Such an assertion is called an appeal to "Church's Thesis"; when used with reasonable prudence, it yields reliable conclusions and dispenses with the tedious details of what was termed "straightforward programming" earlier.

### Exercises

1. (E) (a) If we had defined our machines to have an instruction of the form **decr** $R$ (which decreases by one the number in the register with address $R$), rather than the **clear** $R$ instruction, and to have an instruction of the form **if** $R = 0$ **then** $L$ **else** $L'$ (which compares the number in a register with 0), rather than the **if** $R = R'$ **then** $L$ **else** $L'$ instruction, would the class of

functions computed by such machines be larger, smaller, or the same? (b) What if we made the second of these changes, but not the first?

2. (M) Show that there is a total function $e \in \mathcal{Q}_1^*$ such that that every partial function $f \in \mathcal{P}_k^*$ can be expressed as

$$f(x_1, \ldots, x_k) = e(\mu(y).g(x_1, \ldots, x_k, y))$$

for some function $g \in \mathcal{Q}_{k+1}^*$.

3. (M) What functions $e \in \mathcal{Q}_1^*$ have the property that every partial function $f \in \mathcal{P}_k^*$ can be expressed as

$$f(x_1, \ldots, x_k) = e(\mu(y).g(x_1, \ldots, x_k, y))$$

for some function $g \in \mathcal{Q}_{k+1}^*$?

### 4.2.3. Recursive Cones

We are now ready to characterize the smallest reflexive class by means of closure conditions. We shall say that a class $\mathcal{P}$ of partial functions is a *recursive cone* if it satisfies the following five conditions.

RC$_1$   $\mathcal{P}$ forms a clone (that is, $\mathcal{P}$ contains all projection functions and is closed under composition).

RC$_2$   $\mathcal{P}$ contains the monadic constant function zero, defined by $\mathrm{zero}(x) = 0$.

RC$_3$   $\mathcal{P}$ contains the monadic successor function succ, defined by $\mathrm{succ}(x) = x + 1$.

RC$_4$   $\mathcal{P}$ is closed under *primitive recursion*; that is, if $\mathcal{P}$ contains the $(n-1)$-adic partial function $f$ and the $(n+1)$-adic partial function $g$, then $\mathcal{P}$ also contains the $n$-adic partial function $\mathrm{prim}(f, g)$, defined by

$$\mathrm{prim}(f, g)(x_1, \ldots, x_{n-1}, 0) = f(x_1, \ldots, x_{n-1})$$

$$\mathrm{prim}(f, g)(x_1, \ldots, x_{n-1}, y+1) = g(x_1, \ldots, x_{n-1}, y,$$

$$\mathrm{prim}(f, g)(x_1, \ldots, x_{n-1}, y))$$

RC$_5$   $\mathcal{P}$ is closed under *minimalization*; that is, if $\mathcal{P}$ contains the $(n+1)$-adic partial function $f$, then $\mathcal{P}$ also contains the $n$-adic partial function $\mathrm{minim}(f)$, defined by

$$\mathrm{minim}(f)(x_1, x_2, \ldots, x_n) = \mu(y).f(x_1, \ldots, x_n, y)$$

Let $\mathcal{R}$ denote the smallest class of partial functions satisfying conditions RC$_1$ through RC$_5$, and let $\mathcal{S}$ denote the class $\mathcal{R} \cap \mathcal{G}$ of total functions in $\mathcal{R}$.

**Theorem 4.2.10.** *We have*

$$\mathcal{R} \subseteq \mathcal{P}^*$$

**Proof.** The proof is a matter of straightforward though tedious programming. (The only idea that needs to be added beyond those in the proof of Theorem 4.2.9 is the use of a "stack" or "pushdown store" to keep track of intermediate results when implementing primitive recursion.                                    □

**Theorem 4.2.11.** *We have*

$$\mathcal{P}^* \subseteq \mathcal{R}$$

**Proof.** We begin by showing that the functions pred, cond, pair, left, and right all belong to $\mathcal{S}$. In fact, we shall show this without using condition RC$_5$ (that is, we shall show that they are "primitive recursive"). First, we construct pred by primitive recursion:

$$\mathrm{pred}(0) = 0$$

$$\mathrm{pred}(\mathrm{succ}(x)) = x$$

It will be convenient in what follows to use the triadic function case, defined by

$$\mathrm{case}(x, y, z) = \begin{cases} y, & \text{if } x = 0 \\ z, & \text{if } x \neq 0 \end{cases}$$

We can construct case by primitive recursion:

$$\mathrm{case}(0, y, z) = y$$

$$\mathrm{case}(\mathrm{succ}(x), y, z) = z$$

Next we define the dyadic function diff by

$$\mathrm{diff}(x, y) = \begin{cases} x - y, & \text{if } x \geq y \\ 0, & \text{otherwise} \end{cases}$$

We can construct diff by primitive recursion:

$$\mathrm{diff}(0, y) = 0$$

$$\mathrm{diff}(\mathrm{succ}(x), y) = \mathrm{pred}(\mathrm{diff}(x, y))$$

Next we define the dyadic function eq by

$$\mathrm{eq}(x, y) = \begin{cases} 1, & \text{if } x = y \\ 0, & \text{if } x \neq y \end{cases}$$

We can then construct eq by

$$eq(x, y) = \text{case}(\text{diff}(x, y), \text{case}(\text{diff}(y, x), 1, 0), 0)$$

and construct cond by

$$\text{cond}(w, x, y, z) = \text{case}(eq(w, x), z, y)$$

In order to construct pair, it will be convenient to first define the dyadic function sum by $\text{sum}(x, y) = x + y$. We can construct sum by primitive recursion:

$$\text{sum}(0, y) = y$$

$$\text{sum}(\text{succ}(x), y) = \text{succ}(\text{sum}(x, y))$$

We then define the dyadic function prod by $\text{prod}(x, y) = xy$. We can construct prod by primitive recursion:

$$\text{prod}(0, y) = 0$$

$$\text{prod}(\text{succ}(x), y) = \text{sum}(y, \text{prod}(x, y))$$

Next, we define the monadic function even by

$$even(x) = \begin{cases} 1, & \text{if } x \text{ is even} \\ 0, & \text{if } x \text{ is odd} \end{cases}$$

We can construct even by primitive recursion:

$$even(0) = 1$$

$$even(\text{succ}(x)) = \text{case}(even(x), 0, 1)$$

Next, we define the monadic function half by $\text{half}(x) = \lfloor x/2 \rfloor$. We can construct half by primitive recursion:

$$\text{half}(0) = 0$$

$$\text{half}(\text{succ}(x)) = \text{case}(even(x), \text{half}(x), \text{succ}(\text{half}(x)))$$

Then we can construct pair from succ, sum, prod, and half, by virtue of the formula

$$\text{pair}(x, y) = \binom{x + y + 1}{2} + y + 1$$

Finally, we turn to the functions left and right. We begin by constructing the triadic function $pair_3$:

$$pair_3(x, y, z) = eq(pair(x, y), z)$$

Then we construct a triadic function $right_3$ by primitive recursion:

$$right_3(0, y, z) = 0$$

$$right_3(succ(x), y, z) = case(pair_3(x, y, z), right_3(x, y, z), 1)$$

Then we have $right_3(x, y, z) \neq 0$ if and only if $pair_3(w, y, z) \neq 0$ for some $w < x$. In particular, we have $right_3(z, y, z) \neq 0$ if and only if $right(z) = y$. Then we define a dyadic function $right_2$ by primitive recursion:

$$right_2(0, z) = 0$$

$$right_2(succ(y), z) = case(right_3(z, y, z), right_2(y, z), y)$$

Then we have $right_2(y, z) = w$ if $right(z) = w$ for some $w < y$, and we have $right_2(y, z) = 0$ otherwise. In particular, we can construct the monadic function right by $right(z) = right_2(z, z)$. A similar argument shows that the monadic function left is also primitive recursive.

Suppose now that $f \in \mathcal{P}_k^*$ is computed by $M \in \mathcal{M}_{k,l,m}$. We shall represent configurations of the machine $M$ as natural numbers, by encoding lists of $k + l + 2$ natural numbers (the contents of the $k + l + 1$ registers together with the location of the next instruction, as in the proof of Theorem 4.2.8). The $k$-adic function $i$, defined by

$$i(x_1, \ldots, x_n) = \langle x_1, \ldots, x_n, \underbrace{0, \ldots, 0}_{l+1 \text{ 0's}}, 1 \rangle$$

(giving the encoding of the initial configuration of the $M$ as a function of the arguments of $f$), and a monadic function $e$, defined so that

$$e(\langle x_1, \ldots, x_{k+l}, y, z \rangle) = y$$

(giving the value of $f$ as a function of the encoding of the halting configuration of $M$), are primitive recursive.

Let the monadic function $r$ be such that $r(x)$ equals one of the following: (1) $x$, if $x$ is the encoding of a halting configuration of $M$; (2) the encoding of the configuration following the configuration encoded by $x$ according to $M$, if $x$ is the encoding of a non-halting configuration of $M$; and (3), 0 otherwise. Let the monadic function $h$ be such that $h(x)$ equals 1 if $x$ is the encoding of a halting configuration of $M$, and 0 otherwise. The functions $r$ and $h$ can be constructed from primitive recursive functions as previously constructed, and thus are themselves primitive recursive.

We now construct the dyadic function $s$ by primitive recursion:

$$s(0, x) = x$$

$$s(\text{succ}(n), x) = r(s(n, x))$$

so that $s(n, x)$ is the encoding of the configuration reached after $n$ steps by $M$ when started in the configuration encoded by $x$ (or the first halting configuration reached, if one is reached in fewer than $n$ steps). We then construct the monadic function $t$ by minimalization

$$t(x) = \mu(n).h(s(n, x))$$

so that $t(x)$ is the number of steps taken by $M$ to halt when started in the configuration encoded by $x$. Since $h$ and $s$ are primitive recursive, we have $t \in \mathcal{R}_1$. Finally, we can express $f$ as

$$f(x_1, \ldots, x_k) = e(s(t(i(x_1, \ldots, x_k)), i(x_1, \ldots, x_k)))$$

Since all of the functions on the right-hand side belong to $\mathcal{R}$, so does $f$. $\quad\square$

Our treatment of recursive cones is based on that of Kleene [1938].

### 4.2.4. Register Machines with Oracles

Up to this point, we have seen only one example of a reflexive class, the smallest reflexive class $\mathcal{P}^*$. The time has come to ask what other reflexive classes exist and what the relations among them are. Our answer will involve a notion of "computation relative to an oracle" that was introduced by Turing [1939].

We begin by attempting to formalize the notion of a partial function $f$ being computable "relative to" some other partial function $g$. The theory we shall develop will only deal with the case in which $g$ is a total function. For simplicity, we shall also assume that $g$ is a function of one argument and that it assumes only the values 0 and 1, so that it is the characteristic function of some set $A$ of natural numbers.

The intuitive intent of the theory is to say that a partial function $f$ is "computable relative to $A$" if it is computed by some machine that is augmented by the ability to ask questions about the membership of various natural numbers in $A$. We allow the number of questions, and the subjects of the later questions, to depend on the answers to earlier questions. Since $A$ may not be computable in any sense, we may imagine that the machine asks these questions to an "oracle," who "knows" the set $A$ without having to compute.

To formalize this idea, we consider an expanded class $\mathcal{M}^O$ of machines, which have available to them a fifth type of instruction. This fifth type has the form **if member then** $L$ **else** $L'$, where $L$ and $L'$ are locations. If during the execution of the program the current instruction is of the form **if member then** $L$ **else** $L'$, determine whether the number in the output register is a member of the set $A$; if it is, the next instruction is the one with location $L$; if it is not, the next instruction is the one with location $L'$. (The reason for restricting queries to the number in the output register, rather than a designated register, will become apparent later.)

These augmented machines compute partial functions, which now depend implicitly on the set $A$. If $M \in \mathcal{M}^O$, we shall denote by $f_{M,A}$ the partial function computed by $M$ relative to $A$. Define

$$\mathcal{P}^*(A) = \{f_{M,A} : M \in \mathcal{M}^O\}$$

If the characteristic function $\text{char}_A$ of $A$ belongs to $\mathcal{P}^*$, then clearly $\mathcal{P}^*(A) = \mathcal{P}^*$ (since a machine could compute for itself the answers to any questions it might ask about $A$). If $\text{char}_A$ does not belong to $\mathcal{P}^*$, however, $\mathcal{P}^*(A)$ will be larger than $\mathcal{P}^*$: $\text{char}_A$ will belong to $\mathcal{P}^*(A)$ but not to $\mathcal{P}^*$.

**Theorem 4.2.12.** *If $\mathcal{P}$ is a reflexive class and $\text{char}_A \in \mathcal{P}$, then $\mathcal{P}^*(A) \subseteq \mathcal{P}$.*

The proof is analogous to that of Theorem 4.2.8.

**Theorem 4.2.13.** *There exist $u \in \mathcal{P}_1^*(A)$ and $m \in \mathcal{Q}_2^*(A)$ such that $\mathcal{P}^*(A)$ is a reflexive class by virtue of $u$ and $m$.*

The proof is analogous to that of Theorem 4.2.9. We remark that $u$ and $m$ depend on $A$.

Theorems 4.2.12 and 4.2.13 together show that $\mathcal{P}^*(A)$ is the smallest reflexive class containing $\text{char}_A$. In particular, we have $\text{char}_A \in \mathcal{P}^*(B)$ if and only if $\mathcal{P}^*(A) \subseteq \mathcal{P}^*(B)$.

We have seen that to every set $A$ there corresponds a reflexive class $\mathcal{P}^*(A)$. Does every reflexive class arise in this way? An affirmative answer is given by the following theorem.

**Theorem 4.2.14.** *For every reflexive class $\mathcal{P}$, there is a set $A$ such that $\mathcal{P} = \mathcal{P}^*(A)$.*

**Proof.** Suppose that $\mathcal{P}$ is a reflexive class by virtue of $u$ and $m$. The idea of the proof is to "encode" $u$ and $m$ into $A$. This must be done in such a way that any reflexive class containing $\text{char}_A$ also contains $u$ and $m$, but also in such a way that nothing else is added beyond what is implied by $u$ and $m$.

We set

$$A = \{\langle \pi, t, z \rangle : m(\pi, t) = 1 \text{ and } u(\pi) = z\}$$

To see that $\text{char}_A \in \mathcal{P}$, let $\sigma$ be an index for succ. Then

$$\lambda(\pi, t, z).u(\text{cond}(m(\pi, t), 1, \pi, \text{pair}(\sigma, z)))$$

is a total function in $\mathcal{P}$ that is equal to $z$ if and only if both $m(\pi, t) = 1$ and $u(\pi) = z$. Since $\text{char}_A$ can be obtained by combining this function with selectors that extract $\pi$, $t$, and $z$ from $\langle \pi, t, z \rangle$ and a conditional that tests for equality with $z$, $\text{char}_A$ belongs to $\mathcal{P}$. Thus $\mathcal{P}^*(A) \subseteq \mathcal{P}$ by Theorem 4.2.12.

Conversely, every partial function $f$ in $\mathcal{P}$ is of the form $\lambda(x_1, \ldots, x_k).u_k(\pi, x_1, \ldots, x_k)$ for some index $\pi$. By applying the function pair $k$ times to $\pi$ and $x_1, \ldots, x_k$, a machine can compute an index $\pi'$ such that $u(\pi') = u_k(\pi, x_1, \ldots, x_k)$. A machine with access to an oracle for $A$ can now embark on a sequence of questions that ask if $\langle \pi', t, z \rangle$ belongs to $A$ for all possible combinations of $t = 0, 1, \ldots$, and $z = 0, 1, \ldots$. (By a "programming trick" that exploits the definition of $\langle \cdots \rangle$, this can be accomplished by asking if $\langle \pi', y \rangle$ belongs to $A$ for $y = 1, 2, \ldots$!) If $u(\pi') = \bot$, the answer will always be "no," since then $m(\pi', t) = 0$ for all $t$. If on the other hand $u(\pi') = z$, then the answer will eventually be "yes," since then $m(\pi', t) = 1$ for some $t$. Thus, a machine with access to an oracle for $A$ can halt with $z$ in the output register in precisely those cases for which $f(x_1, \ldots, x_k) = z$. Since this is true for every partial function $f \in \mathcal{P}$, we have $\mathcal{P} \subseteq \mathcal{P}^*(A)$. $\square$

We have now discovered the structure of an arbitrary reflexive class (that is, class $\mathcal{P}$ satisfying conditions $FC_1$ through $FC_7$): it is $\mathcal{P}^*(A)$ for some set $A$ of natural numbers (that is, the class of partial functions computed by register machines with access to an oracle for $A$).

The arguments used to prove Theorems 4.2.10 and 4.2.11 show that $\mathcal{P}^*(A)$ is the smallest recursive cone containing the characteristic function of $A$, and that any principal recursive cone (that is, any recursive cone generated by a single total function) is the reflexive class $\mathcal{P}^*(A)$ for some $A$.

In Theorem 4.2.13 we constructed functions $u \in \mathcal{P}_1^*(A)$ and $m \in \mathcal{Q}_2^*(A)$ such that $\mathcal{P}^*(A)$ is a reflexive class by virtue of $u$ and $m$. The partial function $u$ and the function $m$ depend on $A$; we may write $u^A$ or $m^A$ if we wish to make this dependence explicit. The following proposition shows that this dependence is "uniform" and can be approximated by "absolutely computable" partial functions with access to only initial segments of the sets $A$.

We shall say that a set $A$ *agrees with* a set $B$ *up to* $n$ if, for all $x$ in the range $0 \leq x \leq n - 1$, $x \in A$ if and only if $x \in B$. This definition gives a precise sense in which a possibly infinite set $A$ can be approximated arbitrarily well by the finite sets that agree with it up to increasing thresholds. Unlike possibly infinite sets, finite sets of natural numbers are finite objects. Thus each finite set $\{x_1, \ldots, x_k\}$ can be "encoded" by a natural number $\#\{x_1, \ldots, x_k\}$, in such a way that all of the standard set-theoretic operations correspond to computable functions on the encodings (see Exercise 1 following this section). We shall use the following convention to simplify notation: if a finite set $B$ is written where a natural number should appear, the encoding $\#B$ of the finite set as a natural number should be used.

**Proposition 4.2.15.** *There exist* $u° \in \mathcal{P}_2^*$ *and* $m° \in \mathcal{Q}_3^*$ *such that, for all* $A \subseteq \mathbf{N}$ *and* $\pi, n \in \mathbf{N}$, *if the finite subset* $B \subseteq A$ *agrees with* $A$ *up to* $n$, *then (1)* $m°(\pi, n, B) = m^A(\pi, n)$ *and (2) if the preceding common value is 1, then* $u°(\pi, B) = u^A(\pi)$.

**Proof.** In the construction of Theorem 4.2.13, a computation that terminates in at most $n$ steps can ask the oracle questions only about natural numbers at most $n - 1$. (Since the initial contents of the output register are 0, and each of the $n - 1$ or fewer instructions preceding the halt instruction can increase these contents by at most one.) Thus, the same computation ensues if $A$ is replaced by any set $B$ that agrees with $A$ up to $n$. If $B$ is finite, it can be represented by an additional argument, and access to the oracle is no longer necessary.    □

### Exercise

1. (E)  Associate with each finite set $\{x_1, \ldots, x_k\}$ a natural number $\#\{x_1, \ldots, x_k\}$ in such a way that (a) $\#\{x_1, \ldots, x_k\} = \#\{y_1, \ldots, y_l\}$ if and only if $\{x_1, \ldots, x_k\} = \{y_1, \ldots, y_l\}$, (b) $\#\emptyset = 0$, and (c) there are computable total functions (that is, functions in $\mathcal{Q}^*$) for testing for membership in a set, adjoining an element to a set, finding the smallest element in a set, and deleting an element from a set.

## 4.3. Recursively Enumerable Relations

Our development of recursive function theory has thus far given primacy to the notion of function (partial or total). In this section we shall begin a study of the computability of relations over the domain of natural numbers, and we shall define the most important concepts ("recursively enumerable" and "recursive" relations) in terms of functions.

### *4.3.1. Relations*

A set $A \subseteq \mathbf{N}^k$ of $k$-tuples of natural numbers will be called a $k$-ary *relation*. The set of all $k$-ary relations will be denoted $\mathcal{A}_k$. Since there is just one 0-tuple, 0-ary relations are not very interesting (there are just two of them). The 1-ary relations are in one-to-one correspondence with the sets of natural numbers, and we shall often abuse language by ignoring the distinction between the corresponding sets.

Let $A$ be a $k$-ary relation. The *characteristic function* of $A$ is the $k$-adic function $\mathrm{char}_A$ defined by

$$\mathrm{char}_A(x_1, \ldots, x_k) = \begin{cases} 1, & \text{if } (x_1, \ldots, x_k) \in A \\ 0, & \text{if } (x_1, \ldots, x_k) \notin A \end{cases}$$

for $x_1, \ldots, x_k \in \mathbf{N}$. We shall say that the relation $A$ is *recursive* (or "decidable") if $\mathrm{char}_A$ is a recursive function (that is, belongs to $\mathcal{Q}^*$). The set of all $k$-ary recursive relations will be denoted $\mathcal{R}_k^*$.

Recall that if $f$ is a $k$-adic partial function, the *domain* of $f$ is the relation $\mathrm{dom}(f) = \{(x_1, \ldots, x_k) : f(x_1, \ldots, x_k) \in \mathbf{N}\}$. We shall say that a relation $A$ is *recursively enumerable* if $A = \mathrm{dom}(f)$ for some partial recursive function $f$ (that is, some $f$ that belongs to $\mathcal{P}^*$). The set of all $k$-ary recursively enumerable relations will be denoted $\mathcal{E}_k^*$.

**Example 4.3.1.** Recall the function $d$ defined in Section 4.2.1 by

$$d(x) = \begin{cases} 0, & \text{if } u_1^*(x, x) = \bot \\ 1, & \text{if } u_1^*(x, x) \in \mathbf{N} \end{cases}$$

(We have written $u^*$ rather than simply $u$, since we are currently interested in $\mathcal{P}^*$ rather than an arbitrary reflexive class $\mathcal{P}$.) Since $d$ is a total function assuming only the values 0 and 1, there is a set $K$ such that

$$d = \mathrm{char}_K$$

By Theorem 4.2.2, $d$ is not a recursive function, and so the set $K$ is not recursive. On the other hand, $K = \mathrm{dom}(\lambda(x).u_1(x, x))$, and $\lambda(x).u_1(x, x)$ is a partial recursive function, so that the set $K$ is recursively enumerable.

If $A$ is a $k$-ary relation, we define its *complement* $\mathrm{Compl}(A)$ to be $\mathbf{N}^k \setminus A$, the set of $k$-tuples that are not in $A$. (The empty set $\emptyset$ is unique in being a $k$-ary relation for each $k \geq 0$. We shall regard these relations as being distinct, and write $\emptyset_k$ rather than simply $\emptyset$. We then have $\text{Compl}(\emptyset_k) = \mathbf{N}^k$.)

*Lemma 4.3.1.* (a) If $A$ is recursive, then $\text{Compl}(A)$ is recursive. (b) If $A$ is recursive, then $A$ is recursively enumerable (and, using part (a), $\text{Compl}(A)$ is recursively enumerable). (c) If $A$ and $\text{Compl}(A)$ are both recursively enumerable, then $A$ is recursive (and, using part (a), $\text{Compl}(A)$ is recursive).

**Proof.** The proof of part (a) is trivial, since we have $\text{char}_{\text{Compl}(A)} = 1 - \text{char}_A$; so is the proof of part (b): if we define the partial recursive function $c$ by

$$c(x) = \begin{cases} 1, & \text{if } x = 1 \\ \bot, & \text{if } x \neq 1 \end{cases}$$

then $A = \text{dom}(c \circ \text{char}_A)$.

Part (c) is intuitively clear. Since $A$ and $\text{Compl}(A)$ are recursively enumerable, there are machines $M$ and $M'$ that compute partial recursive functions $f_M$ and $f_{M'}$, respectively, such that $A = \text{dom}(f_M)$ and $\text{Compl}(A) = \text{dom}(f_{M'})$. If we "dovetail" the computations of $M$ and $M'$ on any given input, one of them is bound to halt, revealing whether the input is in $A$ or not.

We shall make this argument precise in a way that does not rely on our discussion of machines, other than through the fact that the recursive function $m^*$ satisfies condition $\text{FC}_7$.

It is convenient to define a sequence $m_0^*, m_1^*, m_2^*, \ldots,$ of functions by induction. Let $m_0^* = m^*$. If $m_k^*$ has been defined, define $m_{k+1}^*$ by setting

$$m_{k+1}^*(\pi, x_1, x_2, \ldots, x_{k+1}, t) = m_k^*(\text{pair}(\pi, x_1), x_2, \ldots, x_{k+1}, t)$$

for all $\pi, x_1, \ldots, x_{k+1}, t \in \mathbf{N}$. Note that $m_k^*$ belongs to $\mathcal{Q}_{k+2}^*$.

Let $\pi$ and $\pi'$ be indices for partial recursive functions with domains $A$ and $\text{Compl}(A)$, respectively. We can then write

$$\text{char}_A(x_1, \ldots, x_k) = m_k^*(\pi, x_1, \ldots, x_k, \mu(t).\text{or}\,(m_k^*(\pi, x_1, \ldots, x_k, t),$$
$$m_k^*(\pi', x_1, \ldots, x_k, t)))$$

where the dyadic function "or" is defined in the obvious way for arguments that are either 0 or 1. $\qquad\qquad\square$

Let $g_1, \ldots, g_k$ be functions in $\mathcal{G}_l$ for some $k, l \geq 0$. Define

$$\text{range}(g_1, \ldots, g_k) = \{(g_1(x_1, \ldots, x_l), \ldots, g_k(x_1, \ldots, x_l)) : x_1, \ldots, x_l \in \mathbf{N}\}$$

*Lemma 4.3.2.* A $k$-ary relation $A$ is recursively enumerable if and only if either $A = \emptyset$ or $A = \text{range}(g_1, \ldots, g_k)$ for some recursive $g_1, \ldots, g_k \in \mathcal{Q}_1^*$.

**Proof.** The proof of the "if" part is trivial if $A = \emptyset$, since $_k = \text{dom}(\text{undef}_k)$. On the other hand, if $A = \text{range}(g_1, \ldots, g_k)$, then

$$A = \text{dom}(\lambda(x_1, \ldots, x_k).\mu(y).\text{and}_k(\text{eq}(x_1, g_1(y)), \ldots, \text{eq}(x_k, g_k(y))))$$

where the dyadic function "eq" and the $k$-adic function "and" are defined in the obvious ways. If $g_1, \ldots, g_k \in \mathcal{Q}_1^*$, then the partial function denoted by the $\lambda$-expression is in $\mathcal{P}_k^*$. This completes the proof of the "if" part.

It remains to prove the "only if" part. If $A = \emptyset$, we are done; otherwise, let $\alpha = (\alpha_1, \ldots, \alpha_k) \in A$. We shall start by constructing functions $h_1, \ldots, h_k \in \mathcal{Q}_{k+1}^*$ with range equal to $A$. Since $A$ is recursively enumerable, there is an index $\pi$ for a partial function with domain $A$. For $j \in [k]$, define $h_j$ by

$$h_j(x_1, \ldots, x_k, t) = \begin{cases} x_j, & \text{if } m_k^*(\pi, x_1, \ldots, x_k, t) = 1 \\ \alpha_j, & \text{if } m_k^*(\pi, x_1, \ldots, x_k, t) \neq 1 \end{cases}$$

Clearly, $A = \text{range}(h_1, \ldots, h_k)$.

It remains to replace the functions $h_1, \ldots, h_k$ with domain $\mathbf{N}^{k+1}$ by functions $g_1, \ldots, g_k$ with domain $\mathbf{N}$. To do this, it suffices to define for each $k \geq 1$ a list of functions $\text{dove}_{k,1}, \ldots, \text{dove}_{k,k} \in \mathcal{Q}_1^*$ such that $\text{range}(\text{dove}_{k,1}, \ldots, \text{dove}_{k,k}) = \mathbf{N}^k$ (see Exercise 1 following this section). Once this has been done, setting $g_j = h_j \circ (\text{dove}_{k+1,1} \ldots, \text{dove}_{k+1,k+1})$ completes the proof. □

For each $k \geq 0$, the set $\mathbf{N}^k$ is totally ordered by the relation $\leq_{\text{lex}}$ (called *lexicographic order*) defined as follows by induction on $k$ as follows. For $k = 0$, the definition is trivial, since there is just one total order on the singleton set $\mathbf{N}^0$. Suppose that $\leq_{\text{lex}}$ has been defined on $\mathbf{N}^k$. Define $\leq_{\text{lex}}$ on $\mathbf{N}^{k+1}$ so that $(x_1, x_2, \ldots, x_{k+1}) \leq_{\text{lex}} (y_1, y_2, \ldots, y_{k+1})$ if and only if either $x_1 < y_1$ or $(x_1 = y_1$ and $(x_2, \ldots, x_{k+1}) \leq_{\text{lex}} (y_2, \ldots, y_{k+1}))$.

We shall say that a list of functions $g_1, \ldots, g_k \in \mathcal{G}_1$ is *lexicographically non-decreasing* if $x \leq y$ implies $(g_1(x), \ldots, g_k(x)) \leq_{\text{lex}} (g_1(y), \ldots, g_k(y))$ for all $x, y \in \mathbf{N}$. We shall say that it is *lexicographically increasing* if $x < y$ implies $(g_1(x), \ldots, g_k(x)) <_{\text{lex}} (g_1(y), \ldots, g_k(y))$ for all $x, y \in \mathbf{N}$. (Clearly, a lexicographically increasing list is also lexicographically non-decreasing.)

*Lemma 4.3.3.* (a) A $k$-ary relation $A$ is recursive if and only if either $A = \emptyset$ or $A = \text{range}(g_1, \ldots, g_k)$ for some lexicographically non-decreasing recursive $g_1, \ldots, g_k \in \mathcal{Q}_1^*$. (b) A $k$-ary relation $A$ is recursive if and only if either $A$ is finite or $A = \text{range}(g_1, \ldots, g_k)$ for some lexicographically increasing recursive $g_1, \ldots, g_k \in \mathcal{Q}_1^*$.

The proof is similar to that of Lemma 4.3.2, and is omitted.

If $A$ is a $(k+1)$-ary relation, we define its *projection* $\text{Proj}(A)$ to be the $k$-ary relation defined by

$$\text{Proj}(A) = \{(x_1, \ldots, x_k) : (x_1, \ldots, x_k, y) \in A \text{ for some } y \in \mathbf{N}\}$$

(The operation "Proj" on relations should not be confused with the projection functions common to all clones. In both cases the name arises from the geometric interpretation in which the coordinates of a relation or arguments of a function are regarded as axes in a multi-dimensional Cartesian space.) We have defined projection on the last $((k+1)$-st) coordinate, but we could have defined a more general operation of projection on the $j$-th coordinate, for $1 \leq j \leq k+1$. This more general operation can be avoided by permutation of the coordinates, which does not affect properties such as recursive and recursively enumerable.

*Lemma 4.3.4.* If $A$ is recursively enumerable, then $\text{Proj}(A)$ is recursively enumerable.

**Proof.** The case $A = \emptyset$ is trivial. Otherwise, by Lemma 4.3.2, $A$ is the range of a list $(g_1, \ldots, g_{k+1})$ of recursive functions. Then $\text{Proj}(A)$ is the range of the list $(g_1, \ldots, g_k)$ of recursive functions and, thus, is recursively enumerable by Lemma 4.3.2.                                                                                    □

The analogue of Lemma 4.3.4 with recursively enumerable replaced by recursive fails.

**Example 4.3.2.** The function $m^*$ is recursive, and it assumes only the values 0 and 1, and so it is the characteristic function of a recursive relation $R$. But $\text{Proj}(R)$ has the function halt as its characteristic function, and so by Corollary 4.2.3 it is not recursive.

Of course, by Lemmas 4.3.1(b) and 4.3.4, the projection of a recursive relation is recursively enumerable. The next lemma shows that all recursively enumerable relations arise in this way.

*Lemma 4.3.5.* If $A$ is recursively enumerable, then $A = \text{Proj}(B)$, for some recursive $B$.

**Proof.** Since $A$ is recursively enumerable, it is the domain of some partial recursive function, which has some index $\pi$. The function

$$\lambda(x_1, \ldots, x_k, t).m_k^*(\pi, x_1, \ldots, x_k, t)$$

is recursive, and it assumes only the values 0 and 1, and so it is the characteristic function of a recursive relation $B$, and $A = \text{Proj}(B)$. □

Our treatment of relations in this section has been parallel to our treatment of functions in Section 4.2: a $k$-ary relation is a set of $k$-tuples, just as a $k$-adic function is a map from $k$-tuples. There is an alternative treatment of relations, according to which a relation is a set of natural numbers $\langle x_1, \ldots, x_k \rangle$ rather than a set of $k$-tuples $(x_1, \ldots, x_k)$. This has some advantages when discussing enumeration (a non-empty $k$-ary relation is the range of a single function, rather than a $k$-tuple of functions), though it has disadvantages at other points (a relation is no longer simply the domain of a partial function).

We have given the definitions of recursive and recursively enumerable in terms of the absolutely computable functions and partial functions $Q^*$ and $P^*$. Everything we have done, however, can be done for an arbitrary reflexive class $P^*(A)$. In this case one uses the qualifying phrase "in $A$" to indicate that computability is with respect to an oracle for $A$; thus a relation $B$ is "recursive in $A$" if its characteristic function is in $Q^*(A)$ and is "recursively enumerable in $A$" if it is the domain of a partial function in $P^*(A)$.

### Exercises

1. (M) Show that for each $k \geq 1$ there exist recursive functions $\text{dove}_{k,1}, \ldots,$ $\text{dove}_{k,k} \in Q_1^*$ such that $\text{range}(\text{dove}_{k,1}, \ldots, \text{dove}_{k,k}) = \mathbf{N}^k$.

2. (M) A relation is *recursively enumerable without repetitions* if it is the range of a list of functions that assumes any list of values for at most one argument. Show that a relation $A$ is recursively enumerable without repetitions if and only if (a) $A$ is infinite and (b) $A$ is recursively enumerable.

3. (M) Prove (a) if $A$ is recursive and $f$ is recursive, then $f^{-1}(A)$ is recursive, and (b) if $A$ is recursively enumerable and $f$ is partial recursive, then $f^{-1}(A)$ is recursively enumerable.

4. (M) (a) If $f$ is one-to-one and recursive, is $f^{-1}$ recursive? (b) If $f$ is one-to-one and partial recursive, is $f^{-1}$ partial recursive?

5. (M) Show that if $A$ is infinite and recursively enumerable, then it contains an infinite and recursive subset $B \subseteq A$.

### 4.3.2. Recursively Enumerable Index Sets

Let $\mathcal{A} \subseteq \mathcal{P}_1^*$ be a set of monadic partial recursive functions. We shall write $v_\pi$ for the partial recursive function $\lambda(x), u_1(\pi, x)$. We shall write $\text{Ind}(\mathcal{A})$ for the set

$$\text{Ind}(\mathcal{A}) = \{\pi \in \mathbf{N} : v_\pi \in \mathcal{A}\}$$

of all indices of functions in $\mathcal{A}$. We have seen in Rice's Theorem (Theorem 4.2.4) which "index sets" $\text{Ind}(\mathcal{A})$ are recursive: the only possibilities are $\text{Ind}(\mathcal{A}) = \mathbf{N}$ and $\text{Ind}(\mathcal{A}) = \emptyset$. We shall write $W_\pi$ for the recursively enumerable set $\{x : v_1^*(\pi, x) \in W\}$. If $\mathcal{B}$ is a set of recursively enumerable sets, we shall write $\text{Ind}(\mathcal{B})$ for the set

$$\text{Ind}(\mathcal{B}) = \{\pi \in \mathbf{N} : W_\pi \in \mathcal{B}\}$$

of all indices of sets in $\mathcal{B}$. Of course, Rice's Theorem also settles the question of which index sets $\text{Ind}(\mathcal{B})$ are recursive, since a non-trivial property of recursively enumerable sets is also a non-trivial property of the partial recursive functions having these sets as their domains.

We shall now enquire as to which index sets are recursively enumerable, rather than recursive. The answer in this case is more complicated, and the cases of partial recursive functions and recursively enumerable sets are best treated separately. We shall deal here with the case of recursively enumerable sets, and state the case for partial recursive functions as a corollary whose proof is left for the reader.

To state our main result, we shall need an encoding of finite sets. There is a one-to-one correspondence between natural numbers and finite sets of natural numbers $F$ and natural numbers $n$ established by

$$\sum_{k \in F} 2^k = n$$

We shall write $F(n)$ for the set encode by $n$ and $n(F)$ for the encoding of $F$ according to this correspondence.

We shall say that a set $\mathcal{A}$ of partial recursive functions or a set $\mathcal{B}$ of recursively enumerable sets is *completely recursively enumerable* if the index set $\text{Ind}(\mathcal{A})$ or $\text{Ind}(\mathcal{B})$ is recursively enumerable.

**Theorem 4.3.6.** *A set $\mathcal{B}$ of recursively enumerable sets is completely recursively enumerable if and only if there exists a recursively enumerable set $I \subseteq \mathbf{N}$ such that $B \in \mathcal{B}$ if and only if $F(n) \subseteq B$ for some $n \in I$.*

For the proof we shall need two lemmas.

*Lemma 4.3.7.* Let $\mathcal{B}$ be completely recursively enumerable. If $B \in \mathcal{B}$, then there exists a finite set $A \subseteq B$ such that $A \in \mathcal{B}$.

**Proof.** Suppose, for the sake of contradiction, that $\mathcal{B}$ is completely recursively enumerable, with $\mathrm{Ind}(\mathcal{B}) = \mathrm{dom}(c)$, and that $B \in \mathcal{B}$, with $B = \mathrm{dom}(b)$, but that no finite subset of $B$ belongs to $\mathcal{B}$. We shall construct a monadic total recursive function $f$ such that $W_{f(x)}$ is finite if $x \in K$, but $W_{f(x)} = B$ if $x \notin K$. We will then have $\mathrm{Compl}(K) = \mathrm{dom}(c \circ f)$, which contradicts the fact that $K$ is recursively enumerable but not recursive.

Let $e^*$ be a monadic recursive function such that $K = \mathrm{range}(e^*)$. Define the dyadic partial recursive function $g$ by

$$g(x, y) = \begin{cases} \bot, & \text{if } x \in K(y) \\ b(y), & \text{otherwise} \end{cases}$$

where $K(y) = \{e^*(0), \ldots, e^*(y)\}$. Let $\gamma$ index $g$. Then $f(x) = \mathrm{pair}(\gamma, x)$ yields the desired function. $\qquad\square$

*Lemma 4.3.8.* Let $\mathcal{B}$ be completely recursively enumerable. If $A \in \mathcal{B}$ and $B \supseteq A$ is recursively enumerable, then $B \in \mathcal{B}$.

**Proof.** Suppose, for the sake of contradiction, that $\mathcal{B}$ is completely recursively enumerable, with $\mathrm{Ind}(\mathcal{B}) = \mathrm{dom}(c)$, and that $A \in \mathcal{B}$, with $A = \mathrm{dom}(a)$, but that $B \supseteq A$, with $B = \mathrm{dom}(b)$ does not belong to $\mathcal{B}$. We shall construct a monadic total recursive function $f$ such that $W_{f(x)} = A$ if $x \in K$, but $W_{f(x)} = B$ if $x \notin K$. We will then have $\mathrm{Compl}(K) = \mathrm{dom}(c \circ f)$, which contradicts the fact that $K$ is recursively enumerable but not recursive.

Let $\alpha$ index $a$. Define the triadic partial recursive function $h$ by

$$h(x, y, z) = \begin{cases} a(y), & \text{if } x \in K(z) \\ b(y), & \text{if } \mathrm{pair}(\alpha, y) \in K(z) \\ h(x, y, \mathrm{succ}(z)), & \text{otherwise} \end{cases}$$

(Note that this definition is coherent, since $a(y) = b(y)$ if both conditions hold.) Let $g(x, y) = h(x, y, 0)$, and let $\gamma$ index $g$. Then $f(x) = \mathrm{pair}(\gamma, x)$ yields the desired function. $\qquad\square$

**Proof of Theorem 4.3.6.** To prove the "if" part, suppose that there exists a recursively enumerable set $I$, with $I = \mathrm{dom}(i)$, such that $B \in \mathcal{B}$ if and only if $F(n) \subseteq B$ for some $n \in I$. We must show that $\mathrm{Ind}(\mathcal{B})$ is recursively enumerable, that is, that the set

$$C = \{x : \exists_n \, n \in \mathrm{dom}(i) \text{ and } F(n) \subseteq W_x\}$$

is recursively enumerable. But the condition on $x$ is equivalent to "there exist $n$ and $y$ such that $n \in W_\iota(y)$ and $F(n) \subseteq W_x(y)$," where $\iota$ indexes $i$. Thus, the set $C$ is the projection of a recursive relation and is, therefore, recursively enumerable.

To prove the "only if" part, suppose that $B$ is completely recursively enumerable, with $\mathrm{Ind}(B) = \mathrm{dom}(c)$. It will suffice to show that the set

$$I = \{n : F(n) \in B\}$$

of encodings of finite sets in $B$ is recursively enumerable, since by Lemmas 4.3.7 and 4.3.8, $B$ must contain all and only the supersets of the finite sets it contains. We shall define a monadic recursive function $f$ such that $W_{f(n)} = F(n)$. We will then have $I = \mathrm{dom}(c \circ f)$, completing the proof.

Define the dyadic partial recursive function $g$ by

$$g(n, x) = \begin{cases} 0, & \text{if } x \in F(n) \\ \bot, & \text{otherwise} \end{cases}$$

Let $\gamma$ index $g$. Then $f(n) = \mathrm{pair}(\gamma, n)$ yields the desired function.          $\square$

**Corollary 4.3.9.** *A set $A$ of partial recursive functions is completely recursively enumerable if and only if there exists a recursively enumerable set $N \subseteq \mathbf{N}$ such that $f \in A$ if and only if $F(n) \subseteq \mathrm{pair}(\mathrm{graph}(f))$ for some $n \in N$.*

Theorem 4.3.6 is due to Rice [1956], who attributed independent proofs to J. Myhill and N. Shapiro.

### 4.3.3. Enumeration without Repetition

We shall conclude this section with a spectacular result due to Friedberg [1958]. It says, roughly speaking, that there is a programming system in which every partial recursive function has one and only one program. Since every partial recursive function has a program, this programming system provide programs for all of the computable functions. But since every partial recursive function has a unique program, all questions concerning the equivalence or optimality of programs disappear! There is a computable partial function that serves an an "interpreter" for programs in this system, and a total recursive "compiler" that translates the programs of this system into indices for the standard interpreter $u^*$. Of course, one cannot have everything: there is no computable compiler that translates indices for the standard interpreter into programs in this new system. Thus, although we know that every partial recursive function has a unique program in this system, there is no systematic way of finding out what it is!

Like Theorem 4.3.6, the result that follows has analogous versions for recursively enumerable sets and partial recursive functions. Again, we shall deal here with the case of recursively enumerable sets, and state the case for partial recursive functions as a corollary whose proof is left for the reader.

***Theorem 4.3.10.*** *There exists a dyadic partial recursive function p such that, for every recursively enumerable set A, there is a unique number $b \in \mathbf{N}$ such that $A = dom(\lambda(x).p(b, x))$.*

**Proof.** Imagine that we have an infinite sequence $B_0, B_1, \ldots$ of "bins." We shall describe a process whereby we put natural numbers into various bins from time to time. Once a number is put into a bin, it will never be taken out. Given this process, we define the partial function $p$ as follows. To compute $p(b, x)$, carry out the process. If at any time the number $x$ is put into the bin $B_b$, halt with the value $p(b, x) = 0$. Otherwise, the process continues indefinitely and $p(b, x) = \bot$. In terms of putting numbers into bins, our goal is as follows: to put each recursively enumerable set into one and only one bin.

To do this, we shall divide the recursively enumerable sets into two classes. We shall say that a recursively enumerable set is *odd* if its cardinality is finite and odd. We shall say that a recursively enumerable set is *even* if its cardinality is either infinite or finite and even. Clearly every recursively enumerable set is either odd or even, but not both. The properties of this division that we shall need are stated in the following three lemmas. □

*Lemma 4.3.11.* There is a monadic recursive function $r$ such that each of the sets $W_{r(0)}, W_{r(1)}, \ldots$, is odd, and each odd set appears exactly once in this sequence.

**Proof.** Define the set $G$ to comprise those $m$ such that $F(m)$ is odd. Then $G$ is infinite and recursive. Define the monadic recursive function $g$ by letting $g(n)$ be the $n$-th element of $G$ in increasing order. Define the dyadic partial recursive function $f$ by

$$f(n, x) = \begin{cases} 0, & \text{if } x \in F(g(n)) \\ \bot, & \text{otherwise} \end{cases}$$

Let $\phi$ index $f$. Then $r(n) = \text{pair}(\phi, n)$ yields the desired function. □

*Lemma 4.3.12.* There is a monadic recursive function $s$ such that each of the sets $W_{s(0)}, W_{s(1)}, \ldots$, is even, and each even set appears at least once in this sequence.

**Proof.** Define the triadic recursive function $f$ by letting $f(n, x, k)$ be 1 if $W_n(k)$ has even cardinality and $x \in W_n(k)$. Define the triadic partial recursive function $g$ by

$$g(n, x, k) = \begin{cases} 0, & \text{if } f(n, x, k) = 1 \\ g(n, x, \text{succ}(k)), & \text{otherwise} \end{cases}$$

Define the dyadic partial recursive function $h$ by $h(n, x) = g(n, x, 0)$. Let $\eta$ index $h$. Then $s(n) = \text{pair}(\eta, n)$ yields the desired function. □

*Lemma 4.3.13.* There is a dyadic recursive function $t$ such that for every $n$ and $m$, $t(n, m) \geq m$ and $W_{r(t(n,m))} \supseteq F(n)$.

**Proof.** Define the tetradic recursive function $f$ by letting $f(n, m, j, k)$ be 1 if $j \geq m$ and $F(n) \subseteq W_{r(j)}(k)$. Define the triadic partial recursive function $g$ by

$$g(n, m, i) = \begin{cases} \text{bileft}(i), & \text{if } f(n, m, \text{bileft}(i), \text{biright}(i)) \\ g(n, m, \text{succ}(i)), & \text{otherwise} \end{cases}$$

This function is, in fact, total, since for every $n$ there are infinitely many $j$ such that $W_{r(j)} \supseteq F(n)$. Thus, $t(n, m) = g(n, m, 0)$ yields the desired function. □

We shall maintain a set of "used" numbers of bins, with the number $b$ designating the bin $B_b$. Initially all numbers are unused. From time to time we shall designate a number as used, but only finitely many numbers will be used at any time during the process. Once a number is designated as used, it remains so forever.

We shall maintain a set of "active" numbers of odd sets, with the number $n$ designating the set $W_{r(n)}$. Initially all numbers are inactive. From time to time we shall designate a number as active, but only finitely many numbers will be active at any time during the process. Once a number is designated as active, it remains so forever.

We shall maintain a set of "active" numbers of even sets, with the number $n$ designating the set $W_{s(n)}$. Initially all numbers are inactive. From time to time we shall designate a number as active, but only finitely many numbers will be active at any time during the process. Once a number is designated as active, it remains so forever.

Each active number designating an even set will at any time be either "uncertified" or "certified," and if it is certified it will be certified by some number called its "certificate." All numbers are initially uncertified. From time to time a number that is uncertified may become certified by a certain certificate, or a number that is certified may become uncertified. A number may alternate between being certified and uncertified any number of times, eventually remaining uncertified, eventually remaining certified, or alternating infinitely many times.

We shall say that $z$ *certifies* $m$ *with respect to* $A$ if (1) $z = \langle y_0, \ldots, y_{m-1} \rangle$ and (2) for each $l$ in the range $0 \leq l \leq m - 1$, we have pair$(s(l), y_l) \in A$ unless and only unless pair$(s(m), y_l) \in A$. Let $B$ be an even recursively enumerable set. Then there exists a $z$ that certifies $m$ with respect to $K$ if and only if $m$ is the smallest number $l$ such that $W_{s(l)} = B$. Furthermore, if $z$ certifies $m$ with respect to $K$, then $z$ certifies $m$ with respect to $K(k)$ for all sufficiently large $k$, and if $z$ does not certify $m$ with respect to $K$, then $z$ does not certify $m$ with respect to $K(k)$ for any sufficiently large $k$. We would like to put into some bin the members of some set $W_{s(m)}$, but to avoid duplications we would like to do this only if $m$ is the smallest number $l$ such that $W_{s(l)} = W_{s(m)}$. If we had access to an oracle for $K$, we could do this after finding a certificate $z$ for $m$ with respect to $K$. Since we do not have access to such an oracle, we shall use the finite sets $K(k)$ as surrogates for $K$, letting $k$ increase with time. This will require us to deal with the consequences of certificates with respect to $K(k)$ ceasing to be certificates for larger values of $k$.

The process of putting numbers into bins will take place in an infinite sequence of "stages." Each stage will consist of two parts, an "odd" part and an "even" part.

The odd part of stage $k$ is as follows. Let $b$ be the smallest unused bin number. Designate $b$ as used. Let $n$ be the smallest inactive odd-set number. Designate $n$ as active. Associate the odd-set $W_{r(n)}$ with the bin $B_b$. For each active odd-set number $m$ and associated bin number $c$, put numbers into $B_c$ if necessary so that $B_c$ contains $W_{r(m)}(k)$.

The even part of stage $k$ is as follows. Let $n$ be the smallest inactive even-set number. Designate $n$ as active. For each active even-set number $m$, treat $m$ as described next.

To treat the active even-set number $m$, we first determine its certified–uncertified status as follows. If $m$ is currently uncertified, check if any of the numbers $0, 1, \ldots, k$ certifies $m$ with respect to $K(k)$. If so, $m$ becomes certified with respect to the smallest such number. If not, $m$ remains uncertified. If $m$ is currently certified by $z$, check if $z$ certifies $m$ with respect to $K(k)$. If so, $m$ remains certified by $z$. If not, $m$ becomes uncertified.

We next describe what action is to be taken after the certified–uncertified status of $m$ has been determined. If $m$ becomes certified, then do the following. Let $b$ be the smallest unused bin number. Designate $b$ as used. Associate the even-set $W_{s(m)}$ with the bin $B_b$. Put numbers into $B_b$ if necessary so that $B_b$ contains $W_{s(m)}(k)$. If $m$ remains certified, then do the following. Let $B_b$ be the bin associated with the even-set $W_{s(m)}$. Put numbers into $B_b$ if necessary so that $B_b$ contains $W_{s(m)}(k)$. If $m$ becomes uncertified, do the following. Let $B_b$ be the bin associated with the even-set $W_{s(m)}$. Disassociate bin $B_b$ from the even-set $W_{s(m)}$. Let $F(i)$ be the current contents of $B_b$. Let $j$ be a number larger than any active odd-set number. Let $h = t(i, j)$. Designate $h$ as active. Associate the odd-set $W_{r(h)}$ with the bin $B_b$. Put numbers into $B_b$ if necessary so that $B_b$ contains $W_{r(h)}(k)$. If $m$, remains uncertified, then do nothing.

**Corollary 4.3.14.** *There exists a dyadic partial recursive function $q$ such that, for every monadic partial recursive function $f$, there is a unique number $b \in \mathbf{N}$ such that $f = \lambda(x).q(b, x)$.*

Our proof of Theorem 4.3.10 follows that of Kummer [1990], which is a substantial simplification of the original proof of Friedberg [1958].

### *Exercise*

1. (M) Let $S$ denote the class

$$S = \{\{2x, 2x + 1\} : x \in K\} \cup \{\{2x\}, \{2x + 1\} : x \notin K\}$$

(a) Show that the sets in $S$ can be enumerated; that is, show that there exists a dyadic partial recursive function $f$ such that the sets $\{x : f(\alpha, x) \in \mathbf{N}\}$ run through all and only the sets in $S$ as $\alpha$ runs through $\mathbf{N}$. (b) Show that the sets in $S$ cannot be enumerated without repetition: that is, show that for every dyadic partial recursive function $g$ such that the sets $\{x; g(\alpha, x) \in \mathbf{N}\}$ run through all and only the sets in $S$ as $\alpha$ runs through $\mathbf{N}$, there exist $\alpha \neq \beta$ such that $\{x; g(\alpha, x) \in \mathbf{N}\} = \{x; g(\beta, x) \in \mathbf{N}\}$.

## 4.4. Turing Reducibility

Of central importance in recursive function theory are notions of reducibility, equivalence, and completeness. These notions come in several versions, the most fundamental of which is the "weak" or "Turing" version, which we shall take up in this section.

### *4.4.1. Reducibility, Equivalence, and Completeness*

The first notion we shall consider is called "Turing reducibility." Though it is possible to define it for $k$-ary relations for any $k$, we shall confine our treatment to $k = 1$; thus, the relations in question may be regarded as sets of natural numbers.

Let $A$ and $B$ be sets of natural numbers. We shall write $A \leq_T B$ (and say "$A$ is Turing reducible to $B$") if $\mathcal{P}^*(A) \subseteq \mathcal{P}^*(B)$ (which, as we have seen, is equivalent to $\text{char}_A \in \mathcal{Q}^*(B)$). (Thus, $A \leq_T B$ is just another notation for the notion "$A$ is recursive in $B$.")

The condition $A \leq_T B$ is intended as a formalization of the assertion "$A$ is at least as easy to compute as $B$"; it means that questions about membership in $A$ may be answered by machines that may ask an oracle questions about membership in $B$. (Of course, the term "easy" is being used in a rather broad sense, since the notion "$A \leq_T B$" will often be employed in situations where both $A$ and $B$ are *impossible* to compute in the usual sense.)

*Lemma 4.4.1.* (a) $A \leq_T A$ (that is, $\leq_T$ is reflexive). (b) If $A \leq_T B$ and $B \leq_T C$, then $A \leq_T C$ (that is, $\leq_T$ is transitive).

The proof is immediate from the definitions.

We shall write $A \equiv_T B$ (and say "$A$ is Turing equivalent to $B$") if $A \leq_T B$ and $B \leq_T A$. The condition $A \equiv_T B$ is intended as a formalization of the assertion "$A$ is exactly as easy to compute as $B$."

*Lemma 4.4.2.* $\equiv_T$ is reflexive and transitive. Furthermore, if $A \equiv_T B$, then $B \equiv_T A$ (that is, $\equiv_T$ is symmetric).

The proof is immediate from Lemma 4.4.1 and the definition of $\equiv_T$. Lemma 4.4.2 may be summarized by saying that $\equiv_T$ is an equivalence on $\text{Pow}(\mathbf{N})$, which partitions the collection of sets of natural numbers into "equivalence classes" called *T-degrees*. If $A$ is a set, the T-degree containing $A$ will be denoted $\deg(A)$. Since, $\mathcal{P}^*(A) = \mathcal{P}^*(B)$ if and only if $A \equiv_T B$ if and only if $\deg(A) = \deg(B)$, there is a one-to-one correspondence between principal recursive cones and T-degrees, with inclusion of cones corresponding to T-reducibility.

*Lemma 4.4.3.* For every set $A$, $A \equiv_T \text{Compl}(A)$.

*Lemma 4.4.4.* Any two of the following conditions imply the third: (1) $A$ is recursive, (2) $B$ is recursive, (3) $A \equiv_T B$.

The proofs are again immediate.

We shall say that $A$ is *T-complete* if (1) $A$ is recursively enumerable and (2) for every recursively enumerable $B$, we have $B \leq_T A$. The condition "$A$ is

T-complete" is intended as a formalization of the notion that $A$ is a "hardest" set to compute among the recursively enumerable sets.

*Lemma 4.4.5.* Let $A$ and $B$ be recursively enumerable sets. Any two of the following conditions imply the third: (1) $A$ is T-complete, (2) $B$ is T-complete, (3) $A \equiv_T B$.

The proof is again immediate from the definitions. We shall see from Proposition 4.4.6 to follow that the set $K$ (defined as the domain of the partial recursive function $u^*$) is T-complete.

**Proposition 4.4.6.** *The set $K$ is T-complete.*

**Proof.** By definition $K$ is recursively enumerable. It remains to show that for every recursively enumerable $B$, we have $B \leq_T K$.

Since $B$ is recursively enumerable, it is the domain of some partial recursive function $b$. Let $\beta$ be an index for $b$. Then we have $x \in B$ if and only if $\operatorname{pair}(\beta, x) \in K$, or equivalently $\operatorname{char}_B(x) = \operatorname{char}_K(\operatorname{pair}(\beta, x))$. This proves $B \leq_T K$. □

The notion of "T-completeness" has been defined for the smallest recursive cone $\mathcal{P}^*$, but it has a relativized analogue for any other principal recursive cone $\mathcal{P}^*(C)$. Specifically, we shall say that $A$ is *T-complete for $C$* if (1) $A$ is recursively enumerable in $C$ and (2) for every set $B$ that is recursively enumerable in $C$, we have $B \leq_T A$. We then have the analogs of Lemma 4.4.5 and Proposition 4.4.6, with "T-complete" replaced by "T-complete for $C$" and $K$ replaced by $K(C) = \operatorname{dom}(u^C)$.

We close this discussion with the observation that we cannot obtain a "weaker" or "broader" equivalence relation by replacing "$A$ is recursive in $B$" by "$A$ is recursively enumerable in $B$," for the resulting relation would not be transitive (see Exercise 1 to follow). Indeed, Post [1944] has argued that T-reducibility is the broadest notion of reducibility that is computationally meaningful.

### Exercise

1. (E) Give an example to show that the relation "$A$ is recursively enumerable in $B$" is not transitive.

#### 4.4.2. T-Degrees

Whenever we have an equivalence, it should be an automatic impulse to consider the structure imposed upon the equivalence classes, ignoring the distinctions among elements in the same class. We shall now follow this impulse with regard to T-equivalence by looking at the structure of the T-degrees.

If $\mathcal{A}$ and $\mathcal{B}$ are T-degrees, and if $A \leq_T B$ for some $A \in \mathcal{A}$ and $B \in \mathcal{B}$, then every set in $\mathcal{A}$ is T-reducible to every set in $\mathcal{B}$. This implies that the relation $\leq_T$ may be used to compare T-degrees as well as sets, and that the T-degrees are ordered by T-reducibility (as defined in Section 1.2.1, this means that the relation $\leq_T$ is reflexive, asymmetric, and transitive on T-degrees).

Lemma 4.4.4 says that all of the recursive sets form a single T-degree (called the *recursive* T-degree, and denoted $\mathcal{O}$). The recursive degree $\mathcal{O}$ is the unique minimum under the relation $\leq_T$.

If $\mathcal{C}$ is a T-degree, and if $A$ is recursively enumerable in $C$ for some $C \in \mathcal{C}$, then $A$ is recursively enumerable in every set in $\mathcal{C}$. Thus, it makes sense to speak of a set $A$ being recursively enumerable in a T-degree $\mathcal{C}$. It is customary to say that a T-degree $\mathcal{A}$ is *recursively enumerable in* a T-degree $\mathcal{C}$ if $\mathcal{A}$ contains a set recursively enumerable in $\mathcal{C}$, but this does not imply that it contains only sets recursively enumerable in $\mathcal{C}$ (for example, the T-degree containing $K$ also contains $\mathrm{Compl}(K)$, which is not recursively enumerable).

If $\mathcal{C}$ is a T-degree, and if $A$ is T-complete for $C$ for some $C \in \mathcal{C}$, then $A$ is T-complete for every set in $\mathcal{C}$. Thus, it makes sense to speak of a set $A$ being T-complete for a T-degree $\mathcal{C}$. The sets that are T-complete for a T-degree $\mathcal{C}$ do not constitute a T-degree, but by the analogue of Lemma 4.4.4 they all belong to a single T-degree, which we shall call the *jump* of $\mathcal{C}$ and denote $\mathcal{C}'$. By the analogue of Proposition 4.4.6, $\mathcal{C}'$ is the T-degree containing the sets $K(C)$ for $C \in \mathcal{C}$.

We have seen that at least two T-degrees contain recursively enumerable sets (the recursive T-degree $\mathcal{O}$, and its jump $\mathcal{O}'$, containing the recursively enumerable but not recursive set $K$). By Example 4.3.1 and Lemma 4.3.1, we have

$$\mathcal{O} < \mathcal{O}'$$

In 1944, Post [1944] asked whether these are the only two recursively enumerable T-degrees. We shall see later that the answer is "no."

It is often desirable to iterate the jump operation. We do this by writing $\mathcal{C}^{(0)} = \mathcal{C}$ and $\mathcal{C}^{(n+1)} = (\mathcal{C}^{(n)})'$ for $n \geq 0$. These T-degrees contain the sets $K^{(n)}$ defined by $K^{(0)} = \emptyset$ and $K^{(n+1)} = K(K^{(n)})$ for $n \geq 0$. By the analogues of Example 4.3.1 and Lemma 4.3.1, we have

$$\mathcal{O}^{(0)} < \mathcal{O}^{(1)} < \cdots < \mathcal{O}^{(n)} < \mathcal{O}^{(n+1)} < \cdots \tag{4.4.1}$$

We shall also define

$$K^{(\omega)} = \{\mathrm{pair}(x, n) : x \in K^{(n)}\}$$

and define $\mathcal{O}^{(\omega)}$ to be the T-degree containing $K^{(\omega)}$. A set $A$ is called *arithmetical* if $A \in \mathcal{O}^{(n)}$ for some $n \in \mathbf{N}$. A T-degree $\mathcal{A}$ is called *arithmetical* if $\mathcal{A} \leq_T \mathcal{O}^{(n)}$ for some $n \geq 0$ (so that $\mathcal{A}$ contains only arithmetical sets).

For sets $A, B \subseteq \mathbf{N}$, define their *join* $A \vee B$ by

$$A \vee B = \{2x : x \in A\} \cup \{2y + 1 : y \in B\}$$

(The join operation encodes $A$ and $B$ into a single set $A \vee B$ in such a way that questions about $A$ or about $B$ can easily be rephrased as questions about $A \vee B$.) The join $A \vee B$ is an upper bound to both $A$ and $B$: we have $A \leq_T A \vee B$ and $B \leq_T A \vee B$. Furthermore, $A \vee B$ is the least upper bound: if $A \leq_T C$ and $B \leq_T C$, then $A \vee B \leq_T C$. The join operation on sets is defined in an asymmetric way: $A \vee B$ is different from $B \vee A$ (if $A$ is different from $B$), though $A \vee B \equiv_T B \vee A$. We can eliminate this asymmetry by transferring our attention from sets to their T-degrees.

If $A \equiv_T C$ and $B \equiv_T D$, then $A \vee B \equiv_T C \vee D$. Thus, it makes sense to define the join $\mathcal{A} \vee \mathcal{B}$ of two T-degrees $\mathcal{A}$ and $\mathcal{B}$ to be the T-degree containing the join $A \vee B$ of some $A \in \mathcal{A}$ and some $B \in \mathcal{B}$. The resulting join operation on T-degrees is associative ($\mathcal{A} \vee (\mathcal{B} \vee \mathcal{C}) = (\mathcal{A} \vee \mathcal{B}) \vee \mathcal{C}$), commutative ($\mathcal{A} \vee \mathcal{B} = \mathcal{B} \vee \mathcal{A}$), and idempotent ($\mathcal{A} \vee \mathcal{A} = \mathcal{A}$), with $\mathcal{O}$ as the unit element $\mathcal{A} \vee \mathcal{O} = \mathcal{A}$. In the light of this success, it is natural to ask if we can define a "greatest lower bound" (or "meet") operation $\wedge$ in such a way as to make the set of T-degrees into a lattice. We shall see later that the answer is "no."

The sequence (4.4.1) provides examples sets of ever increasing impossibility of computation. But it would be wrong to think that impossibility is a numerically quantitative matter. The following theorem shows that two functions can be non-computable for different reasons, so that each remains non-computable even with access to an oracle for the other.

**Theorem 4.4.7 (Kleene and Post [1954]).** *There are sets $A, B \subseteq \mathbf{N}$ (recursive in $K$) such that $A$ is not recursively enumerable in $B$ and $B$ is not recursively enumerable in $A$.*

The sets $A$ and $B$ of this theorem are incomparable, since if $A$ were recursive in $B$ it would certainly be recursively enumerable in $B$, and if $B$ were recursive in $A$ it would certainly be recursively enumerable in $A$.

**Proof.** We shall construct $A$ and $B$ in an infinite sequence of "stages." To keep track of the progress we make, we shall work with the characteristic functions $a$ and $b$ of $A$ and $B$, respectively. For $n \geq 0$, we shall let $a_n$ and $b_n$ be partial functions that describe the decisions we have made about $a$ and $b$, respectively, at the outset of stage $n$. There will be natural numbers $p_n$ and $q_n$ with the following properties: $a_n(x)$ is defined for and only for $x < p_n$, and $b_n(x)$ is defined for and only for $x < q_n$. When $a_n(x)$ or $b_n(x)$ is defined, it will be either 0 or 1. Thus, at the outset of each stage, $a_n$ and $b_n$ are "initial segments" of characteristic functions, for which the values at the first $p_n$ and $q_n$ natural numbers, respectively, have been chosen.

At stage $n$, we shall extend the domain of definition of $a_n$, or $b_n$, or both, to obtain $a_{n+1}$ and $b_{n+1}$. We shall never rescind the decisions we have made in previous stages, however, by changing the values of $a_n$ or $b_n$ at arguments $x$ less than $p_n$ or $q_n$, respectively. Furthermore, we shall only extend $a_n$ and $b_n$ by finitely many values at this stage, so that they will remain undefined at arguments beyond $p_{n+1}$ and $q_{n+1}$, respectively. (Such an extension $a_{n+1}$ of $a_n$ will be called a *finite extension*.) Nevertheless, $a_n$ will be extended during every stage with $n$ even, and $b_n$ will be extended during every stage with $n$ odd. As a result the values of $a_n$ and $b_n$ for any argument will get defined at some stage, so that the infinite sequence of stages uniquely determines characteristic functions $a$ and $b$ that extend each of the $a_n$ and $b_n$, respectively. (Such an extension $a$ of $a_n$ will be called a *complete extension*.)

We begin by setting $a_0 = b_0 = \text{undef}_1$, so that $p_0 = q_0 = 0$. We then proceed as follows.

**Stage $n = 2t$.** The purpose of this stage will be to ensure that

$$A \neq W_t(B) \tag{4.4.2}$$

This will be done by ensuring that

$$p_n \in A \quad \text{unless and only unless} \quad u^B(t, p_n) \in \mathbf{N}$$

To do this, we consider two cases.

**Case 4.4.1.** There is a complete extension $c$ of $b_n$ such that $u^C(t, p_n) \in \mathbf{N}$ for $C = c^{-1}(1)$. This means that the machine described by index $t$, run with input $p_n$ and oracle $C$, halts after some finite number $s$ of steps. During these $s$ steps, the machine queries the oracle only for numbers less than $s$. Thus, there exists a finite extension $e$ of $b_n$ (which is defined for at most $s$ arguments) such that $u^D(t, p_n) \in \mathbf{N}$ for $D = d^{-1}(1)$, where $d$ is any complete extension of $e$. Thus, we set $p_{n+1} = p_n + 1$, $a_{n+1}(p_n) = 0$ (ensuring $p_n \notin A$), $b_{n+1} = e$ (ensuring $p_n \in W_t(B)$), and $q_{n+1}$ equal to the number of arguments in the domain of $e$.

**Case 4.4.2.** There is no complete extension $c$ of $b_n$ such that $u^C(t, p_n) \in \mathbf{N}$ for $C = c^{-1}(1)$. In this case we set $p_{n+1} = p_n + 1$, $a_{n+1}(p_n) = 1$ (ensuring $p_n \in A$), $b_{n+1} = b_n$ (since $p_n \notin W_t(B)$ is assured), and $q_{n+1} = q_n$.

In either case, the condition (4.4.2) is ensured by Stage $2t$ in such a way that it will survive all further stages.

**Stage $n = 2t + 1$.** The purpose of this stage will be to ensure that

$$B \neq W_t(A) \tag{4.4.3}$$

This is accomplished in the same way as for condition (4.4.2), but with the roles of $A$ and $B$, $a$ and $b$, and $p$ and $q$ exchanged.

As already indicated, this infinite sequence of stages uniquely determines the characteristic functions $a$ and $b$ and, thus, the sets $A$ and $B$. Since each of the conditions (4.4.2) and (4.4.3) holds, we have that $A$ is not recursively enumerable in $B$ and $B$ is not recursively enumerable in $A$. It remains to verify the parenthetical remark that $A$ and $B$ are each recursive in $K$. To see this, we observe that to carry out the construction used in the proof, it suffices to be able to decide whether Case 4.4.1 or Case 4.4.2 applies in each stage, and to find a suitable finite extension $e$ when Case 4.4.1 applies. It is routine to construct a machine that takes descriptions of $n$, $a_n$, $b_n$, $p_n$, and $q_n$ as inputs, searches for a suitable finite extension $e$, and halts when and only when it finds one. Thus, the decisions needed to carry out the construction can be performed with access to an oracle for the halting problem for machines (without oracles), and thus with access to an oracle for $K$.      $\square$

The following theorem shows that we cannot define a "greatest lower bound" operation on the set of T-degrees.

***Theorem 4.4.8 (Kleene and Post [1954]).*** *There are sets $A$, $B \subseteq \mathbf{N}$ (recursive in $K^{(\omega)}$) such that (1) any arithmetic set $C$ is recursive in $A$ and recursive in $B$ and (2) any set $C$ that is recursive in $A$ and recursive in $B$ is arithmetic.*

The sets $A$ and $B$ of this theorem can have no meet. For if $C$ were the meet of $A$ and $B$, $C$ would be recursive in $A$ and recursive in $B$ and thus, (by the theorem), arithmetic. By the definition of arithmetic, $C$ would be recursive in $K^{(n)}$ for some $n$. But then $K^{(n+1)}$, which is not recursive in $C$ and (by the theorem) is recursive in $A$ and in $B$, would be a greater lower bound to $A$ and $B$.

We shall not give the proof of Theorem 4.4.8 here; it can be found in the paper of Kleene and Post [1954]. The technique of the proof, based on extensions, is similar to that of Theorem 4.4.7 (though it is necessary to use an infinite sequence of "infinite but incomplete" extensions). The idea of the proof is to arrange that all and only the arithmetical sets are T-reducible to both $A$ and $B$. Since the arithmetical T-degrees have no arithmetical upper bound, the sets $A$ and $B$ can have no greatest lower bound.

We have introduced the relation $\leq_T$ between T-degrees and the operation jump and join operations on T-degrees. We have seen that the join operation can be defined in terms of the relation $\leq_T$, since it yields the least upper bound with respect to this ordering. Kleene and Post [1954] asked whether the jump operation could also be defined in terms of the relation $\leq_T$. Subsequently, Cooper [1990, 1991, 1994] announced that the answer is "yes," and that even the relation "some member of $\mathcal{A}$ is recursively enumerable in $\mathcal{B}$" can be defined in terms of $\leq_T$. His proof, which uses techniques beyond the scope of our treatment of recursive function theory, can be viewed as a strengthening of a result due to Jockusch and Shore [1983, 1984], to the effect that the relation "$\mathcal{A}$ is arithmetical" can be defined in terms of $\leq_T$.

### Exercises

1. (E)  Show that the set $K^{(\omega)}$ is not arithmetical.
2. (M)  Let $\mathcal{A}$ and $\mathcal{B}$ be T-degrees. (a) Show that if $\mathcal{A} \leq_T \mathcal{B}$, then $\mathcal{A}' \leq_T \mathcal{B}'$. (b) Show that $\mathcal{A}' \vee \mathcal{B}' \leq_T (\mathcal{A} \vee \mathcal{B})'$.

#### 4.4.3. Recursively Enumerable T-degrees

We have seen that there is just one T-degree containing recursive sets. There is at least one more containing recursively enumerable sets, namely, the one containing the set $K$. Are there any others, or is every non-recursive, recursively enumerable set T-equivalent to $K$? We shall present a result, due to Friedberg [1957] and Muchnik [1956], which shows that there are others; it even shows that there are pairs of recursively enumerable sets that are incomparable with respect to T-reducibility. This result also marked the introduction of the "priority argument," which has been central to the development of recursive function theory since that time.

**Theorem 4.4.9 (Friedberg [1957]; Muchnik [1956]).** *There exist recursively enumerable sets $A$ and $B$ such that*

$$A \not\leq_T B \qquad \text{and} \qquad B \not\leq_T A.$$

*(It follows that neither A nor B can be recursive (since a recursive set is T-reducible to any set), and that neither A nor B can be T-complete (since any recursively enumerable set is T-reducible to a T-complete set).)*

**Proof.** We shall give a procedure for enumerating the sets $A$ and $B$. We must ensure that $A$ is not recursive in $B$. Since $A$ is recursively enumerable, it will certainly be recursively enumerable in $B$. Thus, to have $A$ not recursive in $B$, we must have Compl($A$) not recursively enumerable in $B$. (We use here the relativized version of Lemma 4.3.1.) This means that we must have, for every $\pi \in \mathbf{N}$, Compl($A$) $\neq W_\pi(B)$. To prove this, we shall show that there is a total function $f \in \mathcal{G}_1$ such that, for all $\pi \in \mathbf{N}$,

$$f(\pi) \in A \quad \text{if and only if} \quad f(\pi) \in W_\pi(B) \qquad (4.4.4)$$

Similarly, we shall show that there is a total function $g \in \mathcal{G}_1$ such that, for all $\pi \in \mathbf{N}$,

$$g(\pi) \in B \quad \text{if and only if} \quad g(\pi) \in W_\pi(A) \qquad (4.4.5)$$

It is an essential feature of the proof that the functions $f$ and $g$ are not recursive.

We shall start by taking $A$ and $B$ to be the empty set. We shall then proceed through an infinite sequence of stages, each of which may add an element to $A$ or $B$. We shall denote by $A_n$ and $B_n$ the finite sets of elements in $A$ and $B$, respectively, at the outset of stage $n$. Thus,

$$A_0 \subseteq A_1 \subseteq \cdots \subseteq A = \bigcup_n A_n$$

and

$$B_0 \subseteq B_1 \subseteq \cdots \subseteq B = \bigcup_n B_n$$

are recursive enumerations of the final sets $A$ and $B$.

We shall specify the values $f(0), g(0), f(1), g(1), \ldots$, of the functions $f$ and $g$ by describing the movements of an infinite sequence of "markers" $F_0, G_0, F_1, G_1, \ldots$. Each marker will eventually be "entered," that is, assigned to some natural number called its "position." Subsequently it may be "bumped" one or more times, that is, reassigned to some larger natural number that becomes its new position. We shall denote the positions of the markers $F_\pi$ and $G_\pi$ at the outset of stage $n$ by $f_n(\pi)$ and $g_n(\pi)$, respectively.

We shall speak of a relation of "priority" among the markers, whereby they are totally ordered as follows:

$$F_0 > G_0 > F_1 > G_1 > \cdots > F_\pi > G_\pi > \cdots$$

thus, $F_0$ has the "highest" priority, $G_0$ has the next highest, and so forth. (This priority ordering is independent of the positions of the markers.)

We shall also describe the movements of two "barriers" $P$ and $Q$. Initially they will have the natural number 0 as their position. Subsequently they may be "advanced," that is, have their position increased by 1. We shall denote by $p_n$ and $q_n$ the positions of $P$ and $Q$, respectively, at the outset of stage $n$.

**Stage $2t$.**

1. Enter marker $F_t$ at the position of the barrier $P$ and advance the barrier $P$.
2. If for each $\pi$ in the range $0 \le \pi \le t$ we have $m^\circ(\pi, f_{2t}(\pi), t, B_{2t}) = 0$ or $f_{2t}(\pi) \in A_{2t}$, do nothing. (The function $m^\circ$ was defined in Proposition 4.2.15.) Otherwise, let $\tau$ be the value of $\pi$ in the range $0 \le \pi \le t$ for which $m^\circ(\pi, f_{2t}(\pi), t, B_{2t}) = 1$ and $f_{2t}(\pi) \notin A_{2t}$, and for which $f_{2t}(\pi)$ assumes its minimum among such values; then do the following:
   (a) Put $f_{2t}(\tau)$ into $A$.
   (b) For each of the markers $G_\sigma$ that has been entered and has priority lower than that of $F_\tau$, do the following: bump $G_\sigma$ to the position of the barrier $Q$ and advance the barrier $Q$. (There are infinitely many markers of lower priority, but only finitely many have been entered by this stage.)

**Stage $2t + 1$.**

1. Enter marker $G_t$ at the position of the barrier $Q$ and advance the barrier $Q$.
2. If for each $\pi$ in the range $0 \le \pi \le t$ we have $m^\circ(\pi, g_{2t+1}(\pi), t, A_{2t+1}) = 0$ or $g_{2t+1}(\pi) \in B_{2t+1}$, do nothing. Otherwise, let $\tau$ be the value of $\pi$ in the range $0 \le \pi \le t$ for which $m^\circ(\pi, g_{2t+1}(\pi), t, A_{2t+1}) = 1$ and $g_{2t+1}(\pi) \notin B_{2t+1}$, and for which $g_{2t+1}(\pi)$ assumes its minimum among such values; then do the following:
   (a) Put $g_{2t+1}(\tau)$ into $B$.
   (b) For each of the markers $F_\sigma$ that has been entered and has priority lower than that of $G_\tau$, do the following: bump $F_\sigma$ to the position of the barrier $P$ and advance the barrier $P$.

Clearly, each marker is eventually entered. Let us consider how many times a marker can be bumped. A marker can bump another marker of lower priority only once for each position it occupies. Thus, a marker can be bumped by a marker of higher priority only one more time than that marker itself is bumped. It follows by induction on the priority of the marker that each marker is bumped only finitely many times. Thus, each marker eventually comes to rest at some position. For all $\pi \in \mathbf{N}$, we define $f(\pi)$ and $g(\pi)$ to be the final positions of the markers $F_\pi$ and $G_\pi$, respectively.

We shall now prove equivalence Eq. (4.4.4). To prove the "only if" part, suppose that $f(\pi) \in A$. Then during some stage $2t$ after the marker $F_\pi$ has reached its final position the element $f_{2t}(\pi) = f(\pi)$ was put into $A$. Thus the condition $m^\circ(\pi, f_{2t}(\pi), t, B_{2t}) = 1$ must have held during that stage. We shall show that $B_{2t}$ agrees with $B$ up to $t$. By Proposition 4.2.15, this will imply $m^B(\pi, f(\pi), t) = 1$, which in turn implies $f(\pi) \in W_\pi(B)$, completing the proof of the "only if" part.

At the outset of stage $2t$, the position of the barrier $Q$ is at least $t$ (since it is advanced during each odd-numbered stage). Suppose that some element $h$ is put into $B$ during some odd-numbered stage $2s + 1$ subsequent to $2t$. We cannot have $h = g_{2s+1}(\tau)$ for some marker $G_\tau$ with higher priority than $F_\pi$, for then $F_\pi$ would be bumped during stage $2s + 1$, contradicting the condition that it has come to rest by stage $2t$. But if $h = g_{2s+1}(\sigma)$ for some marker $G_\sigma$ with lower priority than $F_\pi$, then $h \geq t$, since all these markers are bumped to $t$ or beyond during stage $2t$. Thus, $B_{2t}$ agrees with $B$ up to $t$, which completes the proof of the "only if" part.

To prove the "if" part, suppose that $f(\pi) \in W_\pi(B)$. Thus, for all sufficiently large $r$ we have $m^B(\pi, f(\pi), r) = 1$. We may choose $s \geq i$ sufficiently large that (1) $f_{2s}(\pi) = f(\pi)$ and (2) $B_{2s}$ agrees with $B$ up to $r$. By Proposition 4.2.15, we then have $m^\circ(\pi, f_{2s}(\pi), s, B_{2s}) = 1$.

Suppose, with an eye to contradiction, that $f(\pi)$ is never put into $A$. Then at each stage $2t$ with $t \geq s$, the condition $f_{2t}(\pi) \notin A_{2t}$ holds. There are infinitely many such stages, and each of them puts a new element smaller than $f(\pi)$ into $A$. But there are only finitely many elements smaller than $f(\pi)$, contradicting the assumption that $f(\pi)$ is never put into $A$, and completing the proof of the "if" part.

The proof of Eq. (4.4.5) is analogous.                                      □

Just as Theorem 4.4.9 "scales down" Theorem 4.4.7 into the recursively enumerable degrees, it is also possible to scale down Theorem 4.4.8. The result is the following theorem.

**Theorem 4.4.10.** *There exist recursively enumerable sets A and B such that, for every recursively enumerable C such that $C \leq_T A$ and $C \leq_T B$, there exists a recursively enumerable set D such that $D \leq_T A$ and $D \leq_T B$ but not $D \leq_T C$.*

The proof of Theorem 4.4.10 will not be given here. The first proof was given by Lachlan [1966], using a very complicated elaboration of the priority argument. Soare [1972] and Yates [1966] observed that Lachlan's argument actually applies to the sets constructed in Theorem 4.4.9 (though the argument itself is not simplified very much). Finally, Jockusch [1981] gave a very simple and direct proof of Theorem 4.4.10, which is similar in spirit to (and not much more complicated than) the proof of Theorem 4.4.9.

When is a recursively enumerable set T-complete? We shall present a result due to Arslanov [1981] that relates T-completeness to the Recursion Theorem.

Recall that the Recursion Theorem in its simplest form (Theorem 4.2.6) states that if $f \in \mathcal{Q}_1^*$, then there is a "fixed point" $n \in \mathbf{N}$ such that $u^*(f(n)) = u^*(n)$. The following theorem uses the violation of this property to characterize the T-complete sets among the recursively enumerable sets.

By a *recursive enumeration* of a recursively enumerable set $A$ we shall mean an infinite sequence of finite subsets

$$A_0 \subseteq A_1 \subseteq \cdots \subseteq A = \bigcup_n A_n$$

such that the function $\lambda(n).A_n$ is recursive. Every recursively enumerable set $A$ has a recursive enumeration: if $A = \emptyset$, we may take $A_n = \emptyset$; otherwise, $A$ is the range of a recursive function $g$, and we may take $A_n = \{g(0), \ldots, g(n)\}$.

By a *modulus* for a recursive enumeration

$$A_0 \subseteq A_1 \subseteq \cdots \subseteq A = \bigcup_n A_n$$

we shall mean a partial recursive function $f$ such that $x \in A_{f(x)}$ for all $x \in A$. Every recursive enumeration has a modulus, for we may take $f$, where $f(x)$ is the smallest $n \geq 0$ such that $x$ appears in $A_n$. (This is, in fact, the "smallest" and "least defined" modulus, since all others are obtained from it by extending its domain and increasing its values.) A recursive enumeration has a modulus that is recursive in a set $B$ if and only if the enumerated set is recursive in $B$.

By a *strong modulus* for a recursive enumeration

$$A_0 \subseteq A_1 \subseteq \cdots \subseteq A = \bigcup_n A_n$$

we shall mean a total function $f$ such that, for all $n \in \mathbf{N}$, $A$ agrees with $A_{f(n)}$ up to $n$. A recursive enumeration has a strong modulus that is recursive in a set $B$ if and only if the enumerated set is recursive in $B$.

**Theorem 4.4.11 (Arslanov [1981]).** *Let $A$ be a recursively enumerable set. The following two conditions are equivalent: (1) $A$ is T-complete and (2) there exists a function $f \in \mathcal{Q}_1^*(A)$ with no fixed points: for all $n \in \mathbf{N}$, $u^*(f(n)) \neq u^*(n)$.*

**Proof.** To prove that part (1) implies part (2), we suppose that $A$ is T-complete. Let $\xi$ be an index for zero$_0$. Let $\pi$ be an index for $\lambda(x).\text{succ}(u^*(x))$, and define the function $\eta \in \mathcal{Q}_1^*$ by $\eta(x) = \text{pair}(\pi, x)$. Define the function $f \in \mathcal{G}_1$ by

$$f(x) = \begin{cases} \xi, & \text{if } x \notin \text{dom}(u^*) \\ \eta(x), & \text{if } x \in \text{dom}(u^*) \end{cases}$$

Clearly, $f \in \mathcal{Q}_1^*(\text{dom}(u^*))$. Since $\text{dom}(u^*)$ is recursively enumerable and $A$ is T-complete, $\text{dom}(u^*)$ is recursive in $A$. Thus $f \in \mathcal{Q}_1^*(A)$. It is easy to verify that

$$u^*(f(x)) = \begin{cases} 0, & \text{if } u^*(x) = \bot \\ \text{succ}(u^*(x)), & \text{if } u^*(x) \in \mathbf{N} \end{cases}$$

Thus $f$ satisfies part (2).

To prove that part (2) implies part (1), we suppose that $f \in \mathcal{Q}_1^*(A)$ has no fixed points. Let

$$K_0 \subseteq K_1 \subseteq \cdots \subseteq K = \bigcup_n K_n$$

be a recursive enumeration of $K$, and let the function $k \in \mathcal{P}_1^*$ be the smallest and least defined modulus for this recursive enumeration. Let

$$A_0 \subseteq A_1 \subseteq \cdots \subseteq A = \bigcup_n A_n$$

be a recursive enumeration of $A$, and let $a \in \mathcal{Q}_1^*(A)$ be a strong modulus for this recursive enumeration.

Let $\phi$ be an index for $f$ in $\mathcal{P}_1^*(A)$, so that

$$f(x) = u^A(\phi, x)$$

for all $x \in \mathbf{N}$. Let the function $b \in \mathcal{Q}_1^*(A)$ be defined by

$$b(x) = \mu(n).m^A(\phi, x, n)$$

If the finite set $B$ agrees with $A$ up to $b(x)$, then we have $f(x) = u^\circ(\phi, x, B)$. Thus, we have $f(x) = u^\circ(\phi, x, A_{a(b(x))})$ for all $x \in \mathbf{N}$.

Define the function $c \in \mathcal{Q}_2^*$ by

$$c(x, n) = m^\circ(\phi, x, n, A_n)$$

For all $x \in \mathbf{N}$ and all sufficiently large $n$ (depending on $x$), we have $c(x, n) = 1$. Thus, we may define the function $l \in \mathcal{Q}_2^*$ by taking $L(x, n)$ to be the smallest $t > n$ such that $c(x, t) = 1$.

Define the function $f' \in \mathcal{Q}_2^*$ by

$$f'(x, n) = u^\circ(\phi, x, A_{l(x,n)})$$

Then for all $n \geq a(b(x))$ we have $f(x) = f'(x, n)$.

Let the partial function $p \in \mathcal{F}_2$ be defined by

$$p(x, y) = \begin{cases} u^*(f'(x, k(y))), & \text{if } y \in K \\ \bot, & \text{if } y \notin K \end{cases}$$

Clearly, $p \in \mathcal{P}_2^*$ (to compute $p(x, y)$, search for $y$ in $K_0, K_1, \ldots$; this search, if successful, yields the value of $k(y)$). Let $\pi$ be an index for $p$, and define the function $g \in \mathcal{Q}_2^*$ by

$$g(x, y) = \text{pair}(\text{pair}(\pi, x), y)$$

By the Parametrized Recursion Theorem (Exercise 6, following Section 4.2.1), there is a function $h \in \mathcal{Q}_1^*$ such that, for all $y \in \mathbf{N}$, $h(y)$ and $g(h(y), y)$ index the same partial function in $\mathcal{P}_0^*$. Thus, if $y \in K$ we have

$$u^*(h(y)) = u^*(g(h(y), y)) = u^*(f'(h(y), k(y))) \tag{4.4.6}$$

Now if $y \in K$ and $a(b(y)) \leq k(y)$, then $f(h(y)) = f'(h(y), k(y))$, and Eq. (4.4.6) contradicts the assumption that $f$ has no fixed points. Thus, if $y \in K$, we have $k(y) < a(b(y))$, so that $a \circ b$ is a modulus for the recursive enumeration of $K$. Since $a$ and $b$ are recursive in $A$, so is $a \circ b$ and, therefore, so is $K$. Since $K$ is T-complete, so is $A$. Thus part (1) holds.  □

### Exercise

1. (M) Show that there are three recursively enumerable sets such that none of the six possible T-reducibilities among them holds.

### 4.4.4. An Application

In this section we shall present an application of the incomparable recursively enumerable sets constructed in Theorem 4.4.9. The application concerns a classic theorem due to Ramsey [1930] (which we shall present as Theorem 4.4.12) and shows that certain "non-constructive" features of the proof of this theorem cannot be avoided. Though the proof we give has been superseded by sharper results (which do not use Theorem 4.4.9), it illustrates the relevance of Theorem 4.4.9 to situations that at first glance appear quite unrelated.

A binary relation $E \subseteq \mathbf{N}^2$ is a *graph* if it is irreflexive (that is, $(x, x) \notin E$ for all $x \in \mathbf{N}$) and symmetric (that is, $(x, y) \in E$ if and only if $(y, x) \in E$, for all $x, y \in \mathbf{N}$). A set $C \subseteq \mathbf{N}$ is a *clique* in $E$ if $(x, y) \in E$ for all $x, y \in C$ such that $x \neq y$. A set $C \subseteq \mathbf{N}$ is an *anticlique* in $E$ if $(x, y) \notin E$ for all $x, y \in C$.

**Theorem 4.4.12 (Ramsey [1930]).** *Every graph $E$ has either an infinite clique or an infinite anticlique.*

**Proof.** We shall give a procedure whereby elements are "crossed out," "colored red," or "colored blue" at various stages. What happens in the various stages will not be "computable," however, since it will depend on the graph as a whole, rather than on conditions that can be tested by examining a finite part of the graph.

Initially, no elements will be crossed out or colored. At the outset of each stage, there will be infinitely many elements that have not been crossed out. Of these, finitely many may have been colored red or blue, but infinitely many will have been neither crossed out nor colored.

In each stage, we let $x$ be the smallest number that is neither crossed out nor colored. If there are infinitely many $y > x$ that are not crossed out and for which $(x, y) \in E$, color $x$ red and cross out all $z > x$ for which $(x, z) \notin E$. Otherwise, there must be infinitely many $y > x$ that are not crossed out and for which $(x, y) \notin E$. In this case, color $x$ blue and cross out all $z > x$ for which $(x, z) \in E$.

If, at the completion of all of the stages, infinitely many numbers have been colored red, they form an infinite clique. Otherwise, infinitely many numbers must have been colored blue. In this case, they form an infinite anticlique.  □

Consideration of this proof reveals that it does not tell us how to construct an infinite clique or anticlique, even if we have an oracle for $E$: we cannot determine by asking finitely many questions to the oracle whether an element should be colored red or blue, or whether red or blue will occur infinitely often. This does not mean, however, that there might not be a more constructive proof, whereby the clique or anticlique would be recursively enumerable in $E$

We shall see in this section that no such proof exists: there is a recursive graph with no infinite recursively enumerable clique and no infinite recursively enumerable anticlique. This result is illustrative of the power of recursive function theory in "metamathematics" (the study by mathematical methods of the possibilities and limitations of mathematics).

Let $f, g \in \mathcal{Q}_1^*$ be one-to-one recursive functions. Let $E(f, g)$ be the graph in which, for all $x, y \in \mathbf{N}$ such that $x < y$, $(x, y)$ and $(y, x)$ belong to $E(f, g)$

if and only if

$$\min_{x \leq z < y} f(z) \leq \min_{x \leq z < y} g(z)$$

Clearly, $E(f, g)$ is recursive, and an infinite anticlique in $E(f, g)$ is an infinite clique in $E(g, f)$.

*Lemma 4.4.13.* If $E(f, g)$ has an infinite recursive clique, then range($g$) is recursive in range($f$).

**Proof.** Let $T$ be an infinite recursive clique, and let $t_0 < t_1 < \cdots$ be the elements of $T$. Suppose that we wish to know whether $x \in$ range($g$). If $x = g(y)$ for some $y \in \mathbf{N}$, then either $y < t_0$ or there is a unique $i$ such that $t_i \leq y < t_{i+1}$. Since $T$ is recursive, we can easily find $t_0$ and check the finitely many smaller possibilities for $y$. Suppose that $x = g(y)$ for some $t_i \leq y < t_{i+1}$. Since $T$ is a clique, $(t_i, t_{i+1}) \in E(f, g)$, and thus the minimum of $f(z)$ over $t_i \leq z < t_{i+1}$ is at most the minimum of $g(z)$ over $t_i \leq z < t_{i+1}$, which is at most $g(y) = x$. For each $w$, there is at most one $z$ such that $f(z) = w$, since $f$ is one-to-one. For each value of $w$ that is at most $x$, we can determine whether there is such a $z$ by asking a question to an oracle for range($f$). If there is such a $z$, we can determine it by computing $f(0), f(1), \ldots$, until we find $f(z) = w$. Having found $z$, we can find $t_i$ and $t_{i+1}$ such that $t_i \leq z < t_{i+1}$, and then check the finitely many $y$ such that $y_i \leq y < t_{i+1}$ to determine if there is one such that $g(y) = x$. □

*Theorem 4.4.14.* There is an infinite recursive graph $E$ that has no infinite recursively enumerable clique and no infinite recursively enumerable anticlique.

**Proof.** Let $A$ and $B$ be recursively enumerable sets such that $A$ is not recursive in $B$ and $B$ is not recursive in $A$. (Such sets were constructed in Theorem 4.4.9.) Let $f$ and $g$ be one-to-one recursive functions with range($f$) = $A$ and range($g$) = $B$, respectively. (Such functions were constructed in Exercise 2, following Section 4.3.1, or may be constructed directly as follows: let $f'$ be a recursive function with range($f'$) = $A$, as constructed in Lemma 4.3.2, then let $f(n)$ be the $n$-th new value to appear in the list $f'(0), f'(1), \ldots$, which, being infinite, must continually produce new values.) Let $E = E(f, g)$. If $E$ has an infinite recursively enumerable clique $T'$, then $T'$ has an infinite recursive subset $T$ (by Exercise 5, following Section 4.3.1), and $T$ is also a clique; thus, by Lemma 4.4.13, $B =$ range($g$) is recursive in $A =$ range($f$), a contradiction. If $E$ has an infinite recursively enumerable anticlique, then $E(g, f)$ has an infinite recursively enumerable clique, and an analogous argument yields that $A =$ range($f$) is recursive in $B =$ range($g$), again a contradiction. □

The result of Theorem 4.4.14 was obtained independently by a number of workers: see Specker [1971], Yates [1971], and Jockusch [1972]. The proof we have presented follows Specker's. (Jockusch's proof goes further, and shows that a recursive graph may have no infinite clique or anticlique that is recursively enumerable in $K$, though it always has one whose complement is recursively enumerable in $K$.)

### *Exercises*

1. (M) Prove the following finite analogue of Ramsey's Theorem: In any graph with $2^{2k-2}$ vertices, there exists either a clique with $k$ vertices or an anti-clique with $k$ vertices.
2. (M) Show that there exists $f \in \mathcal{Q}_1^*$ such that range$(f) \not\leq_T$ graph$(f)$ and graph$(f) \not\leq_T$ range$(f)$.

### 4.5. Many-One Reducibility

In this section we shall consider a notion of reducibility that is stronger than Turing reducibility. Like Turing reducibility, it partitions sets into degrees, which (being based on a stronger relation) are refinements of Turing degrees. There are benefits and drawbacks to this strengthening: the structure of individual degrees becomes simpler (this is especially true for the complete degree), but the relationships among degrees become more complicated.

The variant we shall consider is called "many-one," and is denoted by a subscript or prefix "m." Though it is possible to define these notions for $k$-ary relations for any $k$, we shall again confine our treatment to $k = 1$; thus, the relations in question may be regarded as sets of natural numbers.

Let $A$ and $B$ be sets of natural numbers. We shall write $A \leq_m B$ (and say "$A$ is many-one reducible to $B$") if there exists a recursive function $f \in \mathcal{G}_1$ such that, for all $x \in \mathbf{N}$, $x \in A$ if and only if $f(x) \in B$.

The condition $A \leq_m B$, like the condition $A \leq_T B$, is intended as a formalization of the assertion "$A$ is at least as easy to compute as $B$." But $\leq_m$ is stronger than $\leq_T$ in the following way. If $A \leq_T B$, then questions about membership in $A$ can be transformed into questions about membership in $B$, but a single question about $A$ may be transformed into many questions about $B$, with later questions, and even the number of questions, depending on the answers to earlier questions. If $A \leq_m B$, however, a question about $A$ can be transformed into a single question about $B$, and the answers to the two questions will be the same. We observe that if $A \leq_m B$ via the function $f$, then char$_A$ = char$_B \circ f$, and so reducibility is a sort of "factorization" condition, with respect to the non-commutative operation of composition.

*Lemma 4.5.1.* (a) $A \leq_m A$ (that is, $\leq_m$ is reflexive). (b) If $A \leq_m B$ and $B \leq_m C$, then $A \leq_m C$ (that is, $\leq_m$ is transitive). (c) If $A \leq_m B$, then $\text{Compl}(A) \leq_m \text{Compl}(B)$. (d) If $A \leq_m B$ and $B$ is recursive, then $A$ is recursive. (e) If $A \leq_m B$ and $B$ is recursively enumerable, then $A$ is recursively enumerable.

**Proof.** (a) Let $f = \text{proj}_{1,1}$. (b) If $A \leq_m B$ via $f$ and $B \leq_m C$ via $g$, then $A \leq_m C$ via $g \circ f$. (c) The same function reduces the complements as reduces the sets themselves. (d) If $A \leq_m B$ via $f$ and $B$ has the recursive characteristic function $g$, then $A$ has the recursive characteristic function $g \circ f$. (e) If $A \leq_m B$ via $f$ and $B$ is the domain of the partial recursive function $g$, then $A$ is the domain of the partial recursive function $g \circ f$. □

We shall write $A \equiv_m B$ (and say "$A$ is many-one equivalent to $B$") if $A \leq_m B$ and $B \leq_m A$. The condition $A \equiv_m B$ is intended as a formalization of the assertion "$A$ is exactly as easy to compute as $B$" (again in the stronger sense of single questions transforming to single questions with the same answers).

*Lemma 4.5.2.* $\equiv_m$ is reflexive and transitive. Furthermore, if $A \equiv_m B$, then $B \equiv_m A$ (that is, $\equiv_m$ is symmetric).

The proof is immediate from Lemma 4.5.1 and the definition of $\equiv_m$. Lemma 4.5.2 may be summarized by saying that $\equiv_m$ is an equivalence on $\text{Pow}(\mathbf{N})$, which partitions the collection of sets of natural numbers into equivalence classes called *m-degrees*.

The relation $A \leq_m B$ implies $A \leq_T B$, but the converse is false: we have $\text{Compl}(K) \leq_T K$ by Lemma 4.4.3, but Lemma 4.5.1(e) implies $\text{Compl}(K) \nleq_m K$, since $K$ is recursively enumerable while $\text{Compl}(K)$ is not. Since the relation $\leq_m$ is stronger than $\leq_T$, the m-degrees are refinements of the T-degrees: each m-degree is contained within a single T-degree, but a T-degree may contain many m-degrees. The recursive T-degree $\mathcal{O}$, for example, splits into three m-degrees: the empty set $\emptyset$ constitutes an m-degree $\mathcal{O}_{0,\infty}$ by itself, the full set $\mathbf{N}$ constitutes an m-degree $\mathcal{O}_{\infty,0}$ by itself, and all other recursive sets constitute a third m-degree $\mathcal{O}_+$.

If $\mathcal{A}$ and $\mathcal{B}$ are m-degrees, and if $A \leq_m B$ for some $A \in \mathcal{A}$ and $B \in \mathcal{B}$, then every set in $\mathcal{A}$ is m-reducible to every set in $\mathcal{B}$. This implies that the relation $\leq_m$ may be used to compare m-degrees as well as sets, and that the m-degrees are ordered by m-reducibility.

The join $A \vee B$ of sets $A$ and $B$ defined in Section 4.4.2 gives a least upper bound with respect to the relation $\leq_m$, as well as with respect to the relation

$\leq_T$. Furthermore, this operation applies to m-degrees in exactly the same way as to T-degrees. For example, the m-degrees $\mathcal{O}_{0,\infty}$, $\mathcal{O}_{\infty,0}$, and $\mathcal{O}_+$ just defined are ordered as follows, and $\mathcal{O}_+ = \mathcal{O}_{0,\infty} \vee \mathcal{O}_{\infty,0}$:

$$
\begin{array}{ccc}
 & \mathcal{O}_+ & \\
\nearrow & & \nwarrow \\
\mathcal{O}_{0,\infty} & & \mathcal{O}_{\infty,0}
\end{array}
$$

The incomparable m-degrees $\mathcal{O}_{0,\infty}$ and $\mathcal{O}_{\infty,0}$, which are minimal with respect to m-reducibility, show that there are, in general, no greatest lower bounds with respect to the relation $\leq_m$ (much more easily than Theorem 4.4.8 for $\leq_T$).

By Lemma 4.5.1(d) and 4.5.1(e), if an m-degree contains a recursive set or a recursively enumerable set, then it contains only recursive sets or recursively enumerable sets. Thus, we may speak of "recursive m-degrees" or "recursively enumerable m-degrees."

We shall say that $A$ is *m-complete* if (1) $A$ is recursively enumerable and (2) for every recursively enumerable $B$, we have $B \leq_m A$.

The condition "$A$ is m-complete" is intended as a formalization of the notion that $A$ is a hardest set to compute among the recursively enumerable sets.

*Lemma 4.5.3.* Any two of the following conditions imply the third: (1) $A$ is m-complete, (2) $B$ is m-complete, (3) $A \equiv_m B$.

The proof is immediate from the definitions. It follows that there is a unique "complete m-degree."

**Proposition 4.5.4.** *The set $K$ is m-complete.*

**Proof.** We have already seen in Example 4.3.1 that $K$ is recursively enumerable. It remains to show that for every recursively enumerable $B$, we have $B \leq_m K$.                                                        $\square$

Proposition 4.5.4 is, in fact, shown by the proof of the corresponding proposition for T-completeness, Proposition 4.4.6. Again as for T-completeness, it is straightforward to define the relativized notion "$A$ is m-complete for $C$," with the set $K(C)$ playing the role of $K$ in the relativized version of Proposition 4.5.4.

We have seen that the recursive T-degree $\mathcal{O}$ splits into three m-degrees. We shall now study the splitting of the complete T-degree $\mathcal{O}'$. The complete T-degree contains the complete m-degree, since both degrees contain $K$. The complete T-degree also contains the m-degree containing Compl($K$) (since Compl($K$) is also T-complete), and this m-degree is incomparable to the complete m-degree with respect to the order $\leq_m$. Before we seek further m-degrees within $\mathcal{O}'$, let us consider some properties m-complete sets.

Recall that the sequence $W_0$, $W_1$, ..., contains all and only the recursively enumerable sets, indexed in the usual way. We shall say that a set $A$ is *productive* if there exists a recursive function $f \in \mathcal{Q}_1^*$ such that, for all $\pi \in \mathbf{N}$, if $W_\pi \subseteq A$, then $f(\pi) \in A \setminus W_\pi$. (This definition of "productive" is not the standard one, but it is equivalent to the standard one. Its equivalence to other definitions is explored in Exercises 3, 4, and 5 following this section.)

**Remark.** If $A$ is productive, then $A$ is not recursively enumerable (for if it were, it would be equal to $W_\pi$ for some $\pi \in \mathbf{N}$, yielding a contradiction).

*Lemma 4.5.5.* If $A$ is productive and $A \leq_m B$, then $B$ is productive.

**Proof.** Suppose that $A \leq_m B$ via $f$ and that $A$ is productive via $g$. It is routine to construct $h \in \mathcal{Q}_1^*$ such that $W_{h(\pi)} = f^{-1}(W_\pi)$ for all $\pi \in \mathbf{N}$, and easy to check that $B$ is productive via $f \circ g \circ h$.                                                 □

*Lemma 4.5.6.* If $A$ is productive, then $A$ has an infinite recursively enumerable subset.

**Proof.** A finite set $\{x_1, \ldots, x_k\}$ can be described by its unique encoding #$\{x_1, \ldots, x_k\} = \sum_{1 \leq j \leq k} 2^{x_j}$ or by one of its many indices $\pi$ such that $W_\pi = \{x_1, \ldots, x_k\}$. It is routine to construct a recursive function index $\in \mathcal{Q}_1^*$ such that index(#$\{x_1, \ldots, x_k\}$) is an index for $\{x_1, \ldots, x_k\}$. (It is not possible to go the other way, from indices to encodings, of course; that would violate Rice's Theorem, Corollary 4.2.5.)

Suppose that $A$ is productive via $f$. We define a recursive function $g$ by setting $g(0) = f(\text{index}(\#\emptyset))$ and, for $n \geq 1$, $g(n) = f(\text{index}(\#\{g(0), \ldots, g(n-1)\}))$. It is easy to prove by induction on $n$ that $g(n) \in A$. This implies that $g$ is one-to-one, so that range($g$) is infinite. Since $g$ is recursive, range($g$) is recursively enumerable. Thus range($g$) is an infinite recursively enumerable subset of $A$.                                                 □

**Remark.** Every infinite recursively enumerable set contains an infinite recursive subset (Exercise 5, following Section 4.3.1) and so every productive set contains an infinite recursive subset.

We shall say that a set $A$ is *creative* if (1) $A$ is recursively enumerable and (2) Compl($A$) is productive. (If Compl($A$) is "something," we may say that $A$ is "co-something." Thus condition (2) may also be expressed by saying that $A$ is "co-productive.")

**Remark.** If $A$ is creative, then $A$ is not recursive (since its complement, being productive, is not recursively enumerable).

**Example 4.5.1.** The set $K$ is recursively enumerable, and it is easy to check that Compl($K$) is productive via the identity function. Thus, $K$ is creative.

*Lemma 4.5.7.* If $A$ is m-complete, then $A$ is creative.

**Proof.** Since $A$ is m-complete, $A$ is recursively enumerable and, since $K$ is recursively enumerable, $K \leq_m A$. By Lemma 4.5.1(c), Compl($K$) $\leq_m$ Compl($A$). Since Compl($K$) is productive, Lemma 4.5.5 implies that $A$ is productive. Thus $A$ is creative.                                                □

We shall say that a set $A$ is *immune* if (1) $A$ is infinite and (2) $A$ has no infinite recursively enumerable subset.

**Remark.** If $A$ is immune, then $A$ is not recursively enumerable (since an infinite recursively enumerable set has itself as an infinite recursively enumerable subset).

We shall say that a set $A$ is *simple* if (1) $A$ is recursively enumerable and (2) Compl($A$) is immune (that is, $A$ is "co-immune").

**Remark.** If $A$ is simple, then $A$ is not recursive (since its complement, being immune, is not recursively enumerable). Furthermore, if $A$ is simple, then $A$ is not creative (since its complement, being immune, contains no infinite recursively enumerable subset and, thus, is not productive). Thus, if $A$ is simple, then $A$ is not m-complete.

It is not obvious from the definition that simple sets exist; this was first proved by Post [1944]. We shall give a general construction for simple sets due to Dekker [1954].

Let $f$ be a monadic one-to-one recursive function. Define the *deficiency set* of $f$, denoted def($f$), to be the set of $n \in \mathbf{N}$ such that $f(m) < f(n)$ for some $m > n$.

**Theorem 4.5.8 (Dekker [1954]).** *For any one-to-one recursive function $f$, def $(f) \equiv_T range(f)$. Furthermore, if $range(f)$ is not recursive, then $def(f)$ is simple.*

**Proof.** Let $A = range(f)$, so that $A$ is an infinite recursively enumerable set. Let $B = def(f)$. If we are given an oracle for $A$, we can determine whether $y \in B$ as follows. For each of the finitely many $z < f(y)$, ask the oracle if $z \in A$. For each such $z \in A$, find the $w$ such that $z = f(w)$ (there is just one such $w$, since $f$ is one-to-one). Then $y \in B$ if and only if one of these numbers $w$ satisfies $w > y$. Thus, $B \leq_T A$. Now suppose we are given an oracle for $B$ and we wish to determine whether $x \in A$. We first observe that $\text{Compl}(B)$ is infinite: given $x$, let $y$ be such that $f(y)$ is minimum over all $y \geq x$; then $y \notin B$; thus, $\text{Compl}(B)$ contains elements beyond any prescribed bound. To determine if $x \in A$, find an element $y > x$ such that $y \notin B$. Thus, we have $f(z) \geq f(y)$ for all $z > y$. Then $x \in A$ if an only if $x = f(w)$ for one of the finitely many $w \leq y$. Thus, $A \leq_T B$ and, therefore, $A \equiv_T B$.

Suppose that $A$ is not recursive. The definition of $B$ gives a procedure for listing its elements, and so $B$ is recursively enumerable. It remains to show that $\text{Compl}(B)$ contains no infinite recursively enumerable subset. Suppose, with an eye to contradiction, that the infinite recursively enumerable set $C \subseteq \text{Compl}(B)$. Since $f$ is one-to-one and recursive, the set $f(C)$ is also infinite and recursively enumerable. We can determine whether $x \in A$ as follows. List the elements of $f(C)$ until an element $f(y)$ with $f(y) > x$ is obtained. Since $y \in C = \text{Compl}(B)$, we have $y \notin B$; thus, there is some $z > y$ such that $f(z) < f(y)$. Thus, $x \in A$ if and only if $x = f(z)$ for some $z < y$, which can be determined by evaluating $f$ at $y + 1$ points. This contradicts the assumption that $A$ is not recursive. □

By Exercise 2, following Section 4.3.1, there is a one-to one recursive function $k$ such that $range(k) = K$. By Theorem 4.5.8, $def(k) \equiv_T K$, so that $def(k)$ is T-complete, but $def(k)$ is simple, and therefore not m-complete. Therefore, the m-degree of $def(k)$ is another m-degree in $\mathcal{O}'$, different from the m-degrees of $K$ and its complement. Similarly, the m-degree of the complement of $def(k)$ is a fourth m-degree in $\mathcal{O}'$. Since $def(k)$ is not recursive, we see that there are recursively enumerable sets that are neither recursive nor m-complete (much more easily than Theorem 4.4.9 for T-completeness).

We shall now give some further constructions of simple sets that have very natural interpretations. The first two constructions we shall give are based on the notion of "descriptive complexity," which is due to Solomonoff [1964], Kolmogorov [1965], and Chaitin [1966]. (The theory of descriptive complexity emerges when we attempt to formulate a rigorous counterpart to "Berry's

Paradox": What is the smallest natural number not definable by an English sentence with fewer than a thousand words?)

Let $T$ denote the binary relation comprising those pairs $(x, \pi)$ for which $x > \pi$ and $x = u^*(\pi)$. Clearly, $T$ is recursively enumerable. Let $S = \text{Proj}(T)$. By Lemma 4.3.4, $S$ is also recursively enumerable. Let $R = \text{Compl}(S)$. We shall show that $R$ is immune, and thus, that $S$ is simple. (The set $S$ comprises those numbers that can be "described" by numbers smaller than themselves, where "descriptions" are interpreted by $u^*$. Such number may be regarded as "compressible." The complementary set $R$ comprises numbers that are "incompressible," in the sense that they have no descriptions smaller than themselves. The elements of $R$ are sometimes called "random" numbers; this terminology may seem bizarre, since they have been defined in a completely deterministic way, but they in fact have many properties that justify it.)

*Theorem 4.5.9.* *The set $S$ is simple and $T$-complete.*

**Proof.** We have already seen that $S$ is recursively enumerable, and so to prove that $S$ is simple it will suffice to show that its complement $R$ is immune.

First we show that $R$ is infinite. We begin by observing that there are infinitely many indices $\pi$ such that $u^*(\pi) = \perp$. (For if not, $\mathcal{A} = \{\text{undef}_0\}$ would violate Rice's Theorem, Theorem 4.2.4.) Thus, for every $n \geq 0$, there exists $x$ such that the set $I = \{0, \ldots, x\}$ contains $n$ different indices for undef$_0$. It follows that $I$ contains at most $x + 1 - n$ indices for 0-adic constant functions (that is, for natural numbers). In particular, at most $x + 1 - n$ elements of $I$ can appear in $S$. Thus, at least $n$ elements of $I$ belong to $R$. Since this holds for any $n \geq 0$, $R$ is infinite.

It remains to show that $R$ contains no infinite recursively enumerable subset. Suppose that $A$ is an infinite recursively enumerable set. We shall show that $A \cap S \neq \emptyset$, so that $A$ is not a subset of $R$. Using Lemma 4.3.2, let $h$ be a monadic recursive function such that $A = \text{range}(h)$. Define the monadic recursive function $g$ by letting $g(x)$ equal the first element of the sequence $h(0), h(1), h(2), \ldots$, that exceeds $x$. (The function $g$ is total because $A$ is infinite.) Let $\gamma$ be an index for $g$ and define the monadic recursive function $f$ by $f(x) = \text{pair}(\gamma, x)$, so that $f(x)$ is an index for the 0-adic constant function with value $g(x)$. By the Recursion Theorem, Theorem 4.2.6, there exists an $n \in \mathbf{N}$ such that $n$ and $f(n)$ are indices for the same 0-adic function. Thus, we have

$$u^*(n) = u^*(f(n)) = g(n) > n$$

(by the Recursion Theorem, the definition of $f$, and the definition of $g$), so that $g(n) \in S$ (by the definition of $S$). On the other hand, $g(n) \in A$ (since range($g$) $\subseteq$ range($h$) = $A$), and so we have $A \cap S \neq \emptyset$. This completes the proof that $S$ is simple.

It remains to prove that $S$ is T-complete. By Arslanov's criterion, Theorem 4.4.11, it will suffice to show that there is a function $f \in \mathcal{Q}_1^*(S)$ such that $u^*(n) \neq u^*(f(n))$ for all $n \in \mathbf{N}$. Given $x$, let $g(x)$ be the smallest element $y$ of $R$ such that $y > x$. Since $R$ is infinite, $g$ is total, and since $\mathcal{P}^*(R) = \mathcal{P}^*(S)$, we have $g \in \mathcal{Q}_1^*(S)$. Now let $\iota$ be an index for the monadic identity function, and let $f(x) = \text{pair}(\iota, g(x))$, so that $f(x)$ is an index for $g(x)$. We then have $f \in \mathcal{Q}_1^*(S)$. For any $n \in \mathbf{N}$, $f(n)$ is an index for a number $g(n)$ that has no index as small as $n$. Thus, we have $u^*(n) \neq u^*(f(n))$ for all $n \in \mathbf{N}$. □

Let $P$ denote the binary relation comprising those pairs $(\tau, \pi)$ for which $\tau > \pi$ and $u^*(\tau) = u^*(\pi)$. Clearly, $P$ is recursively enumerable. Let $N = \text{Proj}(P)$. By Lemma 4.3.4, $N$ is also recursively enumerable. Let $O = \text{Compl}(N)$. We shall show that $O$ is immune and, thus, that $N$ is simple. (The set $N$ comprises those numbers that, regarded as descriptions for $u^*$, are "non-optimal," in the sense that there is a smaller description for the same number. The set $O$ comprises the numbers that are "optimal" in this sense.) The following theorem is proved by an argument analogous to that for Theorem 4.5.9.

**Theorem 4.5.10.** *The set $N$ is simple and T-complete.*

We shall give one more construction for a simple set that is related to "computational complexity" in the same way that the preceding two constructions are related to descriptive complexity. Let $k$ again be a one-to-one recursive functions such that range($k$) = $K$. Define the "busy beaver" function $b$ (the terminology is due to Rado [1962]) by letting $b(n)$ be the largest number $m$ such that $k(m) \leq n$. Since $k$ is one-to-one, the set $\{m : k(m) \leq n\}$ is finite for every $n$; thus, $b$ is a total function. Let $B = \text{Compl}(\text{range}(b))$.

**Theorem 4.5.11 (Daley [1978]).** *The set $B$ is simple and T-complete.*

The proof, which we shall not give here, can be found in the paper of Daley [1978]. We shall explore both descriptive and computational complexity further in Section 4.7.

### Exercises

1. (E) Exhibit a set $A$ such that $A \leq_m \text{Compl}(A)$, but $A$ is not recursive.
2. (E) Show that if $A \leq_m \text{Compl}(A)$ and $A$ is recursively enumerable, then $A$ is recursive.

3. (M) Say that a set $A$ is *partially productive* if there exists a partial recursive function $f \in \mathcal{P}_1^*$ such that, for all $\pi \in \mathbf{N}$, if $W_\pi \subseteq A$, then ($f(\pi)$ is defined and) $f(\pi) \in A \setminus W_\pi$. (This is the standard definition of "productive.") Show that if $A$ is partially productive, then $A$ is productive. (Hint: Suppose that $A$ is partially productive via $f$. Construct a recursive function $g$ such that

$$W_{g(x,y)} = \begin{cases} W_y, & \text{if } f(x) \in \mathbf{N} \\ \emptyset, & \text{if } f(x) = \bot \end{cases}$$

then apply an appropriate form of the Recursion Theorem to $g$.)

4. (E) Show that if $A$ is productive, then $A$ is productive via a one-to-one function.

5. (M) Say that a set $A$ is *completely productive* if there exists a recursive function $f \in \mathcal{Q}_1^*$ such that, for all $\pi \in \mathbf{N}$, either $f(\pi) \in A \setminus W_\pi$ or $f(\pi) \in W_\pi \setminus A$. Show that if $A$ is productive, then $A$ is completely productive. (Hint: Suppose that $A$ is productive via $f$. Construct a recursive function $g$ such that $W_{g(x,y)} = W_y \cap \{f(x)\}$, then apply an appropriate form of the Recursion Theorem to $g$.)

## 4.6. One-One Reducibility and Recursive Isomorphism

The notions of m-reducibility, m-equivalence, and m-completeness have still stronger variants that are denoted by the subscript or prefix "1" in place of "m." We define $A \leq_1 B$ (read "$A$ is one-one reducible to $B$") by replacing "recursive function $f$" by "one-to-one recursive function $F$" in the definition of $A \leq_m B$. We then define "1-equivalence" $\equiv_1$ and "1-completeness" in terms of 1-reducibility, thus obtaining "1-degrees" and the "complete 1-degree."

Closely connected to 1-reducibility and 1-equivalence is another notion of equivalence of sets, that of "recursive isomorphism." We shall say that a function $f \in \mathcal{F}_1$ is a *recursive permutation* if (1) $f$ is recursive and (2) $f$ is a permutation. (A function is a permutation (or "bijection") if it is (1) one-to-one and (2) onto. A function $f$ is onto (or "surjective") if for every $y \in \mathbf{N}$ there exists an $x \in \mathbf{N}$ such that $f(x) = y$.)

The identity function $\mathrm{id} = \mathrm{proj}_{1,1}$ is a recursive permutation; the inverse $f^{-1}$ of a recursive permutation $f$ is a recursive permutation; and the composition $f \circ g$ of two recursive permutations $f$ and $g$ is a recursive permutation. These observations may be summarized by saying that the set of recursive permutations forms a group under the operation of composition.

We shall write $A \equiv B$ (and say "$A$ is recursively isomorphic to $B$") if there exists a recursive permutation $f$ such that, for all $x \in \mathbf{N}$, $x \in A$ if and only if $f(x) \in B$. The observations of the preceding paragraph imply that $\equiv$ is reflexive, symmetric, and transitive and, thus, that $\equiv$ is an equivalence, which partitions the collection of sets of natural numbers into equivalence classes called "recursive isomorphism classes."

The relation $\equiv$ is defined by a stronger condition than $\equiv_1$, and so we might expect each 1-degree to partition into many recursive isomorphism classes. We shall see later, however, that the relations $\equiv$ and $\equiv_1$ are equivalent and, thus, that each 1-degree forms a single recursive isomorphism class.

If two sets are recursively isomorphic, they differ from one another by a computable relabelling of the natural numbers. Properties of sets that are invariant under recursive isomorphism (such as being empty or full, finite or infinite, recursive or recursively enumerable) are of particular interest in recursive function theory; properties that are not invariant (such as being an interval of consecutive natural numbers, or containing only prime numbers) are less interesting from the viewpoint of recursive function theory (though they may be more interesting from the viewpoint of other disciplines, such as number theory).

### 4.6.1. Recursive Isomorphism of m-Complete Sets

The analogues of Lemmas 4.5.1, 4.5.2, and 4.5.3 and Proposition 4.5.4 hold for 1-notions and are proved by the same arguments.

The relation $A \leq_1 B$ implies the relation $A \leq_m B$, but the converse is false: if a set (or its complement) is finite, then any other set (or its complement) in the same 1-degree must also be finite and must have the same cardinality. Thus, the m-degree $\mathcal{O}_+$ splits into infinitely many 1-degrees: for each $n \geq 1$ there is a 1-degree $\mathcal{O}_{n,\infty}$ comprising the sets of cardinality $n$ and a 1-degree $\mathcal{O}_{\infty,n}$ comprising the sets with complements of cardinality $n$, and finally there is a 1-degree $\mathcal{O}_{\infty,\infty}$ comprising the recursive sets that are neither finite nor co-finite. The m-degrees $\mathcal{O}_{0,\infty}$ and $\mathcal{O}_{\infty,0}$ do not split, of course, since they each contain a single set. Thus we have the following relationships:

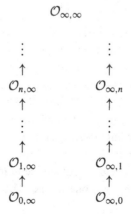

$$\mathcal{O}_{\infty,\infty}$$

$$\vdots \qquad \vdots$$

$$\uparrow \qquad \uparrow$$

$$\mathcal{O}_{n,\infty} \qquad \mathcal{O}_{\infty,n}$$

$$\uparrow \qquad \uparrow$$

$$\vdots \qquad \vdots$$

$$\uparrow \qquad \uparrow$$

$$\mathcal{O}_{1,\infty} \qquad \mathcal{O}_{\infty,1}$$

$$\uparrow \qquad \uparrow$$

$$\mathcal{O}_{0,\infty} \qquad \mathcal{O}_{\infty,0}$$

As for $\leq_m$, any pair of incomparable 1-degrees $\mathcal{O}_{n,\infty}$ and $\mathcal{O}_{\infty,m}$ shows that there are, in general, no greatest lower bounds with respect to the relation $\leq_1$. Such a pair of 1-degrees has the least upper bound $\mathcal{O}_{\infty,\infty}$, but we shall see later that incomparable 1-degrees, in general, have no least upper bounds. (The join operation that gives least upper bounds with respect to $\leq_m$ does not work for $\leq_1$, since the resulting reduction may be "two-to-one" in some cases.)

We shall now consider the complete m-degree, which (perhaps surprisingly) does not split at all. We have the implications

$$A \text{ 1-complete} \Rightarrow A \text{ m-complete} \Rightarrow A \text{ creative}$$

The next theorem show that these are, in fact, equivalences.

**Theorem 4.6.1 (Myhill [1955]).** *If A is creative, then A is 1-complete.*

**Proof.** Suppose that $A$ is creative. Then $A$ is recursively enumerable and $\text{Compl}(A)$ is productive via some recursive function $h \in \mathcal{Q}_1^*$. We shall begin by showing that $A$ is m-complete.

Let $B$ be an arbitrary recursively enumerable set. It is routine to construct a recursive function $f \in \mathcal{Q}_2^*$ such that

$$W_{f(x,y)} = \begin{cases} \{h(x)\}, & \text{if } y \in B \\ \emptyset, & \text{if } y \notin B \end{cases}$$

for all $x, y \in \mathbf{N}$. From the Parametrized Recursion Theorem (Exercise 6, following Section 4.2.1) we obtain a recursive function $g \in \mathcal{Q}_1^*$ such that, for all $y \in \mathbf{N}$, $g(y)$ and $f\big(g(y), y\big)$ index the same partial recursive function in $\mathcal{P}_1^*$, and thus index the same recursively enumerable set:

$$W_{g(y)} = W_{f(g(y),y)} = \begin{cases} \{h(g(y))\}, & \text{if } y \in B \\ \emptyset, & \text{if } y \notin B \end{cases}$$

If $y \in B$, then we have $h(g(y)) \in W_{g(y)}$. We must then have $W_{g(y)} \not\subseteq \text{Compl}(A)$, for if $W_{g(y)} \subseteq \text{Compl}(A)$, then (since $\text{Compl}(A)$ is productive via $h$) we would have $h(g(y)) \notin W_{g(y)}$, a contradiction. Since $W_{g(y)} = \{h(g(y))\}$, $W_{g(y)} \not\subseteq \text{Compl}(A)$ implies $h(g(y)) \notin \text{Compl}(A)$. Thus, $h(g(y)) \in A$.

On the other hand, if $y \notin B$, then $W_{g(y)} = \emptyset$. This implies (since $\text{Compl}(A)$ is productive via $h$) that $h(g(y)) \in \text{Compl}(A)$, and therefore $h(g(y)) \notin A$. Thus, we have $y \in B$ if and only if $h(g(y)) \in A$, so that $B$ is m-reducible to $A$ via $h \circ g$. Thus, $A$ is m-complete.

To show that $A$ is 1-complete, it will suffice to modify this construction so that the recursive function $h \circ g$ is one-to-one. The function $h$ can be taken to be one-to-one by Exercise 4, following Section 4.5 and the function $g$ can be taken to be one-to-one by Exercises 4 and 6, following Section 4.2.1. Thus, $h \circ g$ may be taken to be one-to-one. □

We have the implication

$$A \equiv B \Rightarrow A \equiv_1 B$$

The next theorem shows that this is also an equivalence.

**Theorem 4.6.2 (Myhill [1955]).** *If $A \equiv_1 B$, then $A \equiv B$.*

For the proof, we shall need a definition and a lemma. Let $X$ and $Y$ be sets of natural numbers. We shall say that a finite set $\{(x_1, y_1), \ldots, (x_n, y_n)\}$ of pairs of natural numbers is a *finite correspondence* between $X$ and $Y$ if (1) each natural number appears at most once as the first component of a pair, and at most once as the second component of a pair, and (2) for every $j \in [n]$, we have $x_j \in X$ if and only if $y_j \in Y$.

*Lemma 4.6.3.* Suppose that $X \leq_1 Y$. If $E = \{(x_1, y_1), \ldots, (x_n, y_n)\}$ is a finite correspondence between $X$ and $Y$, and if $x \notin \{x_1, \ldots, x_n\}$, then there exists $y \in \mathbf{N}$ such that $\{(x_1, y_1), \ldots, (x_n, y_n), (x, y)\}$ is a finite correspondence between $X$ and $Y$.

**Proof.** Suppose that $X \leq_1 Y$ via $f$. Set $x' := x$. Set $y' := f(x')$. If $y' \notin \{y_1, \ldots, y_n\}$, take $y = y'$. On the other hand, if $y' = y_j$, set $x' := x_j$ and repeat this procedure.

It is easy to see that no value can be encountered twice as $x'$ or twice as $y'$ (by the fact that $f$ is one-to-one and condition (1) for a finite correspondence). Thus, by the finiteness of $E$, the procedure must eventually terminate with a value for $y$. That this value is satisfactory follows from the fact that $f$ is a reduction and condition (2) for a finite correspondence. □

**Proof of Theorem 4.6.2.** Suppose that $A \leq_1 B$ via $g$ and $B \leq_1 A$ via $h$. We shall construct a recursive permutation $e$ by constructing $\text{graph}(e) = \{(x, y) : e(x) = y\}$. We shall start by taking $\text{graph}(e)$ to be the empty set, which is a finite correspondence between $A$ and $B$. We shall then proceed through an infinite sequence of stages, each of which maintains the condition that $\text{graph}(e)$ is a finite correspondence between $A$ and $B$. The even numbered stage $2t$ will be responsible for ensuring that $t$ appears in $\text{dom}(e)$. The odd numbered stage $2t + 1$ will be responsible for ensuring that $t$ appears in $\text{range}(e)$. Thus, at the completion of all the stages, graph($e$) will be the graph of a recursive permutation $e$.

**Stage 2$t$.** If $t$ is already in dom($e$), do nothing. Otherwise, use Lemma 4.6.3 with $X = A$, $Y = B$, $f = g$, $E = $ graph($e$), and $x = t$ to find $y$, and then put the pair $(t, y)$ into graph($e$).

**Stage 2$t$ + 1.** If $t$ is already in range($e$), do nothing. Otherwise, use Lemma 4.6.3 with $X = B$, $Y = A$, $f = h$, $E = \{(x, y) : (y, x) \in$ graph($e$)$\}$, and $x = t$ to find $y$, and then put the pair $(y, t)$ into graph($e$).                    □

Theorem 4.6.2 is a "computable" version of the Cantor–Schröder–Bernstein Theorem of set theory (see Quine [1969] for a discussion). Taken together Theorems 4.6.1 and 4.6.2 show that all m-complete sets are recursively isomorphic to each other; that is, all m-complete sets differ from each other merely by a computable relabelling of the natural numbers.

### Exercises

1. (E)  Show that the following three conditions are equivalent: (1) $A$ is productive, (2) Compl($K$) $\leq_m A$, and (3) Compl($K$) $\leq_1 A$.
2. (E)  Show that if $K \leq_m A$ via $f$, then $f(K)$ is infinite.
3. (M)  Say that a set $A$ is *doubly productive with respect to finite sets* if there exists a recursive function $g \in \mathcal{Q}_1^*$ such that (1) if $\{x_1, \ldots, x_k\} \subseteq A$ with $k \geq 1$, then $g(\#\{x_1, \ldots, x_k\}) \in A \setminus \{x_1, \ldots, x_k\}$, and (2) if $\{x_1, \ldots, x_k\} \subseteq$ Compl($A$) with $k \geq 1$, then $g(\#\{x_1, \ldots, x_k\}) \in$ Compl($A$) $\setminus \{x_1, \ldots, x_k\}$. Show that if $K \leq_m A$, then $A$ is doubly productive with respect to finite sets. (Hint: Suppose that $K \leq_m A$ via $f$. Construct a recursive function $h \in \mathcal{Q}_1^*$ such that if $x = \#\{x_1, \ldots, x_k\}$, then

$$W_{h(x)} = \begin{cases} f^{-1}(\{x_1, \ldots, x_k\}), & \text{if } \{x_1, \ldots, x_k\} \cap A = \emptyset \\ \mathbf{N}, & \text{if } \{x_1, \ldots, x_k\} \cap A \neq \emptyset \end{cases}$$

Observe that $g(x) = f(h(x))$ is satisfactory if $f(h(x)) \notin \{x_1, \ldots, x_k\}$; use Exercise 2 in the remaining case.)
4. (M)  Say that $A$ is *constructively non-recursive* if there is a recursive function $f \in \mathcal{Q}_1^*$ such that, for all $\pi \in \mathbf{N}$, we have

$$f(\pi) \in A \quad \text{if and only if} \quad f(\pi) \in W_\pi$$

Show that if $A$ is recursively enumerable, then it is constructively non-recursive if and only if it is creative. (Hint: Use Exercise 3.)

5. (M) Say that $A$ is *constructively non-recursive in* $B$ if there is a recursive function $f \in \mathcal{Q}_1^*$ such that, for all $\pi \in \mathbf{N}$, we have

$$f(\pi) \in A \quad \text{if and only if} \quad f(\pi) \in W_\pi[B]$$

(Note that $f$ is to be absolutely recursive.) Show that if $A$ and $B$ are recursively enumerable, then $A$ is constructively non-recursive in $B$ if and only if $A$ is constructively non-recursive and $B$ is recursive.

### 4.6.2. 1-Degrees

We shall now study two aspects of 1-degrees: the structure of 1-degrees within an m-degree, and the lack of least upper bounds for certain pairs of 1-degrees. Our first result is that we may associate with each m-degree $\mathcal{A}$ a 1-degree $\mathrm{Cyl}(\mathcal{A})$ in such a way that $\mathcal{A} \leq_m \mathcal{B}$ if and only if $\mathrm{Cyl}(\mathcal{A}) \leq_1 \mathrm{Cyl}(\mathcal{B})$.

If $A$ is a set of natural numbers, we define its *cylindrification* $\mathrm{Cyl}(A)$ to be the set of natural numbers

$$\mathrm{Cyl}(A) = \{\mathrm{bipair}(x, y) : x \in A, y \in \mathbf{N}\}$$

where $\mathrm{bipair} = \mathrm{pred} \circ \mathrm{pair}$ is a pairing function that establishes a bijection between $\mathbf{N} \times \mathbf{N}$ and $\mathbf{N}$ (the function pair omits 0 and only 0 from its range). We shall say that $A$ is *cylindrical* if $A \equiv \mathrm{Cyl}(C)$ for some set $C \subseteq \mathbf{N}$.

**Remark.** For any set $A$, we have $A \leq_1 \mathrm{Cyl}(A)$ (via $\lambda(x).\mathrm{bipair}(x, x)$), and thus also $A \leq_m \mathrm{Cyl}(A)$. More generally, if $B \leq_m A$ (via $f$), then $B \leq_1 \mathrm{Cyl}(A)$ (via $\lambda(x).\mathrm{bipair}(f(x), x)$). We also have $\mathrm{Cyl}(A) \leq_m A$ (via $\lambda(x).\mathrm{bileft}(x)$) (where, of course, $\mathrm{bileft} = \mathrm{left} \circ \mathrm{succ}$ and $\mathrm{biright} = \mathrm{right} \circ \mathrm{succ}$), but not necessarily $\mathrm{Cyl}(A) \leq_1 A$ (if $A$ is finite, for example).

*Lemma 4.6.4.* The following three conditions are equivalent: (1) $A$ is cylindrical; (2) for every set $B$, if $B \leq_m A$, then $B \leq_1 A$; and (3) $A \equiv \mathrm{Cyl}(A)$.

**Proof.** First we show that condition (1) implies condition (2). Suppose that $A \equiv \mathrm{Cyl}(C)$ and $B \leq_m A$. Then $B \leq_m \mathrm{Cyl}(C)$ (since $\equiv$ implies $\leq_m$), $B \leq_m C$ (since $\mathrm{Cyl}(C) \leq_m C$), $B \leq_1 \mathrm{Cyl}(C)$ (by preceding Remark), and thus $B \leq_1 A$ (since $\equiv$ implies $\leq_1$).

Next we show that condition (2) implies condition (3). Since $\mathrm{Cyl}(A) \leq_m A$, condition (2) implies $\mathrm{Cyl}(A) \leq_1 A$. Since we also have $A \leq_1 \mathrm{Cyl}(A)$, we have $A \equiv_1 \mathrm{Cyl}(A)$. Thus by Theorem 4.6.2 we have $A \equiv \mathrm{Cyl}(A)$.

Finally, condition (3) trivially implies condition (1). □

**Theorem 4.6.5.** *For all sets A and B, $A \leq_m B$ if and only if $Cyl(A) \leq_1 Cyl(B)$.*

**Proof.** Suppose that $A \leq_m B$. Since $Cyl(A) \leq_m A$ and $B \leq_m Cyl(B)$, we obtain $Cyl(A) \leq_m Cyl(B)$. But $Cyl(B)$ is cylindrical, so Lemma 4.6.4 implies $Cyl(A) \leq_1 Cyl(B)$.

Conversely, suppose that $Cyl(A) \leq_1 Cyl(B)$. Then $Cyl(A) \leq_m Cyl(B)$. Since we also have $A \leq_m Cyl(A)$ and $Cyl(B) \leq_m B$, we obtain $A \leq_m B$.   □

Since 1-equivalence implies recursive isomorphism, and since the property of being cylindrical is recursively invariant, a 1-degree that contains a cylindrical set consists entirely of cylindrical sets. If $A$ is a set, then $Cyl(A)$ is a cylindrical set, and if $A \equiv_m B$, then by Theorem 4.6.5 we have $Cyl(A) \equiv_1 Cyl(B)$. Thus "Cyl" maps m-degrees into 1-degrees: within each m-degree $\mathcal{A}$ there is a 1-degree $Cyl(\mathcal{A})$, and the m-reducibilities among m-degrees are exactly mirrored by the 1-reducibilities among the corresponding 1-degrees.

Having seen examples of m-degrees that split into infinitely many 1-degrees, and of m-degrees that do not split at all, we shall now consider the structure of the 1-degrees in a general m-degree. Our next theorem shows that these are the only two possibilities: there are no m-degrees that split into a number of 1-degrees that is finite but greater than one.

*Lemma 4.6.6.* For any set $A$, if $A \vee A \leq_1 A$, then $A$ is cylindrical.

**Proof.** Suppose that $A \vee A \leq_1 A$ via $f$. By Lemma 4.6.4, it will suffice to show that $Cyl(A) \leq_1 A$.

Define the monadic recursive functions $h_0(x) = 2x$ and $h_1(x) = 2x + 1$, so that $A \cup B = h_0(A) \cup h_1(B)$. Define the dyadic recursive function $g$ by primitive recursion as follows:

$$g(x, 0) = f(h_0(x))$$

$$g(x, \operatorname{succ}(y)) = f(h_1(g(x, y))).$$

Then $Cyl(A) \leq_1 A$ via $g \circ$ (bileft, biright).   □

**Theorem 4.6.7.** *An m-degree consists of either a single 1-degree or an infinite number of 1-degrees.*

**Proof.** If an m-degree $\mathcal{A}$ contains only cylindrical sets, these sets, being m-reducible to each other, are also 1-reducible to each other, and thus $\mathcal{A}$ constitutes a single 1-degree. Suppose then that $\mathcal{A}$ contains a non-cylindrical set $A$. It will suffice to show that $A$ contains another non-cylindrical set $B$ such that $A \leq_1 B$ but $B \not\leq_1 A$, for then iteration of this reasoning will yield an infinite ascending sequence of 1-degrees within $A$. If we take $B = A \vee A$, then we have $A \leq_1 B$ but $N \not\leq_1 A$ (since if $B \leq_1 A$, then by Lemma 4.6.6 we have $\text{Cyl}(A) \leq_1 A$ and, thus, $\text{Cyl}(A) \equiv A$, contradicting the assumption that $A$ is non-cylindrical). $\square$

Finally, we shall construct two sets that have no least upper bound with respect to 1-reducibility. We shall need two lemmas.

*Lemma 4.6.8.* If $A$ and $B$ are infinite and recursively enumerable, and if $A \leq_1 B$, then $A \leq_1 B$ via a one-to-one recursive function $f$ such that $f(A) = B$.

**Proof.** Suppose that $A \leq_1 B$ via some one-to-one recursive function $g$. By Exercise 5 following Section 4.3.1, there are infinite recursive subsets $C \subseteq A$ and $D \subseteq B$. By Exercise 2 following Section 4.3.1, $B = \text{range}(h)$ for some one-to-one recursive function $h$. We shall construct $f$ by constructing $\text{graph}(f)$. We shall start by taking $\text{graph}(f)$ to be the empty set. We shall then proceed through an infinite sequence of stages, each of which adds at most one pair to $\text{graph}(f)$. (Thus, at the outset of each stage, $\text{graph}(f)$ contains just a finite number of pairs.) The even-numbered stage $2t$ will be responsible for ensuring that $t$ appears in the $\text{dom}(f)$ (that is, that $t$ appears as the first component of a pair in $\text{graph}(f)$). The odd-numbered stage $2t + 1$ will be responsible for ensuring that $h(t)$ appears in $\text{range}(f)$ (that is, that $t$ appears as the second component of a pair $(x, t)$ in $\text{graph}(f)$). Each stage will maintain the condition that no number appears twice as a first component or twice as a second component of a pair in $\text{graph}(f)$ and that if $(x, y) \in \text{graph}(f)$ then $x \in A$ if and only if $y \in B$.

**Stage 2t.** If $t$ is already in $\text{dom}(f)$, do nothing. Otherwise, put $t$ into $\text{dom}(f)$ as follows. If $g(t) \notin D$, let $y = g(t)$; otherwise, let $y$ be the smallest element of $D$ not yet in $\text{range}(f)$. Put the pair $(t, y)$ into $\text{graph}(f)$.

**Stage 2t + 1.** If $h(t)$ is already in $\text{range}(f)$, do nothing. Otherwise, put $h(t)$ into $\text{range}(f)$ as follows. Let $x$ be the smallest element of $C$ not yet in $\text{dom}(f)$. Put the pair $(x, h(t))$ into $\text{graph}(f)$.

At the completion of all of the stages, $\text{graph}(f)$ will be the graph of a one-to-one recursive function $f$ such that $A \leq_1 B$ via $f$ and $f(A) = B$. (Of course, only a finite number of these stages need be carried out to determine the value $f(x)$ of $f$ for any particular $x$.) $\square$

*Lemma 4.6.9.* Suppose $C$ is simple and that $m \notin C$. Let $D = C \cup \{m\}$. Then $D \leq_1 C$ but $C \nleq_1 D$.

**Proof.** Since $C$ is simple, it is infinite and recursively enumerable. By Exercise 5 following Section 4.3.1, $C$ contains an infinite recursive subset $A$. Let $B = A \cup \{m\}$. Since $A$ and $B$ are both infinite and recursive, they are recursively isomorphic. Let $p$ be a recursive permutation such that $p(B) = A$. Then $D \leq_1 C$ via $f$, where

$$f(x) = \begin{cases} x, & \text{if } x \notin B \\ p(x), & \text{if } x \in B \end{cases}$$

Suppose now, for the sake of contradiction, that $C \leq_1 D$. Then by Theorem 4.6.2, we have $C \equiv D$ via some recursive permutation $q$. Then $m, q(m)$, $q(q(m)), \ldots$, are distinct and form a recursively enumerable subset of Compl $(C)$, contradicting the assumption that $C$ is simple. □

*Theorem 4.6.10.* *There exist two recursively enumerable sets having no least upper bound with respect to 1-reducibility.*

**Proof.** By Theorem 4.4.9, there exist two recursively enumerable sets $A$ and $B$ that are incomparable with respect to T-reducibility. By Theorem 4.5.8, we may assume that $A$ and $B$ are simple. The set $A \vee B$ is an upper bound to $A$ and $B$ with respect to 1-reducibility: we have $A \leq_1 A \vee B$ and $B \leq_1 A \vee B$. Furthermore, $A \vee B$ is simple: $A \vee B$ is clearly recursively enumerable, and if Compl($A \vee B$) contained an infinite recursively enumerable subset, then either it would contain an infinite recursively enumerable subset of even numbers (whence Compl($A$) would contain an infinite recursively enumerable subset), or it would contain an infinite recursively enumerable subset of odd numbers (whence Compl($B$) would contain an infinite recursively enumerable subset).

Suppose, for the sake of contradiction, that $C$ is a least upper bound to $A$ and $B$ with respect to 1-reducibility. Then $C \leq_1 A \vee B$ via some one-to-one recursive function $e$. Furthermore $C$ is simple: $C$ is clearly recursively enumerable, and if Compl($C$) contained an infinite recursively enumerable subset, the image of this subset under $e$ would be an infinite recursively enumerable subset of Compl($A \vee B$).

Suppose that $A \leq_1 C$ via $f$ and that $B \leq_1 C$ via $g$. By Lemma 4.6.8, we may assume that $f(A) = C$ and $g(B) = C$. If we also had $f(\text{Compl}(A)) = \text{Compl}(C)$, then we would have $A \equiv C$ via $f$, contradicting the construction of $A$ and $B$ as incomparable. Thus, there must exist some $m \in \text{Compl}(C) \setminus \text{range}(f)$ and, similarly, there must exist some $n \in \text{Compl}(C) \setminus \text{range}(g)$.

Now consider the set $D = C \cup \{m\}$. We have $A \leq_1 D$ via $f$ as before, and we have $B \leq_1 D$ via $h$, where

$$h(x) = \begin{cases} g(x), & \text{if } g(x) \neq m \\ n, & \text{if } g(x) = m \end{cases}$$

Thus, $D$ is also an upper bound to $A$ ands $B$ with respect to 1-reducibility. But by Lemma 4.6.9, $C \not\leq_1 D$, contradicting the assumption that $C$ was a least upper bound to $A$ and $B$. □

The results of this section are due to Young [1966]. Lemma 4.6.8 is due to S. Tennenbaum (see Dekker and Myhill [1960]).

### 4.6.3. Recursive Isomorphism of Universal Functions

We have seen that all creative sets (or equivalently, all m-complete sets or all 1-complete sets) are recursively isomorphic. Our main result in this section is an analogous result for universal functions. We begin by defining "universal functions" and recursive isomorphism for functions.

Let us say that a monadic partial recursive function $u' \in \mathcal{P}_1^*$ is *universal* if, for every $k \geq 0$ and every $k$-adic partial recursive function $f \in \mathcal{P}_k^*$, there exists $\pi \in \mathbf{N}$ such that

$$f(x_1, \ldots, x_k) = u_k'(\pi, x_1, \ldots, x_k)$$

for all $x \in \mathbf{N}$, where $u_0'(\pi) = u'(\pi)$ and

$$u_{k+1}'(\pi, x_1, x_2, \ldots, x_{k+1}) = u_k'(\text{pair}(\pi, x_1), x_2, \ldots, x_k)$$

The index $\pi$ guaranteed by this definition will be called a "$u'$-index for $f$" (to distinguish it from a "$u^*$-index for $f$").

We shall say that two partial functions $g, h \in \mathcal{F}_1$ are *recursively isomorphic*, and write $g \equiv h$, if there exists a recursive permutation $f$ such that $g = f^{-1} \circ h \circ f$, or equivalently $f \circ g = h \circ f$. More generally, we shall say that two partial functions $g, h \in F_k$ are recursively isomorphic if

$$g = f^{-1} \circ h \circ \underbrace{(f, \ldots, f)}_{k \ f\text{'s}}$$

or equivalently

$$f \circ g = h \circ \underbrace{(f, \ldots, f)}_{k \ f\text{'s}}$$

Recursively isomorphic functions can be be obtained from each other by rearranging the natural numbers in a computable way before applying them, then undoing the rearrangement on the results they yield.

Since the identity function is a recursive permutation, recursive isomorphism is reflexive (that is, $g \equiv g$ for every $g$). Since the inverse of a recursive permutation is another recursive permutation, recursive isomorphism is symmetric (that is, if $g \equiv h$, then $h \equiv g$). Since the composition of two recursive permutations is another recursive permutation, recursive isomorphism is transitive (that is, if $f \equiv g$ and $g \equiv h$, then $f \equiv h$). These observations may be summarized by saying that recursive isomorphism is an equivalence, whereby the class of all partial functions is partitioned into equivalence classes called "recursive isomorphism classes."

A property of partial functions is said to be "recursively invariant" if, whenever it applies to a function $g$ and $g \equiv h$, then it also applies to $h$. Most of the important properties studied in recursive function theory (such as being total, constant, or computable) are recursively invariant. A property of partial functions is said to be "recursively definitive" if any two partial functions to which the property applies are recursively isomorphic.

**Theorem 4.6.11.** *If $u'$ and $u''$ are any two universal functions, then $u' \equiv u''$.*

For the proof of Theorem 4.6.11 we shall need some lemmas.

*Lemma 4.6.12 ("Padding Lemma").* There is a function $\mathrm{pad}_1 \in Q^*$ such that (1) for all $\pi, i \in \mathbf{N}$, both $\mathrm{pad}_1(\pi, i)$ and $\pi$ index the same partial function in $\mathcal{P}_1^*$ and (2) for all $\pi, i, j \in \mathbf{N}$, if $\mathrm{pad}_1(\pi, i) = \mathrm{pad}_1(\pi, j)$, then $i = j$.

**Proof.** We may take

$$\mathrm{pad}_1^*(\pi, i) = \mathrm{pair}(\mathrm{comp}_{1,2}(\pi, \phi), i)$$

where $\phi$ is a $u^*$-index for an appropriate projection function, and $\mathrm{comp}_{1,2}$ is as in Exercise 1, following Section 4.2.1. (The application of $\mathrm{comp}_{1,2}$ turns $\pi$ into an index for a function that ignores its first argument; the application of pair then supplies this argument. The lemma follows from the fact that pair is one-to-one. $\qquad\square$

*Lemma 4.6.13.* Let $u'$ be universal. Then there is a function pair$' \in Q_2^*$ such that for all $\pi, x \in \mathbf{N}$ we have

$$u^*(\mathrm{pair}(\pi, x)) = u'(\mathrm{pair}'(\pi, x))$$

**Proof.** We may take

$$\mathrm{pair}'(\pi, x) = \mathrm{pair}((\mathrm{pair}(\phi, \pi), x)$$

where $\phi$ is a $u'$-index for $u_1^*$.      $\square$

Lemma 4.6.13 allows us to work with one system of indices and two pairing functions, rather than two systems of indices and one pairing function. In particular, the term "index" will henceforth always mean "$u^*$-index."

The next lemma gives an analogue of Lemma 4.6.12 for the "prime-regime" (and functions of zero arguments) rather than the "star-regime" (and functions of one argument).

*Lemma 4.6.14.* Let $u'$ be universal. Then there is a function pad$'_0 \in Q^*$ such that (1) for all $\pi, i \in \mathbf{N}$, we have $u'(\mathrm{pad}'_0(\pi, i)) = u'(\pi)$ and (2) for all $\pi, i, j \in \mathbf{N}$, if $\mathrm{pad}(\pi, i) = \mathrm{pad}(\pi, j)$, then $i = j$.

The proof is similar to that of Lemma 4.6.12, and is left to the reader.

The final lemma does for "inverse functions" what Exercise 1 following Section 4.2.1 does for "composite functions."

*Lemma 4.6.15.* There is a function inv $\in Q_1^*$ such that for all $\pi, y \in \mathbf{N}$, if there exists $x \in \mathbf{N}$ such that $u_1^*(\pi, x) = y$, then $u_1^*(\pi, u_1^*(\mathrm{inv}(\pi), y)) = y$.

**Proof.** The value of the partial function inv for argument $y$ is computed by dovetailing the computations of $u_1^*(\pi, 0), u_1^*(\pi, 1), \ldots$, and producing the value $x$ when it is discovered that $u^*(\pi, x) = y$.      $\square$

We observe that if $\pi$ is an index for a recursive permutation $f$, then $\mathrm{inv}(\pi)$ is an index for its inverse $f^{-1}$. (If the partial function indexed by $\pi$ fails to be total, one-to-one, and onto, then the partial function indexed by $\mathrm{inv}(\pi)$ will be the closest thing to an inverse one might hope for.)

**Proof of Theorem 4.6.11.** It will suffice to prove that $u' \equiv u^*$, for the same argument will prove that $u'' \equiv u^*$, and $u' \equiv u''$ will then follow by transitivity. To this end, we shall first construct a recursive permutation $f$, then prove that

$$f \circ u' = u^* \circ f \tag{4.6.1}$$

We begin by constructing a recursive function $g$ of two arguments; the recursive permutation $f$ will ultimately be obtained from $g$ by substituting an appropriate constant for the first argument. We shall describe how to compute $g(\zeta, x)$ in prose; it should be clear how this description could be formalized to give a proof that $g \in \mathcal{Q}_2^*$.

To compute $g(\zeta, x)$, we construct the recursive permutation $g'$ (which depends on $\zeta$) up to the point at which $g'(x)$ is determined, then set $g(\zeta, x) = g'(x)$.

Let $\zeta \in \mathbf{N}$ be given, and let $z \in \mathcal{P}_1^*$ be the partial recursive function indexed by $\zeta$. Using Lemma 4.6.15, we set $\zeta' = \mathrm{inv}(\zeta)$, and let $z'$ be the partial function indexed by $\zeta'$.

We shall construct $g'$ by constructing graph$(g')$. We shall start by taking graph$(g')$ to be the empty set. We shall then proceed through an infinite sequence of stages, each of which adds at most one pair to graph$(g')$. (Thus, at the outset of each stage, graph$(g')$ contains just a finite number of pairs.) The even numbered stage $2t$ will be responsible for ensuring that $t$ appears in dom$(g')$ (that is, that $t$ appears as the first component of a pair in graph$(g')$). The odd numbered stage $2t + 1$ will be responsible for ensuring that $t$ appears in range$(g')$ (that is, that $t$ appears as the second component of a pair in graph$(g')$). Each stage will maintain the condition that no number appears twice as a first component or twice as a second component of a pair in graph$(g')$. Thus, at the completion of all of the stages, graph$(g')$ will be the graph of a recursive permutation $g'$. (Of course, only a finite number of these stages need be carried out to determine the value $g'(x)$ of $g'$ for any particular $x$.)

**Stage $2t$.**

1. If $t$ is already in dom$(g')$ do nothing. Otherwise, put $t$ into dom$(g')$ through the following steps.
2. Let $\pi$ be an index for the partial function $z \circ u'$. (We may take $\pi = \mathrm{comp}_{1,1}(\zeta, \upsilon')$, where $\mathrm{comp}_{1,1}$ is the recursive function defined in Exercise 1 following Section 4.2.1, and $\upsilon'$ is an index for $u'$.)
3. Using Lemma 4.6.12, generate a sequence $w_0, w_1, \ldots$, of distinct indices for the function indexed by $\pi$. Let $w$ be the first index in this sequence such that pair$(w, t)$ is not yet in range$(g')$. (Such an index must exist, since pair is one-to-one, and so the sequence pair$(w_0, t)$, pair$(w_1, t), \ldots$, has distinct elements, but graph$(g')$ is finite at the outset of this stage.
4. Add the pair $(t, \mathrm{pair}(w, t))$ to graph$(g')$.

**Stage $2t + 1$.**

1. If $t$ is already in range($g'$) do nothing. Otherwise, put $t$ into range($g'$) through the following steps.
2. Let $\eta$ be an index for the partial function $z' \circ u^*$. (We may take $\eta = $ comp$_{1,1}(\zeta', v^*)$, where $v^*$ is an index for $u^*$.) Let $\xi = $ pair$'(\eta, t)$, so that $u'(\xi) = u_1^*(\eta, t)$.
3. Using Lemma 4.6.14, generate a sequence $v_0, v_1, \ldots,$ of distinct elements such that $u'(v_i) = u'(\xi)$ for all $i \in \mathbf{N}$. Let $v$ be the first element in this sequence not yet in dom($g'$).
4. Add the pair $(v, t)$ to graph($g'$).

These instructions define a recursive permutation $g'$ (which depends on $\zeta$) and thus define a recursive function $g$ of two arguments. Let $\gamma$ be an index for $g$, and define the recursive function $h$ by $h(\zeta) = $ pair$(\gamma, \zeta)$ (so that $h(\zeta)$ is an index for $g'$). Apply Corollary 4.2.7 of the Recursion Theorem with $k = 1$ to obtain a natural number $n$ such that $n$ and $h(n)$ index the same partial function. Now define the recursive permutation $f$ by $f(x) = g(n, x)$.

The recursive permutation $f$ is the one constructed as $g'$ when $\zeta = n$. In this construction $z$ is the partial function indexed by $\zeta = n$, and by the Recursion Theorem, this is the same partial function as is indexed by $h(n)$, namely, $f$. Furthermore, $z'$ is the partial function indexed by $\zeta' = \text{inv}(\zeta) = \text{inv}(n)$, namely, the inverse $f^{-1}$ of the recursive permutation $f$.

We are now ready to verify Eq. (4.6.1). We do this by proving, for each $x \in \mathbf{N}$, that $f(u'(x)) = u^*(f(x))$. This proof divides into two cases, depending on whether the value $f(x)$ was determined by adding a pair $(t, \text{pair}(w, t))$ to graph($f$) in stage $2t$ with $x = t$ (Case A), or by adding a pair $(v, t)$ to graph($f$) in stage $2t + 1$ with $x = v$ (Case B).

In Case A, we have

$$f(u'(t)) = z(u'(t))$$
$$= u_1^*(\pi, t)$$
$$= u_1^*(w, t)$$
$$= u^*(\text{pair}(w, t))$$
$$= u^*(f(t))$$

by the identity $f = z$, the definition of $\pi$, the definition of $w$, the definition of $u_1^*$, and the defining condition of Case A, respectively. Thus $f(u'(x)) = u^*(f(x))$ holds in Case A.

In Case B, we have

$$f(u'(v)) = f(u'(\xi))$$
$$= f(u_1^*(\eta, t))$$
$$= f(z'(u^*(t)))$$
$$= f(f^{-1}(u^*(t)))$$
$$= u^*(t)$$
$$= u^*(f(v))$$

by the definition of $v$, the definition of $\xi$, the definition of $\eta$, the identity $f^{-1} = z'$, the identity $f \circ f^{-1} = $ id, and the defining condition of Case B. Thus, $f(u'(x)) = u^*(f(x))$ holds in Case B.                    $\square$

The result of this section is due to M. Blum (see Rogers [1967]).

### Exercises

1. (E) Show that if $u$ and $u'$ are both universal, then there exist functions $g$ and $g'$ in $\mathcal{Q}_1$ such that for all $\pi, x \in \mathbf{N}$ we have

$$u_1'(\pi, x) = u_1(g(\pi), x) \qquad \text{and} \qquad u_1(\pi, x) = u_1'(g'(\pi), x)$$

2. (E) Show that in Exercise 1 the functions $g$ and $g'$ may be constructed so as to be increasing recursive functions. (Hint: Use the Padding Lemma.)

3. (M) (Rogers's Isomorphism Theorem) Show that in Exercise 1 the functions $g$ and $g'$ may be constructed so as to be a recursive permutation and its inverse $g' = g^{-1}$. (Hint: Let the functions $h$ and $h'$ be constructed according to Exercise 2, and note that any sequence of the form $\pi, h^{-1}(\pi), h'^{-1}(h^{-1}(\pi)), \ldots,$ or $\pi, h'^{-1}(\pi), h^{-1}(h'^{-1}(\pi)), \ldots,$ must terminate.)

4. (E) How many recursive isomorphism classes of recursive permutations are there?

### 4.7. Abstract Complexity Theory

In this section, we shall give a foretaste of "complexity theory," which attempts to refine the qualitative comparisons of computability theory into quantitative distinctions. We begin in Section 4.7.1 with "descriptive" complexity theory, which refines the assumption that programs are finite objects by measuring the "size" of programs. In Section 4.7.2 we turn from descriptive complexity measures, which quantify the finiteness of programs, to "computational" complexity measures, which quantify the finiteness of the ensuing computations. The resulting theory, which was founded by Blum [1967a], applies to most of the complexity measures (time, space, and so forth) used in concrete situations, and exposes important limitations in complexity theory (such as the existence of functions with no "best" program). We shall also give an application linking complexity theory with the "predictability" or "learnability" of functions.

### 4.7.1. Descriptive Complexity Measures

A monadic total function $s$ is a *descriptive complexity measure* if (1) $s$ is recursive and (2) there exists a monadic recursive function $\hat{s}$ such that, for all $\pi, n \in \mathbf{N}$, if $s(\pi) \leq n$, then $\pi \leq \hat{s}(n)$. We observe that this definition is equivalent to saying that from $n$ one can compute a finite list comprising all and only the indices $\pi$ such that $s(\pi) \leq n$. It is also equivalent to this latter statement with "$\leq$" replaced by "$=$."

A descriptive complexity measure is intended as a way of measuring the size of a program. A simple example is $s(\pi) = \pi$, which satisfies condition (2) with $\hat{s}(n) = n$. Another way of measuring the size of a program is to count the number of bits in its binary encoding, which corresponds to $s(0) = 0$ and $s(\pi) = 1 + \lfloor \log_2 \pi \rfloor$ for $\pi \geq 1$ and which satisfies condition (2) with $\hat{s}(n) = 2^n - 1$. (This example assumes that 0 is encoded as a word of length zero and that positive integers are encoded without leading zeroes.) Note that the function that assigns to each program the number of ones in its binary encoding is not a descriptive complexity measure, since there are infinitely many programs with a single one in their encodings, namely, the integral powers of two.

**Proposition 4.7.1.** *Let $s$ and $t$ be descriptive complexity measures. There exists a monadic recursive function $f$ such that (1) for all $\pi \in \mathbf{N}$, $s(\pi) \leq f(t(\pi))$, (2) for all $\pi \in \mathbf{N}$, $t(\pi) \leq f(s(\pi))$, and (3) $f$ is strictly increasing, that is, for all $n, m \in \mathbf{N}$, if $n < m$, then $f(n) < f(m)$.*

**Proof.** Define the monadic recursive function $h$ by

$$h(n) = \max\{s(\pi) : t(\pi) \leq n\}$$

(Since $t$ is a descriptive complexity measure, the finite set of $\pi$ such that $t(\pi) \leq n$ is computable from $n$. Since $s$ is a descriptive complexity measure, the corresponding finite set of $s(\pi)$ is computable as well.) Then $h$ fulfills condition (1): for all $\pi \in \mathbf{N}$, $s(\pi) \leq h(t(\pi))$. Interchanging the roles of $s$ and $t$, we obtain a monadic recursive function $g$ fulfilling condition (2). Finally, we define $f$ fulfilling all three conditions by induction: $f(0) = \max\{h(0), g(0)\}$ and $f(n + 1) = \max\{h(n + 1), g(n + 1), f(n) + 1\}$.                    □

Proposition 4.7.1 says that all descriptive complexity measures are similar in that they all tend to infinity at speeds that are recursively bounded in terms of each other. The next proposition shows that, again to within a recursive function, inequalities for one descriptive complexity measure imply inequalities for all others.

**Proposition 4.7.2.** *Let $s$ and $t$ be descriptive complexity measures. There exists a monadic recursive function $h$ such that, for all $\phi$, $\psi \in \mathbf{N}$, (1) if $s(\phi) \leq s(\psi)$, then $t(\phi) \leq h(t(\psi))$ and (2) if $h(s(\phi)) \leq s(\psi)$, then $t(\phi) \leq t(\psi)$.*

**Proof.** The proof is routine, given the choice $h = f \circ f$, where $f$ is provided by Proposition 4.7.1 (see Exercise 1 following this section).                    □

Let us fix a descriptive complexity measure $s$. Let $r$ be a strictly increasing monadic recursive function. We shall say that a program $\phi \in \mathbf{N}$ is $(r, s)$-*decent* if, for every program $\psi \in \mathbf{N}$, if $\phi$ and $\psi$ are indices for the same partial function in $\mathcal{P}_1^*$, then $s(\phi) \leq r(s(\psi))$. A program is decent if there is no other program that computes the same partial function, and is smaller (as measured by $s$) by an application of $r$. A special case is $r(n) = n$, for which a program that is $(r, s)$-decent is called $s$-*optimal*. A program is optimal if there is no smaller program that computes the same partial function. Clearly, every computable partial function has an $s$-optimal program and has $(r, s)$-decent programs for every strictly increasing $r$. The next theorem shows that these programs are not, in general, easy to produce.

**Theorem 4.7.3.** *Let $s$ be a descriptive complexity measure, and let $r$ be a strictly increasing monadic recursive function. The set of $(r, s)$-decent programs contains no infinite recursively enumerable subset.*

**Proof.** Suppose, with an eye to contradiction, that $D$ is an infinite recursively enumerable set of $(r, s)$-decent programs. Let $D$ be the range of the monadic recursive function $d$.

Define the dyadic partial recursive function $p$ by $p(\alpha, x) = u_1^*(d(i), x)$, where $i \geq 0$ is the smallest natural number such that $s(d(i)) > r(s(\alpha))$. Let $\pi$ be an index for $p$ and define the monadic recursive function $f$ by $f(\alpha) = \text{pair}(\pi, \alpha)$. By the Recursion Theorem, there exists $\beta \in \mathbf{N}$ such that $\beta$ and

$f(\beta)$ index the same partial function in $\mathcal{P}_1^*$. Let $b$ denote this partial recursive function.

From the definition of $p$, we see that $b$ may be computed by searching through $i = 0, 1, \ldots$, for an $i$ such that $s(d(i)) > r(s(\beta))$, then computing the value, if any, of the partial function with index $d(i)$. Since the range of $d$ is infinite and $s$ is a descriptive complexity measure, this search must terminate with such an $i$. Thus, $d(i)$ is an index for the same partial function as $\beta$. Since $s(d(i)) > r(s(\beta))$, $d(i)$ is not $(r, s)$-decent, contradicting the assumption that all of the programs in $D = \text{range}(d)$ are $(r, s)$-decent. $\quad\square$

Recall that an infinite set that contains no infinite recursively enumerable subset is called "immune" (see Section 4.5). Such a set is non-computable in a very strong sense, as is illustrated by the following scenario.

Suppose that a programmer adopts a finite (or even a recursively enumerable) set of axioms for proving assertions about programs. The programmer then proceeds to dovetail consideration of all possible programs with consideration of all possible proofs of their optimality. The programmer "releases" all programs that are eventually proved optimal in this way. If the axioms and rules of inference that the programmer uses are "sound" (in the sense that any program proved optimal actually *is* optimal), then by Theorem 4.7.3, only finitely many programs are ever released. This may be interpreted as saying that there are no principles for verifying the optimality of programs that are applicable to infinitely many cases: proofs of optimality are too "deep" for any sound formal system to provide more than a finite number of them. In contrast to this, it is certainly possible for a sound formal system to provide infinitely many proofs of "correctness" of programs (proofs that one program computes the same partial function as another, or computes the partial function given by some other specification); indeed, many such formal systems are studied in courses on program verification.

### Exercise

1. (E) Complete the proof of Proposition 4.7.2.

### 4.7.2. Computational Complexity Measures

We shall say that a monadic partial recursive function $v$ is a *computational complexity measure* if (1) $\text{dom}(v) = \text{dom}(u^*)$, and (2) the binary relation

$$V = \{(\pi, t) : v(\pi) \le t\} \tag{4.7.1}$$

is recursive. We observe that the same notion would be defined if "$v(\pi) \le t$" were replaced by "$v(\pi) = t$" in Eq. (4.7.1).

The definition of a reflexive class guarantees the existence of a computational complexity measure, namely, $v^*$ defined by $v^*(\pi) = \mu(t).m^*(\pi, t)$. Our first result will say that all computational complexity measures are somewhat similar. To state it, it will be convenient to extend to notation for $v$ and $V$ in the same way as for $u$ and $m$.

For $k \ge 0$, we define a $(k+1)$-adic partial function $v_k$ by setting $v_0 = v$ and

$$v_{k+1}(\pi, x_1, x_2, \ldots, x_{k+1}) = v_k(\text{pair}(\pi, x_1), x_2, \ldots, x_{k+1})$$

Similarly, we define a $(k+2)$-ary relation $V_k$ by setting $V_0 = V$ and

$$V_{k+1}(\pi, x_1, x_2, \ldots, x_{k+1}, t) = V_k(\text{pair}(\pi, x_1), x_2, \ldots, x_{k+1}, t)$$

We shall develop most of our results for the case $k = 1$, but very little beyond notation changes for any $k \ge 1$.

Before coming to our first result, we observe that that notions "there exist infinitely many" and "for all but finitely many" (sometimes said "for almost all") are dual to one another in the same sense (stemming from De Morgan's Laws) as the notions "there exist" and "for all."

**Proposition 4.7.4.** *Let $v$ and $w$ be computational complexity measures. Then there exists a dyadic recursive function $g$ such that, for all $\pi \in \mathbf{N}$, (1) for almost all $x \in \mathbf{N}$, $v_1(\pi, x) \le g(x, w_1(\pi, x))$ and (2) for almost all $x \in \mathbf{N}$, $w_1(\pi, x) \le g(x, v_1(\pi, x))$.*

**Proof.** Define the dyadic recursive function $e$ by

$$e(x, t) = \max\{v_1(\pi, x) : \pi \le x \text{ and } w_1(\pi, x) \le t\}$$

We observe that $e$ is indeed recursive: given $x$, there are only finitely many $\pi$ such that $\pi \le x$; for each such $\pi$, the condition $w_1(\pi, x) \le t$ is decidable (since $w$ is a computational complexity measure); and whenever this condition holds, $v_1(\pi, x)$ is computable (since $v$ is a computational complexity measure, and, thus, has the same domain as $w$). Furthermore, for all $\pi$, $e$ fulfills condition (1): for almost all $x$ (indeed, for all $x \ge \pi$) $v_1(\pi, x) \le e(x, w_1(\pi, x))$, since $v_1(\pi, x)$ is included in the maximum defining $e(x, w_1(\pi, x))$. Interchanging the roles of $v$ and $w$, we obtain a dyadic recursive function $f$ fulfilling condition (2). Finally, we define $g$ fulfilling both conditions: $g(\pi, x) = \max\{e(\pi, x), f(\pi, x)\}$.                    □

By its definition, $v^*$ may be interpreted as the "time" needed to carry out the computation for a given index. More generally, we may interpret an arbitrary computational complexity measure $v$ as the amount of some "abstract resource" used by a computation. Proposition 4.7.4 says that all such abstract resources are similar to one another, in that they can all be bounded by recursive functions of one another, with two complications: the recursive functions depend on the argument as well as the resource, and the bounds may fail for finitely many values of the argument. These complications are unavoidable (see Exercises 2 and 3 following this section).

Let $v$ be a computational complexity measure, and let $r$ be a monadic recursive function. We shall say that a monadic recursive function $f$ is $(r, v)$-*easy* if there is an index $\pi$ for $f$ such that, for almost all $x$, $v_1(\pi, x) \leq r(x)$. A function is $(r, v)$-easy if it can be computed by some program that uses an amount of the resource $v$ bounded by the function $r$ (with, as usual, a finite number of exceptions).

**Proposition 4.7.5.** *Let $v$ be a computational complexity measure, and let $r$ be a monadic recursive function. There is a monadic recursive characteristic function $f$ that is not $(r, v)$-easy.*

**Proof.** Let osc be any monadic recursive function (such as left ∘ succ) of "large oscillation," that is, assuming each natural number infinitely many times as value as its argument runs through the natural numbers. We shall define the function $f$ by letting $f(x)$ equal 0 if (1) $v_1(\mathrm{osc}(x), x) > r(x)$ or (2) $u_1^*(\mathrm{osc}(x), x) \geq 1$, and letting $f(x)$ equal 1 otherwise. We observe that $f$ is recursive: condition (1) is decidable; if condition (1) fails, then condition (2) is decidable, since $u^*$ has the same domain as $v$. (Note that if condition (1) holds, there is no need to consider condition (2).)

Suppose, with an eye to contradiction, that $f$ is $(r, v)$-easy. Then there is an index $\phi$ for $f$ such that $v_1(\phi, x) \leq r(x)$ for almost all $x$. Furthermore, we have $\mathrm{osc}(x) = \phi$ for infinitely many $x$. Now a set of "almost all" natural numbers and a set of "infinitely many" natural numbers must have an element in common, say, $y$. For this element, condition (1) fails, and we conclude from the definition of $f$ that $f(y) = 0$ if and only if $f(y) \geq 1$. This contradiction shows that $f$ is not $(r, v)$-easy. $\qquad\square$

We have seen in the preceding Section 4.7.1 that programs that are optimal, or even decent, as regards their size are hard to produce. The situation for programs that are optimal or decent as regards the resources used by their computations is even more discouraging: such programs may not even exist. The next theorem, which we shall state without proof, says that there are functions so perverse that any programs computing them can be vastly improved ("sped-up") for all but a finite number of argument values. (The theorem was first proved by Blum [1967a]. A simpler proof was given by Young [1973].)

**Theorem 4.7.6.** *Let $v$ be a computational complexity measure, and let $r$ be a dyadic recursive function. There is function $f$ such that, for every index $\phi$ for $f$, there exists another index $\psi$ for $f$ such that, for almost all $x$,*

$$v_1(\phi, x) \geq r(x, v_1(\psi, x))$$

Although the functions that fulfill Theorem 4.7.6 are artificial, this theorem nevertheless has a strong influence on the development of complexity theory. One cannot hope to begin by associating with each function an optimal program (as regards time) for computing it, then studying the functions through the associated programs. Rather, the accepted approach has been to define "complexity classes" by associating with each computational complexity measure $v$ and monadic recursive function $r$ the class of all $(r, v)$-easy functions, then studying the relationships among the resulting classes.

Even with this change of tack, care must be exercised. (A good survey of this "Abstract Complexity Theory" is given by Hartmanis and Hopcroft [1971], to which the reader is referred for details of the developments sketched subsequently.) It would be nice, for example, to have a "hierarchy theorem" that says, roughly, that larger resource bounds yield larger classes of easy functions. But this turns out to be false if one starts with an arbitrary recursive resource bound and interprets "larger" in any reasonably computable way; this is shown by the "Gap Theorem" due to A. B. Borodin (which, like the Speed-Up Theorem, discloses a cautionary pathology). The solution to this difficulty can be found by restricting attention to resource bounds satisfying an additional condition, known as "honesty."

If $h$ is a dyadic recursive function, a monadic recursive function $r$ is said to be $(h, v)$-*honest* if there exists an index $\varrho$ for $r$ such that, for almost all $x$,

$$v_1(\varrho, x) \leq h(x, r(x))$$

(Thus, honest functions $r$ are those that can be computed using resources that are bounded by a recursive function of the "input" $x$ and the "output" $r(x)$.) With this definition, abstract complexity theory can be built upon two foundational results. The first of these, the "Honesty Theorem" of E. M. McCreight and A. R. Meyer, says that for every computational complexity measure $v$, there exists an "honesty criterion" $h$ such that every complexity class determined by an arbitrary recursive resource bound is also determined by some $(h, v)$-

honest resource bound. The second, the "Compression Theorem" of Blum [1967a], constitutes the hierarchy theorem sought previously. It says that for every computational complexity measure $v$ and every honesty criterion $h$, there exists a dyadic recursive function $g$ such that, for any $(h, v)$-honest bound $r$, there is a function that is $(g \circ (\text{id}, r), v)$-easy, but not $(r, v)$-easy. Thus, the function $g$ quantifies the sense in which larger resource bounds yield larger complexity classes.

### Exercises

1. (E) Prove or disprove: $u^*$ is a computational complexity measure.
2. (M) Show that Proposition 4.7.1 cannot be simplified by eliminating the first argument of the function $g$.
3. (M) Show that Proposition 4.7.1 cannot be simplified by replacing "almost all" by "all."

### 4.7.3. An Application

In this section, we shall give an application of abstract complexity theory, by showing how it may be used to answer some questions about "learning from examples." We shall describe two situations. The first situation, which concerns the "prediction" of sequences, is as follows.

A computing device is given a sequence $f(0), f(1), \ldots$, of natural numbers, one by one, in the order indicated. These numbers will be called the "data." Its task is to produce a sequence $\hat{f}(0), \hat{f}(1), \ldots$, of natural numbers, with $\hat{f}(x)$ being produced just before $f(x)$ is received. Thus, the interaction of the device with its environment proceeds according to the following protocol. First the device produces its prediction $\hat{f}(0)$, then it receives its first datum $f(0)$, then it produces its second prediction $\hat{f}(1)$, then it receives its second datum $f(1)$, and so forth. The goal of the device is to "catch on" to the sequence after finitely many data have been received, so that $\hat{f}(x) = f(x)$ for almost all $x$.

Each prediction $\hat{f}(x)$ is to be a computable total function of the data $f(0)$, $\ldots, f(x-1)$ received earlier. Thus, we may represent the device as a monadic recursive function $g$ with $\hat{f}(0) = g(\langle\rangle)$, $\hat{f}(1) = g(\langle f(0)\rangle)$, and, in general,

$$\hat{f}(x) = g(\langle f(0), \ldots, f(x-1)\rangle)$$

We shall say that $g$ *predicts* $f$ if $\hat{f}$, defined in this way, satisfies $\hat{f}(x) = f(x)$ for almost all $x$. Let $C$ be a class of monadic total functions. We shall say that $g$ *predicts* $C$ if, for every $f \in C$, $g$ predicts $f$. We seek to characterize the classes $C$ that can be predicted by some recursive $g$.

**Theorem 4.7.7 (Blum and Blum [1975]).** *Let $v$ be a computational complexity measure. (a) If the class $C$ is predicted by some recursive function $g$, then there exists a recursive function $r$ such that every function $f$ in $C$ is $(r, v)$-easy. (b) Conversely, if $r$ is a recursive function, the class $C$ of all $(r, v)$-easy recursive functions is predicted by some recursive function $g$.*

Part (a) of Theorem 4.7.7 will follow from two lemmas. Say that a non-empty class $C$ of monadic recursive functions is *recursively enumerable* if there is a recursive function $h$ whose range contains only indices for functions in $C$ and whose range includes at least one index for each function in $C$. Observe that this is equivalent to saying that there is a dyadic recursive function $c$ such that, for every $\phi$, the function $\lambda(x).c(\phi, x)$ belongs to $C$, and for every $f \in C$, there is a $\phi \in N$ such that $f(x) = c(\phi, x)$ for all $x \in N$. (Thus, $c$ is a "quasi-universal" function, with respect to which every function $f$ in $C$ has a "quasi-index" $\phi$.)

*Lemma 4.7.8 (Barzdin and Freivald [1972]).* If the class $C$ is predicted by some recursive function $g$, then $C$ is recursively enumerable.

**Proof.** Let $C$ be predicted by $g$. We construct a quasi-universal function $c$ for $C$. The value $c(\phi, y)$ is computed as follows. The quasi-index $\phi$ is interpreted as a list $\phi = \langle f(0), \ldots, f(x - 1) \rangle$. This list can be "extrapolated" to an infinite sequence $f(0), f(1), \ldots$, that can be computed by "feeding back" the predictions of $g$ to ensure that they are correct for $f(x), f(x + 1), \ldots, ,$. Let $c(\phi, y)$ equal the term $f(y)$ in this sequence. Clearly, every function that can be predicted by $g$ is generated in this way for some $\phi$ (namely, for any $\phi$ that encodes those values of $f$ for which $g$ would make a mistake), and so $c$ is quasi-universal.                                                                    □

*Lemma 4.7.9.* Let $v$ be a computational complexity measure. If the class $C$ is recursively enumerable, then there exists a recursive function $r$ such that every function $f$ in $C$ is $(r, v)$-easy.

**Proof.** Let $g$ be a recursive function whose range is included in the set of indices for function in $C$ and whose range includes at least one index for each such function. Define $r$ by

$$r(x) = \max\{v_1(g(n), x) : n \leq x\}$$

The function $r$ is recursive, since $g$ indexes only total recursive functions. Furthermore, the function with index $g(n)$ is $(r, v)$-easy, since for almost all $x$ (indeed, for all $x \geq n$), $v_1(g(n), x)$ is included in the maximum defining $r(x)$.   □

**Proof of Theorem 4.7.7(b).** Let $C$ be the class of $(r, v)$-easy functions. Interpret each pair $(\pi, m)$ as the "hypothesis" that (1) for all $z$, $v_1(\pi, z) \leq \max\{m, r(z)\}$ and (2) $\pi$ is an index for $f$, so that for all $z$, $f(z) = u_1^*(\pi, z)$. Let these hypotheses be ordered according to the value of pair$(\pi, m)$. Note that every non-empty set of hypotheses contains a "smallest" hypothesis with respect to this ordering.

Define the recursive function $g$ as follows. Let $g(y)$, where $y = \langle f(0), \ldots, f(x-1)\rangle$, be 0 unless there is a hypothesis $(\pi, m)$ with pair$(\pi, m) \leq y$ that is consistent with the data received thus far: (1) for $z \leq x$, $v_1(\pi, z) \leq \max\{m, r(z)\}$ and (2) for $z < x$, $f(z) = u_1^*(\pi, z)$. If there is such a hypothesis, let $g(y)$ be $u_1^*(\pi, x)$, where $(\pi, m)$ is the smallest such hypothesis. (Note that in this case, $u_1^*(\pi, x)$ is defined because $v_1(\pi, x)$ is defined.)

To see that that this $g$ predicts each $f$ in $C$, observe that if $f$ is $(r, v)$-easy, then there is at least one hypothesis that is correct for all $z$, and therefore there is a least such hypothesis $(\pi, m)$. For all $y \geq$ pair$(\pi, m)$, this least hypothesis will be considered and found consistent, and thus the prediction by $g$ will be correct. □

Theorem 4.7.7 show that the notion of "predictability," which at first sight does not appear to involve complexity at all, is nevertheless completely equivalent to a simple complexity-theoretic notion. We shall now consider a second question about "learning from examples." The second situation, which involves "explanation" of sequences, is as follows.

A computing device is given a sequence $d_0, d_1, \ldots,$ of natural numbers, one by one, in the order indicated. This sequence is interpreted as a description of some partial function $f$ in the following way. A number $d_k = 0$ is to be interpreted as a "dummy" that does not contribute to the description of $f$. A number $d_k \geq 1$ is to be interpreted as a "pair" $d_k = \text{pair}(x, y)$, and it is to be interpreted as asserting that $f(x) = y$. We shall say that a sequence $d_0, d_1, \ldots,$ is an *admissible* sequence of $f$ if (1) every pair in the sequence belongs to the graph of $f$ and (2) every pair in the graph of $f$ appears at least once in the sequence. We shall say that a sequence is *consistent* if it is an admissible sequence for some monadic partial function. (The main reason for allowing dummies as well as pairs is so that the partial function $\text{undef}_1$ will have an admissible sequence, namely, $0, 0, \ldots$.)

The task of the device is to produce a sequence $\pi_0, \pi_1, \ldots,$ of natural numbers, with $\pi_k$ being produced just after $d_k$ is received, such that $u_1^*(\pi_k, x) = y$ for every pair $d_j = \text{pair}(x, y)$ with $0 \leq j \leq k$. Thus, an output of the device may be interpreted as a "theory," and this theory must "explain" all of the data received before it is produced. This task could be accomplished by producing as $\pi_k$ an index for the partial function with finite domain described by the pairs previously received. To avoid this trivial activity, we shall be interested in devices that eventually "settle upon" a single index that describes all of the pairs they ever receive.

As for prediction, we may characterize the behavior of a device by a total recursive function $g$ that assumes the value $\pi_k$ for the argument $\langle d_0, \ldots, d_k \rangle$. We shall say that $g$ *converges* to $\pi$ for the sequence $d_0, d_1, \ldots$, if $g$ produces an output sequence $\pi_0, \pi_1, \ldots$, that is eventually constant, $\pi = \pi_k = \pi_{k+1} = \cdots$ for some $k$. (If a $g$ converges to $\pi$ for a sequence that is admissible for $f$, then $\pi$ must be an index for some partial function that is an extension of $f$.) We shall say that $g$ *explains* $f$ if it converges for every admissible sequence for $f$. Let $C$ be a class of monadic partial functions. We shall say that $g$ *explains* $C$ if, for every $f \in C$, $g$ explains $f$. We seek to characterize the classes $C$ that can be explained by some recursive $g$.

Let $v$ be computational complexity measure, and let $h$ be a dyadic partial recursive function. Let us say that a monadic partial recursive function $f$ is $(h, v)$-*honest* if there is an index $\pi$ for some extension of $f$ such that

$$v_1(\pi, x) \leq h(x, f(x))$$

for almost all $x \in \text{dom}(f)$. (Note that this is a generalization of the definition given in Section 4.7.2, which applied only to total recursive functions.)

***Theorem 4.7.10 (Blum and Blum [1975]).*** *Let $v$ be a computational complexity measure. (a) If the class $C$ is explained by some recursive function $g$, then there exists a dyadic recursive function $h$ such that every partial function $f$ in $C$ is $(h, v)$-honest. (b) Conversely, if $h$ is a dyadic recursive function, the class $C$ of all $(h, v)$-honest partial recursive functions is explained by some recursive function $g$.*

**Proof.** (a) Suppose that $g$ explains $C$. Let $\Sigma(x, y)$ denote the finite set

$$\Sigma(x, y) = \{\langle d_0, d_1, \ldots, d_{k-1}, \text{pair}(x, y)\rangle : 0 < d_0 < d_1$$
$$< \cdots < d_{k-1} < \text{pair}(x, y)\}$$

We then have

$$u_1^*(g(z), x) = y$$

for every $z \in \Sigma(x, y)$, since the theory produced by $g$ explains previously received pairs. Thus, the dyadic function $h$ defined by

$$h(x, y) = \max\{v(g(z), x) : z \in \Sigma(x, y)\}$$

is recursive. Now suppose that $f \in C$. We shall show that $f$ is $(h, v)$-honest. If dom$(f)$ is finite, then $f$ is certainly $(h, v)$-honest (since a finite number of exceptions are allowed). Suppose that dom$(f)$ is infinite. Let $0 < d_0 < d_1 < \cdots$ be the admissible sequence for $f$ in which the pairs appear in strictly increasing order. Since $g$ explains $f$, there exists an index $\pi$ for an extension of $f$ and a natural number $m$ such that for all $k \geq m$ we have $g(\langle d_0, \ldots, d_k \rangle) = \pi$. For almost all $x \in$ dom$(f)$, we have pair$(x, f(x)) = d_k$ for some $k \geq m$. Thus, $z = \langle d_0, \ldots, d_{k-1}, \text{pair}(x, f(x)) \rangle$ belongs to $\Sigma(x, f(x))$. This implies that

$$v_1(\pi, x) \leq h(x, f(x))$$

and thus that $f$ is $(h, v)$-honest.

The proof of part (b) is similar to that of the corresponding part of Theorem 4.7.7. We are given the dyadic recursive function $h$. We interpret pair$(\pi, m)$ as the hypothesis that (1) $\pi$ is an index for an extension of $f$, and (2) for all $x \in$ dom$(f)$ we have

$$v_1(\pi, x) \leq \max\{m, h(x, f(x))\}$$

For any $z = \langle d_0, \ldots, d_k \rangle$, we let $g(z)$ be the $\pi$ in the smallest hypothesis pair$(\pi, m)$ that is consistent with the pairs received thus far: (1) we have

$$v_1(\pi, x) \leq \max\{m, h(x, y)\}$$

for all pair$(x, y) = d_j$ with $j \leq k$, and (2) we have

$$u_1^*(\pi, x) = y$$

for all such pairs. If $f$ is $(h, v)$-honest, there will be an infinite number of hypotheses that are consistent with an admissible sequence for $f$, and $g$ will converge to the smallest of these. □

We have seen that both prediction and explanation, in the technical senses we have described, reduce in principle to complexity theory. It seems remarkable that a theory concocted to study the difficulty of computation should shed light on the difficulties of "learning" as well.

## 4.8. Computable Real Numbers

In Section 2.8.1 we considered sets of natural numbers, and real numbers, described by finite automata. We assumed then that both natural numbers and real numbers were represented to some base $k$ over a finite alphabet $\mathbf{B}_k = \{0, \ldots, k-1\}$. Throughout much of the present chapter we have been discussing computable sets of natural numbers (recursive sets), and we would now like to consider the extension of this theory to real numbers. For $k \geq 2$, let us say that a real number $\xi \in [0, 1]$ is *computable to base $k$* if there exists a monadic recursive function $g : \mathbf{N} \to \mathbf{B}_k$ such that $\xi = \sum_{n \geq 1} g(n) k^{-n}$ (that is, if the $n$-th digit of a base $k$ expansion of $\xi$ is a computable function of $n$). (This is equivalent to saying that there exist recursive sets $R_1 \subseteq \cdots \subseteq R_{k-1}$ such that $\xi = \text{real}_k(R_1, \ldots, R_{k-1})$, in the notation of Section 2.8.1.) We then say that a real number $\xi \in \mathbf{R}$ (positive, negative, or zero) is computable to base $k$ if there exists an integer $n \in \mathbf{Z}$ (positive, negative, or zero) such that $\xi - n$ belongs to $[0, 1]$ and is computable to base $k$. If $\psi$ is an index for the function $g$, the pair $\pi = \text{pair}(n, \psi)$ will be called a *$k$-index* for $\xi$, and we shall write $\text{num}_k(\pi) = \xi$.

We shall also consider a more general definition of the notion "$\xi$ is computable," one which makes no reference to any base. Let $\text{int} : \mathbf{N} \to \mathbf{Z}$ be an encoding of integers as natural numbers, say, by $\text{int}(2t) = t$ and $\text{int}(2t+1) = -t$ (this encoding allows the integer 0 to be represented by the two natural numbers 0 and 1, but these multiple representations will not be important). Let $\text{rat} : \mathbf{N} \to \mathbf{Q}$ be an encoding of rationals as natural numbers, say, by $\text{rat}(n) = \text{int}(\text{bileft}(n))/\text{succ}(\text{biright}(n))$ (again there are multiple representations that are not important). We shall say that a real number $\xi \in \mathbf{R}$ is *computable* if there exists a recursive function $f \in \mathcal{Q}_1^*$ such that

$$|\xi - \text{rat}(f(n))| \leq 1/(n + 1)$$

for all $n \in \mathbf{N}$ (that is, if a rational number that approximates $\xi$ to any desired precision $1/(n + 1)$ can be computed from $n$). If $\pi$ is an index for the function $f$, we shall also call $\pi$ an *index* for $\xi$, and we shall write $\text{num}(\pi) = \xi$.

**Proposition 4.8.1.** *For every $k \geq 2$ and every $\xi \in \mathbf{R}$, $\xi$ is computable to base $k$ if and only if $\xi$ is computable.*

**Proof.** If $\xi$ is computable to base $k$, then $\xi$ is computable, since knowing the integer part and the first $n$ digits in the fractional part of the base $k$ representation of $\xi$ confines $\xi$ to an interval of length $k^{-n}$ with a rational midpoint.

For the converse, we consider two cases. If $\xi$ is rational, then the $n$-th digit in the base $k$ representation of $\xi$ is a periodic function of $n$, and thus certainly a recursive function of $n$. So suppose that $\xi$ is irrational and computable, so that

$$|\xi - \text{rat}(f(n))| \leq 1/(n + 1)$$

for some recursive function $f$ and all $n \in \mathbf{N}$. Then for every rational $\eta \in \mathbf{Q}$, there exists an $n$ such that the interval $[\text{rat}(f(n)) - 1/(n + 1), \text{rat}(f(n)) +$

$1/(n+1)]$ does not contain $\eta$ (it suffices to choose $n \geq 1/|\xi - \eta|$). Thus, the set

$$\Xi = \{m : \mathrm{rat}(m) < \xi\}$$

is recursive: to determine if $m \in \Xi$, compute $\mathrm{rat}(f(0)), \mathrm{rat}(f(1)), \ldots$, until $|\mathrm{rat}(m) - \mathrm{rat}(f(n))| > 1/(n+1)$; then $m \in \Xi$ if and only if $\mathrm{rat}(m) < \mathrm{rat}(f(n))$. Furthermore, we have

$$\mathrm{Compl}(\Xi) = \{m : \mathrm{rat}(m) > \xi\}$$

since the case of equality is excluded: $\xi$ is irrational and $\eta$ is rational. But we can determine each digit of the base $k$ representation of $\xi$ by answering a finite number of questions, each of which asks whether $\xi$ is greater than or less than a given rational (since the endpoints of the intervals corresponding to digit values are rationals). Thus, $\xi$ is computable to base $k$ in this case also. $\quad\square$

Observe that the proof of Proposition 4.8.1 shows that for every $k \geq 2$ there is a recursive function $s_k$ such that $\mathrm{num}(s_k(\pi)) = \mathrm{num}_k(\pi)$ whenever $\pi$ is a $k$-index. It does not, however, yield a recursive function $t_k$ such that $\mathrm{num}_k(t_k(\pi)) = \mathrm{num}(\pi)$ whenever $\pi$ is an index, since it does not give an effective way to determine which of the two cases, $\mathrm{num}(\pi)$ rational or $\mathrm{num}(\pi)$ irrational, holds. For this reason, it is most convenient to work entirely with indices rather than $k$-indices.

Let $\mathbf{S}$ denote the set of computable real numbers. It will be convenient to work also with "computable complex numbers," which may be represented as ordered pairs of computable real numbers (just as the complex numbers are represented as ordered pairs of real numbers).

**Theorem 4.8.2.** *The computable real numbers $\mathbf{S}$ form a field. The computable complex numbers form an imaginary quadratic extension field $\mathbf{D} = \mathbf{S}(\sqrt{-1})$ that is algebraically closed and has countably infinite transcendence degree.*

The algebraic closure of $\mathbf{D}$ means that if a complex number $\zeta \in \mathbf{C}$ satisfies an algebraic equation

$$a_n \zeta^n + \cdots + a_1 \zeta + a_0 = 0$$

where $a_n, \ldots, a_1, a_0 \in \mathbf{D}$ are computable complex numbers and $a_n \neq 0$, then $\zeta$ is also a computable complex number. The infinite transcendence degree of $\mathbf{D}$ means that there exists a sequence $\omega_1, \omega_2, \ldots$, of computable complex numbers (in fact, they may be chosen to be computable real numbers) such that no finite set $\omega_1, \ldots, \omega_k$ satisfies a non-vanishing multivariate polynomial equation with integer coefficients: $P(\omega_1, \ldots, \omega_k) = 0$ with $P(X_1, \ldots, X_k) \in \mathbf{Z}[X_1, \ldots, X_k]$ and $P(X_1, \ldots, X_k) \neq 0$. (Since $\mathbf{S}$ and $\mathbf{D}$ are countable, they have the largest possible transcendence degree.)

We shall not prove Theorem 4.8.2 here, but merely indicate the main ideas. The proof that $\mathbf{S}$ form a field is easy, and only division presents any subtlety. But if we know that the denominator $\eta$ in the quotient $\xi/\eta$ is not 0, then we may safely embark on the search for an interval of approximation to $\eta$ that excludes 0. Having found such an interval, we can then determine how well we must approximate $\xi$ and $\eta$ to obtain the desired approximation to $\xi/\eta$. In fact, for each of the rational operations it is possible to compute an index for the result as a recursive function of indices for the operands. (In the case of division, the value of this recursive function will not be an index if the denominator is 0. In all other cases, the value will be an index provided the arguments are indices.) That $\mathbf{D}$ is algebraically closed follows from the fact that $\mathbf{S}$ is "real-closed" (that is, non-negative numbers have square roots, and algebraic equations of odd degree have solutions). (See Stewart [1988].) For both the square-root and odd-degree polynomials, we can find an interval with rational endpoints within which the polynomial changes sign. By considering two cases (as in the proof of Proposition 4.8.1) we can assume that all solutions in the interval are irrational. Thus, we can approximate the solution as precisely as desired by bisection, since in this case it is possible to determine the sign of the polynomial at any rational point. Finally, to prove that $\mathbf{S}$ has infinite transcendence degree, observe that if $p_1, p_2, \ldots$, are multiplicatively independent integers (for example, if they are distinct primes), then the algebraic numbers $\sqrt{p_1}, \sqrt{p_2}, \ldots$, are linearly independent over the rationals, and thus by Lindemann's theorem the numbers $\exp \sqrt{p_1}, \exp \sqrt{p_2}, \ldots$, are algebraically independent. (The proof of Lindemann's theorem given in Stewart's book is easily generalized to cover this case. See also Beukers, Bézivin, and Robba [1990].) It then suffices to observe that all of these numbers are computable (the square roots because $\mathbf{S}$ is real-closed, and the exponentials by a straightforward argument based on the power-series expansion $\exp x = \sum_{n \geq 0} x^n/n!$).

Theorem 4.8.2 completely characterizes the algebraic structure of the computable complex numbers $\mathbf{D}$, since any two algebraically closed extensions of $\mathbf{Q}$ with the same transcendence degree are algebraically isomorphic (that is, have their elements in a bijective correspondence that preserves all rational operations). What is left unmentioned by Theorem 4.8.2 is the order-theoretic structure (the bijective correspondence just mentioned will not necessarily preserve the order relation among real numbers). In fact, the order relation among computable real numbers is only partially computable: if it is known that two computable real numbers are not equal, then one can compute their order (much as in the proof of Proposition 4.8.1), but there is no way to compute (given indices for the numbers) whether or not they are equal (see Exercise 1 following this section).

The following theorem shows that even the most fundamental order-theoretic properties of the real numbers fail for the computable real numbers. Recall that a bounded and non-decreasing sequence of real numbers converges to a limit (this is an immediate consequence of Dedekind's definition of real numbers).

**Proposition 4.8.3.** *There exists a bounded and non-decreasing sequence* $\xi_0$, $\xi_1, \ldots$, *of computable real numbers (in fact, rational numbers) such that the real number* $\eta = \lim_{n \to \infty} \xi_n$ *is not computable.*

**Proof.** Let $e^*$ be a recursive function such that $K = \text{range}(e^*)$. Define the dyadic recursive function $g \in \mathcal{Q}_2^*$ by

$$g(m, n) = \begin{cases} 1, & \text{if } e^*(x) = m \text{ for some } x \leq n \\ 0, & \text{otherwise} \end{cases}$$

Then for every $m$, we have $g(m, p) \geq g(m, q)$ if $p \geq q$. Thus, if we define

$$\xi_n = \sum_{0 \leq m \leq n} \frac{g(m, n)}{2^m}$$

we have $\xi_p \geq \xi_q$ if $p \geq q$. Since $0 \leq \xi_n \leq 1$ for all $n$, the limit $\eta = \lim_{n \to \infty} \xi_n$ exists. Suppose, for the sake of contradiction, that $\eta$ is a computable real number. Then by Proposition 4.8.1, there is a recursive function $h : \mathbf{N} \to \mathbf{B}$ such that

$$\eta = \sum_{0 \leq m < \infty} \frac{h(m)}{2^m}$$

Furthermore, $h$ must satisfy

$$h(m) = \begin{cases} 1, & \text{if } e^*(x) = m \text{ for some } x \in \mathbf{N} \\ 0, & \text{otherwise} \end{cases}$$

But the condition $e^*(x) = m$ for some $x \in \mathbf{N}$ is equivalent to $m \in \text{dom}(u^*)$, which is in turn equivalent to $m \in K$. Thus, $\text{char}_K = h$ is recursive, a contradiction. □

The notion of computable real numbers goes back to the origins of computability theory, and was described explicitly by Turing [1936/1937]. Proposition 4.8.1 is due to Robinson [1951]. That the computable real numbers form a field was proved by Rice [1954]. Proposition 4.8.3 is due to Specker [1949].

### Exercise

1. (E) Show that the relation $\{(\pi, \tau) : \text{num}(\pi) = \text{num}(\tau)\}$ is not recursive.

# References

W. Ackermann (1928), "Zum Hilbertschen Aufbau der reelen Zahlen," *Math. Ann.*, 99, 118–133.

I. Ágoston, J. Demetrovics and L. Hannak (1983), "On the Number of Clones Containing All Constants (A Problem of R. McKenzie)," *Colloq. Math. Soc. J. Bolyai*, 43, 21–25.

V. B. Alekseev (В. Б. Алексеев) (1989), «О Числе Семейств Подмножеств, Замкнутых Относительно Пересечения», *Дискретная Математика*, 1, 129–136.

M. M. Arslanov (М. М. Арсланов) (1981), «О Некоторых Обобщениях Теоремы о Неподбижной Точке,» *Изв. Высш. Учеб. Завед.*, 228, 5, 9–16.

K. A. Baker and A. F. Pixley (1975), "Polynomial Interpolation and the Chinese Remainder Theorem," *Math. Z.*, 143, 165–174.

Y. Bar-Hillel, M. Perlis and E. Shamir (1961), "On Formal Properties of Simple Phrase-Structure Grammars," *Zeitschrift für Phonetik, Sprachwissenschaft, und Kommunikationsforschung*, 14, 143–177.

Ya. M. Barzdin and R. V. Freivald (1972), "On the Prediction of General Recursive Functions," *Sov. Math. Dokl.*, 13, 1224–1228.

J. Beauquier (1979), «Générateurs algébriques et systèmes de paires itérantes», *Theor. Comp. Sci.*, 8, 293–323.

J. Beauquier (1981), "A Remark about a Substitution Property," *Math. Systems Theory*, 14, 189–191.

J. Beauquier and F. Gire (1987), «Une note sur le théorème de caractérisation des générateurs algébriques,» *Theor. Comp. Sci.*, 51, 117–127.

J. Berman (1980), "A Proof of Lyndon's Finite Basis Theorem," *Discrete Math.*, 29, 229–233.

J. Berstel (1979), *Transductions and Context-Free Languages*, B. G. Teubner, Stuttgart.

F. Beukers, J.-P. Bézivin and P. Robba (1990), "An Alternative Proof of the Lindemann–Weierstrass Theorem," *Amer. Math. Monthly*, 97, 193–197.

G. Birkhoff (1948), *Lattice Theory*, American Mathematical Society, New York.

G. N. Blokhina (Г. Н. Блохина) (1970), «О Предикатном Описании Классов Поста,» *Дискретный Анализ*, 16, 16–29.

M. Blum (1967a), "A Machine-Independent Theory of the Complexity of Recursive Functions," *J. ACM*, 14, 322–336.

M. Blum (1967b), "On the Size of Machines," *Inf. and Control*, 11, 257–265.

234

L. Blum and M. Blum (1975), "Toward a Mathematical Theory of Inductive Inference," *Inf. and Control*, 28, 125–155.

M. Blum and C. E. Hewitt (1967), "Automata on a 2-Dimensional Tape," *Proc. IEEE Symp. on Foundations of Comp. Sci.*, 8, 155–160.

M. Blum and D. Kozen (1978), "On the Power of the Compass (or, Why Mazes Are Easier to Search Than Graphs)," *Proc. IEEE Symp. on Foundations of Comp. Sci.*, 19, 132–142.

M. Blum and W. J. Sakoda (1977), "On the Capability of Finite Automata in 2 and 3 Dimensional Space," *Proc. IEEE Symp. on Foundations of Comp. Sci.*, 18, 147–161.

L. Boasson and M. Nivat (1977), «Le cylindre des langage linéaires,» *Math. Systems Theory*, 11, 147–155.

V. G. Bodnarchuk, L. A. Kaluzhnin, V. N. Kotov and B. A. Romov (1969), "Galois Theory for Post Algebras. I, II," *Cybernetics*, 5, 243–252, 531–539.

M. Boffa (1990), «Une remarque sur les systèmes complets d'identités rationelles,» *Theor. Inf. and Appl.*, 24, 419–423.

M. Boffa (1995), «Une condition impliquant toutes les identités rationelles,» *Theor. Inf. and Appl.*, 29, 515–518.

J. A. Brzozowski (1964), "Derivatives of Regular Expressions," *J. ACM*, 11, 481–494.

J. A. Brzozowski (1968), "Regular-Like Languages Expressions for Some Irregular Languages," *Proc. IEEE Symp. on Switching and Automata Theory*, 9, 278–280.

J. A. Brzozowski and R. Knast (1978), "The Dot-Depth Hierarchy of Star-Free Languages Is Infinite," *J. Comp. and System Sci.*, 16, 37–55.

R. Büchi (1960), "Weak Second-Order Arithmetic and Finite Automata," *Z. Math. Logik Grundlagen Math.*, 6, 66–92.

L. Budach (1978), "Automata and Labyrinths," *Math. Nachr.*, 86, 195–282.

M. Bull and A. Hemmerling (1990), "Finite Embedded Trees and Simply Connected Mazes Cannot Be Searched by Halting Finite Automata," *J. Inf. Process. Cybern.*, 26, 65–73.

G. A. Burle (Г. А. Бурле) (1967), «Классы $k$-значой логики, содержащие все функции одной переменной,» *Дискр. Анализ*, 10, 3–7.

G. Burosch, J. Demetrovics, G. O. H. Katona and A. A. Sapozhenko (1991), "On the Number of Databases and Closure Operations," *Theor. Comp. Sci.*, 78, 377–81.

J. W. Butler (1960), "On Complete and Independent Sets of Operations in Finite Algebras," *Pac. J. Math.*, 10, 1169–1179.

D. G. Cantor (1962), "On the Ambiguity Problem of Backus Systems," *J. ACM*, 9, 477–479.

G. J. Chaitin (1966), "On the Length of Programs for Computing Finite Binary Sequences," *J. ACM*, 13, 547–569.

A. K. Chandra, D. C. Kozen and L. J. Stockmeyer (1981), "Alternation," *J. ACM*, 28, 114–133.

N. Chomsky (1956), "Three Models for the Description of Language," *IRE Trans. on Inf. Theory*, 2, 113–124.

N. Chomsky (1959), "On Certain Formal Properties of Grammars," *Inf. and Control*, 2, 137–167.

N. Chomsky and G. A. Miller (1958), "Finite-State Languages," *Inf. and Control*, 1, 91–112.

N. Chomsky and M. P. Schützenberger (1963), "The Algebraic Theory of Context-Free Languages," in: P. Braffort and D. Hirschberg (eds.), *Computer Programming and Formal Systems*, North-Holland, Amsterdam.

A. Church (1941), *The Calculi of Lambda-Conversion*, Princeton University Press, Princeton, NJ.

A. Cobham (1969), "On the Base-Dependence of Sets of Numbers Recognizable by Finite Automata," *Math. Systems Theory*, 3, 186–192.

R. S. Cohen and J. A. Brzozowski (1971), "Dot-Depth of Star-Free Events," *J. Comp. and System Sci.*, 5, 1–16.

L. Comtet (1964), «Calcul pratique des coefficients de Taylor d'une fonction algébrique,» *Ens. Math. (II)*, 10, 267–270.

J. H. Conway (1971), *Regular Algebra and Finite Machines*, Chapman and Hall, London.

S. B. Cooper (1990), "The Jump Is Definable in the Structure of the Degrees of Unsolvability," *Bull. AMS*, 23, 151–158.

S. B. Cooper (1991), "Definability and Global Degree Theory," *Logic Colloquium '90*, H'elsinki, 25–45.

S. B. Cooper (1994), "Rigidity and Definability in the Noncomputable Universe," in: D. Prawitz, B. Skyrms and D. Westerståhl (eds.), *Logic, Methodology and Philosophy of Science IX*, Elsevier Science, pp. 209–235.

B. Csákány (1983), "All Minimal Clones on the Three-Element Set," *Acta Cybernetica*, 6, 227–238.

R. P. Daley (1978), "On the Simplicity of Busy Beaver Sets," *Zeitschr. für math. Logik und Grundl. der Math.*, 24, 207–224.

J. Dassow (1981), *Completeness Problems in the Structural Theory of Automata*, Akademie–Verlag, Berlin.

M. Davis (1973), "Hilbert's Tenth Problem Is Unsolvable," *Amer. Math. Monthly*, 80, 233–269.

F. Dejean and M. P. Schützenberger (1966), "On a Question of Eggan," *Inf. and Control*, 9, 23–25.

J. C. E. Dekker (1954), "A Theorem on Hypersimple Sets," *Proc. AMS*, 5, 791–796.

J. C. E. Dekker and J. Myhill (1960), "Recursive Equivalence Types," *Univ. Cal. Publ. Math.*, 3, 67–213.

G. C. Denham (1994), "Many-Valued Generalizations of Two Finite Intervals in Post's Lattice," *Proc. Internat. Symp. Multiple-Valued Logic*, 24, 314–318.

E. W. Dijkstra (1960), "Recursive Programming," *Num. Math.*, 2, 312–318.

K. Döpp (1971), "Automaten in Labyrinthen," *Electr. Inf. und Kyb.*, 7, 79–94, 167–190.

W. von Dyck (1882), "Gruppentheoretische Studien," *Math. Ann.*, 20, 1–44.

L. C. Eggan (1963), "Transition Graphs and the Star Height of Regular Events," *Michigan Math. J.*, 10, 385–395.

A. Ehrenfeucht (1961), "Application of Games to the Completeness Problem for Formalized Theories," *Fund. Math.*, 49, 129–141.

S. Eilenberg (1973), "Classes of Semigroups and Classes of Sets," *Proc. ACM Symp. on Theory of Computing*, 5, 266–267.

S. Eilenberg (1974/1976), *Automata, Languages and Machines*, Academic Press, New York, vol. A/vol. B.

S. Eilenberg and M. P. Schützenberger (1976), "On Pseudovarieties," *Advances in Math.*, 19, 413–418.

C. C. Elgot and J. E. Mezei (1965), "On Relations Defined by Generalized Finite Automata," *IBM J. Res. and Dev.*, 9, 47–65.

J. Engelfriet and G. Rozenberg (1980), "Fixed Point Languages, Equality Languages and Representation of Recursively Enumerable Languages," *J. ACM*, 27, 499–518.

C. J. Everett (1944), "Closure Operations and Galois Theory in Lattices," *Trans. AMS*, 55, 514–525.

Ph. Flajolet (1987), "Analytic Models and Ambiguity of Context-Free Languages," *Theor. Comp. Sci.*, 49, 283–309.

R. W. Floyd (1962), "On Ambiguity in Phrase Structure Languages," *Comm. ACM*, 5, 526–534.

R. Fraïssé (1954), «Sur les classification des systems de relations,» *Publ. Sci. de L'Univ. D'Alger*, 1, 35–185.

R. Freese (1980), "Free Modular Lattices," *Trans. AMS*, 261, 81–91.

R. M. Friedberg (1957), "Two Recursively Enumerable Sets of Incomparable Degrees of Unsolvability (Solution of Post's Problem, 1944)," *Proc. Nat. Acad. Sci. USA*, 43, 236–238.

R. M. Friedberg (1958), "Three Theorems on Recursive Enumeration: I, Decomposition, II, Maximal Set, III, Enumeration without Duplication," *J. Symb. Logic*, 23, 309–316.

F. G. Frobenius (1895), "Über endliche Gruppen," *Sitzungber. Preuss. Akad. Wiss. Berlin*, 16–194.

G. P. Gavrilov (1984), "Inductive Representation of Boolean Functions and the Finite Generation of the Post Classes," *Algebra and Logic*, 23, 1–19.

D. Geiger (1968), "Closed Systems of Functions and Predicates," *Pac. J. Math.*, 27, 95–100.

S. Ginsburg and E. H. Spanier (1968), "Derivation-Bounded Languages," *J. Comp. and System Sci.*, 2, 228–250.

S. Ginsburg and E. H. Spanier (1970), "Substitutions in Families of Languages," *Inf. Sci.*, 2, 83–110.

S. Ginsburg and J. Ullian (1962), "Ambiguity in Context-Free Languages," *J. ACM*, 13, 62–88.

P. Goralčik, A. Goralčiková and V. Koubek (1991), "Alternation with a Pebble," *Inf. Proc. Lett.*, 38, 7–13.

S. A. Greibach (1965), "A New Normal-Form Theorem for Context-Free, Phrase-Structure Grammars," *J. ACM*, 12, 42–52.

S. A. Greibach (1966), "The Unsolvability of the Recognition of Linear Context-Free Languages," *J. ACM*, 13, 582–587.

S. A. Greibach (1969), "An Infinite Hierarchy of Context-Free Languages," *J. ACM*, 16, 91–106.

S. A. Greibach (1970), "Chains of Full AFL's," *Math. Systems Theory*, 4, 231–242.

S. A. Greibach (1973), "The Hardest Context-Free Language," *SIAM J. Comp.*, 2, 304–310.

J. Gruska (1971a), "A Characterization of Context-Free Languages," *J. Comp. and System Sci.*, 5, 353–364.

J. Gruska (1971b), "A Few Remarks on the Index of Context-Free Grammars and Languages," *Inf. and Control*, 19, 216–223.

L. Haddad and I. G. Rosenberg (1994), "Finite Clones Containing All Permutations," *Can. J. Math.*, 46, 951–970.

G. Hansel (1966), «Sur le nombre des fonctiones booléennes monotones de $n$ variables,» *C. R. Acad. Sci. Paris*, 262, 1088–1090.

J. Hartmanis and J. E. Hopcroft (1971), "An Overview of the Theory of Computational Complexity," *J. ACM*, 18, 444–475.

T. L. Heath (1931), *A Manual of Greek Mathematics*, Oxford University Press, London.

A. Hemmerling and K. Kriegel (1984), "On Searching of Special Classes of Mazes and Finite Embedded Graphs," *Springer Lect. Notes in Comp. Sci.*, 176, 291–300.

D. Hilbert (1901–1902), "Mathematical Problems," *Bull. AMS*, 8, 437–479.

F. Hoffmann (1981), "One Pebble Does Not Suffice to Search Plane Labyrinths," *Springer Lect. Notes in Comp. Sci.*, 117, 433–444.

C. G. Jockusch, Jr. (1972), "Ramsey's Theorem and Recursion Theory," *J. Symb. Logic*, 37, 268–280.

C. G. Jockusch, Jr. (1981), "Three Easy Constructions of Recursively Enumerable Sets," in: M. Lerman, J. H. Schmerl and R. I. Soare (eds.), *Logic Year 1779–1980: Lect.*

*Notes in Math.*, Springer-Verlag, Berlin, 859, pp. 83–91.

C. G. Jockusch, Jr. and R. I. Shore (1983), "Pseudo Jump Operators I: The R. E. Case," *Trans. AMS*, 275, 599–609.

G. Jockusch, Jr. and R. I. Shore (1984), "Pseudo Jump Operators II: Transfinite Iterations, Hierarchies, and Minimal Covers," *J. Symb. Logic*, 49, 1205–1236.

S. C. Kleene (1938), *Introduction to Metamathematics*, David Van Nostrand, Princeton, NJ.

S. C. Kleene (1956), "Representation of Events in Nerve Nets and Finite Automata," in: C. E. Shannon and J. McCarthy (eds.), *Automata Studies*, Princeton University Press, Princeton, NJ.

S. C. Kleene and E. L. Post (1954), "The Upper Semi-Lattice of Degrees of Recursive Unsolvability," *Ann. of Math.*, 59, 379–407.

A. N. Kolmogorov (1965), "Three Approaches to the Concept 'Quantity of Information,'" *Prob. Inf. Transm.*, 1, 3–11.

A. D. Korshunov (А. Д. Коршунов) (1981), «О Числе Монотонных Булевых Функций,» *Проблемы Кибернетики*, 38, 5–108.

D. Kozen (1994), "A Completeness Theorem for Kleene Algebras and the Algebra of Regular Events," *Inf. and Comput.*, 110, 366–390.

D. Krob (1991), "Complete Systems of B-Rational Identities," *Theor. Comp. Sci.*, 89, 207–343.

V. B. Kudryavtsev (В. Б. Кудрявцев) (1965), «О мощностях множеств предполных множеств некоторыкш функциональных систем, связанных с автоматами,» *Проб. Кибернет.*, 13, 45–74.

V. B. Kudryavtsev, Sh. Ushchumlich and G. Kilibarda (1993), "On Behaviour of Automata in Labyrinths," *Discrete Math. and Appl.*, 3, 1–28.

M. Kummer (1990), "An Easy Priority-Free Proof of a Theorem of Friedberg," *Theor. Comp. Sci.*, 74, 249–251.

A. V. Kuznetsov (А. В. Кузнецов) (1961), «Структуры с замыканием и критерии функциональной полноты,» *Усп. Мат. Наук*, 16, 201–512.

A. H. Lachlan (1966), "Lower Bounds for Pairs of Recursively Enumerable Degrees," *Proc. London Math. Soc.*, 16, 537–539.

R. E. Ladner (1977), "Application of Model Theoretic Games to Discrete Linear Orders and Finite Automata," *Inf. and Control*, 33, 281–303.

M. Latteux (1977), «Produit dans le cône rationnel engendré par $D_1^*$,» *Theor. Comp. Sci.*, 5, 129–134.

M. Latteux and G. Rozenberg (1984), "Commutative One-Counter Languages Are Regular," *J. Comp. and System Sci.*, 29, 54–57.

M. Lerman (1983), *Degrees of Unsolvability*, Springer-Verlag, Berlin.

J. H. Loxton and A. J. van der Poorten (1988), "Arithmetic Properties of Automata: Regular Sequences," *J. reine angew. Math.*, 392, 57–69.

R. C. Lyndon (1951), "Identities in Two-Valued Calculi," *Trans. AMS*, 71, 457–465.

K. Mahler (1929), "Arithmetische Eigenschaften der Lösungen einer Klasse von Funktionalgleichungen," *Math. Ann.*, 101, 342–366.

A. I. Maltsev (А. И. Мальцев) (1966), «Итеративные алгебры и многообразия Поста,» *Алгебра и Логика*, 5, 5–24.

S. S. Marchenkov (1981), "On Homogeneous Algebras," *Sov. Math. Dokl.*, 23, 122–124.

S. S. Marchenkov (1984), "Existence of Finite Bases in Closed Classes of Boolean Functions," *Algebra and Logic*, 23, 66–74.

H. A. Maurer and M. Nivat (1980), "Rational Bijections of Rational Sets," *Acta Informatica*, 13, 365–378.

W. McCulloch and W. Pitts (1943), "A Logical Calculus of the Ideas Immanent in

Nervous Activity," *Bull. Math. Biophys.*, 5, 115–133.

D. McLean (1954), "Idempotent Semigroups," *Amer. Math. Monthly*, 61, 110–113.

R. McNaughton and S. Papert (1971), *Counter-Free Automata*, MIT Press, Cambridge, MA.

R. McNaughton and H. Yamada (1960), "Regular Expressions and State Graphs for Automata," *IRE Trans. Electr. Comp.*, 9, 39–47.

M. L. Minsky (1967), *Computation: Finite and Infinite Machines*, Prentice-Hall, Englewood Cliffs, NJ.

M. L. Minsky and S. A. Papert (1988), *Perceptrons—An Introduction to Computational Geometry*, MIT Press, Cambridge, MA, expanded ed.

A. A. Muchnik (A. A. Мучник) (1956), «Неразрешимость Проблемы Сводимости Теории Алгоритмов,» *Докл. Акад. Наук СССР*, 108, 194–197.

H. Müller (1979), "Automata Catching Labyrinths with at Most Three Components," *Electr. Inf. und Kyb.*, 15, 3–9.

V. L. Murskiĭ (1965), "The Existence in Three-Valued Logic of a Closed Class with Finite Basis, Not Having a Finite Complete System of Identities," *Sov. Math. Dokl.*, 6, 1020–1024.

J. Myhill (1955), "Creative Sets," *Z. Math. Logik und Grundl. der Math.*, 1, 97–108.

A. Nerode (1958), "Linear Automaton Transformations," *Proc. AMS*, 9, 541–544.

J. von Neumann (1966), *Theory of Self-Reproducing Automata*, University of Illinois Press, Urbana, IL.

M. Nivat (1968), «Transductions des langages de Chomsky,» *Ann. de l'Inst. Fourier*, 18, 339–456.

W. F. Ogden (1968), "A Helpful Result for Proving Inherent Ambiguity," *Math. Systems Theory*, 2, 191–194.

Ø. Ore (1944), "Galois Connexions," *Trans. AMS*, 55, 493–513.

R. J. Parikh (1966), "On Context-Free Languages," *J. ACM*, 13, 570–581.

D. Perrin (1990), "Finite Automata," in: J. van Leeuwen (ed.), *Handbook of Theoretical Computer Science—Volume B: Formal Models and Semantics*, MIT Press, Cambridge, MA.

J.-E. Pin (1995), "Finite Semigroups and Recognizable Languages: An Introduction," in: J. Fountain (ed.), *Semigroups, Formal Languages and Groups*, Kluwer Academic.

N. Pippenger (1997), "Regular Languages and Stone Duality," *Theory Comput. Systems* (Formerly, *Math. System Theory*); 30, 121–134.

R. Pöschel and L. A. Kaluzhnin (1979), *Funktionen- und Relationenalgebren*, Deutscher Verlag der Wissenschaften, Berlin.

E. L. Post (1920), "Determination of All Closed Systems of Truth Tables," *Bull. AMS*, 26, 437–437.

E. L. Post (1941), *The Two-Valued Iterative Systems of Mathematical Logic*, Princeton University Press, Princeton, NJ.

E. L. Post (1944), "Recursively Enumerable Sets of Positive Integers and Their Decision Problems," *Bull. AMS*, 50, 284–316.

E. L. Post (1946), "A Variant of a Recursively Unsolvable Problem," *Bull. AMS*, 52, 264–268.

E. L. Post (1947), "Recursive Unsolvability of a Problem of Thue," *J. Symb. Logic*, 12, 1–11.

P. Pudlák and J. Tůma (1980), "Every Finite Lattice Can Be Embedded in a Finite Partition Lattice," *Algebra Universalis*, 10, 74–95.

W. V. O. Quine (1969), *Set Theory and Its Logic*, Harvard University Press, Cambridge, MA.

M. O. Rabin and D. Scott (1959), "Finite Automata and Their Decision Problems," *IBM J. Res. and Dev.*, 3, 114–125.

T. Rado (1962), "On Non-Computable Functions," *Bell Systems Tech. J.*, 41, 877–884.

F. P. Ramsey (1930), "On a Problem in Formal Logic," *Proc. London Math. Soc.*, 30, 264–286.

V. N. Redko (В. Н. Редько) (1964a), «Об определяющей совокупности соотношений алгебры регулярных событий,» *Украин. Мат. Ж.*, 16, 120–126.

V. N. Redko (В. Н. Редько) (1964b), «Об алгебре коммутативных событий,» *Украин. Мат. Ж.*, 16, 185–195.

J. Reiterman (1982), "The Birkhoff Theorem for Finite Algebras," *Algebra Universalis*, 14, 1–10.

H. G. Rice (1953), "Classes of Recursively Enumerable Sets and Their Decision Problems," *Trans. Amer. Math. Soc.*, 95, 358–356.

H. G. Rice (1954), "Recursive Real Numbers," *Proc. AMS*, 5, 784–791.

H. G. Rice (1956), "On Completely Recursively Enumerable Classes and Their Key Arrays," *J. Symbolic Logic*, 21, 304–308.

R. M. Robinson (1951), "Review of Péter, R.: *Rekursive Funktionen*, Akad. Kiadó, Budapest, 1951," *J. Symbolic Logic*, 16, 280–282.

H. Rogers, Jr. (1967), *Theory of Recursive Functions and Effective Computability*, McGraw-Hill, New York.

I. G. Rosenberg (1970), "Über die funktionale Vollständigkeit in den mehrwertigen Logiken," *Rozpr. ČSAV Řada Mat. Přir. Věd*, 80, 4, 3–93.

I. G. Rosenberg (1983), "Minimal Clones I: The Five Types," *Colloq. Math, Soc. J. Bolyai*, 43, 405–427.

G.-C. Rota (1964), "The Number of Partitions of a Set," *Amer. Math. Monthly*, 71, 498–504.

A. Salomaa (1963), "On Basic Groups for the Set of Functions over a Finite Domain," *Ann. Acad. Sci. Fenn.*, 338, 3–15.

A. Salomaa (1966), "Two Complete Axiom Systems for the Algebra of Regular Events," *J. ACM*, 13, 158–169.

S. Scheinberg (1960), "A Note on the Boolean Properties of Context-Free Languages," *Inf. and Control*, 3, 372–375.

J. Schmidt (1952), "Über die Rolle der transfiniten Schlußweisen in einer allgemeinen Idealtheorie," *Math. Nachrichten*, 7, 165–182.

M. Schützenberger (1965), "On Finite Monoids Having Only Trivial Subgroups," *Inf. and Control*, 8, 190–194.

A. Selman (1972), "Completeness of Calculii for Axiomatically Defined Classes of Algebras," *Algebra Universalis*, 2, 20–32.

A. L. Semenov (1977), "Presburgerness of Predicates Regular in Two Number Systems," *Siberian Math. J.*, 18, 289–300.

J. C. Shepherdson (1959), "The Reduction of Two-Way Automata to One-Way Automata," *IBM J. Res. and Dev.*, 3, 198–200.

J. C. Shepherdson and H. E. Sturgis (1963), "Computability of Recursive Functions," *J. ACM*, 10, 217–255.

G. A. Shestopal (1961), "On the Number of Simple Bases of Boolean Functions," *Sov. Math. Dokl.*, 2, 1215–1219.

G. A. Shestopal (1966), "Simple Bases in Closed Classes of Functions of the Algebra of Logic," *Sov. Math. Dokl.*, 7, 792–795.

J. Słupecki (1939), "A Criterion of Fullness of Many-Valued Systems of Propositional Logic," *Studia Logica*, 30, (1972) 153–157; translation of: "Kryterium pełności weilowartościowych systemów logiki zdań," *C. R. Soc. Sci. Lett. Varsovie, III*, 32, 102–109.

R. M. Smullyan (1961), *Theory of Formal Systems*, Princeton University Press, Princeton, NJ.

R. I. Soare (1972), "The Friedberg-Muchnik Theorem Re-Examined," *Can. J. Math.*, 6, 1070–1078.

R. I. Soare (1987), *Recursively Enumerable Sets and Degrees*, Springer-Verlag, Berlin.

R. J. Solomonoff (1964), "A Formal Theory of Inductive Inference," *Inf. and Control*, 7, 1–22.

E. Specker (1949), "Nicht konstruktiv beweisbare Sätze der Analysis," *J. Symb. Logic*, 14, 145–158.

E. Specker (1971), "Ramsey's Theorem Does Not Hold in Recursive Set Theory," in: R. O. Gandy and C. M. E. Yates (eds.), *Logic Colloquium '69*, North-Holland, Amsterdam.

I. Stewart (1988), *Galois Theory*, Chapman and Hall, London, second ed.

J. Stillwell (1982), "The Word Problem for Groups," *Bull. AMS*, 6, 33–56.

M. H. Stone (1936), "The Theory of Representations for Boolean Algebras," *Trans. AMS*, 40, 37–111.

M. H. Stone (1937), "Applications of the Theory of Boolean Rings to General Topology," *Trans. AMS*, 41, 375–481.

J. Stoy (1977), *Denotational Semantics: The Scott-Strachey Approach to Programming Language Theory*, The MIT Press, Cambridge, MA.

H. R. Strong (1968), "Algebraically Generalized Recursive Function Theory," *IBM J. Res. and Dev.*, 12, 465–475.

S. Świerczkowski (1960), "Algebras Which Are Independently Generated by Every $n$ Elements," *Fund. Math.*, 49, 93–104.

A. Tarski (1929), «Sur les classes closes par rapport à certaines opérations élémentaires,» *Fund. Math.*, 16, 181–305.

W. Thomas (1982), "Classifying Regular Events in Symbolic Logic," *J. Comp. and System Sci.*, 25, 360–376.

W. Thomas (1984), "An Application of the Ehrenfeucht-Fraissé Game in Formal Language Theory," *Bull. Soc. Math. de France*, 16, 11–21.

A. M. Turing (1936/1937), "On Computable Numbers, with an Application to the *Entscheidungsproblem*," *Proc. London Math. Soc. (2)*, 42, 230–265/43, 544–546.

A. M. Turing (1939), "Systems of Logic Based on Ordinals," *Proc. London Math. Soc.*, 45, 161–228.

A. B. Ugolnikov (1988), "Closed Post Classes," *Izvestiya VUZ. Matematika*, 32, 79–88.

E. G. Wagner (1969), "Uniformly Reflexive Structures: On the Nature of Gödelizations and Relative Computability," *Trans. Amer. Math. Soc.*, 144, 1–41.

M. Ward (1942), "The Closure Operators of a Lattice," *Ann. of Math.*, 43, 191–196.

P. M. Whitman (1941), "Free Lattices," *Ann. of Math.*, 42, 325–330.

P. M. Whitman (1946), "Lattices, Equivalence Relations, and Subgroups," *Bull. AMS*, 52, 507–522.

S. V. Yablonskiĭ (С. В. Яблонский) (1954), «О функциональной полноте в трехзначном исчислении,» *Докл. Акад. Наук СССР*, 95, 1153–1155.

S. V. Yablonskiĭ, G. P. Gavrilov and V. B. Kudryavtsev (С. В. Яблонский, Г. П. Гаврилов и В. Б. Кудрявцев) (1966), *Функции алгебры логики и классы Поста*, Наука, Москва.

S. V. Yablonskiĭ, G. P. Gavrilov and V. B. Kudryavtsev (S. W. Jablonski, G. P. Gawrilow und W. B. Kudrjawzew) (1970), *Boolesche Funktionen und Postsche Klassen*, Friedr. Vieweg & Sohn, Braunschweig.

Yu. I. Yanov and A. A. Muchnik (Ю. И. Янов и А. А. Мучник) (1959), «О существовании $k$-значных замкнутых классов, не имеющих конечного базиса,» *Докл. Акад. Наук СССР*, 127, 1, 44–46.

C. E. M. Yates (1966), "A Minimal Pair of Recursively Enumerable Degrees," *J. Symb. Logic*, 31, 159–168.

C. E. M. Yates (1971), "A Note on Arithmetical Sets of Indiscernibles," in: R. O. Gandy and C. E. M. Yates (eds.), *Logic Colloquium '69*, North-Holland, Amsterdam.

M. K. Yntema (1967), "Inclusion Relations among Families of Context-Free Languages," *Inf. and Control*, 10, 572–597.

P. R. Young (1966), "Linear Orderings under One-One Reducibility," *J. Symb. Logic*, 31, 70–85.

P. Young (1973), "Easy Constructions in Complexity Theory: Gap and Speed-Up Theorems," *Proc. AMS*, 37, 555–563.

I. I. Zhegalkin (И. И. Жегалкин) (1927), «О технике вычислений предложений в символической логике,» *Матем. Сб.*, 34.

I. I. Zhegalkin (И. И. Жегалкин) (1928), «Арифметизация символической логики,» *Матем. Сб.*, 35.

# Author Index

243

# Subject Index

# Mathematical notations